DIPLOMACY

DIPLOMACY

*New Approaches in History,
Theory, and Policy*

Edited by

Paul Gordon Lauren

THE FREE PRESS
A Division of Macmillan Publishing Co., Inc.
NEW YORK

Collier Macmillan Publishers
LONDON

The Free Press
A Division of Macmillan Publishing Co., Inc.
866 Third Avenue, New York, N. Y. 10022

Collier Macmillan Canada, Ltd.

Library of Congress Catalog Card Number: 79-7352

Printed in the United States of America

printing number

1 2 3 4 5 6 7 8 9 10

Library of Congress Cataloging in Publication Data
Main entry under title:

Diplomacy : new approaches in history, theory, and
  policy.

  Includes index.
  1. Diplomacy--Addresses, essays, lectures.
2. International relations--Addresses, essays, lectures. 3. World politics--Addresses, essays, lectures.
I. Lauren, Paul Gordon.
JX1664.D56   327'.2'09   79-7352
ISBN 0-02-918070-8

To Susan

for her love, patience, and understanding

Contents

Preface

Every major professional meeting of historians and political scientists held during the last several years has arranged sessions for exploring the possibilities offered by interdisciplinary research. Most recently, great interest has been generated in the area of diplomacy where those skilled in traditional historical methods and perspectives and those skilled in contemporary behavioral techniques and theories eagerly searched for new approaches to combine their respective crafts. The Smithsonian Institution, American Historical Association, American Political Science Association, and International Studies Association, among others, have encouraged—and continue to encourage—this interaction. They have been motivated to support these interdisciplinary efforts in part due to the unfortunate problems that existed in the past; but, more important, due to the exciting new possibilites that exist for the future.

Historians working in the field of diplomatic history and political scientists in the field of international relations have long recognized that they both sought to understand the nature of diplomacy. Nevertheless, in the past there was very little interaction between these two disciplines. Faculty and students in each engaged in heated debates over the respective merits of theory or intuition, jargon or prose, numbers or language, analysis or description, hypothetical paradigms or historical facts, the value of present or past events, and the importance of the universal or the unique occurrence. The animosity in these disputes led scholars to emphasize their differences rather than their similarities and to go their own separate ways in isolation. This, in turn, resulted in serious problems for each field, and proved to be harmful for the study and the practice of diplomacy.

In an effort to correct some of these problems, a number of scholars are beginning to probe several new approaches. Diplomatic historians, for example, seeking to write enriched and more sophisticated history are exploring the possibilities suggested by theoretical constructs, methodological experimentation, and the systematic analysis of phenomena. This includes important discoveries in structured and focused comparison, quantification, bureaucratic politics and organizational process, escalation, deterrence, and crisis decision making. Political scientists searching for means to create more enlivened and differentiated theory are exploring the opportunities provided by the empirical evidence of specific historical cases and the perspectives of historians. These include exciting new ways of looking at Bismarck and his generals, the outbreak of World War I, Japanese–American relations, and the Cuban missile crisis. The results of this interdisciplinary work are becoming impressive, and we attempt to present some of them in this unique collection of original essays.

Each chapter that follows has been especially written by a highly respected scholar for this particular book. Using different perspectives, styles, and cases, the authors attempt to demonstrate specific ways in which diplomatic historians and political scientists may learn from each other and thus improve their own scholarship. In order to provide precise examples and avoid mere abstractions, each contributor draws upon his own considerable research for concrete evidence. Moreover, rather than making vast claims and promises of immediate success for a particular methodology or theory, the authors try to provide a balanced and sober assessment of the value and utility of their particular approach. The contributors themselves include some of the most distinguished scholars that exist in the study of diplomacy. All are recognized experts, some as professional historians and some as professional political scientists. All have either national or international reputations, have been recipients of the most prestigious awards available, and have been very active in publishing and presenting the results of their interdisciplinary research to a wide variety of audiences.

This book is designed for those interested in the study and the practice of diplomacy. It is meant primarily for those scholars and their students studying diplomatic history, international relations, foreign policy, conflict and peace, historiography, or methodology and theory from an interdisciplinary perspective. Because of the fact that the chapters also either explicitly or implicitly discuss the policy implications of their particular work, the collection addresses at least some of the concerns of policy makers as well and attempts to assist them in their search for a "usable" past and for "policy-relevant" theory. It is designed to suggest new approaches to diplomatic historians concerned with history, political scientists concerned with theory, and policy makers concerned with policy. Hence, the title of the book, *Diplomacy: New Approaches in History, Theory, and Policy.*

PAUL GORDON LAUREN

Acknowledgments

ONE OF THE GENUINE PLEASURES for an author or editor in publishing a book is the opportunity it affords to acknowledge publicly the many individuals who offered encouragement and assistance along the way. In this regard, I am pleased to be able to thank those who made this volume possible:

~ The contributors themselves for eagerly accepting their respective assignments and believing in the significance of the project from the very beginning, especially Gordon Craig and Alexander George, from whom I have learned so much first as a student, then as a colleague, and now as a friend;

~ Joel Colton and Lydia Bronte of the Rockefeller Foundation and Samuel F. Wells, Jr., of the Woodrow Wilson International Center for Scholars for sponsoring a special conference at the Smithsonian Institution which enabled us to present our chapters before a most distinguished audience of historians, theorists, and policy makers;

~ Zara Steiner of Cambridge University, Joseph Kruzel of Duke University, John P. Crecine of Carnegie–Mellon University, Brent Scowcroft (former Assistant to the President for National Security Affairs), Morton Halperin of the Center for National Security Studies, Ernest May of Harvard University, Ray Cline of Georgetown University, and Robert Art of Brandeis University for presenting formal comments on the chapters at the conference;

~ James Austin, William Bader, William Becker, Geoffrey Best, James Billington, I. M. Destler, John Gaddis, Alan Henrikson, Richard Hewlett, Edythe Holbrook, David Holloway, John Huizenga, Tomas Kelly, James King, John Koehler, Michael Lacey, Abraham Lowenthal, David MacIsaac, Charles Maier, Murrey Marder, Robert Osgood, David Painter, Stephen Pelz, James Pryzstrup, A. James Reichley, John Roberts, David Rosenberg, Francis Sayre, Stanley Sloan, S. Frederick Starr, John Steinbruner, David Trask, M. S. Venkataramani, and Sherry Wells for making valuable suggestions as participants in the conference;

~ Colin Jones, Senior Editor of The Free Press, for providing constant support and encouragement;

~ Sharyn Barrington-Carlson, Sue Rabold, and Jeanie Anderson for providing efficient and cheerful staff support;

~ and my wife, Susan, for giving so much of herself, to whom this book is dedicated.

Notes on the Contributors

GORDON A. CRAIG, J. E. Wallace Sterling Professor of Humanities and
Chairman of the Department of History at Stanford University, is the
doyen of European diplomatic historians in this country. Born in Scotland,
he received his Ph.D. from Princeton University in 1941. He has pub-
lished extensively in the fields of diplomatic history, German history, and
military history,and has received many awards. His books include *The
Politics of the Prussian Army, 1640–1945* (1955), *From Bismarck to Adenauer:
Aspects of German Statecraft* (1958), *The Battle of Königgrätz* (1964), *Europe
Since 1815* (1961, 1966, and 1971), *War, Politics, and Diplomacy: Selected
Essays* (1967), and, most recently, *Germany, 1866–1945* (1978). Professor
Craig has also edited two influential works, one with E. M. Earle and
Felix Gilbert, *Makers of Modern Strategy: Military Thought from Machiavelli to
Hitler* (1943), and with Felix Gilbert, *The Diplomats, 1919–1939* (1953). He
was made *Honororprofessor* of the Free University of Berlin in 1962, re-
ceived the degree of Doctor of Letters *honoris causa* from Princeton in 1970,
and was awarded a Dinkelspiel Award for Outstanding Service to
Undergraduate Education at Stanford in 1973.

ROGER V. DINGMAN, Associate Professor of History at the University of
Southern California, received his Ph.D. from Harvard University in
1969. He also studied at the Inter-University Center for Japanese Studies.
He has received a Woodrow Wilson Fellowship, the Harvard Canaday
Award, and a Haynes Foundation award. Professor Dingman has been a
National Fellow of the Hoover Institution and a visiting faculty member
of the U.S. Naval War College. His publications focus upon
Japanese–American diplomatic relations and include *Power in the Pacific:
The Origins of Naval Arms Limitation, 1914–1922* (1976), an edited volume
with Satō Seizaburō entitled *Kindai Nihon no taigai taido* (1974), and
chapters or articles in *American–East Asian Relations: A Survey,* and *Kokusai
Seiji.*

xiii

DIPLOMACY

ALEXANDER L. GEORGE is Graham H. Stuart Professor of International Relations in the Department of Political Science at Stanford University. Born in Illinois, he received his Ph.D. from the University of Chicago in 1958. He has been a Rockefeller Fellow, Fellow at the Center for Advanced Study in the Behavioral Sciences, and President of the International Studies Association. His books include *Woodrow Wilson and Colonel House* (1956) written with Juliette George, *Propaganda Analysis* (1959), *The Chinese Communist Army in Action* (1967), *The Limits of Coercive Diplomacy: Laos, Cuba, Vietnam* (1971) with David Hall and William Simons, *Deterrence in American Foreign Policy: Theory and Practice* (1974) with Richard Smoke, and *Towards a More Soundly Based Foreign Policy: Making Better Use of Information* (1975). His book, *Deterrence*, was awarded the prestigious Bancroft Prize for 1975. Articles have appeared in *World Politics, Public Opinion Quarterly, International Studies Quarterly, Policy Science,* and *American Political Science Review,* among others.

OLE R. HOLSTI is George V. Allen Professor in the Department of Political Science, Duke University. Born in Switzerland, he received his Ph.D. from Stanford University in 1962. He has received awards from the National Science Foundation, Ford Foundation, and the Canada Council, and has been a Fellow at the Center for Advanced Study in the Behavioral Sciences. His books include *Content Analysis: A Handbook with Application for the Study of International Crisis* (1963) with others, *Enemies in Politics* (1967) with David Finlay and Richard Fagen, *Content Analysis for the Social Sciences and Humanities* (1969), *The Analysis of Communication Content: Developments in Scientific Theories and Computer Techniques* (1969) edited with G. Gerbner and others, *Crisis, Escalation, War* (1972), and *Unity and Disintegration in International Alliances: Comparative Studies* (1973) with P. Terrence Hopmann and John Sullivan. Chapters have appeared in many books and articles have been published in *The Journal of Conflict Resolution, Behavioral Science,* and *American Political Science Review,* among others.

ROBERT JERVIS is Professor of Political Sciences at the University of California, Los Angeles. A native of New York, he received his Ph.D. from the University of California at Berkeley in 1968. Prior to receiving his position at UCLA, he taught at Yale and at Harvard. He has received a Guggenheim Fellowship and has been an International Affairs Fellow of the Council on Foreign Relations. Professor Jervis' books include *The Logic of Images in International Relations* (1970), *International Politics: Anarchy, Force, and Imperialism* (1973) edited with Robert Art, and the highly influential *Perception and Misperception in International Politics* (1976). His chapters have appeared in *In Search of Global Patterns, Thought and Action in Foreign Policy, Contending Approaches to International Politics,* and *Coercion, NOMOS XIV.* Articles have been published in *World Politics, Polity,* and *International Studies Quarterly.*

PAUL GORDON LAUREN is Associate Professor of History at the University of Montana. Born in Washington, he received his Ph.D. from Stanford University in 1973. He has taught in the international relations program at Stanford, and now teaches courses on diplomacy, European diplomatic history, war and peace, and the Cold War. He began his graduate career as a Woodrow Wilson Fellow and has received awards from the Danforth Foundation, *Deutscher Akademischer Austauschdienst,* and the Foreign Area Fellowship Program of the Social Science Research Council and the American Council of Learned Societies. He has been a Peace Fellow of the Hoover Institution, and has recently been awarded a Rockefeller Foundation Humanities Fellowship. His publications include a book entitled *Diplomats and Bureaucrats: The First Institutional Responses to Twentieth-Century Diplomacy in France and Germany* (1976), a chapter in *The Politics of National Power: Essays on the History of Foreign Policy and International Relations,* and articles in *Diplomatic History* and *International Studies Quarterly.*

MELVIN SMALL is Professor of History at Wayne State University. A native of New York, he received his Ph.D. from the University of Michigan in 1965. Professor Small has been a Fellow at the Center for Advanced Study in the Behavioral Sciences and has received an award from the American Council of Learned Societies. From 1972 to 1974 he was a Visiting Lecturer at the University of Aarhus in Denmark. He writes and teaches in the areas of American diplomatic history, international relations, and peace research, and is one of the leading authorities on Quantitative International Politics. His publications include the edited book *Public Opinion and Historians* (1970) and *The Wages of War* (1972), with J. David Singer. His many articles have appeared in the *Journal of Common Market Studies, The Historian, Jerusalem Journal of International Relations, Policy Sciences, Kölner Zeitschrift für Soziologie und Socialpsychologie, Societas, World Politics, Film and History, The Americas, Journal of Conflict Resolution, Journal of Peace Research,* and the *Annals of the American Academy of Political and Social Science.*

RICHARD SMOKE is a member of the faculty at the Wright Institute in Berkeley, California. Born in Pennsylvania, he received his Ph.D. from the Massachusettes Institute of Technology in 1972. His dissertation received the Helen Dwight Reid Award of the American Political Science Association in 1971–1972. He has been a Fellow at the Center for Advanced Study in the Behavioral Sciences, a Postdoctoral Fellow at the Institute of Personality Assessment and Research, and has served as Instructor and Assistant Dean for Research at the Kennedy School of Government at Harvard. His books include *Deterrence in American Foreign Policy: Theory and Practice* (1974), with Alexander L. George, which won the Bancroft Prize, and *War: Controlling Escalation* (1977). Currently he is writing a textbook entitled *National Security: An Introduction,* due to appear in 1980.

SAMUEL F. WELLS, JR. is Secretary of the International Security Studies Program of the Woodrow Wilson International Center for Scholars at the

Smithsonian Institution. Born in South Carolina, he received his Ph.D. from Harvard University in 1967. He has taught at Wellesley and at the University of North Carolina, and has been a Woodrow Wilson Fellow, Danforth Fellow, Peace Fellow of the Hoover Institution, and Fellow at the Woodrow Wilson Center. He has received awards from the American Philosophical Society, the Kittredge Educational Fund, and the Ford Foundation. His publications include *The Ordeal of World Power: American Diplomacy Since 1900* (1975) with Robert Ferrell and David Trask, and articles in *The Historian, Canadian Historical Review, Perspectives in American History, World Issues, Wilson Quarterly,* and *Proceedings of the First National Symposium of the Civilian–Military Institute.*

SAMUEL R. WILLIAMSON, JR. is Dean of the College of Arts and Sciences and Professor of History at the University of North Carolina at Chapel Hill. A native of Louisiana, he received his Ph.D. from Harvard University in 1966. Prior to accepting his present position, he taught at the U.S. Military Academy at West Point and Harvard, and served as Assistant to the Dean at Harvard and as Director of the Curriculum in Peace, War, and Defense at North Carolina. He has been a Woodrow Wilson Fellow, Fulbright Scholar, and Danforth Fellow, and has received awards from the American Philosophical Society and the American Council of Learned Societies. His book, *The Politics of Grand Strategy: Britain and France Prepare for War, 1904–1914* (1969), was awarded the prestigious George Louis Beer Prize of the American Historical Association in 1970. Dean Williamson has also published a chapter in *The Military in a Democracy* and an article in the *Historical Journal.*

INTRODUCTION

1
Diplomacy:
History, Theory, and Policy

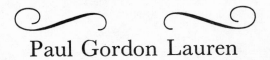

Paul Gordon Lauren

IN THE CHALLENGING and complex realm of diplomacy a unique place is accorded to the astute and renowned French diplomat, François de Callières. Having spent a lifetime in public service, he became acutely concerned early in the eighteenth century when his country faced an uncertain future with unfavorable treaty conditions and a leader untried in foreign affairs. Even though he was over seventy years old at the time, a sense of dedication presumably compelled de Callières to reflect upon his long experience as a negotiator and to publish his thoughts regarding the principles of successful diplomacy. The result was his masterful treatise entitled *De la manière de négocier avec les Souverains* (1716), described by Sir Ernest Satow as "a mine of political wisdom"[1] and judged by Sir Harold Nicolson as a work that "remains to this day the best manual of diplomatic method ever written."[2] He concisely stated the purpose of the book in his introduction:

> To give an idea of the personal qualities and general knowledge necessary in all good negotiators; to indicate to them the paths which they should follow and the rocks which they should avoid; and to exhort those who destine themselves to the foreign service of their country, to render themselves capable of discharging worthily that high, important, and difficult office before entering upon it.[3]

De Callières complained that good diplomats were rare because there had been "no discipline or fixed rules" by which "good citizens destined to become negotiators might instruct themselves in the knowledge necessary for this kind of employment."[4] He resented the fact that unskilled and untrained people were sent to embassies and entrusted with the conduct of diplomacy. "And yet I may hazard a guess," he stated with both caution and conviction,

> that there is perhaps no employment in all his Majesty's service more difficult to discharge than that of negotiation. It demands all the penetration, all the dexterity, all the suppleness which a man can possess. It requires a wide-spread understanding and knowledge, and above all a correct and piercing discernment.[5]

3

In order to provide part of this understanding, knowledge, and discernment, de Callières strongly advised that those involved in and concerned with foreign affairs intimately study diplomatic history. Implicit in his advice was also the recommendation that diplomatic historians make every effort to understand the craft of the theoreticians and practitioners of diplomacy as well.[6]

Problems of the Past

Unfortunately, these sagacious recommendations of de Callières are often unheeded. Despite their mutual interest in understanding the interaction among nations, political scientists working in the area of international relations and historians in the field of diplomatic history frequently disparage the value of synthesis or exaggerate the contrasts in perspective and methodology between their two disciplines. Political scientists often accuse their historian colleagues of simply "scratching around" and lacking any rigorous methodology at all, failing to be concerned with contemporary problems, and being "mere chroniclers" of an "embalmed past." Historians, not to be outdone, frequently criticize the theorists for erecting artificial models *ex nihilo,* creating smoke screens of jargon, and becoming infatuated with computer paraphernalia instead of human beings. The conflicting opinions and rancor in this dispute only encourages scholars to emphasize their differences rather than their similarities and thus to go their separate ways in isolation.

The results of this internecine conflict are harmful to the work of scholars in each discipline and to the study and practice of diplomacy. Political scientists, for their part, generally lose the valuable perspective of time and proportion by concentrating almost exclusively on events during the atomic era and ignoring the wealth of human practice in diplomacy during earlier periods. They miss many sources of evidence by focusing primarily upon American experiences and neglecting the vast array of material from other geographical or cultural areas. They forfeit an appreciation for the many practical complexities and subtleties of diplomacy by largely failing to use foreign languages, to consult some of the classic works on diplomatic method, and to read the diplomatic documents themselves. Moreover, and perhaps more serious, they sacrifice much depth and variety by eschewing complex historical facts for abstract models, hypothetical paradigms, and logically (or mathematically) plausible solutions. If history is consulted at all, it is generally ransacked for "data" or employed in the way candidly admitted by theorist Thomas Schelling: "I have used some historical examples but usually as illustration, not evidence."[7]

This is a dangerous practice, for to indiscriminately jerk—or even to surgically slice—variables out of their historical or human context generates

4

not only a misunderstanding of, but also a lack of appreciation for, the traditions of the past and the complexities of the human condition. One recent study of diplomatic practice goes so far as to assert that crisis management "is an innovation of nuclear diplomacy" and "has come to mean solely the personalization of international diplomacy, the technique developed by Henry Kissinger."[8] This view simply discounts the rich experience of classical diplomacy and the management techniques developed during crises by such statesmen as Castlereagh, Aberdeen, and Bismarck. Similarly, efforts to index, chart, code, program, or "Z-score" data to determine standard deviation from mean activity,[9] all too easily lose people in their paradigms, graphs, and jargon. An analysis of the balance of power, for example, recently summarized its findings in the following way:

> Considering both the base 50 graphs and the systematic mean graphs, there are 110 semicycles, including 30 dyads and 80 triads. . . .
>
> Combining these two variables, balance and strength of bond, we get a good view of the dynamics of the triad over the five time periods. . . . Of the 110 semicycles, 50 underwent a change in balance in the following time period. The number of balanced cycles was 68 out of a possible 110 for a β of .62. . . .
>
> Enlarging our analysis to the pentadic level, we find . . . a dyadic relationship is unbalanced, it signifies that nation X is friendly to Y while Y is hostile to X.[10]

The impersonal Xs and Ys of this kind of theory have only a tenuous existence in history, if they have any existence at all. Historical experience demonstrates time and time again that state policy is determined—as it only can be—by the decisions and the actions of men and women. Formal alliances have no meaning unless the human actors feel bound by their obligations. Weapons have bargaining influence only if people are willing to use them, or if others think they are willing. The whole concept of diplomacy itself is significant only insofar as it is understood and put into practice by people.[11] For these several reasons, the human actors in their own particular historical context cannot be folded, stapled, mutilated, or shunted aside when inconvenient for abstract printouts, models, or theories.

Diplomatic historians suffer from a number of problems of their own as well. By concentrating primarily on the unique circumstances of events, they neglect the observable patterns of human behavior. They often deliberately reject Wilhelm Dilthey's proposition that *"the manifest meaning of history must, first of all,* be sought *in what is always present,* in what always recurs. . . in the composite patterns of interactions."*[12] By chauvinistically insisting upon utilizing traditional techniques alone, they deprive themselves of some of the demonstrated advantages of the behavioral sciences' more precise computations, methodologies, and theories. In this sense, they "go a-wandering in the dark forest of the past, gathering facts like nuts and berries," according to David Hackett Fischer in his book, *Historian's Fallacies* (1970),[13] and find themselves subject to his following criticism:

5

The work of too many professional historians is diminished by an antirational obsession—by an intense prejudice against method, logic, and science. . . . In the process of this reaction, historians have not merely severed their ties with the natural sciences, but have also turned away from science in the large sense of a structured, ordered, controlled, empirical, rational discipline of thought.[14]

In addition, by drawing most of their evidence from the more ancient past, diplomatic historians discover that they isolate themselves and their work from the legitimate concerns of policy makers dealing with contemporary issues.[15] Perhaps it is for reasons like these that G. M. Young issued his famous—or infamous—indictment that "the greater part of what passes for diplomatic history is little more than the record of what one clerk said to another clerk."[16]

To describe diplomatic history as a mere record of clerks is a harsh, but occasionally appropriate, judgment of many works in the field. As Gordon A. Craig observes:

With the exception of specialists in military affairs, who have always been second-class citizens of the historical profession, none of the practitioners of political history have been charged more often with myopic vision and analytical superficiality than those who have taken the world of diplomacy as their province.[17]

Much of this criticism is justified due to the fact that a great deal of diplomatic history has been indifferent to the problems of methodology and conventionally narrative. In any traditional textbook or study, for example, we could readily find the relatively simple facts of each historical case: the personalities and actions of the leading statesman, the specific provisions of treaties then in effect, the crisis or war that emerged, the formal instructions issued to chiefs of mission, and a description of what eventually happened. This approach by its very nature is *descriptive* and narrative rather than *analytical*. As a consequence, we would find it much more difficult to discover an explicit treatment of the influence of stress or organizational process upon decision making, the characteristics of alliance politics, or the diplomatic system as a whole, or upon the dynamics of bargaining with threats of force and escalation during intense international crises. Similarly, we would find it difficult to discover the use of quantitative techniques or of focused comparisons between different cases. "The general reaction of most diplomatic historians to these innovative efforts," writes one observer, "has been akin to the papal response to Galileo."[18] Frequently, this has resulted in "any number of arid monographs . . . literally copied out of the bound volumes of Foreign Office papers in the Public Record Office, tricked out with Latin tags (*sub spe rati, rebus sic stantibus,* and the like) and impressive footnotes (FO France/1749; from Lyons, no. 249, very confidential, March 4, 1869), and sent forth to grace the lower shelves of university libraries."[19]

These various problems in each discipline when dealing with diplomacy have been recognized by theorists, historians, and policy makers alike.

Several leading political scientists, for example, have called for the creation of new and more sophisticated theory based not upon abstract, deductive conjecture as in the past but rather upon empirical evidence from specific historical cases.[20] Similarly, a growing number of diplomatic historians have encouraged their professional colleagues to consider broadening their focus, drawing upon theory, and utilizing methodological experimentation.[21] Policy makers, for their own part, have recently sought the advantages of external research and pleaded with both theorists and historians to make theory and history "usable" in order to help solve contemporary problems in diplomacy.[22] They have begun to recognize the validity of Marc Bloch's statement that "to act reasonably, it is first necessary to understand."[23]

The "Use" of History and Theory for Policy

The "use" of history and theory for policy purposes is an issue that is attracting increasing attention.[24] It is usually extremely difficult to establish the direct connection between theory and/or history, on the one hand, and practice or policy, on the other. Nevertheless, policy makers in need of diagnosis and prediction either explicitly or implicitly use theoretical generalizations or historical analogies. In the absence of sophisticated assistance from scholarship, they tend to apply dangerously oversimplified or unrelated notions to their present crisis or problem.[25] As Ernest May observes in his insightful book, *"Lessons" of the Past* (1973), policy makers do not ordinarily take the time or make the effort to analyze the full nature of their immediate international concern:

> When resorting to an analogy, they tend to seize upon the first that comes to mind. They do not search more widely. Nor do they pause to analyze the case, test its fitness, or even ask in what ways it might be misleading. Seeing a trend running toward the present, they tend to assume that it will continue into the future, not stopping to consider what produced it or why a linear projection might prove to be mistaken.[26]

He blames not only policy makers for this phenomenon, but also scholars: "By and large, those of us professionally occupied in teaching and writing history [and presumably theory as well] have put out little effort to help them."[27]

This matter of helping policy makers by the use of theory and history, however, provokes among scholars a wide variety of different responses, each of which must be respected.[28] Some regard the use—or abuse—of their work as abhorrent, either because they disagree with a particular foreign policy (witness the gulf that existed between campuses and policy makers at the time of the Vietnam War), or strongly disapprove of someone else using their own work for political purposes which they did not intend. Others view the use of their scholarship as essentially irrelevant, and argue that they write only for the sake of pure theory or history, or for themselves, or for their own students in the classroom. Still other scholars take great pleasure in seeing their analytical skills or research abilities utilized in such a way as to influence the actual course of events, and actively encourage policy makers to seek the best professional advice they can offer. The number of those in this latter category is growing, for as one recent article states with approval, more and more scholars are moving "from a stance toward the world that emphasizes detached observation and analysis to a stance in which observation is increasingly mixed with participation, analysis with judgment and advice."[29] The ability of those scholars who do wish to provide such assistance, of course, is a function of the type and quality of theory or history they write and the kinds of questions they address.

Theory in international relations comes in a variety of forms. As Alexander George and Richard Smoke among other scholars have noted, there is a generally recognized tripartite distinction, although few theories fit exclusively into one category or the other.[30] One kind of theory is *empirical theory*. This attempts to understand the nature of international relations; it is the kind of theory that absorbs the attention of most scholars specializing in the field. It tries to explain processes, develop propositions, and discover correlations in the world of interaction among nations. Operating on the assumption that experience includes not only single, isolated events, but also elements of regularity and patterns in human behavior, empirical theory seeks to identify, describe, and/or explain these. Such theory is normally the ideal of the social scientist as scientist, and is noted fot its absence of values.

Another variety is *normative theory*, which deliberately does concern itself with values. It possesses an inescapably philosophical dimension, and addresses the "ought" rather than the "is" of international affairs. This may take the form of a reasoned critique or comment upon a particular line of foreign policy or a proposal for a different course to be followed. On another level of abstraction, it may take the form of the identification of long-range goals for the international system as a whole. This would include works, for example, such as Immanuel Kant's *Zum ewigen Frieden* (1795), Grenville Clark's and Louis Sohn's *World Peace Through World Law* (1958), Rajni Kothari's *Footsteps Into the Future: Diagnosis of the Present World and a Design for an Alternative* (1974), or recent studies by the peace research movement.[31]

Finally, there is *policy science theory* in international relations. This kind of theory, unlike nearly all empirical theory, is deliberately cast in action-oriented terms. It attempts to provide explicit guidance for the specific tasks of policy makers. Toward this end, it tries to provide directly comprehensive and usable insights and aids for coping with concrete problems of the present or expected future. This may include the identification and clarification of goals, techniques, and perhaps even values. Policy science theory says to policy makers: "In order to achieve your stated objective, you must employ these particular means." As such, this kind of theory is more concerned about the "how" rather than the "what" of policy.

Policy makers can use such theory to assist them in comprehending or diagnosing the meaning of the information they possess and in identifying various means and then matching those to the ends they seek. Yet, as George and Smoke point out, even the theory of policy science is "notably underdeveloped" and characterized mainly by "free-floating generalizations and isolated insights."[32] What policy makers need, they argue, is more sophisticated and differentiated theory—theory that can discriminate among different cases and classes of cases to present variables of direct diagnostic and predictive significance. They do not find this quality in present theory, and perceptively observe the nature of the problem in the following words:

> It is the nature of any theory that it must simplify some aspects of the reality it seeks to comprehend. But if policy use is to be made of a theory, those elements of the real-life phenomenon that were left out or oversimplified in the formulation of the theory must be identified, and their implications for the theory's content and its use must be noted . . . . Reasoning deductively . . . investigators have offered . . .relatively abstract theory . . . which has received little testing against historical reality.[33]

This "historical reality" of which they speak is the business of history and historians. Theirs is the realm of "the real-life phenomenon." Wilhelm Dilthey expressed this same idea over a century ago. "The historians of a nation," he wrote, "stand in a more direct relationship to its political life than any other group of pure intellectuals."[34] Nevertheless, the history that historians write is subject to any number of different interpretations by those in political life. The "lesssons of history" are not at all clear, and people often disagree as to the correct lesson to be learned from a particular historical experience or misapply those lessons to a new situation that differs from the past in important respects.[35] In addition, some policy makers claim that they never would consider making a decision without consulting history, while others assert that they "don't consider history to be of any practical use.[36] Regardless of their claims, however, policy makers do in fact use history in making decisions. As Robert Jervis convincingly argues: "What one learns from key events in international history is an important factor in determining the images that shape the interpretation of incoming information . . . . We cannot make sense out of our environment without assuming that, in some sense, the future will resemble the past."[37]

History can help statesmen understand their world by providing detailed evidence of the range of situations that have occurred and of causal links in human behavior. It is not always easy to know, however, how the study of history does this. The works of historians do not lend themselves to quick delineation or categorization as do theories of international relations. This is due in part to the complexity of the subject matter, wide variety of ap-

9

proaches, and disagreements among historians about the nature of history itself. Historians differ strongly, for instance, on whether all events are *sui generis,* whether there are recurring and constant phenomena throughout time, or whether both universal and unique characteristics are evident in each circumstance.[38] There are, nevertheless, certain patterns in the kinds of questions or issues that historians address which can assist policy makers in their use of history. Perhaps it is in this sense that we can best appreciate the attitudes of those "who believe in the relevance of the past to present, who believe that there is something to be learned from historical experience, and above all . . . those who insist that we must first know what really happened in the past before we can make useful judgments about it, before we can hope to apply the experience of yesterday to the problems of today and tomorrow."[39]

Historical studies, for example, examine past *processes.* The unique enterprise that separates historians from other students of the past, according to David Trask, Historian of the U.S. Department of State, is that he or she thinks not structurally but rather processionally—in terms of time passing.[40] In this regard, their detailed examination of past process concentrates on those elements which do not alter over time and on those elements which do, whether they are discussing the diplomacy of Frederick the Great or Willy Brandt, or the diplomatic advice of de Callières or Charles de Gaulle. The focus of history, in short, is first and foremost on continuity and change. This is directly related to the task of the policy maker who attempts to employ a strategy to achieve desirable continuities and changes by shaping present and future processes. For precisely this reason, Trask concludes, history is not a mere interesting diversion but, rather, an indispensable element of policy making: "The policy maker has no alternative but to make use of historical information and historical thought simply because he is specifically concerned with processes, the bread and butter of historians."[41]

History also studies the crucial importance of *people:* the statesmen and diplomats, the soldiers and sailors, the politicians and bureaucrats, the wise and foolish, and the villains and occasionally even the heroes. It is people who make the decisions, take the actions, and thus breathe life into the processes. History deals with the complex interaction among human actors and observes the role of strengths, weaknesses, abilities, emotions, vices, and, in the words of Zara Steiner, "the personalities and casts of mind of the people."[42] They may be wise, foolish, compassionate, vengeful, good, or evil, but because of plan or chance, office or character, people matter. The great Eurpoean diplomatic historian, Federico Chabod, clearly and explicitly expressed this idea in the introduction to his masterpiece when he wrote that "history, at least up to the present, has been made by men, and not by automata."[43] "In a given situation," he continued, "the work of the individual statesman always intervenes incisively in the course of events."[44] History can make policy makers sensitive to this fact.

The work of historians, if properly done, can also teach policy makers something about *proportion*. In a brief but marvelous essay several years ago entitled "The Historian's Opportunity," Barbara Tuchman argued that the task of historians is to tell what human history is about and what the forces are that drive us. History, she wrote, "being concerned as it is with reality and subject as it is to certain disciplines," must see these various elements "in proportion to the whole":[45]

> Distillation is selection, and selection . . . is the essence of writing history. It is the cardinal process of composition, the most difficult, the most delicate, the most fraught with error as well as art. Ability to distinguish what is significant from what is insignificant is *sine qua non.*[46]

This is precisely the task of policy makers in foreign affairs as well who, when deluged with paper and pressed for time, must be able to make intelligent, objective judgments about what is important and what is not.[47] It has been said that one of the qualities which made Bismarck such a successful statesman was his extraordinary sense of proportion.[48] He understood the importance of being able to discern the salient feature of a given problem, to respect the limitations imposed upon choice and action, and to recognize that diplomacy is the art of the possible. The study of history can be excellent training for just such skills.

Historians and theorists are thus in a position to provide certain unique contributions to policy makers seeking to practice diplomacy. If they have not done so in the past, it may well be due to the numerous problems and deficiencies in each discipline as described previously. Policy makers have called for "usable history" and "policy-relevant theory," yet have received little assistance. This state of affairs has been recognized by May who concludes: "If history [and one could add theory] is to be better used in government, nothing is more important than that professional historians [and theorists] discover means of addressing directly, succinctly, and promptly the needs of people who govern."[49] The first step toward achieving such a goal may depend upon the willingness and ability of both historians and theorists to engage in interdisciplinary research.

New Approaches in History and Theory

Recognizing both their unfortunate problems of the past and their opportunities for improving theory and history in the future, a number of scholars are beginning to probe the possibilities offered by new approaches in interdisciplinary research. Most recently, a great deal of interest is being generated in the area of diplomacy and international relations where those skilled in contemporary behavioral techniques and theories and those skilled in traditional historical methods and ideas are searching for ways to fruitfully

11

combine their respective crafts. Political scientists eager to discover more about the nature of alliances, crisis management, or deterrence are looking to diplomatic historians for specific information and evidence about the United States–Japanese Alliance, the outbreak of World War I, or the formation of the North Atlantic Treaty Organization. Diplomatic historians interested to learn of the wider implications of Bismarck's relations with the generals, decision making in Austria–Hungary, or Kennedy's ultimatum to Khrushchev during the Cuban missile crisis are seeking the advice of those theorists writing in the areas of escalation, bureaucratic process, or coercive diplomacy.

The results of this interdisciplinary work suggest a number of exciting possibilities, and we attempt to present some of them in this unique collection of original essays. By discussing both techniques and theories, we make an effort to demonstrate specific ways in which historians in the field of diplomatic history and political scientists in the field of international relations may learn from each other and thus enhance their own work. Our concern is with exploring a two-way research strategy in which the past is studied in new ways with theory, and theories, in turn, are examined more critically with historical evidence. We believe it is intellectually untenable to maintain that any single discipline or research method has a monopoly on truth. Fundamentally, both fields seek to understand the relations among nations and toward this end they either explicitly or implicitly make comparisons, offer explanations, and formulate theories or generalizations, whether their attention is devoted to the single case or to many. Historically, cumulative knowledge has been achieved in a perpetual cycle moving from empirical research to theorizing, back to empirical research, and then again to theorizing. In this process, there is an interdependence of researchers, and their work should be considered as complementary rather than competitive. As E. H. Carr once wrote:

> Scientists, social scientists, and historians are all engaged in different branches of the same study: the study of man and his environment, of the effects of man on his environment and of his environment on man. The object of study is the same: to increase man's understanding of, and mastery over, his environment.[50]

To suggest a fruitful interchange between disciplines is certainly not to minimize the difficulties. It is not easy to develop competence in the skills of both the historian and the political scientist. Moreover, historians frequently disagree among themselves in the explanations of past events, just as theorists dispute the value of different theories. Nor is it to suggest that the wisdom of the great classical writers on the subject of diplomacy has somehow been superseded as a result of recent developments in psychology or computer technology.[51] Indeed, this essay began with a discussion of de Callières during the eighteenth century and Gordon A. Craig's chapter is appropriately subtitled "The Relevance of Some Old Books." Nor is it to argue that all of the techniques of the past are antiquated. Each scholar should keep his or her mind open to new approaches, but at the same time maintain a healthy skepticism of easy promises, quick fixes, and fads.[52] The paradigms, models, theories, and methods are only the instruments of conducting research, raising questions, and making policy. They should not be enshrined as ends in themselves, and should always remain the servants rather than the master.[53] As Clausewitz with a keen appreciation for this matter declared years ago: "Theory should be study, not doctrine."[54]

Nor is the suggestion of an interchange to argue that the distinctive objectives, perspectives, and qualities of either discipline be discarded. A mutual respect of diversity is essential. The theorists of international relations, for example, need not and should not abandon their search for constants to create theory and make policy recommendations. The task of the theorist is to identify the many conditions, variables, and causal patterns associated with historical outcomes. To deal in a world of intellectual speculation, to create theory, to discover relationships between variables, or to be consulted for advice on foreign policy is challenging and rewarding, and few theorists would voluntarily give up these benefits. Similarly, historians need not and should not neglect the complexities of the human condition or refrain from warning theorists about the dangers of arbitrarily superimposing models upon reality or reminding policy makers that it may be inappropriate or misleading to view a particular current problem as analogous to an earlier historical case. The task of the diplomatic historian is to construct a clear and accurate record of the formal relations and interactions among sovereign nations, analyzing and interpreting the ways in which they formulate their policies, the foreign and domestic factors with which they must contend, the techniques and modalities they employ, and the results they achieve in attempting to realize their objectives. The excitement of reading that original handwritten document, of finding that long-lost dispatch, of discovering that key that unlocks the meaning of some past policy, or of carefully reconstructing events with the available evidence is the substance of why historians study diplomatic history. Few historians would deliberately forego even the form of conducting research in, say, the *Archives diplomatiques* of the Quai d'Orsay: gaining entrance from the smartly dressed guards after a careful examination of your own "letter of credence" from the embassy, ascending the circular marble stairway lighted by chandeliers and adorned with tapestries, walking down the red-carpeted hall decorated with leather-padded doors and portraits of all the illustrious French foreign ministers in history, and then being invited to be the first scholar ever to open that box of just-released diplomatic dispatches.

A closer interdisciplinary collaboration between history and political science should not be considered in terms of ever losing any of these unique qualities, but of enhancing the work of each scholar and of the study of diplomacy and international relations. The contributions of this interchange should be seen as supplementing, rather than replacing, the valuable features of each discipline. The exploration by historians and political scientists into the works of each other can raise probing questions about previous assumptions and methodologies, suggest means of distinguishing the general from the specific, generate alternative explanations or hypotheses, encourage considerations of both qualitative and quantitative factors, and facilitate looking at old problems in new ways. Theory, for example, could become much more extended, qualified, differentiated, and highly enlivened from its abstract conceptualization by drawing upon the empirical evidence of historical cases and the perspectives of historians. Diplomatic history could become much more sophisticated and enriched by drawing upon theory, methodological experimentation, systematic analysis of phenomena, sharper identification of variables, and explicit definitions of problems and concepts. Such an interdisciplinary approach, which combines some elements of the theorist's craft with those of the historian, may thus lead to better history, better theory, and perhaps, in turn and through use, even better policy.

Notes

1. Sir Ernest Satow, *A Guide to Diplomatic Practice,* 2 vols. (London: Longmans, Green, 1917 ed.). I:x.

2. Sir Harold Nicolson, *The Evolution of Diplomacy* (New York: Collier, 1962 ed.), p. 85.

3. François de Callières, in translation under *On the Manner of Negotiating with Princes* (Notre Dame: University of Notre Dame Press, 1963), p. 3.

4. Ibid, p. 8.

5. Ibid., p. 9.

6. Ibid., pp. 44, 62, 64, 95, 112, 118.

7. Thomas C. Schelling, *Arms and Influence* (New Haven: Yale University Press, 1966), p. vii. An early criticism of these developments provoked an influential article by Hedley Bull, "International Theory: The Case for a Classical Approach," *World Politics* 18 (April 1966):361–377, which in turn led to a stimulating discussion reproduced in Klaus Knorr and James Roseman (eds.), *Contending Approaches to International Politics* (Princeton: Princeton University Press, 1969). See also Davis B. Bobrow, *International Relations: New Approaches* (New York: Free Press, 1972).

8. Amos Perlmutter, "Crisis Management: Kissinger's Middle East Negotiations," *International Studies Quarterly* 19 (September 1975):316, 318.

9. See L. Hazlewood et al., "Planning for Problems in Crisis Management"; Stephen Andriole and Robert Young, "Toward the Development of an Integrated Crisis Warning System"; and Wayne Martin, "The Measurement of International Military Commitments for Crisis Early Warning"; all in *International Studies Quarterly* 21 (March 1977):75–180; and Stephen Andriole, "Computers and Na-

tional Security,'' a paper presented at the International Studies Association, Washington, D.C., 1978.

10. Brian Healy and Arthur Stein, ''The Balance of Power in International History: Theory and Reality,'' *Journal of Conflict Resolution* 17 (March 1973):56–58.

11. For more discussion of this matter, see Paul Gordon Lauren, ''Crisis Management: History and Theory in International Conflict,'' in Gaines Post, Jr., and Roger Chickering (eds.), *The Politics of National Power: Essays on the History of Foreign Policy and International Relations* (forthcoming).

12. Wilhelm Dilthey, *Pattern and Meaning in History*, edited with an introduction by H. P. Rickman (New York: Harper and Brothers, 1962 ed.), p. 161. A similar point of view is expressed in Thucydides, *The Peloponnesian War*, Introduction by M. I. Finley (New York: Penguin Books, 1972 ed.), Book I, p. 48.

13. David Hackett Fischer, *Historian's Fallacies: Toward a Logic of Historical Thought* (New York: Harper and Row, 1970), p. 4.

14. Ibid., p. xxi.

15. For a very thoughtful discussion of the advantages for the historian in dealing with more contemporary matters, see Arthur Schlesinger, Jr., ''The Historian as Participant,'' in Felix Gilbert and Stephen R. Graubard (eds.), *Historical Studies Today* (New York: Norton, 1972), pp. 393–412.

16. G. M. Young, *Victorian England: Portrait of an Age* (London: Oxford University Press, 1953 ed.), p. 103.

17. Gordon A. Craig, ''Political and Diplomatic History,'' in Gilbert and Graubard, *Historical Studies Today*, p. 360. See also the essay by Peter Paret, ''Assignments Old and New: A Review Article,'' *American Historical Review* 76 (February 1971):119–126.

18. Thomas J. McCormick, ''The State of American Diplomatic History,'' in Herbert J. Bass (ed.), *The State of American History* (Chicago: Quadrangle Books, 1970), p. 123.

19. The words are those of Craig, ''Political and Diplomatic History,'' p. 360.

20. See, for example, Alexander L. George and Richard Smoke, *Deterrence in American Foreign Policy: Theory and Practice* (New York: Columbia University Press, 1974), especially pp. 66–103; Richard Smoke, *War: Controlling Escalation* (Cambridge: Harvard University Press, 1977); Robert Jervis, *Perception and Misperception in International Politics* (Princeton: Princeton University Press, 1976); Ole Holsti, *Crisis, Escalation, War* (Montreal: McGill–Queen's University Press, 1972); and Alexander L. George, David Hall, and William Simons, *The Limits of Coercive Diplomacy: Laos, Cuba, Vietnam* (Boston: Little, Brown, 1971).

21. Craig, ''Political and Diplomatic History,'' especially pp. 364–368; Melvin Small, ''The Applicability of Quantitative International Politics to Diplomatic History,'' *The Historian* 38 (February 1976):281–304; the papers and comments of Samuel R. Williamson, Roger Dingman, Stephen Pelz, Jamie Moore, and Paul Gordon Lauren at the panel entitled ''New Approaches to Diplomatic History,'' 90th Annual Convention of the American Historical Association, Atlanta, December 28, 1975; and Paul Gordon Lauren, ''Ultimata and Coercive Diplomacy,'' *International Studies Quarterly* 16 (June 1972):131–165.

22. Most recently, the comments made by those with extensive policy experience at a

special conference entitled "History as an Instrument of Policy Analysis," held at the Wilson Center, the Smithsonian Institution, Washington, D. C., September 11–12, 1978; papers presented at the panel entitled "The Scholar–Policy Maker Nexus in International Affairs: The Use, Misuse, and Disuse of External Research by the Foreign Policy Establishment," 19th Annual Convention of the International Studies Association, Washington, D.C., February 23, 1978; and Raymond Platig and Pio Uliassi, presentation entitled "External Research and the Policy-Making Process," Scholar–Diplomat Seminar on European Affairs, U.S. Department of State, Washington, D.C., May 17, 1977. This view is also confirmed by personal discussions with policy makers in this country and in Europe. See also Alexander L. George, *Towards a More Soundly Based Foreign Policy: Making Better Use of Information,* Appendix D, vol. 2, *Report of the Commission on the Organization of the Government for the Conduct of Foreign Policy* (Washington D.C.: Government Printing Office, 1975).

23. Marc Bloch, *The Historian's Craft: Reflections on the Nature and Uses of History* (New York: Vintage Books, 1953 ed.), p. 11.

24. For more discussion of this matter, see the chapter by Samuel F. Wells, Jr., in this book.

25. See George and Smoke, *Deterrence in American Foreign Policy,* p. 625.

26. Ernest May, *"Lessons" of the Past: The Use and Misuse of History in American Foreign Policy* (New York: Oxford University Press, 1973), p. xi.

27. Ibid, p. xiv.

28. For two stimulating discussions of this age-old dilemma of an intellectual either to become involved or to remain aloof from politics, see Gordon A. Craig, "Johannes von Muller: The Historian in Search of a Hero," *American Historical Review* 74 (June 1969):1487–1502; and "Engagement and Neutrality in Weimar Germany," *Journal of Contemporary History* 2 (April 1967):49–63. See also Justus D. Doenecke, "Harry Elmer Barnes: Prophet of a 'Usable' Past," *The History Teacher* 8 (February 1975):26–276.

29. Nathan Glazer, "Theory and Practice in the Social Sciences," *The Chronicle of Higher Education,* July 31, 1978, p. 28.

30. This distinction was initially proposed by Walter Lippmann, as indicated in Kenneth Thompson, "Toward a Theory of International Politics," *American Political Science Review* 49 (September 1955):733–746. See also Stanley Hoffmann, *Contemporary Theory in International Relations* (Englewood Cliffs, N.J.: Prentice-Hall, 1960); and, most recently, Richard Smoke and Alexander L. George, "Theory for Policy in International Relations," *Policy Sciences* 4 (December 1973):387–413; and George and Smoke, *Deterrence in American Foreign Policy,* pp. 616–620. My discussion here draws primarily upon the two latter sources.

31. Immanuel Kant, *Zum ewigen Frieden,* in *Immanuel Kants Werke,* ed. by Ernst Cassirer, 11 vols. (Berlin: Cassirer, 1912–1922), VI: 427–474; Grenville Clark and Louis Sohn, *World Peace Through World Law* (Cambridge: Harvard University Press, 1958); and Rajni Kothari, *Footsteps Into the Future: Diagnosis of the Present World and a Design for an Alternative* (New York: Free Press, 1974). For an interesting discussion of further aspects of this moral approach to world politics, see also Smoke, *War: Controlling Escalation,* pp. 408–409.

32. George and Smoke, *Deterrence in American Foreign Policy,* pp. 619, 620.

33. Ibid., p. 598. They make this statment in the specific context of theories on deterrence, but I think the point possesses the wider applicability with which I use it here.

34. Wilhelm Haffner (Wilhelm Dilthey), "Deutsche Geschichtschreiber: Johannes von Muller," *Westermanns Jahrbuch der Illustrirten Deutschen Monatshefte* 19 (1866):246, as cited in Craig, "Johannes von Muller," p. 1501.

35. See George, Hall, and Simons, *The Limits of Coercive Diplomacy*, especially p. ix; and May, *"Lessons" of the Past, passim.*

36. The words are from Theophile Delcassé, as cited in Maurice Paleologue, *Un grand tournant de la politique mondiale, 1904-1906* (Paris: Plon, 1934), p. 83.

37. Jervis, *Perception and Misperception*, p. 217. His whole chapter, "How Decision Makers Learn from History," pp. 217-287, is fascinating.

38. See Adrian Kuzminski, "The Paradox of Historical Knowledge," *History and Theory* 12 (1973):269-280. See also the interesting discussion by diplomatic historian Alan K. Henrikson, "Thinking Historically," *The Fletcher Forum* 2 (May 1978):225-232.

39. The words are those of Francis Loewenheim in the preface to his edited book, *The Historian and the Diplomat* (New York: Harper and Row, 1967), p. vii. See also Klaus Knorr in the introduction "On the Utility of History" to his edited collection, *Historical Dimensions of National Security Problems* (Lawrence: University Press of Kansas, 1976), especially p. 3. For the suggestion that this problem might be even more critical in a democracy, see Laurence Evans, "The Dangers of Diplomatic History," in Bass, *The State of American History*, pp. 155-156.

40. David F. Trask, "A Reflection on Historians and Policymakers," a speech delivered at the Bicentennial Foreign Policy Conference, Columbus, Ohio, August 1976, and released by the Department of State, Bureau of Public Affairs.

41. Ibid.

42. Zara Steiner, *The Foreign Office and Foreign Policy, 1898-1914* (Cambridge, England: Cambridge University Press, 1969), p. ix.

43. Federico Chabod, *Storia della politica estera italiana dal 1870 al 1896* (Bari: Laterza and Figli, 1951), I:xii. The other factors that he considers are the ideas, the historical content, and the materials available to diplomats.

44. Ibid., p. xiv.

45. Barbara Tuchman, "The Historian's Opportunity," *Saturday Review* (February 1967):28.

46. Ibid., p. 71.

47. One recent manual of diplomacy states the problem in the following words: "No diplomatic skill is more critical than the power of objective analysis. A diplomat must be able mentally to encircle any situation, to examine it from every possible vantage point. He must know how to dissect each problem dispassionately, to identify each of its elements, and to weigh these with complete objectivity." William Macomber. *The Angels' Game: A Handbook of Modern Diplomacy* (New York: Stein and Day, 1975), p. 52.

48. See Gordon A. Craig, *From Bismarck to Adenauer: Aspects of German Statecraft* (New York: Harper and Row, 1965 ed.), especially pp. 15-19.

49. May, *"Lessons" of the Past*, pp. 189-190.

50. Edward Hallett Carr, *What Is History?* (New York: Vintage Books, 1961), p. 111.

51. A brief mention of this idea is made in Herbert Butterfield and Martin Wright (eds.), *Diplomatic Investigations: Essays in the Theory of International Politics* (London: Allen and Unwin, 1966), pp. 12–13.

52. This is the general theme running throughout Charles Delzell (ed.), *The Future of History* (Nashville: Vanderbilt University, 1977).

53. See Wayne S. Cole, "Commentary," presented at a session entitled "Paradigms and Models: What Utility for Diplomatic History?", Southern Historical Association, Dallas, Tex. November 7, 1974; and McCormick, "The State of American Diplomatic History," pp. 123–124. For a discussion of this problem in a larger context, see Abraham Kaplan, *The Conduct of Inquiry* (San Francisco: Chandler, 1964), especially pp. 25–26.

54. Carl von Clausewitz, *On War,* trans. and ed. by Michael Howard and Peter Paret (Princeton: Princeton University Press, 1976 ed.), Book II, Chapter 2, p. 141. For a similar but more recent conclusion with specific reference to history, see Henry Kissinger, "The Lessons of the Past," *The Washington Review* 1 (January 1978):3–9.

PART I

2
On the Nature of Diplomatic History: The Relevance of Some Old Books

Gordon A. Craig

In 1936, when I chose diplomatic history as the field in which I would work for a research degree, Humphrey Sumner, my tutor in Balliol College,[1] suggested that I begin by reading D. P. Heatley's *Diplomacy and the Study of International Relations.*[2] I hunted the book down in the Bodleian without difficulty but was perplexed by what I found. It began with an essay on the history of diplomacy that defied all my powers of concentration because of the meandering course followed by the author and his frequent pauses to engage in dialogue with his footnotes, a practice that had the distracting effect of recalling a recent piece by Frank Sullivan in *The New Yorker,* called "A Garland of Ibids."[3] Apart from this, the volume was made up of bibliographical essays on subjects in which I had no compelling interest, like juristic literature, maps and treaties, and international ethics, and it concluded with a long appendix of quotations, mostly French, about ambassadorial functions and negotiations, as well as a number of extracts from parliamentary reports on subjects like the effects of telegraphic communication on the conduct of British foreign policy.

All in all, this didn't look very promising. Still, I had been led to believe that Oxford tutors knew what they were about, so I persisted; and somewhat to my surprise I had soon stopped worrying about the book's eccentric organization and had acquired a respect and admiration for it that have not diminished with the years. It was, in fact, the first book that made me realize that becoming a diplomatic historian involved more than sitting in a library for a while and then writing a monograph about some aspect of foreign affairs on the basis of the materials I had found there. Heatley did not, to be sure, deny the importance of that operation. In his pawky Scottish way, he admitted that "for such mastery as is attainable of international policy at any point of time and contact in the relations of State to State particularity of knowledge is indispensable, and that must be sought in special works and in the sources that bear upon each problem." But he insisted that there was an antecedent

21

stage. Before he plunged into his archival work, the historian must endeavor to acquire what Heatley called "the habit of mind that is required for appreciating questions of foreign policy."[4]

He never explained exactly what he meant by this, but light was thrown on his thinking by a statement made with some emphasis in his introductory essay. "We must never," he wrote, "separate the study of policy . . . from the appreciation of the instruments on the understanding and use of which success depends; and we must test the character of the instruments by the work they have to do."[5] The implication was clear. Before he began to write about international relations, the historian must make every effort to understand the nature of the diplomatic process itself. Since it was unlikely that he would be able to gain this understanding from practical experience, he would have to do so by reading; and Heatley undertook to facilitate the process. In the most comprehensive of his bibliographical essays, he suggested appropriate reading on the traditions and practices of diplomacy, on the gifts required of, and the problems confronting, the persons who were charged with the formulation and execution of foreign policy, on the limitations imposed upon them by the nature of the international context of their work, and on the relationship between their craft and that other more drastic instrument of policy, the art of war. His list should be consulted in its entirety,[6] but some of his recommendations deserve special attention.

From Wicquefort to Satow

Of those that dealt with the formal aspects of diplomacy, the most important were Charles de Martens' famous *Guide Diplomatique* (1832) and Sir Ernest Satow's *A Guide to Diplomatic Practice* (1917). The son of the author of one of the most influential eighteenth-century treatises on international law,[7] Martens preferred the world of practical politics to that of theory and published his handbook as a service to *"les jeunes gens qui se vouent à la carrière diplomatique."*[8] The importance of this calling was, in his view, beyond question. To it fell the responsibility for regulating the problems and adjudicating the conflicts of interest that resulted from the relations of independent states with each other; its task was to maintain their respective security, tranquility, and dignity; its goal, the promotion of peace and international harmony.[9] When it failed, the results were more serious than those that flowed from delinquencies in domestic policy. The price of a concession too hastily made, or a treaty imprudently drafted, was always high and sometimes prohibitive. "The least of inconsidered words can wound a whole nation; an ill-judged démarche, a mistaken calculation, a combination that is unsound or speculative, a simple indiscretion can compromise both the dignity of a government and the national interest."[10]

It was understandable, therefore, that those who chose diplomacy as a career should be proficient in those branches of learning that would enable them to move in the world of international politics with confidence and efficiency and prudence. These, Martens felt, should include the law of nations; European public law (that is, treaty law, as expounded by his father); the constitutions and public law of the principal European states; history, particularly that of war, and of such modern treaties and negotiations as illustrated the policies of the various powers; political systems (domination, equilibrium, confederation, etc.); political economy; the geography and statistics of the various states; the technique of negotiation and the procedures to be followed in protecting the national interest; and the act of drafting instructions and other diplomatic notes.[11]

Martens did not elaborate on this formidable catalogue, restricting himself to the subjects mentioned on his title page.[12] His first volume was devoted to a description of the functions of the foreign office and its chief, the classification of diplomatic agents, the composition, rights and prerogatives of diplomatic missions, diplomatic ceremonial (rank, order, the etiquette governing audiences and private and formal visits), the duties and functions of diplomatic agents (representations, reporting, negotiation in its varied forms), and the organization and functions of consular agencies. The second and larger volume dealt with the style of diplomatic documents of every kind—proclamations and protests, instructions and dispatches, *pleins-pouvoirs* and *lettres de faire-part*, memoranda and conference protocols—and provided the apprentice diplomat with models from distinguished hands. These were chosen with an eye to their political interest as well as their literary merits, and they included Louis XV's instruction to his minister in St. Petersburg at the time of the accession of Catherine II in 1762,[13] George Canning's instruction to Stratford Canning in September 1826 concerning steps to conclude the war between Greece and Turkey,[14] Thouvenel's letter to his ambassador in Washington protesting the American behavior in the *Trent* affair in 1861,[15] and two powerful examples of diplomatic advocacy, Metternich's circular memorandum to the Austrian missions in 1846, arguing that the incorporation of Cracow in the Habsburg empire was not a breach of treaty,[16] and Cavour's letter of November 9, 1860, to his envoy in Berlin, seeking to alleviate Prussian concern over recent Piemontese annexations and denying that these changes in the map, which were justified by the principle of nationality, threatened the public law of Europe.[17]

Sir Ernest Satow's diplomatic handbook,[18] the first of its kind in English, owed a great deal to Martens, and, indeed, the contents of its first volume much resembled that of his predecessor, concerning itself with the functions, rights, and immunities of diplomatic agents and describing the organization, administration, and termination of missions and the constitution and traditions of the Corps Diplomatique, that is, the body of ambassadors resident in a national capital at any given time. Because Satow hoped, however, that his book would be useful not only "to members of the services but also to the general public and to writers who occupy themselves with international affairs,"[19] he felt the necessity of writing also about matters that Martens tended to take for granted. Thus, his first volume included a chapter on the Latin and French phrases used in diplomatic correspondence and engagements, an amusing and helpful essay where one could learn the meaning of the often misused term *démarche,* the distinction between a *casus belli* and a *casus foederis,* and the subtle differences between *uti possidetis* and *status quo,* and where some interesting examples of the use of *ultimata* were presented, including the formulae used by the Austrian and German governments in 1914.[20]

Satow was also less interested than Martens—national temperament may have had something to do with this—in teaching his readers how to draft elegant diplomatic notes. His consideration of diplomatic intercourse was brief and dealt largely with the languages used in diplomatic communication (he tells us that Bismarck filed notes from the Russian government that were written in Russian without reading them, until the Russians saw the point and switched to French) and with the various forms of communication in current usage.[21] The greater part of his second volume Satow devoted not to stylistic models, as Martens had done, but to a discussion of congresses and conferences, on which he was his country's leading expert.[22] This included lists of the most important modern gatherings of this kind, with brief descriptions of their proceedings that emphasized form and procedure rather than substance, and a series of chapters describing the various kinds of treaties, compacts, and engagements and their appropriate uses, as well as a discussion of good offices and mediation.

To supplement these treatises on the procedures and forms of diplomacy, Heatley recommended two earlier works about the way diplomacy was actually practiced by the diplomat on mission: Wicquefort's *L'ambassadeur et ses fonctions* (1679) and Callières' *De la manière de négocier avec les Souverains* (1716). The first of these has been called one of the most remarkable books published during the seventeenth century, a judgment doubtless influenced by the circumstances of its composition and the checkered career of its author. Abraham de Wicquefort, a Dutch subject, was minister resident of the Elector of Brandenburg in Paris from 1628 to 1658, when he was declared *persona non grata* by the French government because of uncomplimentary references to Cardinal Mazarin found in dispatches of his that had been intercepted. He sought to cling to his post but was, after a brief imprisonment in the Bastille, put on a boat to England, whence he made his way back to his own country, where he became historiographer of the Dutch republic and secretary interpreter of dispatches. This did not dissuade him from accepting a secret pension from Louis XIV and from agreeing also to serve as resident envoy for the Duke of Luneburg; and it was not long before this conflict of interest made him vulnerable to charges of espionage for foreign powers. He was arrested

and in 1675 sentenced to life imprisonment—as a writer of the next generation said smugly, *"damnatus . . . ad perpetuas carceres, publicatis bonis'*[23]—but
escaped with the aid of his daughter four years later and lived his life out in
Hanover, where he died at the age of eight-five in 1682.[24]

Wicquefort's book on the ambassador[25] was written while he was in
prison, and, given the circumstances, it was a remarkably lively account and
astonishingly rich in historical detail. It was also refreshingly matter of fact.
The author wrote in his preface that it was high time that someone wrote a
book of practical advice for diplomats, since most of the existing works on
diplomacy were idealized descriptions of the "perfect ambassador" that
showed little understanding either of the diplomat's job or of the nature of the
real world.[26] He was not going to waste his time arguing that ambassadors
should be men of unqualified moral virtue, for, given the corruption of the
age, such envoys might be hard to find. It was, after all, not so long ago that
the emperor's ambassador at the Venetian court had to be recalled because he
had made a bordello of his mission, manufactured counterfeit money, and,
after failing in an attempt to kill his wife, succeeded in murdering his chief of
chancellery.[27] The best ambassadors were neither moral paragons nor liber-
tines but men with a normal quotient of viruties and vices who possessed, in
addition, however, qualities of mind and feeling—Wicquefort would have
agreed with Satow's definition of diplomacy as "the application of intelligence and tact to the conduct of official relations between the governments
of independent states"[28]—that made them competent to represent their country in a foreign land.

Of fundamental importance to the diplomat was a clear understanding of
the nature of his job and a realization that it had nothing to do with personal
gratification or self-aggrandizement. The ambassador's princcpal function,
Wicquefort wrote, "consists in maintaining effective communication between
the two Princes, in delivering letters which his Master writes to the Prince at
whose court he resides, in soliciting answers to them . . . , in protecting his
Master's subjects and conserving his interests."[29] He was, on the one hand, a
"messenger of peace" and, on the other, an "honorable spy," and in the latter capacity it was his duty to ferret out information that would reveal threats
to his master's interests or opportunities for advancing them. He must possess
the ability to gauge the temperament and intelligence of those with whom he
had to deal and to use this knowledge profitably in negotiation. "Ministers
are but men and as such have their weaknesses, that is to say, their passions
and interests, which the ambassador ought to know if he wishes to do honor to
himself and his Master."[30]

In pursuing this intelligence, the qualities he should cultivate most
assiduously were *prudence* and *modération*. The former Wicquefort equated with
caution and reflection, and also with the gifts of silence and indirection, the
art of "making it appear that one is not interested in the things one desires the
most," of moving toward an objective as rowers do, with one's back to it.[31]

The diplomat who possessed *prudence* did not have to resort to mendacity or deceit or to rely on the *artifices* and *tromperies* that Louis XI and his minister Commines used so often and with such unfortunate effect.[32] *Modération* was the ability to curb one's temper and to remain cool and phlegmatic in moments of tension. "Those spirits who are compounded of sulphur and saltpeter, whom the slightest spark can set afire, are easily capable of compromising affairs by their excitability, because it is so easy to put them in a rage or drive them to a fury, so that they don't know what they are doing." One of Mazarin's supreme talents was his ability to goad antagonists into losing their temper and their objectivity.[33]

The possession of these gifts was particularly important in the conduct of negotiations and the drafting of treaties, subjects on which Wicquefort had interesting things to say.[34] He pointed out, however, that in the last analysis their effectiveness would depend upon the relationship that existed between the ambassador and his master. The ambassador's loyalty to his prince required a reciprocal feeling of confidence and trust. Reluctance on the part of the prince to allow his envoy to act, whenever necessary, upon his own initiative was a reflection on the wisdom of his choice of representation and could result only in the destruction of the prestige and authority of his envoy's position. In negotiations particularly, nothing was more infuriating to participating powers than the realization that their vis-à-vis had no authority to treat. Wicquefort cited the ill results of the Spanish attempt to slow down negotiations at Münster in 1644 by sending ambassadors without *plein pouvoirs*,[35] an interesting illustration of a truth that was to prove itself again many years later, when the British and French governments sent a similarly disarmed delegation to Moscow in August 1939.

Wicquefort's book caused a considerable stir in its time but was soon forgotten, largely because it was eclipsed by François de Callières' book on negotiation,[36] which possessed a literary grace and sophistication to which Wicquefort could not pretend. This seems a bit unfair, since much of what Callières had to say about the personal qualities of the competent diplomat, about the cardinal importance of caution and reflection, and about the advantages that can be derived from careful analysis of the passions and prejudices of those with whom one must deal were little more than reformulations of points made by his predecessor.[37] Some of Wicquefort's best illustrative anecdotes turn up in Callières' text, as does the description of the ambassador as an honorable spy; and one of Callières' most frequently cited passages, which speaks of the ambassador as an "actor placed before the eyes of the public in order that he may play a great part . . . [who] must be able to simulate a dignity even if he possess it not" is merely an elaboration of Wicquefort's suggestion that the ambassador, who is called upon to play many roles, "ought to have the tincture of a comedian."[38]

What distinguishes Callières' treatise is, first of all, the passion with which the author argues that a nation's foreign relations should be handled by professionals. Anticipating a remark made more than two centuries in the future by Harold Nicolson about the way in which diplomacy, like water colors, suffered from the fascination it exerted on amateurs,[39] Callières complained bitterly of the grave harm done to the public interest by "novices in negotiation." "Instead of gradual promotion by degrees and by the evidence of proved capacity and experience, as is the case in the usages of war, one may see often men who have never left their own country, who have never applied themselves to the study of public affairs, being of meagre intelligence, appointed so to speak over-night to important embassies in countries of which they know neither the interests, the laws, the customs, the language, nor even the geographical situation."[40]

Governments should reflect, he insisted, upon the story of the Duke of Tuscany who, upon complaining to a Venetian visitor of the inadequate intellectual and personal capacities of a Venetian resident at his court and receiving the answer, "I am not surprised. We have many fools in Venice," retorted with spirit, "We also have fools in Florence, but we take care not to export them."[41] An incompetent envoy could do harm to the interests of his country that would take years of hard work to repair, and for that reason the most extreme care must be taken in the selection of one's foreign representatives. Since public offices are always at the mercy of nepotism, cabals, and court intrigue, safety lay in the imposition of objective criteria of competence. "Diplomacy is a profession by itself which deserves the same preparation and assiduity of attention that men give to other recognized professions."[42]

The second salient characteristic of Callières' book was what he had to say about the way in which international agreements are achieved. Here he was on familiar ground, for, as one of Louis XIV's most experienced diplomats, he was the veteran of many protracted and wearying sessions at the bargaining table and had ended his career as head of the French delegation during the negotiations at Ryswick in 1697.[43] He had no illusions about large conferences, "vast concourses of ambassadors and envoys," which were generally too clumsy to achieve anything very useful. Most successful conferences were the result of careful preliminary work by small groups of negotiators who hammered out the essential bases of agreement and secured approval for them from their governments before handing them over, for formal purposes, to the *omnium-gatherums* that were later celebrated in the history books.[44]

Success in negotiation, moreover, generally depended upon a number of other conditions. The negotiator should be given a clear set of instructions and a carefully defined set of objectives, and communication between him and his government should be intimate and frank. But even in the best of circumstances, his chances of carrying out his instructions successfully were not good unless he approached his task with the right temperament. "Despite all disappointments and exasperations he must act with *sang-froid;* he must work with patience to remove all obstacles that lie in his path, whether they are placed there by accident or act of God or by the evil design of men; he must

27

preserve a calm and resolute mind when the conjunctures of events seem to conspire against him; and, finally, he must remember that, if once he permit his own personal or outrageous feelings to guide his conduct in negotiation, he is on the sure and straight road to disaster."[45]

Even more essential was the readiness on his own part and that of his government to accept the knowledge that if one sought victory in negotiation this could only defeat one's best interests. The only practical desideratum was mutual advantage, and this was also the best guarantee of the results a-chieved. The key to success lay in harmonizing the interests of the parties concerned. "An ancient philospher," Callières wrote, "once said that friend-ship between men is nothing but a commerce in which each seeks his own in-terest. The same is true or even truer of the liaisons and treaties which bind one sovereign to another, for there is no durable treaty which is not founded on reciprocal advantage, and indeed a treaty which does not satisfy this condi-tion is no treaty at all, and is apt to contain the seeds of its own dissolution."[46]

This was by no means the whole story. Successful negotiation and, in-deed, the nature of international relations in general depended also to a very large extent upon the nature of the international context. Callières suggested this, when he spoke of the states of Europe as being "members of one Republic" and said that "no considerable change can take place in any one of them without affecting the condition, or disturbing the peace, of all the others,"[47] but he did not elaborate on it, and one must turn to two other books on Heatley's list for fuller treatment of the question of international systems.

The first of these was a work that enjoyed considerable fame in its time, was frequently reprinted and translated from the original German into several languages including Swedish and Polish, and was approved in more than one country (in England, for instance, as late as the 1850s) as part of the prepara-tion for examinations for the foreign service.[48] This was A. H. L. Heeren's *History of the Political System of Europe and its Colonies* (1809).[49] The author, who was professor of history at Göttingen, set out to write not an ordinary history of the Eurpoean nations but, rather, the story of the way in which those states, which "resembled each other in manners, religion and culture and [were] connected by reciprocal interests," came to form a union characterized by "internal freedom [and] reciprocal independence amidst all inequalities of power."[50]

In Heeren's view, this process, which he felt had been consummated in the eighteenth century, was made possible, not only by the cultural homo-geneity of the European states, but also by their variety, "which preserved practically in circulation a greater compass of political ideas" and which created a general repugnance to the idea of dominance by a single power. "A rightful condition among the several states, such as may be projected in theory, was at all times far from being formally established; yet as a gradual result of the progress of culture, a system of international law was developed, which, reposing not merely on express treaties, but also on silent agreements, enjoined the observance of certain maxims in peace, but more especially in times of war, and which, though often violated, were still eminently beneficial. Even the strict, and sometimes excessive etiquette, mutually observed by the states towards one another, was by no means a matter of indifference, if considered only as a mutual acknowledgement of independence on the part of states, often the most unlike in power and constitution."[51] The first fruit of all this, "and the support of the whole system," was the "sacredness of recognized rightful possession"; equally important was the principle of preserving the balance of power, "that is, the mutual preservation of freedom and independence, by guarding against the preponderance and usurpation of an individual." In Heeren's view, maintenance of the balance was "the constant problem for higher policy" and the principal preoccupation of the diplomats who made and executed it; and the consequences of that preoccupation were "a constantly wakeful attention of the states to one another, and various consequent relations by means of alliances and counter-alliances, especially of the more distant states; the greater importance of states of the second and third order in the political system; and, in general, the preservation of a feeling of the value of independence, and the elevation of politics above gross selfishness."[52]

The first edition of Heeren's book appeared in 1809, at a time when, with Austria's crushing defeat at the hands of Napoleon and the conquest of most of Germany by the Corsican, the system whose emergence he had postulated was shaken to its foundations. While describing this catastrophe, he was far from believing that it had been necessary or that it might not be merely a preface to "a greater and more glorious futurity";[53] and by the time his fourth edition was ready, in 1822, he could write happily of a reconstructed system based upon the Final Act of the Congress of Vienna, the procedures for the preservation of the balance that were stipulated in the Treaty of Chaumont and the Quadruple Alliance, the readmission of France to the European concert at the Conference of Aix la Chapelle, and the religious sanctions provided by the Holy Alliance.[54] "Thus," he pronounced with satisfaction, "the grand drama of the history of the political system of Europe for three hundred years concluded with its restoration."[55]

Heeren's view of the eighteenth century was sharply contested by Albert Sorel in the first volume of his *L'Europe et la Révolution française* (1885).[56] Sorel came to history late, after his career at the Ministry of Foreign Affairs, which had begun in 1866, was cut short after the Franco–Prussian war by his marriage to a German citizen. He was appointed in 1872 to the chair of diplomatic history at the Ecole des Sciences politiques, although he had no historical training or publications to his credit. The last deficiency he corrected quickly with a diplomatic history of the recent war (1875) and a study of the eastern question in the eighteenth century (1877), after which he turned to the work that was to be his masterpiece.[57]

The first and most widely read of the eight volumes of *L'Europe et la Révolution française* was an entended discussion of the political traditions of the old regime, the first chapter of which included a description of *les moeurs politiques* of the eighteenth century that was intended to reveal the stark realities that lay behind the grandiloquent formulations of an age in which, as La Bruyère had written, diplomats "spoke only of peace, alliances, public tranquility . . . and thought only of their selfish interest."[58] Far from seeing themselves as members of a commonwealth with mutual rights and obligations, the European rulers were guided only by private ambitions and seized on any opportunity to gratify them. As Voltaire once said: *"Le temps, l'occasion, l'usage, le prescription, la force font tous les droits.'"*[59] What was called an Age of Reason was in reality dominated by the passions of princes and by deceit and intrigue and treachery.[60] Peace was always "precarious and perfidious," and war always atrocious.[61] As a regulating principle, balance of power operated not to prevent the outbreak of violence but, rather, to appease those who had condoned aggression after it had succeeded, and it did so at the expense of smaller states that could not defend themselves.[62]

One cannot read Sorel's account of eighteenth-century diplomacy without being forced to consider the possibility that Heeren's picture of the European system was overdrawn and that he was describing a system *in spe,* an aspiration that was not in fact actualized until the period 1815–1848, when written and unwritten conventions had much more binding force than earlier and the principle of the balance of power worked effectively. At the same time, the vigor with which Sorel attacked the idea of an eighteenth-century collaborative system as an *"auguste abstraction,'"*[63] makes one suspect that his somber view of the old regime was perhaps colored by his concern over tendencies in his own time, a dangerous age that had resulted from the destructive work of system-breakers like Bismarck, who said in 1876: "To speak of Europe is a mistake—*notion géographique"* and "I always hear the word Europe in the mouths of politicans who want something from other powers that they dare not ask in their own name."[64] This is not the place to seek to reconcile their differences; but it is clear at least that, however misplaced their emphases may have been, both Heeren and Sorel were correct in sensing the importance of the international climate of opinion at any given time and in seeing that the existence or nonexistence of consensus about the means of defending or advancing one's interest will determine the general nature of international relations as well as the specific preoccupations and capabilities of diplomats.

Such is the human tendency to dichotomize, and so long lived is the liberal tendency to consider war as an aberration in history that should not be dwelt upon, that the inclusion of Clausewitz's essay *On War* in a list of readings on diplomacy may still seem odd to persons who have never read it. Yet Clausewitz's work is more than "the most profound, comprehensive, and systematic examination of war and its conduct" that has ever been written.[65]

It is often forgotten that this dedicated professional soldier, the high point of whose life was reached when, as a Russian liaison officer attached to Blücher's staff, he stood in the center of the maelstrom at Gross-Görschen in May 1813 and risked his life repeatedly in cavalry fights,[66] was also a sensitive political observer and a keen analyst of international tendencies.[67] Indeed, we might never have had the essay *On War* at all, if his political enemies at the Prussian court had not collaborated in 1819 with the British envoy in Berlin, Sir George Henry Rose, to balk his ambition to become Prussian minister to the Court of St. James.[68] The masterpiece that he wrote in his years of disappointment, when he held an unexciting position in the War Academy, leaves little doubt that he would have been a distinguished diplomat, for it is a mine of political shrewdness and insight, most of which was, sadly, lost upon his own countrymen.

So impregnated is the work with politics, and so convinced was Clausewitz of the interconnectedness of politics and war, that chapters that at first reading seem specifically military in content can by simple verbal substitution be made to apply to diplomacy as well. This is true of the striking *aperçu* in the chapter on "Friction in War," that "everything in war is very simple, but the simplest thing is difficult. . . . Countless minor incidents—the kind you can never really foresee—combine to lower the general level of performance, so that one always falls far short of the intended goal." Action in war (diplomacy) "is like movement in a resistant element. Just as the simplest and most natural of movements, walking, cannot easily be performed in water, so in war [diplomacy] it is difficult for normal efforts to achieve even moderate results."[69] The good general (diplomat) "must know friction in order to overcome it whenever possible. . . . It is a force that theory can never quite define. Even if it could, the development of instinct and tact would still be needed, a form of judgement much more necessary in an area littered by endless minor obstacles than in great momentous questions which are settled in solitary deliberation."[70]

Similarly, Clausewitz's chapter "On Military Genius," which describes the intellectual gifts and the qualities of character and temperament that mark the great commander, needs only minor revision to describe the statesman as well. For he should also possess "a sense of unity and power of judgement raised to a marvellous pitch of vision, which easily grasps and dismisses a thousand remote possibilities which an ordinary mind would labor to identify and wear itself out in so doing"; and, to make this power of divination effective, he too must have "the ability to keep [his] head in times of exceptional stress and violent emotion,"[71] as well as the strength of mind, in such moments, "to stick to his first opinion and to refuse to change unless forced to do so by a clear conviction."[72]

Clausewitz's most striking formulation was the statement in his note of July 10, 1827, that "war is nothing but the continuation of policy with other means,"[73] from which it followed that the initiating, the objectives, and the

31

termination of war must all be the result of political decisions made with the best interests of the state in mind. "The political object is the goal, war is the means of reaching it, and means can never be considered in isolation from their purpose"[74]—it was this profound truth that was so drastically neglected by the German leadership in World War I, when the insubordination of the military chiefs, backed by inflamed public and parliamentary opinion, destroyed the ability of Chancellor Theobald von Bethmann Hollweg to maintain rational control over the course of operations. But it can also be argued that their greater fault was failure to ponder the extraordinary sixth chapter of Book Six, in which Clausewitz, pursuing his idea that, when it came to actual conflict, the defense had a natural superiority in the use of means, alluded to the natural resistance of the international community to aggression. In words that revealed his general affinity with his contemporary Heeren, he wrote: "If we consider the community of states in Europe today, we . . . find major and minor interests of states and peoples interwoven in the most varied and changeable manner. Each point of intersection binds and serves to balance one set of interests against the other. The broad effect of all these fixed points is obviously to give a certain amount of cohesion to the whole. Any change will necessarily weaken this cohesion to some degree. The sum total of relations between states thus serves to maintain the stability of the whole rather than to promote change; at least, that tendency will generally be present."[75]

One should not, therefore, underestimate the force of balance that is inherent in the international community even when it seems most disorganized and most vulnerable to aggression. Other things being equal, the victim of aggression will find that it has more friends than enemies; and attempts to subvert the public order will always be dangerous gambles.

> If it were not for that common effort toward maintenance of the *status quo,* it would never have been possible for a number of civilized states to coexist peacefully over a period of time; they would have been bound to merge into a single state. The fact that Europe, as we know it, has existed for over a thousand years can only be explained by the operation of these general interests; and if collective security has not always sufficed to maintain the integrity of each individual state, the fact should be ascribed to irregularities in the life of the system as a whole which instead of destroying were absorbed into it.[76]

Past Precepts and Present Practice

What relevance do books like these have for the study of diplomatic history and international relations today? Heatley's purpose in recommending them, we remember, was to give the apprentice historian the kind of understanding of the world of diplomacy and of the instruments of foreign policy that would inform his research and writing. Yet even as he compiled his book, changes were taking place that were, in the decades that followed, to transform that world and its modalities. The small Eurocentric diplomatic community that had dominated world affairs for centuries was forced to open its doors to new members, a change first made evident at the Paris Peace Conference of 1919 and demonstrated more dramatically a year later in the first General Assembly of the League of Nations, when almost fifty nations, the majority of them non-European, made evident their desire to be heard in the great questions of world affairs. This process of expansion did not stop— by the 1970s there were more than 130 nations that maintained permanent delegations at the United Nations—and it was inevitably accompanied by a deterioration of the internal homogeneity of the community. Its members no longer drew on a common fund of history. Ideological differences, virtually unknown in the old diplomatic system, complicated communication and understanding, for totalitarian governments made a fine art of defying the rules and conventions that had been inherited from the past, which led the United States Secretary of State, Bainbridge Colby, to protest in 1920 that "the existing regime in Russia is based upon the negation of every principle of honor and good faith and every usage and convention underlying the whole structure of international law . . . in short, of every principle upon which it is possible to base harmonious and trustful relations,"[77] and which caused similar reactions on the part of democratic statesmen to Fascist and National Socialist diplomacy. Similarly, new nations, liberated from a colonial past, were apt to express their independence by studied disregard of the standards and procedures of their former masters. All of this added up to a high degree of incoherence in international discourse.

These changes made new demands on the professional diplomat. It became clear that the kind of education prescribed in Martens' *Guide Diplomatique* would not prepare him to be an effective representative of his country in a multicultural and highly ideologized environment. Whereas negotiation had to Wicquefort and Callières been the diplomat's key function, in the expanded community it was often replaced by cross-cultural interpretation, proficiency in which was more likely to be aided by some knowledge of anthropology, sociology, and comparative value systems than by mastery of international law.[78] Yet even in those countries where strenuous efforts were made to train diplomats to cope with the new conditions, the recipients of that preparation found that the authority once inherent in their profession was challenged and their role diminished. In democratic countries, the popular demand for open diplomacy and parliamentary control so reduced the envoy's independence that at crucial points in negotiation he was forced to surrender his functions to political ministers. At the same time, even his claim to be his government's best source of information about the country to which he was accredited was contested by the intelligence community and other government agencies, as well as by the hordes of junketing politicians, consultants to international corporations, journalists, television teams, and peripatetic academicians that are a feature of modern life.

It was reflection upon the totality of these changes that led Nevile Bland, the editor of the fourth and greatly reduced edition of Satow's *Guide to Diplomatic Practice,* to write in 1968: "There has been a growing tendency since 1933 to supersede the professional diplomat with the creature of the local ideology and to substitute for the discreet exchange of notes tendentious press conferences and abuse over the air. Whatever the disadvantages of the so-called secret diplomacy may have been, can it be claimed that the airing of national dislikes and prejudices in uncontrolled language, whether at the United Nations or over the radio, is less likely to lead to international friction? I will put another question: can these practices rightly be called diplomacy?" Warming to the task, he continued in a manner reminiscent of Callières:

> What are left of the old canons of diplomacy are continuously subject to change, both deliberate and unconscious. Increasing questioning in parliament and press; a growing tendency of Ministers dealing with foreign affairs to travel about the world and take into their own hands consultations which a few decades back could, and would, have been conducted by the heads of the diplomatic missions concerned; the vastly increased speed and facility of communication between the Foreign Office and Her Majesty's Missions abroad; the growing habit of parliamentary and other groups of paying visits to foreign countries—all these tend to undermine the confidence and independence of members of the Foreign Service and in some cases to usurp, in favour of an amateur hotel and travel agency, time and money formerly, and more usefully, devoted by members of Her Majesty's Embassies, Legations and Consulates to the cultivation of local contacts.

In these circumstances, Mr. Bland seemed to doubt the advisability of issuing a new edition of Satow, since it included little in the way of guidance for those foreign service officers who had to deal with "this type of non-diplomacy."[79]

Does it also have little to offer the diplomatic historian of our time, and is this also true of the other books discussed above, all of which, like Satow, deal with a diplomatic system that seems to have in large part disappeared? To answer this question in the affirmative would be to take a very narrow and utilitarian view of relevance, and one that a historian can ill afford to accept. As Thomas Nipperdey has written, the historian of the modern period looks to the past for general perspective and evidence of continuity. But that is not all. Discontinuity also has its lessons, and the fact that things are no longer done as they once were is no excuse for not studying the old procedures. "Turning toward the different and strange, which has no relationship of continuity with us, and attempting to understand it in the light of its own assumptions helps us understand our position and our own susceptibility to continuity and change; indeed, it is indispensable for such understanding."[80] The historian who has studied the diplomatic rules and methods of the period before World War I will, other things being equal, tend to have more understanding, and to be a more critical analyst, of the diplomacy of his own day. He has acquired a standard of comparison, however much he must qualify it by his appreciation of differences in the objective circumstances of the periods being compared.

During the past fifty years, the nature of diplomatic history has changed as radically as diplomacy itself. A branch of study that was once criticized by other historians for its narrowness and its excessive concentration on diplomatic correspondence and the story of negotiations, it has in recent years shown an increasing tendency to embrace more general questions, like the moral and intellectual roots and assumptions of national policy; domestic factors as a determining factor (what the Germans have been calling *Der Primat der Innenpolitik*) and the use by governments of action abroad to alleviate or solve problems at home; interagency competition in the decision-making process; the role of bankers and export firms in influencing the external behavior of governments; movements of public opinion and the way in which opinion on foreign policy is influenced by the press and television;[81] the effect on international relations of national stereotypes and how they are made and communicated; cultural and other nonpolitical forms of international contact; comparative political systems and ideological convergence; and much else. Upon subjects like these, the works discussed above have little bearing.

On the other hand, while the broadening of the focus of diplomatic history is commendable and to be encouraged, its principal preoccupation will continue to be with the kind of international relations that one reads about in the daily newspapers—with the story of the formal relations between governments, with the way they formulate their policies in specific cases, with the modalities they employ and the combinations they form in order to protect and advance their interests, with their conflicts and the ways in which they are or are not resolved, with the ways they get in and out of wars.[82] And on all these subjects Heatley's recommended reading list will have some relevance.

This becomes clear if we consider for a moment some important books that still have to be written. When the time comes, for instance, to write a full-scale history of the North Atlantic Treaty Organization, its author will have to deal with the part played by John Foster Dulles in the European Defense Community crisis of 1954, which led in the end to an enlargement of the treaty organization, and in the Suez crisis of 1956, which came close to destroying it. It would be worth his while, before he makes his assessment of Dulles' competence as the director of United States policy, to ponder Callières' view that "in general, the training of a lawyer breeds habits and dispositions of mind which are not favorable to the practice of diplomacy. And though it be true that success in the law courts depends largely upon a knowledge of human nature and an ability to exploit it—both of which are factors in diplomacy—it is nonetheless true that the occupation of the lawyer, which is to split hairs about nothing, is not a good preparation for the treatment of grave public affairs."[83]

The future historian of the Strategic Arms Limitations Talks will doubtless emphasize the unprecedented amount of scientific knowledge that underlay the negotiation of the treaty of May 1973 and the fact that, in contrast to all previous arms limitation agreements between major powers, this one, instead of seeking to limit offensive weapons, did the opposite, the signatories agreeing not to build new defensive nuclear systems and accepting a condition of mutual vulnerability. If, at the same time, he remembers Martens' definition of good diplomatic style as *"bien dire dans l'ordre convenable tout ce qui doit être dit, et rien au delà"*[84] and has read Wicquefort and Callières on the mutuality of advantage that treaties must provide, he will appreciate both the skill with which momentous issues were compressed into unambiguous literary form and the reasons why ideological differences did not prevent the treaty's consummation.

Should his interest extend to the negotiations for a second SALT agreement, he may have occasion to note that, whereas the earlier negotiations had in general followed the rules of classical diplomacy, those for SALT II suffered a serious setback as a result of President Carter's deliberate and amateurish flouting of them in March 1977—his departure from bases of negotiation that had already yielded forty-five pages of agreed text, his submission through the Secretary of State, who had played no part in the earlier talks, of a new set of proposals which appeared to give a decided advantage to the United States, and, when the Russians refused to discuss these, his expression, in a press conference held before the Secretary had returned home to report, of veiled threats about what the United States government would do if it felt that the Russians were "not acting in good faith."[85] It was precisely to discourage this kind of diplomacy that Martens and Satow, Wicquefort and Callières wrote their books.

Similarly, the future author of a monograph on the Conference on Security and Cooperation in Europe in 1975 will find more than enough in those works to explain why the Western powers did not win the concessions that they thought they had won from the Soviet Union at Helsinki and why they were powerless to correct this at the Belgrade meeting of February 1978. Wicquefort's chapter on treaties includes a crushing judgment on the Helsinki negotiators: "If equivocal words and ambiguities are inconvenient in conversation, they ought for more compelling reasons to be banned from treaties, where one cannot speak too clearly and where it is necessary to employ terms that do not leave the slightest scruple or doubt in the mind or the slightest opening for an interpretation contrary to the intentions of those who treat."[86] As for the meeting in Belgrade, which was supposed to provide a review of compliance with the Helsinki agreement, it degenerated into a profitless ideological slanging match, which was what the Soviet government wanted, in part because the United States government violated every principle of conference and negotiating technique emphasized in the older literature—

sending a delegation composed not of professional diplomats but of persons chosen to appeal to various shades of domestic opinion, which was not clearly briefed at the outset and was the recipient of subsequent instruction from agencies with different points of view, and which never seems to have had a clear idea of its precise objectives or its fallback position in case they were not attained. The Belgrade meeting should be regarded by anyone with a historical sense as a case study in the degeneration of diplomatic standards and a striking illustration of the old rule, valued by Wicquefort and Callières and Satow, that it is unwise to go into conference unless one is reasonably sure what the results are going to be.

It would be idle to comment on the importance of Clausewitz for the diplomatic historian of our time, for it is clearly impossible to write the political history of either the Korean War or the conflict in Vietnam without keeping the precepts of the German philosopher of war in mind. Both conflicts demonstrate the difficulty that a democratic state has in maintaining the kind of coordination between policy and war that Clausewitz considered essential, and the long struggle in Southeast Asia is an interesting example of the fateful results that can flow from a failure to weigh the factors discussed in his chapter on "Scope of the Means of Defense."[87]

Finally, it is possible that one book on our list will assume increasing relevance in the years ahead. There is already a growing interest in regionalism and federalism ("The Federal State" has been announced as one of the *Grands Thèmes* of the International Congress of Historical Sciences that will meet in Bucharest in 1980), and we shall doubtless see an increase in the number of monographs dealing with the movement toward European unity since 1945. It would be possible, in approaching that important subject, to regard the years 1866–1945 as a great aberration in European history and to interpret the post–1945 movement as a resumption of a development that was rudely interrupted in the 1860s by what Robert C. Binkley once called "the crisis of federative polity."[88] A historian who thought along those lines would find it profitable to read Heeren's *History of the European System*, perhaps tempering it with a little of Albert Sorel's skepticism, for, at the very least, it would provide him with an example of how people, before the age of integral nationalism, could think of themselves as belonging to a federative community with "a greater and more glorious futurity."

But these are trivial illustrations. The important point is that if the diplomatic historian of our time is to be more than a mere chronicler of how nations deal with each other, if he is to be a critical analyst of foreign relations and an interpreter of the great events of our recent past to the lay public, he is going to have to make a practice of thinking about how governments in earlier times went about their diplomatic business. It is this habit of mind that will give him perspective and a basis for judgment. Which is, of course, precisely what Heatley was driving at.

Notes

1. Benedict Humphrey Sumner, Fellow and Tutor in Modern History at Balliol, 1925–1944, Professor of History at Edinburgh University, 1944–1945, and Warden of All Souls from 1945 until his death in 1951, was a diplomatic historian of distinction. His masterpiece, *Russia and the Balkans,* with its superb reconstruction of the origins and proceedings of the Congress of Berlin, was published in 1937.

2. D. P. Heatley, *Diplomacy and the Study of International Relations* (Oxford: Clarendon Press, 1919). Heatley was Lecturer in History at the University of Edinburgh.

3. This piece, which pretended to be a review of Van Wyck Brooks's *The Flowering of New England,* appeared in the spring of 1936. It has been reprinted in E. B. White and Katharine S. White (eds.), *A Sub-Treasury of American Humor* (New York: Coward-McCann, 1941), pp. 263–266.

4. Heatley, *Diplomacy,* pp. 86–87.

5. Ibid., pp. 4–5.

6. Ibid., pp. 149–167.

7. This was G. F. von Martens, whose *Précis du Droit des Gens moderne de l'Europe fondé sur les Traités et l'Usage,* was first published in 1788.

8. The edition used here is the fifth, Charles de Martens, *Le Guide Diplomatique. Précis des Droits et des Fonctions des Agents diplomatiques et consulaires, suivi d'un Traité des Actes et Offices divers, qui sont du Ressort de la Diplomatie, accompagné de Pièces et Documents proposés comme Examples,* ed. by M. F. H. Geffcken, 2 vols. in 3 (Leipzig: Brockhaus, 1866).

9. Ibid., I: 1n. Here Martens is following a well known definition by the Comte de Garden.

10. Ibid., I: 25.

11. Ibid., I: 6–7.

12. See note 8.

13. Martens, *Guide,* II, pt. 1, 292–298.

14. Ibid., pp. 298–305.

15. Ibid., II, pt. 2, 181–184.

16. Ibid., pp. 8–20.

17. Ibid., pp. 152–156.

18. Sir Ernest Satow, *A Guide to Diplomatic Practice,* 2 vols. (London: Longmans, Green, 1917). A second and revised edition was published in 1922; a third, in one volume, with the historical sections severly cut and chapters on the League of Nations and the British Commonwealth, in 1932; a fourth, edited by Nevile Bland, also in one volume and with the League material replaced by chapters on the United Nations and associations of the Western states, in 1968. Satow was a professional diplomat with long years of service in Japan, whose language, religion, economy, and culture he studied and wrote about. The second edition is used here.

19. Satow, *Diplomatic Practice,* 2nd ed., I: vii.

20. Ibid., pp. 158–180.

21. Ibid., pp. 68–110.

22. He wrote the study *International Congresses,* which was one of the series of handbooks prepared for the guidance of the British delegation at the Paris Peace Conference of 1919.

23. Bynkershoek, *De Foro Legatorum* (The Hague, 1721), chapter XI.

24. Henry Wheaton, *History of the Law of Nations in Europe and America; from the earliest times to the Treaty of Washington, 1842* (New York: Gould, Banks, 1845), pp. 234–235.

25. First published in 1679. The edition used here is of 1690: *L'Ambassadeur et ses fonctions par Monsieur de Wicquefort, Conseiller aux Conseils d'Estat et Privé du Duc de Brunswic et Luneburg Zelle etc., Dernière Edition, augmentée des Reflexions sur les Mémoires pour les Ambassadeurs, de la Réponse à l'Auteur et du Discours Historique d'Election de l'Empereur et des Electeurs* (Cologne: Marteau, 1690). An English translation by John Digby, entitled *The Ambassador and his Functions,* was published in 1716.

26. He may have been thinking of *Le parfait Ambassadeur,* traduit de l'Espagnol en Français, par le Sieur Lancelot (Paris, 1642), although there were other works of this kind.

27. Wicquefort, *L'Ambassadeur,* p. 5.

28. Satow, *Diplomatic Practice,* I:1.

29. Wicquefort, *L'Ambassadeur,* p. 6.

30. Ibid., p. 7.

31. Ibid., pp. 58ff., 61f.

32. Ibid., pp. 12, 65.

33. Ibid., p. 91.

34. Ibid., pp. 125ff.

35. Ibid., pp. 178ff.

36. François de Callières, *De la Manière de négocier avec les Souverains. De l'Utilité des Négociations, du choix des Ambassadeurs et des Envoyez, et des qualitez nécessaires pour reüssir dans ces emplois* (Paris, 1716). A new and enlarged French edition in two volumes was published in London in 1750. The first English edition, under the title *The Art of Negotiating with Sovereign Princes,* appeared in London in 1716. In 1919 a new English translation by A. F. Whyte, somewhat but not significantly abbreviated, appeared in London, with the title *The Art of Diplomacy.* The edition used here is a reprint of this, *On the Manner of Negotiating with Princes* by Monsieur de Callières (Notre Dame: University of Notre Dame Press, 1963).

37. Callières, *Negotiating,* pp. 18ff., 47–48.

38. Cf. ibid., pp. 21f., 27, 35; Wicquefort, *L'Ambassadeur,* pp. 5, 6, 91.

39. Harold Nicolson, *Curzon: The Last Phase, 1919–1925* (New York: Harcourt, Brace, 1939), p. 54.

40. Callières, *Negotiating,* p. 9.

41. Ibid., p. 59.

42. Ibid., p. 56.

43. One of Callières' colleagues at Ryswick was the poet Matthew Prior, who was secretary to the British plenipotentiaries. Prior's *Journal* and correspondence include interesting memoirs on the preliminaries and the negotiations (see Satow, *Diplomatic practice,* II: 27ff.), which are also alluded to in one his verses, which indicates that the diplomatic career was strenuous but had its lighter moments.

> While with Labour Assiduous due pleasure I mix
> And in one day attone for the Busyness of Six
> In a little Dutch Chaise on a Saturday Night
> On my left hand my Horace and—on my right
> No Memoire to compose and no Post-boy to move
> That on Sunday may hinder the softness of Love.

The Literary Works on Matthew Prior, ed. by H. Bunker Wright and Monroe K. Spears, 2 vols. (Oxford: Clarendon Press, 1959), I: 158.

44. Callières, *Negotiating,* p. 68.
45. Ibid., p. 108.
46. Ibid., p. 109.
47. Ibid., p. 11.
48. Heatley, *Diplomacy,* p. 13.
49. A. H. L. Heeren, *Handbuch der Geschichte des europäischen Systems und seinen Kolonien* (Göttingen, 1809). A fourth edition, published in 1822, was the basis of the American edition, which is used here, *History of the Political System of Europe and its Colonies,* with an introduction by George Bancroft, 2 vols. (Northampton, Mass.: S. Bulter and Son, 1829). A British edition under the title *A Manual of the Political System of Europe* appeared in 1834.
50. Heeren, *Political System,* I: v (Author's preface to the first edition).
51. Ibid., p. 11.
52. Ibid., pp. 12–13.
53. Ibid., p. viii.
54. Heeren's view of the Holy Alliance differed from that of later historians. He wrote: "Politicians, accustomed only to the language and forms of modern diplomacy, were startled at this strange phenomenon. Had they forgotten that the diplomacy of the 16th and 17th centuries was wont to say much respecting Christianity and its welfare?" Ibid., II: 396.
55. Ibid., p. 398.
56. Albert Sorel, *L'Europe et La Révolution française,* 8 vols. (Paris: Plon, Nourrit, 1885–1904). The edition used here is the fourth edition of the first volume (Paris, 1897). An English edition of the first volume, translated and edited by Alfred Cobban and J. W. Hunt, was published in 1969.
57. Editors' introduction to Albert Sorel, *Europe and the French Revolution* (London: Colins, 1969), pp. 9–10.
58. La Bruyère, *Les Caractères ou les Moeurs de ce Siècle,* 8th ed. (Paris, 1694), Chapter 10 ("Du Souverain ou de la République," with its famous description of the diplomat as a chameleon and a Proteus).
59. Sorel, *Révolution,* I: 13.

60. Ibid., pp. 16–20.

61. Ibid., p. 81.

62. Ibid., pp. 37–41.

63. Ibid., p. 9.

64. Erich Eyck, *Bismarck. Leben und Werk,* 3 vols. (Zürich: Eugen Rentsch Verlag, 1941–1944), III: 244.

65. Herbert Rosinski, *The German Army,* ed. by Gordon A. Craig (New York: Praeger, 1966), p. 110.

66. See Roger Parkinson, *Carl von Clausewitz* (London: Stein and Day, 1971), pp. 213ff.

67. See, for instance, Carl von Clausewitz, *Politische Schriften und Briefe,* ed. by Hans Rothfels (Munich: Drei Masken Verlag, 1922); and, for the best discussion, Peter Paret, *Clausewitz and the State* (New York: Oxford University Press, 1976), especially pp. 147ff.

68. See Peter Paret, "Bemerkungen zu dem Versuch von Clausewitz zum Gesandten in London ernannt zu werden," *Jahrbuch für die Geschichte Mittel-und Ostdeutschlands* 26 (1977): 161–172. In letters to Castlereagh, Rose accused Clausewitz of harboring revolutionary sentiments.

69. Carl von Clausewitz, *On War,* ed. and trans. by Michael Howard and Peter Paret with introductory essays by Peter Paret, Michael Howard, and Bernard Brodie, and with a commentary by Bernard Brodie (Princeton: Princeton University Press, 1976), p. 119. This edition is based largely on the first edition of 1832, supplemented by the annotated German text of 1952, edited by Werner Hahlweg.

70. Ibid., p. 120.

71. Ibid., p. 105.

72. Ibid., p. 108.

73. Ibid., p. 69.

74. Ibid., pp. 87, 605ff.

75. Ibid., p. 373.

76. Ibid., p. 374f. Clausewitz agreed that some would consider these ideas utopian but attacked those "who ridicule the very idea of political balance" in the eighteenth century, as Sorel was later to do, by refusing to admit the validity of the evidence they cited to support their argument. Ibid., pp. 374–376. On the importance of this chapter, often neglected even by Clausewitz scholars, see James E. King, "On Clausewitz: Master Theorist of War," *Naval War College Review* 25 (Fall 1977): 31–32.

77. Historical Office, Department of State, *Foreign Relations of the United States, 1920* (Washington, D.C.: Government Printing Office, 1936), III: 463ff.

78. See F. S. C. Northrop, *Philosophical Anthropology and Practical Politics* (New York: Macmillan, 1960).

79. Satow, *Diplomatic Practice* (London: Longmans, Green, 1968 ed.), pp. v–vi. The editor was head of the Treaty Department of the Foreign Office from 1935 to 1938 and from 1938 to 1948 minister and later ambassador at the court of the Netherlands.

80. Thomas Nipperdey, "Über Relevanz," in *Aus Theorie und Praxis der Geschichts-wissenschaft: Festschrift für Hans Herzfeld zum 80. Geburtstag*, ed. by Dietrich Kurze (Berlin: De Gruyter, 1972), pp. 23ff.

81. See, for instance, Peter Blaestrup, *Big Story*, 2 vols. (Boulder: Westview Press, 1977), for an account of the way in which the Tet offensive came to be regarded as a disaster for American forces because of exaggerated press and television treatment and the failure of the media to reassess the estimates of damage by a new look at the evidence after the offensive was halted, and an analysis of the domestic effects of this.

82. The weakness of Ernst Nolte's *Deutschland und der kalte Krieg* (Munich: Piper Verlag, 1974) is, as Felix Gilbert has pointed out in the *American Historical Review* 81 (June 1976): 619, that the author provides no detailed treatment of diplomatic negotiations and government actions, preferring to concentrate upon movements of public opinion and failing adequately to document the effect of these upon policy in either the United States or the Soviet Union. A diplomatic history of the Cold War has still to be written.

83. Callières, *Negotiating*, pp. 55–56. Wicquefort felt that businessmen were equally unfitted for diplomacy, as were people "with too strong a connection with the prejudices of scholars," by which he presumably meant former professors. *L' Ambassadeur*, pp. 77–78.

84. Martens, *Guide*, II: 5.

85. See the excerpts from the President's remarks in the press conference in *New York Times*, March 31, 1977, and Andrei Gromyko's caustic remarks about them as reported on 1 April.

86. Wicquefort, *L'Ambassadeur*, p. 143. Throughout the spring of 1975 the British weekly *The Economist* warned that such ambiguities would result from the conference and would vitiate the agreement.

87. Clausewitz, *On War*, pp. 372–376.

88. Robert C. Binkley, *Realism and Nationalism, 1852–1871* (New York: Harper and Brothers, 1935), pp. 181ff.

3
Case Studies and Theory Development: The Method of Structured, Focused Comparison

Alexander L. George

THE DISTINGUISHED HISTORIAN of the Renaissance, Jacob Burckhardt, once remarked that the true use of history is not to make men more clever for the next time but to make them wiser forever. Admittedly, it is not easy to learn from history, though almost every statesman and general has professed to have done so. In the first place, people often disagree as to the correct lesson to be drawn from a particular historical experience. For example, quite different lessons regarding military strategy for fighting limited wars were drawn from the frustrating experience of the Korean War and once again, quite ominously, from the failure of American military power in the Vietnam War.[1] Second, even if people agree on the correct lessons to be drawn from a particular historical case, they often misapply those lessons to a new situation that differs from the past one in important respects.[2]

From Lessons of History to Theory

If it is hazardous to draw lessons of broader applicability from single historical cases, how then can historical experience be utilized to understand better and to deal effectively with contemporary situations that bear a certain resemblance to past historical cases? The answer lies in stating lessons in a *systematic and differentiated way* from a *broader range* of experience that deliberately draws upon a variety of historical cases. In other words, the task is to convert "lessons of history" into a comprehensive *theory* that encompasses the complexity of the phenomenon or activity in question. Achievement of this

Copyright © 1979 by Alexander L. George.

Preparation of this manuscript was supported by a research grant (No. SOC 75-14079) from the National Science Foundation. The author expresses his appreciation also to the Center for Advanced Study in the Behavioral Sciences, where he was a Fellow during 1976-1977.

goal will be furthered by intellectual cooperation between historians, who are well equipped to provide detailed and discriminating explanations of single historical outcomes, and political scientists, who specialize in techniques for generalizing from and explaining the variance among historical outcomes. Let us consider further the contribution that historians and political scientists can make to the development of policy-relevant theory that is grounded in systematic examination of historical experience.

As any historian or literate person knows, the "lessons" of history are often inconsistent, if not contradictory, and generalizations are hazardous if not carefully qualified. The lesson drawn from a particular case may be contradicted by the lesson that springs from another case. Since historians know this better than others, they are perforce the custodians of relevant historical memory. Historians can make an important contribution to policy making by providing timely reminders that the lessons of history relevant to a current policy problem are not always clear and that to view the current situation as analogous to an earlier historical case (or cases) may be inappropriate or misleading and lead to policy error.

The formulation of theory by political scientists builds upon, but also attempts to go beyond, this minimal but important contribution that historians can make. Theory attempts to absorb the "lessons" of a *variety* of historical cases within a single comprehensive analytical framework; it is the task of theory to identify the many conditions and variables that affect historical outcomes and to sort out the causal patterns associated with different historical outcomes. By doing so, theory accounts for the variance in historical outcomes; it clarifies the apparent inconsistencies and contradictions among the "lessons" of different cases by identifying the critical conditions and variables that differed from one case to the other.

Until recently, development of this kind of historically grounded theory has lagged for several reasons. In the first place, such an approach requires scholars capable of drawing upon and blending the perspectives and special methods of both the historian and political scientist. To this end, some training in both disciplines is necessary. In an earlier era, the education of political scientists included training in history; but in the modern era the two disciplines, which once shared a common epistemological and methodological approach, drifted steadily apart as political science responded to the challenge of the scientific "behavioral" movement in the social sciences. Recent years, however, have seen the beginnings of a reversal of this trend. The intially overly optimistic expectations of political scientists that the behavioral–scientific approach could be easily and productively applied to problems of importance in the study of international relations has given way to greater sobriety. While research methods associated with the behavioral approach have produced interesting results and continue to hold promise, many political scientists now believe that a variety of methods, qualitative as well as quantitative, must be employed in developing knowledge and theory.[3] The

44

often bitter arguments that divided the field of international studies into "traditionalists" and "behavioralists" have gradually given way to a growing awareness that these "contending" approaches are not really antithetical but, rather, are "complementary"—that is, they perform different tasks, both of which are needed.[4]

The drawing back together of history and political science has been facilitated also by developments in the training of historians which have encouraged a more sympathetic view of, and willingness to experiment with, the concepts and methods of the other social sciences. Many historians now believe that their own work can be enhanced considerably by employing a more systematic analysis of phenomena. In the study of diplomatic history, this includes drawing upon certain theories or quantitative techniques developed by political scientists in the field of international relations.

Development of historically grounded theory of the kind needed in the study of international relations and foreign policy was delayed for other reasons as well. Historians often viewed with suspicion efforts by political scientists or others to generalize from historical case studies. It is true, as the historian never tires of reminding us, that history does not repeat itself and that each case possesses unique features. The usual rebuttal by the scientifically oriented political scientist has been that, nonetheless, one can deal with unique cases by treating them as members of a "class" or type of phenomenon that one is interested to understand better—that is, as instances of "alliance formation," "deterrence," "war initiation," "negotiation," "escalation," "war termination," "revolution," and so on. These are types of undertakings and phenomena that occur repeatedly throughout history and hence, the political scientist argues, the many instances of each type can be grouped together and studied as a class of similar events rather than an unique occurrences. By doing so, one may then be able to employ methods of statistical analysis to discover correlations among different variables that might prove to be of causal significance or, at least, that might serve as "indicators" of predictive value. By following this research strategy, it might be possible to develop scientific generalizations and general laws of at least a probabilistic character covering all of the many instances/cases of each type of phenomena.

To this, of course, historians can offer the objection that to take an instance of a certain type of phenomenon out of its individual historical context may well distort explanation and understanding of the single case. Further, this practice can also lead to spurious or misleading generalizations or, if not that, to trivial generalizations which, even though true, characterize the least interesting and significant features of the phenomenon in question.

At one time this intellectual disagreement appeared to be a formidable, unbridgeable obstacle to formulation of an approach to theory development that would synthesize some of the perspectives and methods of both history and political science. But this obstacle, too, has been largely overcome in re-

45

cent years. For one thing, political scientists employing statistical methods for analyzing a large number of cases have come to recognize the necessity for assessing whether the correlations among variables discovered in such studies are genuinely causal or spurious. To this end they employ a variety of research strategies, some involving advanced statistical techniques which we need not consider here. Of more immediate relevance is the fact that some political scientists have developed an alternative research strategy that employs a qualitative procedure that makes use of the historian's methodology of explanation. Thus, to assess whether a statistical correlation between independent variables and the dependent variable is of causal significance, the investigator subjects a single case in which that correlation appears to more intensive scrutiny, as the historian would do, in order to establish whether there exists an *intervening process,* that is, a causal nexus, between the independent variable and the dependent variable. If a connection between the two variables can be established in this way, then it comprises relevant evidence of the causal importance of the independent variable—at least in that single case and, therefore, *possibly* in other cases in which the statistical correlation was established.[5] (On the other hand, whether the independent variable constitutes either a necessary or sufficient condition for the outcome of the dependent variable cannot be easily determined in a single case study of this kind.)[6]

A reappraisal of the relevance of historical method for theory construction has been encouraged by other developments in modern behaviorally oriented political science research. The effort to develop explanatory generalizations via statistical analysis of a large number of cases of a given type or phenomenon has proved to be more difficult than expected. On occasion, it has led investigators to rediscover and to respect the importance of the unique features of each case. As Sidney Verba, a distinguished political scientist specializing in comparative politics, has put it:

> To be comparative, we are told, we must look for generalizations or covering laws that apply to all cases of a particular type. But where are the general laws? Generalizations fade when we look at particular cases. We add intervening variable after intervening variable. Since the cases are few in number, we end up with an explanation tailored to each case. The result begins to sound quite idiographic or configurative. . . . In a sense we have come full circle. . . . As we bring more and more variables back into our analysis in order to arrive at any generalizations that hold up across a series of political systems, we bring back so much that we have a "unique" case in its configurative whole.[7]

It is important to recognize, however, that the dilemma reported by Verba has not led him or others to conclude that the quest for theory and generalizations is infeasible, or that henceforth we must undertake to do only atheoretical, purely idiographic single case studies. Rather, the solution to this apparent impasse is to *formulate the idiosyncratic aspects of the explanation for each case in terms of general variables.* In this way the "uniqueness" of the explanation is recognized but it is described in more general terms, that is, as a particular value of a general variable that is part of a theoretical framework of independent, intervening, and dependent variables.[8] "The 'unique historical event' cannot be ignored," Verba notes, "but it must be considered as one of a class of such events *even if it happened only once.*"[9]

The recognition that even unique cases can contribute to theory development strengthens, of course, the linkage between history and political science. The only remaining hurdle for an effective synthesis and working relationship has to do with the already noted suggestion that the "uniqueness" of a single case be described not only in the specific terms that historians employ but also in terms of variance in the value of independent, intervening, and/or dependent variables. Some (though certainly not all) historians may quarrel with this suggestion, arguing that some unique qualities are inevitably lost in the process of moving from a specific to a more general description and explanation. This is undoubtedly often true; some loss of information and some simplification is inherent in generalization and in any effort at theory formulation. The critical question, however, is whether the loss of information and simplification entailed jeopardizes the validity of the theory and its utility. This question cannot be answered abstractly or on an *a priori* basis. Much depends upon the sensitivity and judgment of the investigator in choosing and conceptualizing his variables and also in deciding how best to describe the variance in each of his variables. It is particularly the latter task—the way in which variations for each variable are formulated—that may be critical for capturing the essential features of the "uniqueness." It is for this reason that investigators would do well to develop the categories for describing the variance in each of their variables not on an *a priori* basis but inductively, via detailed examination of how the value of a particular variable varies in many different cases.

Not all historians would quarrel, in any case, with the necessity of proceeding in this direction if one seeks to formulate historical generalizations and not merely specific explanations for each case. The point is that historians themselves often attempt to formulate generalizations, and such generalizations are simply not possible if the explanation of each single case is couched in purely idiosyncratic and highly specific terms. Indeed, the comparative method, as developed and employed by historians themselves, requires that they find ways of describing and explaining individual cases that render them comparable.[10]

To distinguish between explanation of a "unique" case couched in idiosyncratic terms that are specific only to that case, and those couched in terms of general variables, political scientists have coined the terms "configurative-idiographic" and "disciplined-configurative."[11] We shall shortly discuss these and other types of case studies.

The effort by political scientists and others to develop theory about important problems of strategy, foreign policy, and international relations was

47

handicapped for a number of years by a belief that reliance on modern decision theory and game theory (and its adaptations) would not only provide a powerful impetus and framework for the development of such theories, but also make it possible to make minimal use of historical experience. In the fifties and sixties, for example, deterrence theory was developed substantially as a deductivist product of decision theory and/or game theory. Investigators applied the premises and logic of these two general theories to the problem of deterrence and constructed abstract models which were presented as embracing the essential analytical and policy issues. In early formulations of deterrence theory and coercion theory, investigators cited episodes from history selectively to illustrate general points they had deduced from the more abstract models; they did not attempt to use historical cases to assess these general theorems more systematically. Some specialists employing this deductivist approach to theory formulation recognized, it is true, the danger in "too much abstractness" and the necessity, for developing a stronger empirical basis for their theories.[12] However, for many years very little effort was made to study historical cases of deterrence and coercion in any careful or systematic way as a means of testing, elaborating, and/or qualifying the formal deductivist theoretical models.

The *analytical inductive* approach to theory development—one that would examine how deterrence and coercion had actually worked in various historical cases, why and under what conditions strategies had succeeded or failed—was largely neglected. As a result, early deterrence and coercion theories were not well grounded in historical experience: they offered the most rudimentary explanations for why and when deterrence and coercive efforts could be expected to be successful. This might not have had worrisome consequences had deterrence and coercion theories been offered merely for heuristic purposes. But in fact they were presented as prescriptive, policy-relevant theories—guides to policy making. Subsequent empirical work based on systematic analysis of historical cases revealed serious shortcomings in these formal deductivist theories. This experience serves to emphasize that prescriptive theories that purport to provide guidelines for policy must have a strong empirical base; good *explanatory* theory regarding phenomena such as deterrence, coercion, and so on is a precondition for the development of *prescriptive* theory covering these activities.[13]

As a result of this experience, many political scientists now have a better appreciation of the limits of formal deductivist approaches as a strategy for developing policy-relevant theory and the utility of analytical induction as an alternative approach for this purpose. The perils of bypassing systematic study of relevant historical cases are now better understood and so for this reason, too, many political scientists are mindful of the necessity to incorporate some of the perspectives and methods of historians into their research strategy.

48

Last but not least among the reasons for the slow development of historically grounded theory was the unexpected difficulty encountered in making
effective use of single case studies for development of theory. Following the
end of World War II, political scientists were quite favorably disposed to use
case studies for this purpose. Many case studies were turned out, not only in
the field of international relations but also in public administration, comparative politics, and American politics. Although individual case studies
were often well done and instructive, they did not lend themselves readily to
strict comparison and to orderly cumulation. As a result, the inital en-
thusiasm for case studies gradually faded, and the case study as a strategy for
theory development fell into disrepute.[14]

But in this respect, too, more recent developments—some of which we
have already described—have revived interest in using case studies for theory
development and, what is more important, scholars have now identified ways
of making more effective use of case studies for this purpose. Even among
behaviorally oriented political scientists, the single case study and the method
of "controlled comparison" of a few cases has become a respectable,
legitimate research strategy that can contribute to theory development. The
other two basic methods or strategies are, of course, the experimental and the
statistical approaches.[15] The statistical method itself is an alternative to experimental research designs, the requirements for which are often impossible
or extremely difficult to meet in political science research. While the statistical
method is not strictly controlled experimentation, it can often be employed in
ways that enable the investigator to approximate the essential logical functions of a quasi-controlled experiment.[16]

It is important to recognize that the revival of interest in case studies is by
no means confined to political scientists. In the last decade, a number of
scientifically oriented scholars in other social science disciplines have come to
take a more positive view of the contribution to theory development that case
studies can make. This is particularly noteworthy among eminent
psychologists who have come to recognize the limitations of experimental and
statistical research approaches for development of scientific knowledge and
theory about human behavior.[17]

The Controlled Comparison Research Strategy

The controlled comparison (or comparative) method, in turn, as Lijphart
notes, resembles the statistical method in all respects but one: "The critical
difference is that the number of cases it deals with is too small to permit
systematic control by means of partial correlations."[18] As a result, the controlled comparison method encounters certain problems having to do with the

fact that while the investigator is interested in many variables he has only a few cases to work with. But, as Lijphart notes, these weaknesses of the method can be minimized and, besides, the controlled comparison method has certain distinct advantages over the statistical method. Thus, intensive analysis of a few cases may be more rewarding than a more superficial statistical analysis of many cases.[19] And, in general, the problems of reliability and validity may be smaller for the investigator working with the comparable-cases approach: "He can analyze his smaller number of cases more thoroughly, and he is less dependent on data that he cannot properly evaluate."[20]

The ability of single case studies or controlled comparison of a few cases to contribute to theory development depends in the first instance upon employing the "disciplined-configurative" mode of analysis, already discussed, rather than the "configurative-idiographic" mode. Unlike the latter, the disciplined-configurative type of case study employs general variables for purposes of description and explanation. As noted earlier, this is necessary to permit comparison and cumulation of findings.

A second prerequisite is that the investigator define adequately the "class" of events/phenomena for which he is attempting to develop explanatory theory. This is essential in order to select appropriate cases for intensive analysis. The historical cases must all be instances either of deterrence, of coercive diplomacy, of crisis managment, of alliance formation, of war termination, of outbreak of war, of negotiation, of the impact of domestic politics on policy making, of the impact of personality on decision making, or of whatever else it is the investigator wishes to study and to theorize about.

A third prerequisite is that the investigator be selective and focused in his treatment of a case. It is the investigator's theoretical and/or practical interest which should define what aspects of a historical case he singles out for description and explanation. One reason why single case studies in the past contributed so little to theory development was that they either lacked a common focus or a common approach to the study of a given type of problem. In analyzing a historical case, the investigator often attempted to do justice to all those aspects of it that were particularly interesting or unusual, or on which reasonably good historical data was available. There was no assurance, therefore, that those aspects of the case relevant for developing a particular kind of theory would be included or treated adequately in the case study. It is not surprising, therefore, that contemporary investigators with a well defined theoretical interest in a particular historical case often find earlier treatments of it of little value and have to redo the case study of it in order to extract its theoretical relevance.

In this connection, it is important to recognize that a single historical case can be relevant for a variety of theoretical interests. For example, the Cuban missile crisis offers useful material for developing many different theories;

thus, it is an instance of deterrence, coercive diplomacy, crisis management, negotiation, domestic political influence on foreign policy, personality involvement in decision making, and so on. Each of these theoretical interests in the Cuban missile crisis requires the case study analyst to adopt a somewhat different focus and to identify and satisfy a different set of data requirements. Treatment of the Cuban crisis in a case study must be selectively focused in accord with the type of theory that the investigator is attempting to develop.[21]

These observations remind us that a "case study," in the rigorous sense in which the term is used in clinical psychology and medical research, is meant to be a scientific observation. As Hugh Heclo notes, a scientific observation is designed to use selected data rather than merely whatever data is obtained: "Such a study is intended to monitor or explicate some larger phenomenon and thus is to be planned under the impetus of theory rather than the excrescent accumulation of whatever data happen to turn up. In an idealized analogue to natural science, political science can then use an extended series of these observations to test the operational deductions from its theoretical hypotheses. . . . Of course, deductive and inductive uses are not mutually exclusive, and a case study may contain elements of both processes."[22]

Types of Case Studies That Contribute to Theory Development

In this spirit Harry Eckstein, reflecting upon trends in research on comparative politics, has argued that case studies are valuable at all stages of the theory-building process beginning with hypothesis formation and extending to rigorous hypothesis testing via what he calls the "crucial case study."[23] He distinguishes among several types of case studies and the different uses which they have. The disciplined-configurative case study employs available general hypotheses (whether cast in the form of general laws or statements of probability) to explain the outcome in a particular case. In contrast to the configurative-idiographic type of study, as we have already noted, the disciplined-configurative study describes and analyzes the case in terms of theoretically relevant general variables.

The third type that Eckstein identifies is the "heuristic" case study, which goes beyond the effort at explanation in a disciplined-configurative study in an important respect. Thus, the case study is used as a means of stimulating the imagination in order to discern important *new* general problems, identify possible theoretical solutions, and formulate potentially generalizable relations that were not previously apparent. In other words, the case study is regarded as an opportunity to learn more about the complexity of the problem studied, to develop further the existing explanatory framework, and to refine and elaborate the initially available theory employed by the investigator in order to provide an explanation of the particular case examined.

Eckstein notes, somewhat cryptically, that the "heuristic" case study can be part of a "building-block" approach to the construction and development of theory, but he does not elaborate on this important point. Actually, a *series* of heuristic case studies or a simultaneous comparison of two or more cases, if each comprises an instance of the same class of events, can be an excellent research strategy for the cumulative development of theory. In this way the investigator can move beyond a preoccupation with the single case study to comparative case studies—what Lijphart and others refer to as the method of "controlled comparison," which Eckstein, given his focus on the different uses of single case studies, fails to discuss. We shall return to this point below when we discuss the method of structured, focused comparison and the strategy of treating each single case in a well selected group of comparable cases as a "deviant" case that may be prototypical for the development of a typological theory.

The fourth type of case study noted by Eckstein is the "plausibility probe." Here the investigator employs a case study at a preliminary stage of inquiry before he is ready to undertake a more rigorous testing of general hypotheses. The purpose of a "plausibility probe" is to enable the investigator to judge whether the potential validity of those hypotheses is great enough to warrant his making a major investment in more thorough, hopefully more decisive hypothesis-testing studies. As Eckstein notes, many significant case studies in political science have actually made only a partial effort at assessing a theory or general hypothesis and can properly be regarded, therefore, as some form of a plausibility probe.

While Eckstein does not develop his discussion of the utility of plausibility probes further, it would be useful to consider how their contribution to theory development might be enhanced even in the absence of follow-up research that provides a more rigorous testing of the general hypotheses in question. Since the latter type of study is often very difficult to arrange or to carry out satisfactorily, one might consider how a *series* of heuristic and plausibility probe case studies might be employed in order to achieve cumulation. By viewing heurisitic cases and plausibility probes within the framework of the strategy of controlled comparison it may be possible to cumulate the findings and to employ them as an admittedly weak, but still useful, form of hypothesis assessment that falls short of rigorous hypothesis testing. Thus, proceeding in this fashion, one could regard "theory" as a set of working hypotheses which have survived a series of plausibility probes and which have been reformulated and refined as necessary in accord with results of individual probes that called into question the initial hypotheses. Employed in this way, the plausibility probe takes on some of the functions and uses of the heuristic type case and fits into the "building-block" strategy.

The fifth type of case study to which Eckstein gives particular emphasis is the "crucial case" study. As he notes, it is possible for a single case study, *if* it is strategically selected and properly carried out, to invalidate or to confirm a theory. In other words, a single case study by itself is capable—at least in principle—of providing a rigorous, decisive form of hypothesis testing. How, then, can a candidate case, one that will provide a crucial test of the theory, be identified? As Eckstein notes, such a case must "fit" closely the existing theory and not fit equally well any other rule or theory. If it meets these criteria, the crucial case study fulfills the function of a well designed experiment. Thus, the existing theory which is being tested must generate a prediction;[24] if the theory is valid, such-and-such an outcome in the candidate crucial case should (or should not) occur.

Efforts to select and design a crucial case study, and to interpret its results as a test of the theory under consideration, encounter various problems and objections.[25] While the possible use of case studies as crucial cases should be considered, it should also be recognized that a fully satisfactory use of a single case study for testing a theory is often not possible.[26]

Eckstein's discussion focuses on the different uses of single case studies; he does not make explicit in this particular essay the ways in which single case studies link up with the comparative method. Nor does he discuss the strategy of employing "controlled comparison" of a few appropriately selected cases for theory development. These broader questions are discussed to some extent in Lijphart's two articles, which usefully complement Eckstein's impressive brief for the utility of single case studies. But Lijphart, in turn, does not discuss the *specific tasks* that must be addressed by an investigator in designing a controlled comparison, tasks which must be properly handled if the controlled comparison is to contribute effectively in some way to theory development. Nor do Eckstein and Lijphart discuss the procedures for carrying out a controlled comparison study, once it has been properly designed.

What, then, *are* the appropriate procedures for utilizing a single case study or a controlled comparison of a small number of cases for theory development? Granted that case studies can contribute usefully in several ways to the development of theory, and granted that one can point to a number of reasonably successful studies of this kind, is there a rigorous case study methodology, or is it an art form? Can one learn how to do theoretically oriented case studies? Can one explicate in sufficient detail a set of tasks, requirements, and procedures that, if followed, will increase the likelihood of successful use of case studies for this purpose? Can one codify from the successful case studies a general set of methodological principles that will be useful to those who want to design and carry out new case studies or controlled comparisons? Another question we shall want to keep in mind: Is the research strategy of case study and controlled comparison competitive with or, rather, complementary to the experimental and statistical modes of research?

Controlled Comparison: Design and Implementation

We are not addressing here the task of designing a disciplined-configurative type of study, one which merely uses an existing theory to explain a new case. Rather, we wish to address the task of designing what Eckstein calls heuristic and plausibility probe case studies and using them as building blocks for theory development.[27] It is useful to distinguish three phases in any such study. In Phase 1 the design and structure of the study are formulated. In Phase 2 the individual case studies are carried out in accord with the design. In Phase 3 the investigator draws upon results of the case studies in order to assess, reformulate, or elaborate the initial theory stated in Phase 1.

PHASE 1: DESIGN

Five tasks must be performed at the outset of the study to achieve a well designed single case or controlled comparison study:

Task 1. The specification of the research problem and the research objectives of the study: (a) What kind of phenomenon or behavior is the investigator singling out for examination—that is, what is the class of events on which the study will focus? (b) What is the *existing theory,* if any, that bears on those aspects of the phenomenon in question? (c) Which aspects of the existing theory will be singled out for assessment and/or refinement and elaboration?

For example, if the investigator is interested in (a) the phenomenon of coercive diplomacy, and (b) the existing theory seems to imply that stronger powers can always or usually coerce weaker powers, he may choose (c) to identify the conditions and critical variables that help explain those cases in which the stronger power fails to coerce the weaker one. (This research objective, in turn, may require a research strategy of comparing cases in which the stronger power succeeded in coercing a weaker power with cases in which it failed to do so.)

Task 2. Specification of the elements (conditions and variables) that will enter into a controlled comparison of instances (cases) of the class of events in question: (a) What is the dependent (or outcome) variable to be explained? (b) What independent and intervening variables comprise the theoretical suppositions and framework of the study? (c) Which variables will be held constant and which allowed to vary across the cases to be compared?

If one were analyzing the phenomenon of "war termination," for instance, (a) one would have to decide whether the dependent (outcome) variable to be explained was merely a cease-fire or a settlement of outstanding issues over which the war had been fought; (b) one might include as variables to be considered in explaining the success or failure of efforts to terminate a war the fighting capabilities and morale of the armed forces, the availability of economic resources for continuing the war, the type and magnitude of pressures from more powerful allies, the policy makers' expectation that the original war objective was no longer attainable at all or only at excessive cost, the pressures of prowar and antiwar opinion at home, and so on; and (c) one might choose to hold constant the outcome of the dependent variable (i.e., study only cases in which efforts to achieve a cease-fire or settlement failed) in order to identify the independent and intervening variables associated with such failures; or, alternatively, one might vary the outcome, choosing cases of both success and failure in order to identify the conditions and variables that seemed to account for this difference in the outcome.

Task 3. Selection of *appropriate* cases for controlled comparison—appropriate in the light of the specifications made in tasks 1 and 2. The "universe" from which cases are selected must be well defined; this can be done only by stipulating clearly the type of phenomenon/event/behavior that is to be studied. Thus, the cases must all be instances of the same class or universe; one must not mix apples, oranges, and pears.

If one is interested in developing *deterrence* theory the cases selected must be examples of deterrence, not of coercive diplomacy; or they must be cases that contribute to one or another of the different segments of deterrence theory.[28]

Task 4. Consideration of ways in which variance in the dependent variable (outcome) and independent variables can best be described to further theory development—that is, to increase the likelihood of discovering causal patterns between various outcomes of the dependent variable and various configurations of independent and intervening variables.

In the study of coercive diplomacy, for example, one might regard it as satisfactory, to begin with,[29] to define the variance in outcomes of efforts to employ this strategy simply in terms of "success" or "failure" (leaving it open for further investigation later to reveal the possible usefulness of identifying more specific types of success and failure that might help to develop a more discriminating explanatory theory). Similarly, to start with, one might define the variance in the independent variables (such as "asymmetry of motivation" between the coercing power and the target of coercive diplomacy; the sense of time urgency for compliance with the demands of the coercing power experienced by the target; the target's fear of unacceptable escalation) simply in terms of the presence or absence of these conditions or states of mind—i.e., treating them as dichotomous attributes rather than as values on a continuum.

Task 5. Formulation of the data requirements to be satisfied in the analysis of the cases—that is, the *general questions* to be asked of each case in the controlled comparison.

For example, in a comparative study of policy makers' approaches to strategy and tactics vis-à-vis their political opponents in the international arena, one might start by asking the general questions developed in the "operational code" approach. These questions are designed to illuminate the orientations of a leader to the fundamental issues of history and politics that presumably influence his calculation and choice of foreign policy. In this type of study the investigator examines an appropriate body of material in order to infer the "answers" a political leader gave to the following questions (i.e., his beliefs on these fundamental issues):

A. *Philosophical Questions (Issues):*
 1. What is the essential nature of political life? Is the political universe essentially one of harmony or conflict? What is the fundamental character of one's political opponents?
 2. What are the prospects for eventual realization of one's fundamental political values and ideological goals? Can one be optimistic or pessimistic?
 3. Is the political future predictable? In what sense, and to what extent?
 4. How much "control" or "mastery" can one have over historical developments? What is the political leader's (elite's) role in "moving" and "shaping" history?
 5. What is the role of "chance" in human affairs and in historical development?

B. *Instrumental Questions (Issues):*
 1. What is the best approach for selecting goals or objectives for political action?
 2. How are the goals of action pursued most effectively?
 3. How are the risks of political action best calculated, controlled, and accepted?
 4. What is the best "timing" of action to advance one's interests?
 5. What is the utility and role of different means for advancing one's interests?[30]

Several observations need to be made before proceeding. First, in any given study these five tasks should be viewed as comprising an integrated whole. They are interrelated in important ways that must be kept in mind in designing a controlled comparison study. That is to say, the way in which Task 2 is handled must be consistent with the specification of Task 1; Similarly, both the selection of cases in Task 3 and the theoretical framework developed in Task 4 must be appropriate from the standpoint of the determinations made in Tasks 1 and 2; and, finally, the identification in Task 5 of the data requirements to be met in each case study must be guided by the specifications in Tasks 1, 2, and 3.

Second, it is prudent to keep in mind that such a close integration of the five tasks cannot usually be accomplished on the first try; considerable iteration and respecification of the various tasks will probably be necessary before an integral research design comprising the five tasks is formulated. The investigator will have to gain considerable familiarity with the phenomenon in

56

question and to undertake a preliminary examination of a variety of cases before selecting those for the controlled comparison. The exploratory and learning experience required in order to develop a good research design have in fact some of the characteristics of Eckstein's heuristic and plausibility probe types of case studies.

Third, despite the investigator's best efforts, the formulation of the design is likely to remain imperfect in some respects. It will be difficult to develop a research design that deals with all of these five tasks in an optimal manner. But one can hope to learn from experience; at the conclusion of a case study or controlled comparison, the investigator himself or others may be able to state the "lessons" for a better design of such studies in the future.

PHASE 2. THE CASE STUDIES

Formulation of the research design—that is, the five tasks described above—constitutes the first phase of a controlled comparison study. The second phase is, of course, the undertaking of the case studies. Each of the cases singled out for controlled comparison is studied from the standpoint of the data requirements identified in Task 5. The value (or outcome) of the dependent variable in that case is established through standard procedures of historical inquiry. This is expressed in terms of the specifications for describing the variance in the dependent variable determined in Task 4. The investigator then proceeds to develop a historical explanation for the outcome in this case, again utilizing the methods of historical inquiry but transforming the specific explanation into the concepts comprising the conditions, the independent and the intervening variables of the theoretical framework that was specified in Task 2. (That is to say, in Eckstein's terms, the investigator does a disciplined-configurative case study, not a configurative-idiographic one.)

Quite obviously, the investigator's theoretical framework must be comprehensive enough to capture the major elements of the historical explanation—that is, the independent and intervening variables must be adequate to absorb enough of the richness of the historical explanation, to capture and record the essentials of a causal explanation of the outcome in that case. If not, the investigator must redesign the framework (Task 2) and redo his case studies.[31]

In seeking to formulate an explanation for the outcome in each case, the investigator employs the historian's method of causal imputation, which differs from the mode of causal inference in statistical-correlational studies. The causal interpretation gains plausibility if it is consistent with the available data and if it can be supported by relevant generalizations for which a measure of validity can be claimed. The plausibility of an explanation is enhanced *to the extent that alternative explanations are considered and found to be less consistent with the data and/or less supportable by available generalizations.* If the data and generalizations available to the investigator do not permit him to choose from competing explanations, then both explanations for the case should be retained as equally plausible and the implications of both for theory development should be considered later on in Phase 3 of the study.

As this implies, the utility of the explanations developed in the case studies for theory development rests upon their plausibility. The explanations should meet the standards of historical scholarship. If later on competent historians successfully challenge the plausibility of the explanation advanced in a case study, the investigator will have to reassess the implications which he has drawn from that case for theory development. Such a reassessment would be necessary also in the event that new historical material bearing on the case in question becomes available and leads to a successful challenge to the investigator's interpretation of the case.

In other words, the implications drawn from the case studies for theory development are provisional; they depend upon the plausibility of the explanations for the outcomes in the individual cases.

PHASE 3. DRAWING THE THEORETICAL IMPLICATIONS OF THE CASE STUDIES

Recall that Task 1 of the first phase of the investigation was to state the existing theory that bears on those aspects of the phenomenon singled out for examination. Having performed the case studies in Phase 2, the investigator concludes the study by drawing upon their results—that is, the explanations for the outcomes and other findings regarding the nature and complexity of the phenomenon in question—in order to assess, refine, and/or elaborate the initial theory stated in Phase 1.[32]

There are limitations and advantages as to what controlled comparison can accomplish in this respect. As noted earlier in the discussion of Eckstein's crucial case type of study, controlled comparison is seldom likely to provide a fully satisfactory confirmation or invalidation of an existing theory. Among the reasons why decisive theory testing in controlled comparison studies is often not possible is the fact that few available theories in international politics are as yet clearly or fully enough formulated to permit rigorous testing. Rather, most theories are in need of sharper formulation and a fuller statement of the network of the parameters, independent and intervening variables that influence the variation in outcomes of the dependent variable. It is precisely one of the advantages of controlled comparison and single case studies, particularly those having a heuristic function, that they can facilitate this task.

But the ability of case studies to contribute to theory development goes beyond this. Controlled comparison can also be used to identify the variety of different causal patterns that can occur for the phenomenon in question. In a controlled comparison study, the investigator is interested as much in the differences among the cases as he is in their similarities. (In fact, it is one of the criteria employed in selecting cases for controlled comparison that they should differ in one or a few of the variables of theoretical interest.) Each case that differs from other cases is used to identify a variation, a different causal pattern, within the system of variables forming the initial theoretical framework. In other words, each case is dealt with by the investigator as if it were a "deviant" case.[33]

Proceeding in this way, using each case to generate possibly a different causal pattern, the investigator gradually develops a fuller "typological" theory of the phenomenon. Cumulation in theory development is possible, therefore, via a systematic progression of well selected controlled comparisons. (This is perhaps what Eckstein has in mind when he refers, somewhat cryptically, to the possible use of heuristic case studies in a building-block approach to the construction and development of theory.)

It is important to recognize that cumulation of theory in this fashion is *open-ended*; the "typological" theory that a particular controlled comparison study produces may not be comprehensive, since the study of additional cases may identify new causal patterns or variants of patterns already identified.

Typological Theory

Controlled comparison, as Diesing notes,[34] is particularly suited for developing typological theory and what I have called "rich, differentiated theory" which, in contrast to a general explanatory theory, is cast in the form of contingent generalizations and has the capability for more discriminating explanations.[35] Contrast, for example, a general explanatory theory such as "war is the result of miscalculation" with a richer, more differentiated theory comprised of contingent generalizations that identify the different conditions under which different types of miscalculations lead to different types of war outbreaks. Quite obviously, the second type of differentiated theory not only has greater explanatory power, it also has far greater practical value for policy makers because it enables them to make more discriminating diagnoses of emerging situations in which some kind of miscalculation might lead to outbreak of violence.

Indeed, investigators who favor the controlled comparison research strategy are often attracted to it precisely because it enables the development of this type of differentiated, policy-relevant theory.[36] Thus, political scientists who employ the controlled comparison method of analyzing cases have in common with historians and clinicians generally an interest in developing the kind of theory that enriches understanding of each particular case—that is, each instance of the class events in question.[37]

The research strategy of controlled comparison is suited to the development of what Diesing calls "particularized holistic theory" rather than the production of general theories or statistical generalizations. This is the case for several reasons. First, a controlled comparison deals with a relatively small number of cases, whereas a statistical-correlative approach to theory development deals with a large number of cases. The large N in the latter type of study either includes all instances of the class of events in question (the entire statistical universe) or constitutes a representative sample of that universe. The small n in a controlled comparison (which may be limited to as few as two cases) is not necessarily representative of the universe of instances belonging to that class of events; what is more, *it need not be* representative in the statistical sampling sense in order to contribute to theory development. The desideratum that guides selection of cases in the controlled comparison approach is not numbers but *variety,* that is, cases belonging to the same class that differ from each other. Thus, the investigator in designing the study will either seek cases in which the outcome of the dependent variable differed or cases having the same outcome but a different explanation for it.

The investigator who employs the controlled comparison strategy seeks to identify *the variety of different causal patterns* that can occur for the phenomenon in question. He seeks to identify *the conditions under which each distinctive type of causal pattern occurs* rather than attempting to address the question of *how often* each outcome and/or causal pattern does occur or can be expected to occur. Thus, controlled comparison is useful for developing a differentiated theory comprised of conditional generalizations rather than frequency distributions.

Controlled Comparison and Statistical-Correlative Studies

It is important to recognize that the results of controlled comparison investigations are comprehensible and useful from the standpoint of the seemingly rival methodolgy of statistical-correlative analysis. Controlled comparison investigations not only identify various "cells" for a potential statistical-correlational study; it is highly likely, in addition, that these "cells" are of theoretical and causal significance. Controlled comparison studies, therefore, accomplish some of the objectives of a statistical-correlational analysis of a large N that seeks to identify causal relationships. Controlled comparison does this insofar as each case identifies an outcome for the dependent variable and provides a historical explanation for it that is couched in terms of the independent and intervening variables of theoretical interest.

In the absence of controlled comparison studies on which to draw for this purpose, investigators employing the statistical approach would be obliged to rely solely upon quantitative data analysis in an attempt to discover causal patterns and relationships of the kind already developed via controlled comparison.

Thus, controlled comparison analysis of a small n is neither competitive with nor a substitute for quantitative analysis of a large N. Rather, the two approaches are genuinely complementary. Controlled comparison studies of a particular phenomenon should facilitate development of more sophisticated quantitative studies. The latter type of study, in turn, contributes in two ways: it can subject the causal hypotheses developed via use of historical explanation in the controlled comparison study to a different kind of statistical test of causal significance; and it can attempt to establish frequency distributions for the different causal patterns identified via controlled comparison.

Clearly, both controlled comparison and statistical modes of research are of value for theory development. They can and should become part of a more complex long-range research strategy for theory development in which investigators interested in a phenomenon move back and forth between intensive analysis of one or a few case studies to quantitative (and less intensive) analysis of a large number of cases.[38]

To be sure, the mode of causal imputation in single case studies differs from the mode of causal inference in statistical analysis. On the other hand, the *design tasks* encountered in the two types of studies are similar, though handled somewhat differently by the investigator. The five design tasks identified earlier in discussing the first phase of a controlled comparison are problems that must also be dealt with satisfactorily in a statistical-correlative approach to development of explanatory theory.

Investigators employing the statistical-correlational method of analysis often limit themselves to establishing possible causal relationships of independent variables with a dependent variable and to inferring the causal weight of individual or groups of independent variables rather than attempting, as in controlled comparison, to identify the configuration of different causal patterns (i.e., the typological theory). But, in principle, techniques of statistical analysis can be employed to develop such typological theory.

The Method of Structured, Focused Comparison

In the preceding pages I have attempted to show how the standpoint of the political scientist can be combined with that of the historian in employing the strategy of controlled comparison for the development of theory. To this end, some features of the historian's methodology for intensive, detailed explanation of the single case are combined with aspects of the political scientist's conception of the requirements for theory and his procedures for scientific inquiry.

I have called the resulting synthetic approach the "method of structured, focused comparison" since the comparative analysis of cases is both structured and focused—focused because it deals selectively with only certain aspects of the historical case (e.g., with President Kennedy's unsuccessful effort to deter Soviet deployment of offensive missiles into Cuba), and structured because it employs general questions to guide the data collection and analysis in that historical case.

From the statistical (and survey) research model, this method borrows the device of asking a set of *standardized, general questions* of each case. These standardized questions—as noted in discussing design Task 5—must be carefully developed to reflect adequately the research objectives and theoretical focus of the inquiry. These questions must be of a general nature, not couched in overly specific terms relevant to only one or another case but applicable to all cases within the class of events in question. (Asking the same questions of each case does not prevent the investigator from asking specific questions of each case as well to bring out idiosyncratic features that are of possible interest in and of themselves, if not also for theory development.)

Using a standardized set of questions in the controlled comparison is necessary to assure acquisition of comparable data from the several cases. In this way, the method of structured, focused comparison will avoid the all-too-familiar and disappointing experience of traditional, intensive single case studies in the past which, even when they were instances of a single class of events, were not performed in a comparable way and hence did not contribute to an orderly, cumulative development of knowledge and theory about the phenomenon in question. Instead, as conducted in the past, each case study tended to go its own way, reflecting the special interests of each investigator and often, somewhat opportunistically, being guided by the readily available historical data rather than by a well defined theoretical focus. As a result, the idiosyncratic features of each case tended to shape the research questions differently. It is not surprising that single case studies, lacking "scientific consciousness," did not cumulate.[39]

The controlled comparison approach offers an opportunity to overcome this disappointing experience with single case studies. But comparative studies vary widely in their conceptualization and the procedures employed, and the result have often fallen short of what might have been attained. In the present chapter I have tried to explicate the methodological requirements that one should strive to meet, however imperfectly, in order to enhance the utility of the controlled comparison approach for theory development. Since controlled comparison studies often do not attempt to meet these methodological requirements, I have used the term "method of structured, focused comparison" to refer to controlled comparisons which deal explicitly with these requirements and which also distinguish clearly between the three phases of this kind of investigation.

While innumerable studies employ some variant of comparative case methodoolgy, thus far very few have met the full set of design and procedural requirements of the method of structured, focused comparison. There is, as a result, relatively little experience to draw upon at this time in order to develop a more detailed handbook-type discussion of how best to employ this method.

On the other hand, it is already clear that merely a formalistic use of the method of structured, focused comparison cannot guarantee good results. For example, the important procedural device of formulating a set of standardized, general questions to ask in each case study will be of value only to the extent that these questions are grounded in, and reflect adequately, the starting theory and the research objectives for improving upon it. (I have tried to emphasize this earlier in this chapter in discussing the need to integrate the five design tasks in Phase 1 of a structured, focused comparison.) Thus, a set of general questions that does not link up with existing theory and is not well designed to further the research objectives is not very likely to produce the kinds of incisive case study results that contribute optimally to theory reformulation in Phase 3 of the study.

Similarly, the results achieved in a structured, focused comparison will inevitably depend on how well the investigator deals with the other four design tasks that were discussed earlier in this chapter.[40]

Finally, while controlled comparison is an essentially qualitative approach to theory development, there is such a thing as "qualitative methodology." Its requirements, while they differ in a few respects from those of quantitative methodology, share many of the same rigorous, exacting tasks needed to establish a sound empirical base on which to ground theory development.

Notes

1. See, for example, Ole R. Holsti and James N. Rosenau, "The Meaning of Vietnam: Belief Systems of American Leaders", *International Journal* 32 (Summer 1977):452–474.

2. For an incisive discussion of the problem see Ernest R. May, *"Lessons" of the Past: The Use and Misuse of History in American Foreign Policy* (New York: Oxford University Press, 1973); and Robert Jervis, *Perception and Misperception in International Politics* (Princeton: Princeton University Press, 1976), Chapter 6, "How Decisionmakers Learn From History," pp. 217–287.

3. For an incisive recent statement see Gabriel A. Almond and Stephen J. Genco, "Clouds, Clocks, and the Study of Politics," *World Politics* 29 (July 1977): 489–522.

4. See, for example, Klaus Knorr and James N. Rosenau (eds.), *Contending Approaches to International Politics* (Princeton: Princeton University Press, 1969); especially Chapter 1.

5. The utility of single case studies for assessing the causal status of statistical correlations has been discussed in some detail by Bruce Russett. He also recommends that investigators make greater use of an iterative research strategy, one that alternates statistical-correlational studies of large numbers of cases with intensive single case analysis. See his "International Behavior Research: Case Studies and Cumulation," in M. Haas and H. S. Kariel (eds.), *Approaches to the Study of Political Science* (San Francisco: Chandler, 1970), pp. 425–443.

6. These problems are discussed in Alexander L. George, "The Causal Nexus Between Cognitive Beliefs and Decision-making Behavior: The 'Operational Code' Belief System," in Lawrence Falkowski (ed.), *Psychological Models and International Politics* (Boulder, Colo.: Westview Press, 1970).

7. Sidney Verba, "Some Dilemmas in Comparative Research," *World Politics* 20 (October 1976): 113.

8. Some writers prefer to reserve use of the word "variable" for concepts that are subjected to measurement. The refinement of concepts should in any case precede measurement. For an incisive discussion see Giovanni Sartori, "Concept Misinformation in Comparative Politics," *American Political Science Review* 64 (December 1970): 1033–1053.

9. Verba, "Some Dilemmas," p. 114 (underlining supplied). In this passage, it may be noted, Verba is taking issue with investigators who, in employing statistical techniques of analysis, have often been extremely reluctant to develop "cells" into which only one or a few cases from their larger sample would fall, since this would provide too few numbers for statistical analysis. For this reason investigators often group their cases into larger and broader "cells," thereby providing enough instances to permit statistical analysis. Thereby, however, the investigator loses the opportunity for a more discriminating analysis of the differences among these cases and has to focus on the more general characteristics which place them in the broader "cell." This common practice in statistical analysis, dictated by technical considerations, has had adverse consequences for the development of theory. Systematic avoidance of more discriminating cells excludes development of a richer, more differentiated theory.

10. See, for example, the writings on comparative history by the eminent French historian, Marc Bloch. A useful commentary is provided by William Sewell, "Marc Bloch and the Logic of Comparative History," *History and Theory* 6 (1967): 208–218. As many historians have noted, the method of comparison of historical cases is their substitute for experimentation.

   Of the many studies by historians which employ the comparative method, one may cite such varied ones as Crane Brinton, The *Anatomy of Revolution* (New York: Norton, 1938); Paul Schroeder, "Alliances, 1815–1945: Weapons of Power and Tools of Management," in Klaus Knorr (ed.), *Historical Dimensions of National Security Problems* (Lawrence: University of Kansas Press, 1976), pp. 227–262; Paul Gordon Lauren, *Diplomats and Bureaucrats: The First Institutional Responses to Twentieth-Century Diplomacy in France and Germany* (Stanford: Hoover Institution Press, 1976).

11. Verba, "Some Dilemmas," p. 114. See also Harry Eckstein, "Case Study and Theory in Political Science," in F. I. Greenstein and N. W. Polsby (eds.), *Handbook of Political Science* (Reading, Mass.: Addison-Wesley, 1975), VII: 79–138.

12. For example, Thomas C. Schelling, *Strategy of Conflict* (New York: Oxford University Press, 1966), p. 163.

13. For a more detailed discussion see A. L. George and R. Smoke, *Deterrence in American Foreign Policy: Theory and Practice* (New York: Columbia University Press, 1974), especially chapters 3, 16.

14. For a sober evaluation of the earlier nonscientific, noncumulative character of case studies of foreign policy, see James N. Rosenau, "Moral Fervor, Systematic

Analysis, and Scientific Consciousness in Foreign Policy Research,'' in Austin Ranney (ed.), *Political Science and Public Policy* (Chicago: Markham, 1968), pp. 197–238. Case studies of the type that many historians and political scientists have done, Rosenau observed, are not necessarily appropriate to scientific inquiry. Most of these case studies, he held, lacked ''scientific consciousness'' and hence did not cumulate. Rosenau went on to make a number of suggestions for imbuing case studies with ''scientific consciousness'' and for making them more comparable.

Similarly sober evaluations of case studies in other fields of political science were offered by other writers. See, for example, R. Macridis and B. C. Brown (eds.), *Comparative Politics: Notes and Readings* (Homewood, Ill.: Dorsey Press, 1955), who criticized the old ''comparative'' politics for being, among other things, not genuinely comparative—i.e., concerned mainly with single case studies which were essentially descriptive and monographic rather than theory oriented. In the field of public administration similar concerns were expressed, for example, by Herbert Kaufmann, ''The Next Step in Case Studies,'' *Public Administration Review* 18 (Winter 1958): 52–59. And in the field of American politics an important critique of the atheoretical case study was presented by Theodore J. Lowi, ''American Business, Public Policy, Case-Studies and Political Theory,'' *World Politics* 16 (July 1964): 677–715.

15. For a comparison and lucid discussion of these three basic scientific methods, see for example Arend Lijphart's two articles: ''Comparative Politics and the Comparative Method,'' *American Political Science Review* 65 (September 1971): 682–693, and ''The Comparable-Case Strategy in Comparative Research,'' *Comparative Political Studies* 8 (July 1975): 158–177. The latter article also refers to earlier descriptions of the comparative method.

16. See, for example, Richard A. Brody and Charles N. Brownstein, ''Experimentation and Simulation,'' in *Handbook of Political Science,* VII: 211–263.

17. See, for example, Donald T. Campbell, '' 'Degrees of Freedom' and the Case Study,'' *Comparative Political Studies* 8 (July 1975): 178–193; and the same author's ''Qualitative Knowing in Action Research,'' paper presented to the annual meeting of the American Psychological Association, New Orleans, September 1974. See also Lee Cronbach, ''Beyond the Two Scientific Disciplines of Scientific Psychology,'' *American Psychologist* 30 (February 1975): 116–127; and Richard S. Lazarus, ''The Self-Regulation of Emotions,'' University of California at Berkeley, unpublished manuscript, no date.

18. Lijphart, ''Comparative Politics and the Comparative Method,'' p. 684.

19. Ibid., p. 685.

20. Lijphart, ''The Comparable-Case Strategy,'' p. 171.

21. Thus, the Cuban missile crisis is treated as an example of deterrence failure in George and Smoke, *Deterrence in American Foreign Policy;* as an example of coercive diplomacy in A. L. George, D. K. Hall, and W. E. Simons, *The Limits of Coercive Diplomacy* (Boston: Little, Brown, 1971); as an example of crisis management in Ole R. Holsti, *Crisis, Escalation, War* (Montreal: McGill–Queen's University Press, 1972).

22. H. Hugh Heclo, ''Review Article: Policy Analysis,'' *British Journal of Political Science* 2 (January 1972): 83–108.

23. Eckstein, "Case Study and Theory in Political Science." An excellent discussion of critical issues in efforts to utilize case studies for theory development is provided by James F. Keeley, "Comparative Case Studies and Theory-Building," Stanford University, unpublished manuscript, January 1976.

24. The discussion of crucial cases appears on pp. 113–123 of Eckstein's article. Earlier (p. 89), he draws a useful distinction between "experimental prediction," "concrete prediction," and "forecasting," and calls attention to the fact that not all are equally conclusive for theory testing: "The failure of a single forecast, for example, is generally (not always) less conclusive than that of an experiemental prediction, although related forecasting failures are pretty definitive."

25. Eckstein discusses some of the specific objections raised to his brief for crucial case studies on pp. 123ff.

26. The various uses and types of case studies are also discussed by Lijphart, "Comparative Politics and the Comparative Method," pp. 691–693. Lijphart's terminology for identifying the various types differs from Eckstein's but his discussion of the types closely parallels Eckstein's, with two exceptions: Lijphart does not designate a separate category for Eckstein's "plausibility probe"; and Lijphart adds a quite important type of case study, the analysis of the "deviant" case, for which Eckstein does not make explicit provision. The similarities and differences between these two listings of types of case studies are as follows:

Lijphart	*Eckstein*
"atheoretical case study" ⟷	"configurative-idiographic"
"interpretative case study" ⟷	"disciplined-configurative"
"hypothesis-generating case study" ⟷	"heuristic"
? ⟶	"plausibility probe"
"theory-confirming" case study / "theory-infirming" case study ⟷	"crucial case"
"deviant" case study ⟷	?

27. If the existing literature on the problem singled out for study does not contain much by way of theoretical formulation or hypotheses, the major objective of the study may be "heuristic" (rather than hypothesis testing). Hence, the investigator's research strategy may be to examine a *variety* of cases—what is sometimes called "the method of differences"—in order to identify independent variables that are of possible causal significance in explaining different outcomes. The investigator's research objective in such a study, in other words, is to formulate a theoretical framework and some hypotheses.

On the other hand, if the investigator's research objective is to assess the causal significance of one major independent variable his research strategy may be to examine cases which are highly similar in all other respects—what is sometimes called "the method of similarities."

28. The three segments of deterrence theory are "commitment theory," "initiation theory," and "response-to-warning theory." Cases which are not instances of attempted deterrence, strictly speaking, may nonetheless be included in the study if they illuminate one or another of these three segments of the theory. See chapters 17, 19, and 20 of George and Smoke, *Deterrence in American Foreign Policy.*

29. As in the study by George, Hall, and Simons, *The Limits of Coercive Diplomacy;* see especially the Appendix, pp. 255–259.

30. These questions were originally formulated in Alexander L. George, "The 'Operational Code': A Neglected Approach to the Study of Political Leaders and Decision-Making," *International Studies Quarterly* 13 (June 1969): 199–222. A variety of case studies have been undertaken employing these questions.

31. Partial reanalysis of the case studies may be necessary, even though during the design phase the investigator familiarized himself with the phenomenon in question and examined a variety of cases before final specification of the five tasks.

    It should be emphasized that to engage in this type of iteration is *not* to engage in "circularity." The investigator can take a preliminary look at the cases in order to improve the theoretical framework—i.e., by identifying additional independent variables and/or better ways of describing the variance in the variable (see the previous discussion of the advantages of an inductive approach for this purpose). Thus, the preliminary look at the cases amounts to making a specific *heuristic* use of them to learn more about the problem and to improve the research design before proceeding with hypothesis testing and/or hypothesis development. To do so is *not* to engage in the indefensible practice of imposing the initial theory or hypotheses identified in Phase 1 on the explanation of the cases developed in Phase 2; nor is it to fall into the unacceptable practice of deriving explanatory hypotheses from the cases that should be used later to assess those same hypotheses.

32 For an illustration of how this can be done, see "Part Three: Toward a Reformulation of Deterrence Theory," in George and Smoke, *Deterrence in American Foreign Policy*, pp. 50ff.

33. On the logic of deviant case analysis and the role it can play in the development of theory see, for example, Patricia Kendall and Katherine M. Wolf, "The Analysis of Deviant Cases in Communications Research, "in Paul F. Lazarsfeld and Frank Stanton (eds.), *Communications Research, 1948-49* (New York: Harper and Brothers, 1949), pp. 152–157.

34. Paul Diesing, *Patterns of Discovery in the Social Sciences* (Chicago and New York: Aldine-Atherton, 1971), p. 196.

35. George, Hall, and Simons, *Limits of Coercive Diplomacy*, p. xvi; George and Smoke, *Deterrence in American Foreign Policy*, p. 511.

36. See in this connection Paul Diesing's discussion of "particularized holistic theory," i.e., typological theory that describes typical patterns and ranges of variation. "The holist's primary theoretical interest," Diesing notes in *Patterns of Discovery*, pp. 195–196, "is in the development of more complex and detailed types." What Diesing refers to as "types" are what I am referring to here as different causal patterns.

    Another useful discussion of single case analysis from a methodological standpoint is provided by Steven R. Brown, "Intensive Analysis in Political Research," *Political Methodology* 1 (Winter 1974): 1–25.

37. See also Eckstein's useful remarks on clinical studies which are associated more with action objectives than those of pure knowledge. Eckstein, "Case Study and Theory," pp. 81–82.

38. As Bruce Russett has emphasized in reflecting on his own research experience, neither of these two research strategies is complete without the other; neither can alone provide a basis for reliable and valid generalizations about international politics of the type that will be helpful in policy making. See his "International Behavior Research: Case Studies and Cumulation."

Of course, it may be difficult in practice for any given investigator to make use of both research strategies since the skills involved differ, but a division of labor between investigators specializing in one and the other research strategy should be feasible.

39. James N. Rosenau, "Moral Fervor, Systematic Analysis, and Scientific Consciousness in Foreign Policy Research."

40. My own work, *Deterrence in American Foreign Policy* (with Richard Smoke), best exemplifies the structured, focused method. An earlier book, *The Limits of Coercive Diplomacy,* employed an abridged variant of the method. Important elements of structured, focused comparison have also been utilized in a series of operational code belief system studies under way since 1969. (For a summary, see A. L. George and O. R. Holsti, "Operational Code Belief Systems and Foreign Policy Decision-Making," research proposal submitted to the National Science Foundation, December 1974.) Exemplary use of the structured, focused method is evident in Richard Smoke's *War: Controlling Escalation* (Cambridge: Harvard University Press, 1977); see particularly his careful formulation of a set of theoretically relevant general questions and his selection of historical cases in Chapter 3 and Appendix B, pp. 36–45, 316–326. Other significant uses of the structured, focused method include Joseph J. Kruzel, "The Preconditions and Consequences of Arms Control Agreements," Ph.D dissertation, Harvard University, 1975; Dan E. Caldwell, "American–Soviet Détente and the Nixon–Kissinger Grand Design and Grand Strategy," Ph.D., dissertation, Department of Political Science, Stanford University, May 1978.

4
The Quantification of Diplomatic History

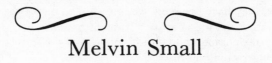

Melvin Small

DESPITE A GOOD DEAL OF INITIAL SKEPTICISM, a large number of historians have adopted many of the statistical techniques of modern social scientists.[1] In the fields of political, social, economic, legal, and even intellectual history, quantitative methods are being used, and used successfully. Although some historians still contend that zealous quantifiers claim too much for their particular methods, few today would deny a place for such techniques in the subdisciplines of history. The only major exception appears to be diplomatic history. In this prosaic field, the guardians of the barricades have maintained fealty to traditional approaches and have resisted infiltrators armed with computers and calculators. In part, the traditionalists have been successful because even historians who advocate the new methodologies do not feel that diplomatic history has much in common with the behavioral sciences.[2]

The application of quantitative techniques to diplomatic history, of course, does not represent a "new approach" for all scholars. Although historians of diplomacy may consider it all new, unorthodox, and perhaps even bizarre, other students of international politics have been applying such techniques to historical data for several scholarly generations. They have been systematically mining historical monographs and official documents for all periods from the Congress of Vienna to the present in order to analyze such issues of direct concern to historians as the dynamics of arms races, national military capabilities during different epochs, and early warning indicators for approaching crises. For the most part, however, this poaching in Clio's domain has gone unnoticed by historians.

Diplomatic historians, to be sure, are aware of the contributions of social science to theories of personality, bureaucratic politics, and opinion formation, and some have employed such theories in their own work,[3] but few have even thought about employing the methods of the quantifiers. Such methods seem to work in political history where there are votes to count, in social history where demographic movements must be measured, in economic

69

history where Cliometricians play with price indices, in intellectual history where content analysis is appropriate—but not in diplomatic history. Those that have employed quantitative techniques in that subdiscipline are not card-carrying historians but are found, rather, in political science, sociology, and other behavioral sciences. In fact, when diplomatic historians do begin to flirt with numbers, they have generally wound up read out of the profession, in both the figurative and literal sense.[4] It might be that when they try to wed the dispatch or memorandum to the chi square and the correlation coefficient they are no longer doing history.

Whether or not they are "doing" history, these scholars investigate such historical topics as the Cuban missile crisis and the origins of World War I, the policies of statesmen like Bismarck and Dulles, and international activity during crucial epochs such as the Cold War and the decade of the 1870s.[5] Of course, their diplomatic histories involve data-based descriptions or explanations of the international system derived from the application of research methods of the harder sciences to historical materials. In style, such studies do not resemble traditional diplomatic history. For one thing, they devote an inordinate (for historians) amount of time to discussions of assumptions, procedures, coding rules, and methods, so that others can replicate the study. Indeed, replicability is one of the chief qualities that distinguishes most sciences from humanistic disciplines. Further, they are more concerned with the aggregation and statistical description of events than with chronological narratives. Yet most practitioners of Quantitative International Politics (QIP) see their work as directly related to, and a logical extension of, the sort of diplomatic history done by Thucydides or Barbara Tuchman.

In this chapter, I plan to examine the relationship between diplomatic history and Quantitative International Politics and to evaluate some of the studies that have been produced by the quantifiers.[6] At the least, diplomatic historians should become familiar with their work for they and their empirically oriented colleagues may have something to say to one another.

Studying Diplomacy with Numbers

Communication in the past has been frustrated for several reasons. Foremost may be a perceived lack of common purpose. Both groups of scholars seek to describe the same phenomena—wars, ultimata, crises, foreign ministers—but they begin from different premises. Most diplomatic historians deal with a specific country or system over a brief period of time, and they seek to tell the story of their subject in complete, sometimes overwhelming, detail. Indeed, they are so thorough that their monographs are often the primary sources for social scientists. The limited terrain they cover relates directly to their purposes. Historians claim to study the past not only because it is there, but to understand better where we are through a more complete knowledge of where we have been. Nevertheless, after introducing their subject with generalizations about its universal importance and applicability to the Cold War, they usually move abruptly into a narrative for the next three hundred pages and rarely attempt to relate their period to the present or to some general theory of human behavior. They explain the cause of a particular war and not the causes of war.

Those engaged in the study of QIP generally eschew the microscopic case study for a macroscopic examination of scores of cases over a broad temporal and spatial canvas. To some of them, the specific incidents they aggregate are unimportant except in terms of what they may contribute to a pattern that might have bearing on a theory of international behavior. Even those studying primary documentation over a relatively limited period of time offer little to the historian since they began from such radically different premises. Thus, in one examination of the diplomacy of the major powers during the decade of the 1870s, political scientist Richard Rosecrance and his colleagues list five objectives:

> 1) to formulate different clusters of "power," "balance of power" and "status" theories . . . 2) to develop valid approximations or measures of "power," "status," "balance of power," . . . 3) to formulate valid measures of international "cooperation and conflict" . . . 4) to seek to establish a relationship among "power," "balance of power," "status," and the dependent variables of "cooperation" and conflict thereby testing the theories sketched in (1); and 5) to draw conclusions about the general applicability of such theories in the nineteenth century, with comments upon the results of such an investigation for twentieth century practice.[7]

Diplomatic historians no doubt would ask, "Is that all?" Why study the 1870s if not to shed new light on the manner in which Bismarck isolated France or on the complicated vagaries of British Near Eastern policy from 1877 through 1880? Compare William Leonard Langer's introduction to his classic on the diplomacy of the same period:

> I have written this book . . . as a study of the evolution of the European states system. . . . I have tried . . . to describe and explain the broad course of development in international relations and to analyze the factors that brought about the great international groupings and alignments.[8]

One may search in vain through Langer's seminal study for any explicit attempt to build theories or to offer a prescription for contemporaries. Conversely, it is rare to find in the quantitative longitudinal studies of the social scientists any new interpretations of specific historical events.

The situation is not hopeless. Implicit in both approaches are ideas and insights of mutual interest. In describing systemic changes during the 1870s, Rosecrance and his colleagues illuminate the background conditions for specific decisions. In explaining in detail the decision-making processes (with-

71

out quite calling them that) during the 1870s and 1880s, Langer suggests contributions to theory. The problem is to develop a diplomatic history that includes the best of both worlds—a diplomatic history that contributes to our understanding both of the way foreign relations work and what happened during a particular event.

The development of such a diplomatic history is also frustrated by a language problem. Diplomatic history, whether written by Pierre Renouvin or A. J. P. Taylor, can be understood by most adult readers. What passes for QIP, however, is unintelligible to all but a small community of social scientists who understand differential equations or spectral analysis. Why not then learn the language as we once learned the lingua franca of diplomatic history, French? There are glossaries, handbooks, and even summer programs, such as those run at the University of Michigan and the Newberry Library in Chicago, to facilitate comprehension. Yet for purists this is not enough. One converted political historian feels quickie courses are insufficient to get along in these new languages.[9] For him, our education must be more sophisticated as he compares the summer programs to Berlitz courses, where you might learn how to buy some leather on the Ponte Vecchio but be unable to discuss the meaning of the Renaissance with a professor from the University of Florence.

This is an extreme position. Even if historians constantly "tooled up" in statistics, they would always find themselves at least a half year behind the latest fad in packaged programs or innovations. Further, the social scientists are just as contentious about the appropriate statistic to employ as diplomatic historians are about the writings of Fritz Fischer. QIP has borrowed techniques from more technologically advanced social sciences that have, in turn, borrowed them from the physical sciences. Consequently, many of the methods used by political scientists are vigorously assailed as inappropriate by some members of their own guild.[10]

What then are the untutored, untrained, and overburdened diplomatic historians to do? In the 1930s, a judicious William Langer hired graduate students to translate Japanese documents rather than attempt to learn the language himself. Contemporary historians can easily acquire enough concepts and jargon to communicate with a specialist who may assist with "translation" or methodological advice. But how do we know that his or her advice is correct? We do not, given the confusion in the area. Thus, we must assume simply that those who use such techniques honestly have explored all possiblities and then concentrate our attention on the plausibility of their findings.[11] Such an approach might horrify a physicist, as well as some quantifiers, but the state of the art is so primitive in the social sciences that we would be spinning our wheels were we to devote too much time to the pursuit of methodological expertise.

The lack of common purpose and language are not the only factors separating diplomatic historians from those who use quantitative methods to study international interactions. History is said to be an ideographic and not a nomothetic discipline and thus any attempt to search for patterns and cycles is impossible. Almost all of the critics of Quantitative International Politics— not just historians—express dismay about the cavalier manner in which events are compared across time and space. According to them each war, alliance, foreign minister, or crisis is said to represent a discrete, unique oc-currence. After surveying the major alliances from 1816 through 1945, and emphasizing their diverse purposes during different periods, one diplomatic historian concludes that "analyzing and categorizing alliances according to their provisions are not likely to be very fruitful in describing what alliances really do; nor are attempts to establish statistical correlations between numbers and types of alliances existing at various times and the cor-responding levels of international conflict and tension likely to be very fruit-ful."[12] Similarly, contend others, it is dangerous to assume much similarity between the Franco–Spanish War of 1823 that resulted in an estimated one thousand battle deaths and the Football War of 1969 in Central America that caused a comparble number of deaths.[13]

This problem of comparability worried historian–diplomat Harold Nicolson, who expressed concern that some might look for too many "lessons" in his study of the post-Napoleonic period. For him, "events are not affected by analogies; they are determined by the combinations of cir-cumstances. And since circumstances vary from generation to generation it is illusive to suppose that any pattern of history, however similar it may at first appear, is likely to repeat itself exactly in the kaleidoscope of time."[14] With this comment, the argument is clearly joined. The social scientist must re-spond that Nicolson's assertion is just that—an assertion that we need not take on faith. At bottom, the question of the comparability of historical events is an empirical one that should be put to the test. In the physical sciences, we can describe precisely the commonalities and differences between apples and oranges, two members of the family of fruits, and we certainly know something about the relative distance between those items and, let us say, an egg or a potato. Why not determine the differences and commonalities be-tween the Congress of Vienna and the Conference of Versailles or the Yalta Conference?

It is important to note that Nicolson had been asked by the British Foreign Office to study the Congress of Vienna in order to offer guidance for those who were preparing for peace in the 1940s. Whether Nicolson liked it or not, the statesman of his day were consciously looking for historical analogues. They have always done so, occasionally with disastrous results. Ernest May, among others, has demonstrated how the architects of American foreign policy during the Cold War applied improper analogies to the dynamics of the international system.[15] Earlier, Franklin Delano Roosevelt is alleged to have constructed an Asian policy based, in part, on romantic images picked up from grand-uncle Delano who had been engaged in the China trade in the nineteenth century.[16]

If statesmen insist on using historical analogies in the formulation of policy, then, ask the quantifiers, why not arm them with the proper ones? They should be presented with a usable past derived operationally from reproducible evidence and not just from a few prominent anecdotes. Unlike traditional diplomatic history, QIP is explicitly policy oriented, and, in fact, overlaps with the peace research movement.[17] Behind much of the work in QIP is the notion that an accurate rendering of the past might lead to a more peaceful world. For peace researchers, wars and international conflict are caused, in part, by leaders' highly selective and inaccurate readings of history. Thus, for example, the QIP approach can be used to test the famous dictum, *si vis pace, para bellum*.[18] Do nations that are well prepared for war end up in military conflict less frequently than those that are inadequately prepared? This is an empirical question that must be answered with more than a vague reference to Prussia in 1870 or Russia in 1904. Of course, one danger in this approach may be that as we become more accurate in our predictions, we will be helping policy makers not to make peace but to make war more effectively.[19]

This is not yet a serious problem since decision makers, like many humanists, doubt whether a quantitative approach can yield meaningful results. Some have likened the quantifiers to the proverbial drunk who loses his keys at the dark end of a street but insists on looking for them under a lamppost at the other end where the light is better.[20] Undoubtedly, one can count a wide variety of things in diplomatic history, but are those the relevant things? One explanation for the vast number of quantitative studies of the United Nations relates to the excellent bookkeeping job performed by the Secretariat. Those easy-to-come-by voting data that ultimately yield information on blocs in the General Assembly reveal little about Soviet diplomacy or policies made in the inner sanctums of multinational corporations.

And even were we able to count adequately Soviet or ITT's diplomatic interactions, would our findings be valid? Paul Schroeder offers an example of a sequence of events that a quantifier might count:

1. A man takes a woman by the hand.
2. He puts his arms around her.
3. He draws her close to him.
4. He kisses her.
5. He strangles her.[21]

Some might choose to code these five interactions as four cooperative actions and one conflictful one and perhaps conclude that, on the eve of the strangulation, the two actors had been behaving in a cooperative manner. One thinks of Japanese envoys Kurusu and Nomura setting up a negotiating meeting with Secretary of State Hull for December 7, 1941.

There is no easy solution to this problem. The demands of operational procedures and reproducible coding rules mean that a good deal of the richness and subtlety of specific events will be lost as they are categorized and aggregated by unromantic and insensitive coders. For example, in attempting to develop a measure of military strength, we found it difficult to locate meaningful figures for reserve and militia units for all countries for all time periods.[22] Consequently, we used standing armies for one of our indicators, a category that obviously does not tell the entire story about a nation's armed services. Confronted with difficult-to-interpret data on reserves for some countries, and missing data for others, as well as limited time and money to collect those data, we made a compromise and employed the best possible indicator available to us. Historians who pick their way through our materials find a favorite country or two that may be under- or overvalued during a certain period and proclaim our work a fraud. For the social scientist, the question is how valid is the indicator for the thousands of cases in the sample, not whether each figure represents absolute historical reality. To be sure, traditional historians have to make comparable compromises along the way to the production of a monograph. Some may run out of money before they can get to the archive in Tirana and thus have to reconstruct Albanian activity from documents in other archives. Others must work around missing or destroyed documents in archives they do examine. But the scrupulous historian calls attention to these problems and his or her level of confidence in the narrative or notes. Once the coding rules have been explained, the social scientist has little inclination to discuss individually the thousands of data points in terms of their bona fides. In this area, then, the gap between the two cultures is wide, and will remain so until the diplomatic historian recognizes the different types of demands and needs of the data gatherer in QIP as well as the practical problems entailed in producing a 99 and 100 percent pure datum for each event or indicator. We must remember that, whereas the diplomatic historian may be trying to explain what happened in 1877 between Russia and Turkey, the QIP investigator may be concerned with all countries in Europe from 1816 to 1900, every year.

One advantage of the application of an often rigorous and perhaps rigid scientific method to diplomatic history is the opportunity others are given to replicate the quantitative studies. For many social scientists, traditional history, based as it is upon intuitive and invisible coding rules and an almost spiritual immersion in the sources, can never get at "historical truth." It is impossible to replicate or even understand the procedures and assumptions of a Bradford Perkins or a C. K. Webster. Of course, most historians presently see little need for replication of their efforts. Interestingly enough, neither do the quantifiers. At least, while most of the studies in the genre can be replicated, few have taken the original authors up on it.[23] In general, each scientist-scholar is still operating according to the most individualistic of research strategies.

Two results of this failure have been a distressing lack of cumulativeness in this new science and much wasteful duplication of effort.[24] Thus, one project in the East might spend hundreds of person-hours and thousands of dollars compiling a set of population figures that had been put together in the Midwest or maybe in Mannheim, Germany, three years earlier. When we examine the output of the projects and scholars in QIP, we discover a multitude of different lists of wars, competing catalogues of events during the Cold War, and a wide and mutually inconsistent series of categorizations of regime types. In the end, at least for the present, QIP is not much better off than diplomatic history where we might have five or six leading competitive interpretations of the origins of the Cold War.

Most likely I am being unfair. The QIP movement is barely twenty years old and has struggled to develop in the often insecure and inhospitable environment of academic politics and careerism. Further, over that short period of time, it has experimented imaginatively with a variety of new methods and has produced hundreds of articles, books, dissertations, and reports that illuminate the nature of international relations and even diplomatic history. It is to some of these methods and findings that I now turn as we try to determine where diplomatic history and QIP intersect.

The Methods and Data of QIP

Turning first to tools that might be of assistance to the historian, QIP researchers have employed content analysis in many different contexts. Content anlysis is used to search through communications for order or patterns that might be missed in impressionistic examinations.[25] It features highly standardized procedures for sampling, measurement, and analysis. Typically, this method is used to examine a large volume of material according to an explicit set of coding rules. Adherence to these rules helps to control for both sample bias and the perceptual biases of the individual investigator.

A continuing area of interest to diplomatic historians has been the role of public opinion in affecting a nation's foreign posture. Passing over the knotty problem of determining the impact of opinion on policy, we encounter difficulties when we try to select and evaluate the almost infinite variety of opinions that appear in the mass media. What is a representative sample? How do we look at sufficient materials in sufficient media to be certain that patterns are accurately gauged? Content analysis offers some partial answers to these questions. In a study of American opinion of Russia during World War II, I employed several assistants to read every article listed under "Russia" in the *Reader's Guide to Periodical Literature* (N = 796), and to code them according to a rather simple set of instructions. When the results of this content analysis were arranged according to different periods and types of journals, I was able to buttress my impressionistic narrative with hard evidence.[26] In a follow-up study, I demonstrated that, in the absence of public opinion polls, content analysis of the media might enable us to "poll" past generations.[27]

Content analysis may also be used in the examination of diplomatic documents. The Stanford Studies in International Conflict and Integration is well known for its work with this tool.[28] In this case, project researchers used both human coders and computers to scan published documents relating to the six weeks that preceded the outbreak of World War I. As they well knew, what they made up for in precision and speed by using a computer instead of human coders, may have been lost in terms of coding flexibility.[29] In any event, they searched through more than six thousand odd communications (1.4 million words) for the perceptions and rhetorical behaviors of key decision makers during the crisis. Of course, the six thousand documents still represent the tip of the iceberg of relevant materials available to the intrepid researcher who visits all of the continental archives. Further, as might have been expected, the Stanford project ran into some tricky problems when it came to translating the documents precisely into English. Whether the massive effort was worth a candle will be considered below.

Others have turned to content analysis in their studies of the philosophies and psychologies of specific leaders. Contending that dipping into the papers of prominent figures is not likely to produce scientifically based findings, they have, for example, content-analyzed the writings and speeches of Franklin Roosevelt, Adolf Hitler, and John Foster Dulles.[30] Again, as is the case in this genre, these behaviorially oriented scholars have not bothered to mine the archives for unpublished materials since they feel that the private individual may be found between the lines of his or her public record.

A variation of content analysis is cognitive mapping, or the "representation of the causal beliefs or assertions of a specific individual through a close analysis of the way he links concepts in his writings or speeches."[31] This method is especially useful in comparing the belief systems of decision makers as it may uncover subconscious assumptions and reasoning processes that help us to understand diplomatic interactions. Thus, if we discover that the belief systems of contending leaders are different, we may better appreciate the dynamics of a conflict situation.

Another empirical approach used to uncover patterns in diplomacy that might be overlooked by those with preoperational methodologies involves events data.[32] Here researchers attempt to collect and code all diplomatic events or interactions between a set of states, often in terms of their conflictful or cooperative aspects. Instead of merely looking at obvious crisis activity, those who work in this area scale every word or deed that leaders of countries direct toward the international environment over an extended period of time. Using either monographs for earlier periods or newspapers for the Cold War years, events data projects have mapped interactions for long-term crises like the Arab–Israeli dispute or for entire decades in the nineteenth century.[33] As with content analysis, this tool may not be immediately relevant to the historian who examines all salient documents in an archive pertaining to an event. For the most part, social scientists who use events data are less concerned about the specific events they examine than they are about how patterns in interstate relationships offer early warning indicators of impending conflict.

Practitioners of QIP offer more than methodological tools to the diplomatic historian. They have devoted an enormous portion of their energies to the gathering of data that they use to make longitudinal quantitative assessments of such factors as national wealth, power, conflict, alliance activity, and political culture.[34] As with most of their research, they create massive data banks from published materials and not archival sources.[35] Thus, government yearbooks and annuals such as the *Statesman's Year Book* and the *Almanach de Gotha* have been mined for statistical information. Some of these secondhand (for historians) sources were surprisingly accurate and were used by penurious governments for their own intelligence surveys in much the same way as contemporary defense ministers carefully study publications of London's Institute for Strategic Studies. For example, one of the treasure troves for nineteenth-century statistical data is the *Almanach de Gotha,* a paragon of "Teutonic thoroughness." One observer noted that "the thoroughness and accuracy of its statistics and diplomatic fourth part make it . . . indispensable in every newspaper office and reference library, as in every chancellery, embassy, and consular agency of the civilized world" because of "its unequalled equipment for the gathering and orderly presentation of government information."[36]

Nevertheless, data handbooks are of marginal utility for diplomatic historians. Those working on monographic treatments of limited periods still need to examine the archives, when available, for data on the size of armed forces, population distribution, or national income. Further, they must be wary of interpolations and extrapolations. Missing data is the bane of longitudinal cross-national researchers. Most try to complete their series whenever possible through the use of statistical procedures that generate missing numbers through curve fitting. Consequently, while one data handbook may provide "real" figures for the population of Austria–Hungary in 1870 and 1880, the figure for 1875 may have been generated artificially. The best of the handbooks flag such entries while others may be more obscure about their origins. We must also remember that the so-called real figures, gleaned from an Austrian yearbook, may merely represent the best "guesstimate" of a harried and ill equipped demographer who had not been in the field for ten years.

Even more difficult to employ are derived indicators, measures of abstract concepts such as power, status, or democracy, constructed from data on iron production, diplomatic representation, or percent of voters participating in elections. The best of these may be very helpful in providing the diplomatic historian with a broader view of the total system in which he or she is working, as well as long-term trends that are often obscured when attention is concentrated upon a specific crisis.

The Correlates of War Project, for one, provides the international rela-

TABLE 1. Diplomatic Importance in 1869 and 1899

1869			1899		
1.	France	57	1.	Germany	79
2.	England	51	2.	England	78
3.	United States	44	3.	France	76
4.	Prussia	37	4.	Italy	65
5.	Italy	35	5.	United States	63
6.	Spain	33	6.	Spain	60
7.	Russia	32	7.	Austria	56
			8.	Russia	53
8.	Brazil	31	9.	Belgium	42
9.	Turkey	31	10.	Turkey	39
10.	Austria	30	11.	Brazil	38
11.	Holland	27	12.	Holland	35
12.	Denmark	26	13.	Japan	34
13.	Portugal	26	14.	Argentina	33
			15.	Portugal	33
14.	Bavaria	25	16.	Switzerland	33
15.	Belgium	25			
16.	Sweden	24	17.	Sweden	32
17.	Württemberg	19	18.	Paraguay	29
18.	Argentina	17	19.	Uruguay	29
19.	Baden	17	20.	Denmark	27
20.	Greece	17	21.	Mexico	27
			22.	Peru	27
21.	China	16	23.	China	24
22.	Switzerland	16	24.	Greece	24
23.	Chile	14	25.	Rumania	24
24.	Peru	13			
25.	Japan	12	26.	Chile	23
26.	Colombia	9	27.	Serbia	21
27.	Venezuela	9	28.	Siam	20
			29.	Colombia	19
28.	Bolivia	8	30.	Persia	19
29.	Persia	8	31.	Morocco	18
30.	Mexico	7	32.	Guatemala	17
31.	Ecuador	6	33.	Bolivia	16
32.	Guatemala	5	34.	Venezuela	16
33.	Haiti	5			
34.	Morocco	2	35.	Ecuador	15
			36.	Haiti	11
			37.	Korea	10
			38.	Dominican Republic	9
			39.	Ethiopia	6
			40.	Honduras	2
			41.	Salvador	2

tions community with a wealth of data and derived indicators on magnetic tape or in printouts that may help to place the work of historians in some context. For example, using the ranks and numbers of diplomats represented in each country's capital, the project was able to put together an index of diplomatic importance. In Table 1 are scores for 1869 and 1899.[37] While the margin of error is such that one should not make anything of the fact that Germany has one more point in 1899 than England or that England has two more than France, it is clear that these three powers are considered to be more important than Italy and the United States. As we examine both lists, we find much that appears to be intuitively reasonable to the historian who specializes in these epochs.

The project has also produced comparable listings of the capabilities of nations over time. Employing an index composed of scores for population and urban population, armed forces size and defense expenditures, and iron and steel production and energy consumption, it reveals rankings that again conform to the historian's impressionistic evaluations. In Table 2 are national capability scores expressed in terms of the percentage of all the capabilities in the system that each nation controls.[38]

The two rankings accurately reflect some of the changes in the distribution of power from 1860 to 1890, with England showing a relative decline and the United States and Prussia/Germany moving up toward top rank. Such scores that seek to measure objective capability may prove useful as benchmarks

TABLE 2. **Percentage Shares of Capabilities for the Most Active Members of the Interstate System in 1860 and 1890**

1860 % Share of Capabilities		1890 % Share of Capabilities	
1. England	25	1. England	19
2. Russia	15	2. United States	18
3. France	13	3. Germany	14
4. United States	8	4. Russia	11
5. Austria–Hungary	8	5. France	11
6. Prussia	7	6. Austria–Hungary	6
7. Italy	6	7. Italy	6
8. Spain	5	8. Spain	3
9. Turkey	4	9. Turkey	3
10. Belgium	2	10. Belgium	2
11. Sweden	2	11. Sweden	2
12. Holland	1	12. Holland	1
13. Switzerland	1	13. Switzerland	1
14. Denmark	.8	14. Portugal	1
15. Portugal	.6	15. Rumania	.9
16. Greece	.2	16. Denmark	.8
		17. Greece	.6
		18. Persia	.5

against which historians might want to compare evaluations made by the statesmen themselves.[39] After all, it is the subjective perceptions of contemporaries, no matter how erroneous, that determine the course of interstate interactions.

While historians might accept with caution some of the mountains of data produced by QIP research teams, they are probably more wary of the use to which these data have been put and the resultant findings. One efficient way to present representative findings is to turn to major projects in the field, the Stanford Studies, the Situational Analysis Project, and the Correlates of War Project.[40]

Some Findings of QIP

Scholars associated with the Stanford Studies on International Conflict and Integration have studied intensively the outbreak of World War I as well as the period from 1870 to 1914.[41] As for the oft-examined six-week crisis itself, their content analysis of the diplomatic correspondence suggests several conclusions with which historians would probably agree.[42] Here was a case in which, though few of the participants desired a world war, none took the necessary steps to avert the catastrophe. Indeed, most of the decision makers behaved in a way that could only exacerbate tensions. Observers have been interested in why otherwise rational leaders could not see the handwriting on the wall that appears so clear from historical hindsight.

The Stanford team addresses this question directly. Applying theories from psychology to their data, they report that the more involved the participants became in the crisis, the more they perceived hostility in the messages of their adversaries and the more they responded to that perceived hostility with hostility of their own. Under increasing stress as the crisis escalated, decision makers displayed less tolerance for ambiguity and presented increasingly more rigid positions. The pace of the crisis during the last two weeks, with foreign ministers suffering from information overload, or mental and physical fatigue, was a contributory factor to the outbreak of a war no one desired. Interestingly, not all participants behaved in the same manner. According to the Stanford researchers, Germany and Austria–Hungary were involved earlier in hostile crisis behavior than were the Triple Entente powers, a conclusion that might warm the hearts of those who see the greatest culpability in Vienna and Berlin.[43]

The examination of behavior during the six weeks after Sarajevo does not explain why there was a crisis in the first place. Looking back to the underlying causes of conflict, Choucri and North analyzed the systemic and structural factors in the European state system from 1870 to 1914, using rather sophisticated statistical tools, and came up with some interesting, if unspectacular, results.[44] Their model moves nations from the growth of population and technological bases that produce demands on the leadership that result, in some cases, in foreign expansion and a concomitant rise in military expenditures that was often followed by the formation of alliances and a propensity to enter into conflicts fraught with danger. The role played by domestic lateral pressure producing a movement to the Third World supports, to some degree, general Marxist models and especially the theory of unequal development in capitalist societies.[45]

This broader aspect of the project's activities is less satisfying to historians than the study of the 1914 crisis. In the first place, the indicators used for power, pressure, and expansion, and the way they are measured, may not pass historians' validity tests. More important, while one might accept the importance of lateral pressure in industrial societies as predicting to imperialist expansion, the study does not explain how we get from that point to the crisis of 1914. Why, for example, was there no war in 1911 during the second Moroccan Crisis, or in 1913 during the crises attendant to the Balkan wars? Structural factors that produce conflict, according to Choucri and North, were present then as well as in 1914—or in 1906, for that matter.

Despite such criticisms, the Stanford project represents a brave and imaginative attempt to apply quantitative methods to one of our most "popular" questions: Why World War I? Its contributions must be taken as seriously as those offered by the Fays, Schmidts, Albertinis, and Fischers.

Another project that should be of direct interest to historians is the Situational Analysis Project (SAP), located primarily at Cornell University.[46] Under the direction of Richard N. Rosecrance, scholars have been employing a variation of an events data technique to examine diplomatic interactions among the major powers from 1870 through 1890. SAP considers its research in nineteenth-century diplomacy to be relevant for today's statesmen.[47] Employing the monographs of diplomatic historians, project workers coded almost five thousand actions in terms of their cooperative or conflictful components. After cleaning and refinement, they ended up with 2,046 interactions for the 1870s, including both physical and verbal events.[48] Dyadic scores for conflict and cooperation were then statistically associated with power, status, and alliance measures in order to discover what types of nations behaved in what sorts of ways during different periods.[49]

How does such an approach differ from that of the historian? First of all, historians would probably labor in several archives for several years instead of using other historians' works for their primary data. And while SAP scores every interaction, historians, who might very well take notes on five thousand dispatches, report only the most dramatic ones. In addition, the "coding" of events by the historian is idiosyncratic and nonreplicable while often ahistorical research assistants code SAP data according to a predetermined set of explicit rules. In projects such as these, assistants tend to agree more than 90 percent of the time on a coding decision. Indeed, if pretests of intercoder reliability fall below 90 percent agreement, the rules are usually redrafted.

One difficulty in evaluating SAP's contribution to our understanding of diplomatic history is that its interest in what happened is often obscured by its overriding concern with theories of the balance of power. Nevertheless, SAP describes the decade of the 1870s in ways that should prove interesting to historians. During the decade, the major power system moved from multipolarity to unipolarity under the direction of Bismarck. But this shift was not accomplished smoothly. The project points to a good deal of instability from subperiod to subperiod. In fact, according to SAP, the diplomacy of this decade was a good deal more dynamic than historians usually indicate. Interestingly, in 1963, in his influential nonquantitative monograph, project director Rosecrance reported that the Bismarckian concert system was rather stable.[50] Here, then, is an example of how one student of diplomatic history, albeit a political scientist, altered his views after subjecting his data to an empirical technique. Among other specific findings, SAP demonstrates that France, the isolated power, was clearly the least active of the majors in terms of either her own initiatives or those directed toward her. More surprising, perhaps, is the discovery that Austria–Hungary received her largest number of cooperative gestures from Russia during the decade.[51]

The work of the project is incomplete. Over the next few years, it will have more to contribute to the way historians look at the period from 1870 to 1890, and, to some degree, SAP may affect they way we evaluate parallel work done by Choucri and North from the Stanford project.

A third major research enterprise in QIP is the Correlates of War Project (COW) at the University of Michigan's Mental Health Research Institute.[52] The location of an international relations project at such an institute appears at first glance to be peculiar. However, this institute is staffed by scholars ranging from animal biologists to students of diplomatic history, all of whom are concerned with conflict, most of whom believe in a general systems approach to their disciplines.

Under the guidance of political scientist J. David Singer, the Correlates of War Project began in 1963 to chart empirically diplomatic history since 1816. Through the 1960s, the project devoted the bulk of its energies to the development of a massive data base relating to wars, alliances, intergovernmental organizations, diplomatic representation, and components of national power. Once some of the data sets were completed, a variety of analyses were run, using increasingly more sophisticated statistical tools. Unlike the Stanford and SAP projects, COW is macrohistorical and not of immediate interest to most historians since it does not examine specific events or even limited time periods.

The project has not yet discovered the correlates, let alone the causes, of war. It has, however, produced results that merit attention from the historical community. Most important to date is the project's analysis of the 93 international wars that resulted in at least one thousand battle deaths from 1816 to 1965.[53] COW is not the first to examine statistically the frequency and severity of war in modern times. In fact, its work has been built upon the solid contributions of Quincy Wright and Lewis F. Richardson.[54] As with earlier researchers, COW reports that international war is primarily the province of major powers. They participated in over 60 percent of the 93 wars from 1816 through 1965 and, more significantly, more than 50 percent of all nations did not participate in an interstate war during that period. Diplomatic historians who have concentrated their attention on the major powers have not been off the mark, as this is where the diplomatic and martial activity appears to be.

Since 1816, according to COW, there has been no noticeable trend in the frequency of war. And when we control for the size of the system, there is no evidence that wars are becoming any more lethal. While such news may be welcome to those who fear that we are living in a century of total war, COW notes pessimistically that patterns in the incidence of war may relate to cycles of from twenty to forty years. This finding also reinforces the notion that it takes a generation or so for a nation to forget the horror of war and prepare once again for the romance of international combat. Another pattern that holds across time is the greater likelihood of wars breaking out in the spring and autumn than in the summer and winter. Further, despite changes in weapons technology and military strategy since 1816, the initiator of an attack consistently has had about a 70 percent chance of victory. Finally, dealing with wars, despite our mythology about the relatively pacific record of democracies compared to authoritarian polities, there is little to choose between the two sets of nations, even if we include war initiation.[55]

In addition, COW has devoted a considerable amount of attention to categorizing and analyzing alliances consummated since 1816.[56] Alliances are also the playthings of major powers, as up to the post–World War II era's "pactomania," very few system members belonged to an alliance that was not dominated by a major power. More interesting is the fact that, despite our anecdotal references to perfidious alliance partners, in the main, most have lived up to their commitments, at least through benevolent neutrality.

Perhaps COW's most intriguing tentative finding to date is the appearance, in disparate analyses, of a marked difference in diplomatic interactions in the nineteenth and twentieth centuries. Thus, COW reports that in the nineteenth century, the incidence of war seems to be associated with a low level of alliance participation, whereas the opposite appears to be true in the twentieth century.[57] Or, in the nineteenth century, as power in the system became more concentrated, war was more likely, a pattern that did not hold up in the twentieth century.[58] Although the intercentury difference does not show up in all of the project's studies, it appears with sufficient frequency to challenge the original assumption that we can crudely compare nineteenth-century events with their counterparts in the twentieth century. Of course, it is likely that certain decades in the twentieth century resemble others in the nineteenth, as SAP suggests, and that further analyses will reveal such complementarities.[59]

Along with the other projects in QIP, COW depends heavily upon diplomatic historians' monographs for information on alliances, wars, and dispute behavior. On occasion, it has had to alter listings, and subsequent analyses because of new data turned up in the archives by historical researchers. In the *Wages of War,* Singer and Small did not include the Changkufeng incident of 1938 as a qualifying war because they believed, according to the best printed sources available to them, that fewer than one thousand soldiers perished in combat. In 1977, after more than twenty years of research, much of it in virgin territory in the Japanese archives, Alvin D. Coox published a meticulous study indicating that more than one thousand Russian and Japanese soldiers died in the obscure incident.[60] Would that COW could have worked through the archives the way Coox did, but no longitudinal macrohistorical projects have the funds or time to send researchers into the archives to check every data point. Naturally, all QIP scholars would benefit from increased cooperation and interest from historians who are specialists in specific wars and eras in the quantifier's broad research domain.[61] Although there is no single project explicitly involved in longitudinal analyses of the relationship between domestic and foreign conflict, many QIP scholars have worked with this problem. In their own case studies, historians often talk about nations solving their domestic misfortunes through foreign adventures. Mussolini, for one, is said to have launched his imperialist program in the 1930s because of economic failures. Or, conversely, one explanation for increased domestic violence during the years of American military involvement in Southeast Asia was that the war experience contributed to a violent climate at home.

Several early examinations of actors in the international system of the late 1950s found no linkage between foreign and domestic conflict.[62] More recently, others reported that there may be a link between foreign and domestic conflict in some types of countries under certain conditions.[63] The jury is still out on the theory. Both groups of scholars used comparable strategies as they aggregated, scaled, and compared statistically thousands of incidents of nations' domestic and foreign violent activites. Here is another example of quantitative studies that might not be of interest to the historian concerned about the causes of just one conflict. Suppose we could establish categorically that there is no link between foreign and domestic conflict? Such a finding might mean that for 95 percent of the nations during 95 percent of the period such a link does not exist. The historian interested in one nation during one period may discover that his falls into the 5 percent that do not fit the QIP model.[64]

The Road Ahead

Our survey of the field does not exhaust the range of scholarship in QIP. It does, however, touch on the sorts of quantitative research most salient to diplomatic historians. The vast majority of the books, articles, monographs, and theses that fall under the QIP rubric are either too contemporary or mac-rohistorical to be of immediate interest to the case-study-oriented historian. Nevertheless, aside from the works discussed in detail above, other research in the field offers both methodological and substantive suggestions for historians.

A more complete sampling of relevant studies in QIP would include: Russett's effort to measure empirically the degree of closeness between the United States and England over a period of seventy years; Gamson and Modigliani's content analysis of Soviet–American interactions reported in the press during the early Cold War years; Naroll, Bullough, and Naroll's Toyn-bean examination of different societies from 216 B.C. to the present to test the efficacy of deterrence; Alker and Puchala's demonstration of how one might employ trade data to assess changing political relationships; Mueller's imag-inative consideration of poll data to enhance our understanding of opinion and policy during the fifties and sixties; and Rieselbach's use of scal-ing techniques to explain the phenomenon of isolationism in Congress from the late 1930s through to the 1950s.[65]

Most of the aforementioned works do not look like the sort of thing a historian should be doing, yet all offer insights that, for example, students of Anglo–American relations, the Cold War, or isolationism will find helpful. But it is unlikely that diplomatic historians will wholeheartedly embrace the methodology of QIP in the foreseeable future. As long as the historian con-centrates on the idiographic, the disciplines will remain distinct. And why should they not? Ironically, despite some quantifiers' evangelical desire to turn the historian–humanist into a rigorous social scientist, they would be lost without the rich case studies provided by their colleagues who labor for years in dingy archives to describe Danish–German relations in the 1840s. If histo-rians moved away from their detailed monographic narratives to more longitudinal, policy-relevant, comparative studies, where would the data come from?

What, then, is the prospect for the application of quantitative techniques to diplomatic history? Clearly, there are subjects within the discipline that can be successfully examined through the use of such techniques. In general, though, much of what historians do cannot be quantified, unless the basic paradigms within which they work are altered, an unlikely, and perhaps undesirable, prospect.

What is needed on the part of historians is a greater awareness of the social scientists poring over their data. Increased awareness should lead to mutually beneficial cooperation between the two styles of diplomatic history, with the result being a more valid representation of the past on the part of the quantifiers and a somewhat more rigorous and operational methodology on the part of the historians. Both disciplines will be the richer for this coopera-tion, as will, naturally, the millions of people who constitute the audience for historical scholarship.

Such cooperation might take several forms. For example, diplomatic historians and social scientists interested in international relations are beginning to talk with one another in the Diplomatic History and World Politics Network of the Social Science History Association. Among other things, the network circulates an informational roster in which members describe their research and offer to share their data sets with others in the field. This is an especially important function in times of limited resources for extracontinental scholarly jaunts. Undoubtedly, such sharing is inhibited by historians' concern about the purity of social scientists' data, but this will be overcome when more historians begin to participate in enterprises in QIP that produce longitudinal and cross-national data.

Indeed, the absence of historians in projects in QIP has been a major problem for scholars trained as political scientists who work with historical materials. Many lack both the substantive knowledge of diplomatic history and an understanding of the historical method. They desperately need historians to evaluate their research designs, sources, and, especially, the validity of their statistical results. Social scientists involved in projects in the quantitative mode who have tried to recruit historians to serve as consultants and co-investigators have enjoyed little success.

Historians tend to reject such requests not only because they see scant merit in the work of QIP or little professional payoff for themselves, but also because the two scholarly cultures are quite different. While social scientists are at home with team research, historians work by themselves. An interesting indicator of the relatively collective nature of scientific research and the individualistic approach of the humanities can be seen when one compares the number of jointly authored articles in the *Journal of Conflict Resolution* with those that appear in the *Journal of Modern History* or *Diplomatic History*. Historians may find that a bit more teamwork will enhance the quality of both QIP and their own studies.

For their part, students of international relations are able to help historians understand how some of their research problems might be addressed through the use of statistical tools. One can imagine a variety of contexts in which diplomatic historians might employ content analysis or sophisticated sampling techniques. The day may be dawning when reviewers will no longer be able to say that they do not understand why an author of a monograph failed to look at certain sources or how that author could possibly have interpreted a document in such a peculiar manner.

Diplomatic historians who are clumsy with numbers should be able to find statistically savvy colleagues either in their own department or in social science departments down the hall. The adoption of some of these tools will not necessarily detract from the flow of the narrative. It might merely result in the replacement of one quantitative phrase with another. Literary quality is not lost when we replace the traditional quantitative statement, ''Most people in the United States supported Polk's request for a declaration of war in

1846," with the more precise, empirically based conclusion, "Of the newpapers and magazines sampled, more than 80 percent supported Polk's war message."

By being among the last of their guild to deal with numbers, diplomatic historians will be able to learn from their colleagues' errors and excesses and make judicious use of the tools of modern social science. The future of both QIP and diplomatic history will be exciting as that most stodgy of fields catches up with the rest of the historians and recognizes that statistics and computers, in their proper place, will contribute not only to understanding diplomatic history but may make that history more useful for policy by statesmen who constantly search for guidance from the past to safeguard our present and future.

Notes

1. I have discussed this subject previously in Melvin Small, "The Applicability of Quantitative International Politics to Diplomatic History," *The Historian* 38 (February 1976): 281–304; and Melvin Small, "Doing Diplomatic History By the Numbers: A Rejoinder," *Journal of Conflict Resolution* 21 (March 1977): 23–34.

2. None of the following excellent volumes discuss the application of social science techniques to diplomatic history: Val Lorwin and Jacob Price (eds.), *The Dimensions of the Past* (New Haven: Yale University Press, 1972); David S. Landes and Charles Tilly, *History as Social Science* (Englewood Cliffs, N. J.: Prentice-Hall, 1971); William O. Aydelotte, Allen G. Bogue, and Robert W. Fogel (eds.) *The Dimensions of Quantitative Research in History* (Princeton: Princeton University Press, 1972); and Roderick Floud, *An Introduction to Quantitative Methods for Historians* (Princeton: Princeton University Press, 1973). Moreover, when the Social Science History Association organized its divisions in 1975, it failed to include one for diplomatic history.

3. Some works by diplomatic historians that consciously use social scientific models or approaches are Ernest R. May, *American Imperialism: A Speculative Essay* (New York: Atheneum, 1968); Paul Gordon Lauren, *Diplomats and Bureaucrats: The First Institutional Responses to Twentieth-Century Diplomacy in France and Germany* (Stanford: Hoover Institution Press, 1976); Robert D. Schulzinger, *The Making of the Diplomatic Mind: The Training, Outlook, and Style of United States Foreign Service Officers, 1908-1931* (Middletown, Conn.: Wesleyan University Press, 1975); Ralph B. Levering, *American Opinion and The Russian Alliance 1939-1945* (Chapel Hill: University of North Carolina Press, 1976); and several of the contributions to Klaus Knorr (ed.), *Historical Dimensions of National Security Problems* (Lawrence: University Press of Kansas, 1976).

4. Very few practicing diplomatic historians have published work in the quantitative mode. On the other hand, some major reference figures in the field—Karl Deutsch, Robert North, and Charles McClelland—who are political scientists began their careers as historians.

5. A useful introduction to the field is Susan Jones and J. David Singer, *Beyond Conjecture in International Politics: Abstracts of Data Based Research* (Itasca, Ill.: Peacock, 1972), a volume that carefully abstracts 158 articles written in the genre to 1970. An examination of some of the same material in narrative form is Patrick J. McGowan and Howard Shapiro, *The Comparative Study of Foreign Policy* (Beverly Hills: Sage, 1973). An exhaustive dissection of four major projects in the field is Francis Hoole and Dina A. Zinnes (eds.), *Quantitative International Politics: An Appraisal* (New York: Praeger, 1976). A thoughtful review article is Harvey Starr, "The Quantitative International Relations Scholar as Surfer: Riding the Fourth Wave," *Journal of Conflict Resolution* 18 (June 1974): 336–368. An excellent introduction geared to the undergraduate is Ted Robert Gurr, *Politimetrics: An Introduction to Quantitative Macropolitics* (Englewood Cliffs, N.J.: Prentice-Hall, 1972). Gurr takes the student from the inception of three projects to their conclusion as he explains and comments on assumptions, methods, research designs, and results. His two chapters on statistics are painless. A critical view of the field is Robert Jervis, "The Costs of the Quantitative Study of International Relations," in Klaus Knorr and James N. Rosenau (eds.), *Contending Approaches to International Relations* (Princeton: Princeton University Press, 1969), pp. 177–217. A witty, scathing attack is Edmund Ions, *Against Behavoralism: A Critique of Behavioral Science* (Totowa, N.J.: Rowman and Littlefield, 1977), pp. 76–97. The Russians are beginning to show some interest in the overall approach as well. See Juhan Kahk and Ivan Kovalchenko, "Quantitative Methods in Historical Research," *Social Sciences* 2 (1976): 102–116, and B. N. Mironov and Z. V. Stepanov. *Istorik i Matematika* (Leningrad: Izdatel'stvo "Nauka" Leningradskoe otdelenie, 1975).

6. One political scientist prefers SSIP, the Scientific Study of International Politics, to QIP. Dina A. Zinnes, *Contemporary Research in International Relations* (New York: Free Press, 1976), p. 15. Her discussion of the proper labeling for empirical studies of international relations is probably correct for her concerns but, in this exercise, since we are interested only in quantitative historical studies, QIP is quite appropriate. There are, of course, a wide range of studies in Zinnes' field that are "scientific" but not particularly historical and quantitative, including computer simulations such as Stuart A. Bremer, *Simulated Worlds: A Computer Model of National Decision Making* (Princeton: Princeton University Press, 1976); game theory, such as Anatol Rapaport, *Fights, Games, and Debates* (Ann Arbor: University of Michigan, 1960); or modeling, such as Michael D. Intriligator, "Some Simple Models of Arms Races," *General Systems* 9 (1964): 143–147.

7. Richard Rosecrance, Alan Alexandroff, Brian Healy, and Arthur Stein, *Power, Balance of Power, and Status in Nineteenth Century International Relations* (Beverly Hills: Sage, 1974), p. 7

8. Langer, *European Alliances and Alignments, 1871–1890* (New York: Vintage Books, 1964 ed.), p. vii.

9. J. Morgan Kousser, "The Agenda for 'Social Science History,'" *Social Science History* 1 (Spring 1977): 389.

10. The first time I delivered a paper that employed statistics (prepared for me by an expert), I was astonished to discover many of my social scientific listeners much less interested in my results than in whether it was advisable to use a Pearson or a Spearman correlation coefficient. Indeed, the discussion period was one of the

most heated I have experienced, but it had nothing to do with my substantive findings. I have since discovered that there is often little consensus among statisticians, as well as social scientists, on the correct statistic for specific analytical problems.

11. A commentator at a conference pointed out that the standardized format used by one well known political scientist always included a dense section on the details of the latest avant garde method employed, a section that one had to skip over for lack of expertise. But he advised his listeners that one could trust this scholar to be careful and prudent in such matters. (Richard Rosecrance, commenting on Michael Wallace's "The Role of Arms Races in the Escalation of Disputes into Wars: Some New Evidence," at the Social Science History Conference, Ann Arbor, Mich., October 21, 1977.) Diplomatic historians might be able to pick up enough technical expertise to be able to communicate with quantifiers in the brief piece by J. David Singer, *On the Scientific Study of Politics: An Approach to Foreign Policy Analysis* (New York: General Learning, 1973).

12. Paul Schroeder, "Alliances, 1815–1945: Weapons of Power and Tools of Management," in Knorr, *Historical Dimensions of National Security Problems,* p. 255.

13. See, for example, the interesting and balanced review article by André Corvisier, "L'étude de la guerre entre la sociologie et l'historie," *Revue Historique* 522 (April–June 1977): 362–363.

14. Harold Nicolson, *The Congress of Vienna: A Study in Allied Unity: 1812–1822* (New York: Viking Press, 1961), p. ii.

15. *Lessons of the Past: Uses and Misuses of History in American Foreign Policy* (New York: Oxford University Press, 1973).

16. Harold R. Isaacs, "Sources for Images of Foreign Countries," in Melvin Small (ed.), *Public Opinion and Historians: Interdisciplinary Perspectives* (Detroit: Wayne State University Press, 1970).

17. One may see this clearly in Juergen Dedring, *Recent Advances in Peace and Conflict Research: A Critical Survey* (Beverly Hills: Sage, 1976), or in many of the contributions to such publications as the *Journal of Peace Research* or the *Journal of Peace Science.* For more discussion of the use of history for policy purposes, see Paul Gordon Lauren's introduction to this volume and the chapter by Samuel Wells.

18. See an explicit attempt to test Kissinger–Nixon readings of history in J. David Singer and Melvin Small, "Foreign Policy Indicators: Predictors of War in History and in the State of the World Messages," *Policy Sciences* 5 (1974): 271–296.

19. After delivering a talk on peace research at the Air Force War College in Montgomery, Alabama, in 1971, I was asked, somewhat churlishly, could not our findings be used to assist generals in determining the most propitious time to launch an attack?

20. For a discussion of the quantitative fallacy see David Hackett Fischer, *Historians' Fallacies: Toward a Logic of Historical Thought* (New York: Harper, 1970), pp. 90–94. See also a review by Rein Taagerpera in *Behavioral Science* 19 (March 1974): 143; Robert P. Swierenga, "Computers and American History: The Impact of the 'New' Generation," *Journal of American History* 60 (March 1974): 1064–1065.

21. Paul W. Schroeder, "Quantitative Studies in the Balance of Power: An Historian's Reaction," *Journal of Conflict Resolution* 21 (March 1977): 8. See also in

the same issue Alan Alexandroff, Richard Rosecrance, and Arthur Stein, "History, Quantitative Analysis, and the Balance of Power," pp. 35-56, and Schroeder, "A Final Rejoinder," pp. 57-74. The entire debate in the *Journal of Conflict Resolution* illuminates many of the cultural and intellectual differences between the two types of diplomatic history. For a broader discussion that supports Schroeder, see Maurice Mandlebaum, *The Anatomy of Historical Knowledge* (Baltimore: Johns Hopkins University Press, 1977).

22. Here I am referring to my work with the Correlates of War Project at the University of Michigan, where, since 1964, I have served as historian–gadfly and co-investigator. I will discuss the project in detail below.

23. Karl W. Deutsch, "Recent Trends in Research Methods in Political Science," in James Charlesworth (ed.), *A Design for Political Science* (Philadelphia: American Academy of Political and Social Sciences, 1966), p. 42. In 1968 Bruce Russett, J. David Singer, and Melvin Small suggested ("National Political Units in the Twentieth Century: A Standardized List," *American Political Science Review* 62 [September 1968]: 932–951) that scholars might employ a standardized numbering system for nations to facilitate exchange of data, but few researchers took them up on their time-and energy-saving proposition.

24. For pessimistic comments on the lack of cumulativeness in QIP see selections in James N. Rosenau (ed.), *In Search of Global Patterns* (New York: Free Press, 1976), pp. 145–216.

25. For historians, the best introduction to the way content analysis is done is Richard L. Merritt, "Perspectives on History in Divided Germany," in Small, *Public Opinion and Historians,* pp. 139–174. A skeptical eye is cast upon Merritt's work in the "Comment" by John Higham in the same volume, pp. 175–179, and in Ions, *Against Behavioralism,* pp. 104–107. A recent use of content analysis by historians in which the method is carefully explained is Louis A. Galambos and Barbara R. Spence, *The Public Image of Big Business, 1880-1940: A Quantitative Study in Social Change* (Baltimore: Johns Hopkins University Press, 1975). See also Robert C. North, Ole R. Holsti, M. George Zaninovich, and Dina A. Zinnes (eds.), *Content Analysis* (Evanston, Ill.: Northwestern University Press, 1963).

26. Melvin Small, "How We Learned to Love the Russians: American Media and the Soviet Union during the Second World War", *The Historian* 36 (May 1974): 455–478. Compare this approach with that in Levering, *American Opinion and the Russian Alliance,* a study that is informed by social science theory but does not use quantitative methods.

27. Melvin Small, "When Did the Cold War Begin: A Test of An Alternate Indicator of Public Opinion," *Historical Methods Newsletter* 9 (March 1975): 61–73. Other studies that employ content analysis of media are Quincy Wright and Carl J. Nelson, "American Attitudes toward Japan and China, 1937-38," *Public Opinion Quarterly* 3 (January 1939): 46–62; Frank L. Klingberg, "The Historical Alternation of Moods in American Foreign Policy," *World Politics* 4 (January 1952): 239–273; Bernard C. Cohen, "Mass Communication and Foreign Policy," in James N. Rosenau (ed.), *Domestic Sources of Foreign Policy* (New York: Free Press, 1967), pp. 196–212; Peter Hansen, Melvin Small, and Karen Siune, "The Structure of the Debate in the Danish EC Campaign: A Study of an Opinion–Policy Relationship," *Journal of Common Market Studies* 15 (December 1976): 93–129.

28. See Dina A. Zinnes, "The Expression and Perception of Hostility in Pre-War Crisis: 1914," in J. David Singer (ed.), *Quantitative International Politics: Insights and Evidence* (New York: Free Press, 1968), pp. 85–122; Ole R. Holsti, Robert C. North, and Richard A. Brody, "Perception and Action in the 1914 Crisis," in *ibid.*, pp. 123–158; and Ole R. Holsti, *Crisis, Escalation, War* (Montreal: McGill-Queen's University Press, 1972).

29. For a presentation of computer coding see Philip Stone, Robert F. Bales, J. Zvi Namenwirth, and Daniel M. Ogilvie, "The General Inquirer: A Computer System for Content Analysis Based on the Sentence as a Unit of Information," *Behavioral Science* 7 (October 1962): 484–497.

30. Ralph K. White, "Hitler, Roosevelt, and the Nature of War Propaganda," *Journal of Abnormal and Social Psychology* 44 (April 1949): 154–174; William Eckhardt, "War Propaganda, Welfare Values, and Political Ideologies," *Journal of Conflict Resolution* 3 (September 1965): 345–358; Ole R. Holsti, "Cognitive Dynamics and Images of the Enemy: Dulles and Russia," in David Finlay, Ole R. Holsti, and Richard R. Fagan (eds.), *Enemies in Politics* (Chicago: Rand McNally, 1967), pp. 25–96; Peter Suefeld, Philip E. Teltlock, and Carmenza Ramirez, "War, Peace, and Integrative Complexity; United Nations Speeches on the Middle East Problem, 1947–1976", *Journal of Conflict Resolution* 21 (September 1977): 427–442.

31. Jeffrey A. Hart, "Cognitive Maps of Three Latin American Policy Makers," *World Politics* 30 (October 1977): 116. See articles in Robert Axelrod (ed.), *The Structure of Decision* (Princeton: Princeton University Press, 1976), and Stephen G. Walker, "The Interface Between Beliefs and Behavior: Henry Kissinger's Operational Code and the Vietnam War," *Journal of Conflict Resolution* 21 (March 1977): 129–168. An older but comparable work that originally was used by American intelligence services is Nathan Leites, *The Operational Code of the Politburo* (New York: Macmillan, 1951).

32. Useful as an introduction are Philip M. Burgess and Raymond W. Lawton, *Indicators of International Behavior* (Beverly Hills: Sage, 1972). For a sampling of the wares of the field, see Charles W. Kegley, Gregory A. Raymond, Robert M. Rood, and Richard A. Skinner (eds.), *International Events and the Comparative Analysis of Foreign Policy* (Columbia: University of South Carolina Press, 1975). An interesting introduction to a major project is Charles F. Hermann, Maurice A. East, Margaret G. Hermann, Barbara G. Salmore, and Stephen A. Salmore (eds.), *CREON: A Foreign Affairs Data Set* (Beverly Hills: Sage, 1973). CREON has coded 12,000 events from 36 nations from 1959 to 1968 using the annual *Deadline Date in World Affairs*. Another important events data study of crises from Schleswig-Holstein to Cuba is Russell D. Long and Robert A. Goodsell, "Behavioral Indicators of War Proneness in Bilateral Conflicts," in Patrick J. McGowan (ed.), *Sage International Yearbook of Foreign Policy Studies* (Beverly Hills: Sage, 1974), II: 191–266.

33 .One distressing problem with the data banks developed by events data scholars is the manner in which the patterns discovered depend upon the type and number of sources used. Charles F. Doran, Robert F. Pendley, and George E. Antunes, "A Test of Cross-National Event Reliability: Global Versus Regional Data Sources," *International Studies Quarterly* 17 (June 1973): 175–203.

34. In a critical aside, political scientist Klaus Knorr refers to the way behaviorists

"ransack [history] in their quest for suitable data." Knorr, "Introduction: On the Utility of History," in Knorr, *Historical Dimensions of National Security Problems,* p. 2.

35. Published data handbooks dealing with a lengthy historical period include Arthur Banks, *Cross-Polity Time-Series Data* (Cambridge: MIT Press, 1971); J. David Singer and Melvin Small, *The Wages of War: 1816-1965: A Statistical Handbook* (New York: Wiley, 1972). Many of the projects in international relations have put their data on tape in the University of Michigan's ICPR International Relations Data Archive. See also Michael Hudson, "Data Problems in Quantitative Comparative Analysis," *Comparative Government* 5 (July 1973): 611-629; Ted Robert Gurr, "The Neo-Alexandrians: A Review Essay on Data Handbooks in Political Science," *American Political Science Review* 67 (March 1974): 243-252. Traditional scholars have also contributed valuable handbooks. See B. R. Mitchell, *European Historical Statistics* (New York: Columbia University Press, 1975).

36. A. Schade Van Westrum, "Europe's Social Registers," *Bookman* 24 (February 1907): 575-860; Paul Meuriot, "L'Almanach de Gotha," *Journal de la Societé de Statistique de Paris* (June 1912): 167-179.

37. J. David Singer and Melvin Small, "The Composition and Status Ordering of the International System: 1815-1940," *World Politics* 18 (January 1966): 258-259. See also, for changes made in the original indicator, Small and Singer, "The Diplomatic Importance of States; an Extension and Refinement of the Indicator," *World Politics* 25 (July 1973): 577-599. William Roosen has applied a similar approach to status in "A Computerized Assessment of Louis XIV's Diplomatic Service," paper delivered at France in the Seventeenth Century Conference, Newberry Library, Chicago, October 9, 1976.

38. The Correlates of War Project has not yet published a final report on its capabilities index. These scores were used in J. David Singer, Stuart Bremer, and John Stuckey, "Capability Distribution, Uncertainty, and Major Power War, 1820-1965," in Bruce Russett (ed.), *Peace, War, and Numbers* (Beverly Hills: Sage, 1972), pp. 19-48. The rankings may change a bit when the method in which the scores are computed is altered.

39. Our empirically based scores should not be confused with the superficially scientific procedures used by Ray S. Cline in *World Power Assessment: A Calculus of Strategic Drift* (Washington, D.C.: Center for Strategic Studies, 1975). Cline employs an indicator of perceived power composed of hard data such as population, area, economic, and military figures, and his own intuitive scores for strategic purpose and will to pursue national strategic goals.

40. A useful quantitative summary of the results of QIP is John A. Vasquez, "Statistical Findings in International Politics: A Data-Based Assessment," *International Studies Quarterly* 20 (June 1976): 171-218.

41. For an excellent, exhaustive analysis of the project see the several articles in Hoole and Zinnes, *Quantitative International Politics,* pp. 349-459. See also Gordon Hilton, "The 1914 Studies: A Reassessment of the Evidence and Some Further Thoughts," *Peace Research Society (International) Papers* 7 (1970): 117-141.

42. On the 1914 crisis, most important here are Holsti, *Crisis Escalation, War;* Zinnes, "The Expression and Perception of Hostility in Prewar Crisis"; Holsti, Robert C. North, and Richard Brody, "Perception and Action in the 1914 Crisis"; Holsti,

"The 1914 Case," *American Political Science Review* 59 (June 1965): 365–378. From the same project on the Cuban missile crisis is Holsti, Brody, and North, "Measuring Affect and Action in International Reaction Models: Empirical Materials from the 1962 Missile Crisis," *Peace Research Society (International) Papers* 2 (1965): 170–190. See also Holsti's chapter in this volume.

43. Of less interest to historians is Eugenia V. Nomikos and Robert C. North, *International Crisis: The Outbreak of World War I* (Montreal: McGill–Queen's University Press, 1976). In this volume, the authors present a non-numeric narrative that adds little to what we know about the crisis.

44. Nazli Choucri and Robert C. North, *Nations in Conflict: National Growth and International Violence* (San Francisco: Freeman, 1975). Using a comparable model, the authors examined peaceful societies in "In Search of Peace Systems: Scandinavia and the Netherlands, 1870–1970," in Russett, *Peace, War, and Numbers,* pp. 239–274.

45. Samir Amin, *Unequal Development* (New York: Monthly Review Press, 1976).

46. For the major studies from SAP see Peter DeLeon, James MacQueen, and Richard N. Rosecrance, "Research Report: Situational Analysis in International Politics," *Behavioral Science* 14 (January 1969): 51–58; Brian Healy and Arthur Stein, "Balance of Power in International History: Theory and Reality," *Journal of Conflict Resolution* 17 (March 1973): 33–61; Jeffrey Hart, "Symmetry and Polarization in the European International System, 1870–1879: A Methodological Study," *Journal of Peace Research* 11, No. 3 (1974): 229–244; Rosecrance *et al., Power, Balance of Power, and Status in Nineteenth Century International Relations;* Alan S. Alexandroff, "Symmetry in International Relations: An Empirical Analysis of the Behavioral Interaction of the European Powers from 1870–1890," paper prepared for delivery at the Social Science History Association Conference, Ann Arbor, Mich., October 22, 1977.

47. Rosecrance et al., *Power, Balance of Power, and Status in Nineteenth Century International Relations,* pp., 9–10.

48. Although SAP covers two decades, most of its published work to date relates to the 1870s.

49. SAP's assumptions, measures, and procedures are discussed in detail in the excellent "Quantitative International History: An Exchange," *Journal of Conflict Resolution* 21 (March 1977): 3–74. Compare this approach to the 1870s to traditional historian Mihailo D. Stojanovic, *The Great Powers and the Balkans* (Cambridge, Eng.: Cambridge University Press, 1939).

50. Richard N. Rosecrance, *Action and Reaction in World Politics: International Systems in Perspective* (Boston: Little, Brown, 1963), p. 147.

51. Rosecrance et al., *Power, Balance of Power, and Status in Nineteenth Century International Relations,* pp. 30–32.

52. For the history of the project during its first decade see J. David Singer, "The Correlates of War Project: Interim Report and Rationale," *World Politics* 24 (January 1972): 243–270. A report directed to historians is Melvin Small and J. David Singer, "Historische Tatsachen u. Wissenschaftliche Daten am Beispiel der Erforschung von Kriegen" [Historical Facts and Scientific Data in the Study of War], in Peter Christian Ludz (ed.), *Soziologie und Sozialgeschichte: Aspekte und Pro-*

bleme, Sonderheft 16, Kölner Zeitschrift fur Soziologie und Sozial-Psychologie (1973): 221–241.

53. On the wars see Singer and Small, *The Wages of War, 1816–1965;* Small and Singer, "Patterns in International Warfare, 1816–1965," *Annals of American Adademy of Political and Social Science* 311 (September 1970): 145–155. The basic patterns reported here obtain when the war list is brought up throught 1977. For information on the ten wars fought from 1966 to 1978, see Small and Singer, "Trends in International Conflict," in Charles Kegley and Patrick McGowan (eds.), *Challenges to America: United States Foreign Policy in the 1980's* (Beverly Hills: Sage, 1979).

54. Quincy Wright, *A Study of War* (Chicago: University of Chicago Press, 1965); Lewis F. Richardson, *Statistics of Deadly Quarrels* (Chicago: Quadrangle, 1960). Other older statistical studies of the frequency and severity of wars are Jean de Bloch, *The Future of War* (New York: Doubleday and McClure, 1899); Pitirim A. Sorokin, *Social and Cultural Dynamics* (New York: American Book, 1937), III. Since World War II, Gaston Bouthoul of the Institut de la Polemologie in Paris has been studying violent conflicts in comparable fashion. For the results of his study of 366 wars since the eighteenth century see Bouthould and Réné Carrère, *Le Defi de la Guerre (1740–1974): Deux Siècles de Guerres et de Revolutions* (Paris: PUF, 1976). A Marxist with a statistical approach is Boris T. Urlanis, *Voeni i Narodo-Nacelenie Evropi* [Wars and the Population of Europe] (Moscow: Government Publishing House, 1960). See also David Wood, *Conflict in the Twentieth Century,* Adelphi Papers, No. 48 (London: Institute for Strategic Studies, 1968); and a useful compendium, Milton Leitenberg, *A Survey of Studies of Post World II Wars, Conflicts, and Military Coups,* prepared for the Nordic Cooperation Committee for International Politics Symposium, Helsinki, September 1977.

55. Melvin Small and J. David Singer, "The War Proneness of Democratic Regimes, 1816–1965," *Jerusalem Journal of International Relations* (Summer 1976): 50–69. On the same subject see Bruce M. Russett and R. Joseph Monsen, "Bureaucracy and Polyarchy as Predictors of Performance: A Cross National Examination," *Comparative Political Studies* 8 (April 1975): 3–31.

56. J. David Singer and Melvin Small, "Formal Alliances, 1815–1939," *Journal of Peace Research* 3 (1966): 1–32; Small and Singer, "Formal Alliances, 1816–1965; An Extension of the Basic Data, *Journal of Peace Research* 6 (1969): 267–282. Alan Ned Sabrosky, "The War-Time Reliability of Inter-State Alliances, 1816–1965," paper prepared for International Studies Association Conference, Washington, D. C., February 19-22, 1975.

57. J. David Singer and Melvin Small, "Alliance Aggregation and the Onset of War, 1815–1940," in Singer, *Quantitative International Politics,* pp. 247–286.

58. Singer, Bremer, and Stuckey, "Capability Distribution, Uncertainty, and Major Power War, 1820–1965."

59. A preliminary analysis of war and dispute data since 1816 shows the period from 1966 to 1977 to resemble the periods from 1816 to 1849 and 1871 to 1890 in the incidence and magnitude of violent interactions. Small and Singer, "Trends in International Conflict."

60. Alvin D. Coox, *The Anatomy of a Small War; The Soviet-Japanese Stuggle for Changkufeng/Khasan* (Westport, Conn.: Greenwood, 1977).

61. COW has had some useful cooperation from historians. In one study, a member of the project team polled a group of 25 diplomatic historians to ascertain whether they agreed with his classification of the major powers from 1816 through 1965. Charles M. Gochman, "Status, Capabilities, and War: 1820–1970," Ph.D. thesis, University of Michigan, 1976.

62. Rudolph J. Rummel, "Dimensions of Conflict Behavior Within and Between Nations," *General Systems Yearbook* 8 (1963): 1–50; Rummel, "Testing Some Possible Predictors of Conflict Behavior Within and Between Nations," *Peace Research Society (International) Papers* 1 (1963): 79–111; Raymond Tanter, "Dimensions of Conflict Behavior Within and Between Nations, 1958–1960," *Journal of Conflict Resolution* 10 (March 1966): 41–64. More recently, the original studies have been supported by Robert Burrowes and Bertram Spector, "The Strength and Direction of Relationships Between Domestic and External Conflict and Cooperation: Syria, 1961–1967," in Jonathan Wilkenfeld (ed.), *Conflict Behavior and Linkage Politics* (New York: McKay, 1973), pp. 294–324.

63. Dina Zinnes and Jonathan Wilkenfeld, "An Analysis of Foreign Conflict Behavior of Nations," in Wolfram H. Hanreider (ed.), *Comparative Foreign Policy* (New York: McKay, 1972), pp. 167–213; Wilkenfeld and Zinnes, "A Linkage Model of Domestic Conflict Behavior," in Wilkenfeld, *Conflict Behavior and Linkage Politics,* pp. 251–293. Andres D. Onate, "The Conflict Interactions of the People's Republic of China, 1950–1970, "*Journal of Conflict Resolution* 18 (December 1974): 578–594.

64. Of course, it is possible that this general method, and events data technique, can be used successfully by historians of, for example, contemporary Syria, China, or the United States. See Burrowes and Spector, "The Strength and Direction of Relationships Between Domestic and External Conflict and Cooperation: Syria, 1961–1967"; Onate, "The Conflict Interactions of the People's Republic of China, 1950–1970", Michael Stohl, "War and Domestic Political Violence: The Case of the United States, 1890–1970," *Journal of Conflict Resolution* 19 (September 1975): 379–415. For a variation on this theme, see how domestic instability is related to American foreign policy in the Cold War era in Charles F. Doran, *Domestic Conflict in State Relations: The American Sphere of Influence* (Beverly Hills: Sage, 1976).

65. See Bruce M. Russett, *Community and Contention: Britain and American in the Twentieth Century* (Cambridge: MIT Press, 1963); William A. Gamson and Andre Modigliani, *Untangling the Cold War: A Strategy for Testing Rival Theories* (Boston: Little, Brown, 1971); Raoul Naroll, Vern C. Bullough, and Frada Naroll, *Military Deterrence in History: A Pilot Cross-Historical Survey* (Albany, N. Y.: SUNY Press, 1974); Hayward R. Alker, Jr., and Donald Puchala, "Trends in Economic Partnership in the North Atlantic Area," in Singer, *Quantitative International Politics,* pp. 287–316; John E. Mueller, *Wars, Presidents, and Public Opinion* (New York: Wiley, 1973); and Leroy N. Rieselbach, *The Roots of Isolationism* (Indianapolis: Bobbs-Merrill, 1966).

PART II

5
Theories of Crisis Decision Making

Ole R. Holsti

IN MEMOIRS WRITTEN SOME YEARS BEFORE HE ASSUMED THE PRESIDENCY, Richard Nixon wrote of crises as "mountaintop experiences" in which he often performed at his best: "Only then [in crises] does he discover all the latent strengths he never knew he had and which otherwise would have remained dormant."[1] He added:

> It has been my experience that, more often than not, taking a break is actually an escape from the tough, grinding discipline that is absolutely necessary for superior performance. Many times I have found that my best ideas have come when I thought I could not work for another minute and when I literally had to drive myself to finish the task before a deadline. Sleepless nights, to the extent that the body can take them, can stimulate creative mental activity.[2]

Others have appraised the effects of crisis on decision making in a similar vein, suggesting, for example, that "a decision maker may, in a crisis, be able to invent or work out easily and quickly what seems in normal times to both the 'academic' scholar and the layman to be hypothetical, unreal, complex or otherwise difficult."[3] More important, theories of nuclear deterrence presuppose rational and predictable decision processes, even during intense and protracted international crises. They assume that threats and ultimata will enhance calculation, control, and caution while inhibiting recklessness and risk-taking.[4] Deterrence theories, in short, tend to be sanguine about the ability of policy makers to be creative when the situation requires it—and never is that requirement greater than during an intense international crisis.

These observations appear to confirm the conventional wisdom that in crisis decision making necessity is indeed the mother of invention. Is there any reason to question the universal validity of that view? Fortunately, scenarios of inadequate decision making resulting in a nuclear war are thus far limited to novels and movies, but otherwise the evidence is less than totally reassuring. The recollections of those who have experienced intense and protracted crises suggest they may be marked at times by great skill in policy

99

making, and at others by decision processes and outcomes that fail to meet even the most permissive standards of rationality. Some recall the "sense of elation that comes with crises,"[5] whereas others admit to serious shortcomings in their own performance during such situations. Indeed, although the definitive history of the Watergate episode remains to be written, available evidence suggests that Nixon's performance during the culminating crisis of his presidency was at best erratic, certainly falling far short of his own self-diagnosis as described above.

But anecdotes do not provide a sufficient basis for addressing the question: How do policy makers respond to the challenges and demands of crises? Do they tend to approach such situations with high motivation, a keen sense of purpose, extraordinary energy, and an enhanced capacity for creativity? Or, is their capacity for coping with complex problems sometimes impaired, perhaps to the point suggested by Richard Neustadt's phrase, "the paranoid reaction characteristic of crisis behavior"?[6]

This chapter will address these questions by describing and analyzing several major theories of crisis decision making. It will begin with a discussion of the various definitions of the much abused term, "crisis," and review theoretical models of behavior during crises. This will be followed by the presentation of several hypotheses concerning some of the effects of intense and protracted crisis on decision making, utilizing recent evidence from several social sciences, especially the field of psychology. Some of these hypotheses of crisis-induced stress will then be examined in the light of evidence from two classic case studies in diplomatic history: the 1914 crisis leading to the outbreak of World War I and, more briefly, the Cuban missile crisis of 1962. Finally, the conclusion will discuss some of the advantages and disadvantages of interdisciplinary research for psychologists, political scientists, and diplomatic historians.

Crisis: Definitions, Descriptive Theories, and Prescriptive Theories

One of the first requirements in establishing any viable body of theory is that of providing workable definitions. In this regard, theories of crisis behavior have been plagued with the fact that "crisis" is a much overused term that has become burdened with a wide range of meanings, some of them quite imprecise. In common usage it is victim of the age of hyperbole, becoming a synonym for virtually every problem of even moderate difficulty. Even in foreign policy research and diplomatic history, diversity is more in evidence than uniformity. As one of the pioneers in crisis research, Charles McClelland, observes:

> So many studies of crisis have been published in the last fifteen years from so many different angles of inquiry that it is more difficult than it once was to be sure about

100

the denotations and connotations of the term. Not only is there a heavy popular usage of the word in ordinary discourse but also there are indications that historical change has brought about an expansion of the variety of situations that are called readily by the crisis name.[7]

In order to resolve this problem, scholars have been working to establish an acceptable definition of a crisis. These efforts fall into two very broad groups. Common to the first is a systematic perspective in which crisis represents a signficant change in the quantity, quality, or intensity of interactions among nations. As McClelland describes this approach, it "looks on the whole configuration of parties participating back and forth" and observes changes in the patterns of interaction.[8] Special attention is given to any significant step-level change or turning point. This might be a dramatic increase in the number of border incidents, verbal challenges, or physical threats. After a crisis, the number and type of these exchanges may return to a more "normal" state. Accordingly, one way to identify crises analytically in diplomatic history is through a *post hoc* search for changed interaction patterns between nations.[9]

A second approach to defining a crisis—the decision-making perspective—focuses on the human participants themselves rather than the system. Here, a situation is a crisis when it is so defined by those who are responsible for coping with it. It is thus possible that in a confrontation between nations X and Y, decision makers in the former will believe themselves to be facing a crisis, whereas those in the latter will not. Although differences may be found among those who adopt a decision-making approach to crisis, one definition developed by Charles Hermann has gained a number of adherents: A crisis is a situation characterized by *surprise,* a *high threat* to important values, and *short decision time.*[10] This definition is not without its critics, but most of them tend to disagree only with one or another of the three criteria, usually either surprise,[11] or short decision time.[12] Nevertheless, the Hermann definition offers some important advantages to both theorists and historians, not the least of which is the existence of at least some evidence linking each of the defining criteria with some consequences for decision making.

Most of the extensive literature on crisis extends far beyond this initial problem of definition and concentrates its attention on actual behavior during crisis situations. This proceeds from a wide variety of theoretical and empirical perspectives. It can perhaps be understood best by following the approach of Hermann and Brady, and systematically identifying four rather distinct, *descriptive* theories.[13]

The first of these is the *organizational response* model. It is directed at decision-making groups and the bureaucratic organizations which may shape and constrain policy choices in crisis. Studies at the level of the decision-making group reveal that the concomitants of crisis—for example, smaller groups or greater cohesion—can have both positive and negative consequences for the quality of decision processes. Leadership skills often determine whether, for example, group cohesion becomes a vehicle for constructive cooperation, or whether it takes on a more pathological form such as "groupthink."[14] Organizational theorists have often regarded crises as occasions in which greater than normal rationality prevails because decisions are made at the top of organizational hierarchies by persons less constrained by narrow parochial views.[15] Moreover, limited time reduces opportunities to adopt bargaining and incremental strategies that may reduce the quality of decisions.[16] But others have shown that not even in crisis situations is decision making free of the organizational processes and bureaucratic politics that may constrain rational choice.[17]

A second approach may be found in the *hostile interaction* model, which examines the antecedents and consequences of interactions among nations in crises, with special attention to the role of perceptions in exacerbating, sustaining, or mitigating the pattern of relations between contending parties. According to this model, those involved in a crisis perceive accurately any hostility directed toward them, and they respond in kind. Thus, crisis is viewed as an occasion that is likely to trigger a "conflict spiral." Stated somewhat differently, this conception of crisis highlights the processes by which hostility breeds more hostility, and it focuses less attention on the means by which such a pattern of interactions may be arrested.[18]

The *cost calculation* model emphasizes the strategic and tactical choices associated with maximizing gains and minimizing losses in crisis management. Crises that pose significant threats to such central goals as national existence are likely to engender greater caution in decision makers, as well as more vigorous efforts to reach peaceful settlements. Conversely, in crises posing threats of lesser magnitude, policy makers will feel less constrained and, therefore, they may be more willing to resort to high-risk strategies and tactics; for example, they may undertake actions that convey irrationality or loss of control in an effort to force concessions from the adversary. Thus, the hostile interaction and cost calculation models differ in some significant ways, especially with respect to the prospects for attenuating escalation in a crisis.[19]

The *individual stress* model focuses upon the impact of crisis-induced stress on certain aspects of cognitive performance that are critical in decision making. Theories and research at the individual level generally emphasize the negative effects of intense and protracted crises on decision processes and outcomes. It should be noted, however, that this model is not merely a variant of a frustration–aggression theory. As will be evident in later sections of this chapter that deal with the individual stress model in much more detail, the probable consequences of intense and protracted stress are by no means confined to or even most clearly manifested by the release of aggressive impulses.

Other theories address themselves to the *consequences* of crisis. These are also marked by diversity. Among those with a systemic perspective, crisis has been viewed both as a prelude to war[20] and as a surrogate for war that offers a means of effectuating needed change.[21] There are also competing views on the consequences of *multiple* crises. The first, suggested by Quincy Wright, among others, states that the more frequent the crises, the greater the likelihood that war will result. "If p_1, p_2, p_3, etc., indicate the probability of war in successive crises in the relations of two states and P indicates the probability of war for n crises, then $P = 1 - (1 - p_1)(1 - p_2)(1 - p_3) \cdots (1 - p_n)$. . . . Even though p is very small, as n approaches infinity the probability of war approaches certainty."[22] This might be labeled the "actuarial" view of crises. An insurance company typically charges a higher premium for the person who drives thirty thousand miles a year than for one who logs only a quarter of that distance, on the theory that greater exposure to the highways will increase the probability of a claim. The Wright formulation assumes that each crisis can be thought of as a discrete event and that there is little or no learning from episode to another; that is, the participants can be thought of as beginning each time with a "crisis mangement tabula rasa." Thus, the cumulative probability of crises leading to war increases with each incidence of such an event.

An alternative position denies that decision makers begin with a blank slate at the onset of each crisis. Because the participants learn from their experiences, crises become "routinized." "Outputs received from occurrences and situations in the international environment and from sequences of international interaction are processed by the advanced modernizing social organizations according to their perceived characteristics: if these outputs are recognized as familiar and expected experiences met repeatedly in the remembered past, they will be treated in a highly routine fashion."[23] The participants gain experience in ways of coping with environment and adversaries and, although threats and challenges may continue to characterize relations between parties, uncertainty is reduced. Thus, "repeated exposure to acute crises may reduce the probabilities of an outbreak of general war."[24]

Finally, *prescriptive theories*—that is, theories that emphasize how to achieve one's purposes—of crisis management span an equally broad range. For present purposes, it may be sufficient to identify some basic features of two rather different perspectives. This is done merely for the purpose of illustration, and it should not be construed as an adequate treatment of the various positions or of all aspects of crisis management.

One position holds that the primary task of crisis management is to communicate one's interests and demands as unambiguously as possible, in order to prevent miscalculation on the part of adversaries. With a clear exposition of one's interests, the adversary will either avoid further provocation (ending the crisis) or demonstrate a calculated willingness to escalate the conflict (and thus reveal no interest in resolving it except on one's own terms). Strategies of crisis management include "burning one's bridges" and other forms of seemingly irrational behavior that are intended to convey to adversaries an unambiguous message of one's resolve and commitment.[25]

A rather different theory of crisis management places emphasis not only on protecting one's primary interests, but also on avoiding actions that might drive an opponent into a mutually undesirable process of escalation. Those in the group described in the previous paragraph believe that the primary danger of crisis mangement is that unwise concessions will mislead a thoroughly rational opponent into making further demands (the "appeasement model"); the opposing view is that an overly rigid policy may lead the adversary, whose rationality is not without limits under circumstances of crisis-induced stress, to strike back in ways that are disadvantageous to both sides.[26]

Perhaps this cursory review of a large literature is sufficient to establish the point that even if there are fewer than a hundred flowers contending for the attention of those undertaking crisis studies, consensus remains an elusive goal rather than an established condition. Stated somewhat differently, the diplomatic historian who ventures into neighboring disciplines with expectations of finding broad agreement on key concepts that are linked together in well established theories, and solidly buttressed by empirical evidence, is likely to be somewhat disappointed.

Lest this appraisal paint an overly pessimistic picture, it is also worth pointing to some signs of genuine progress toward the goals of cumulative knowledge. There is a convergence around, and refinements of, certain key terms and definitions (e.g., Hermann's definition of crisis) in the literature. There is also a growing willingness to undertake comparative studies in which a single crisis is viewed from several, rather than from a single, theoretical perspective,[27] or in which two or more crises are examined in a systematic and rigorous comparative manner.[28] Moreover, there is evidence that the crisis literature that has been heavily skewed toward studies of postwar crises involving one or more of the superpowers, is now being significantly broadened by research which includes both pre-and post-1945 cases well as small- and middle-range powers.[29] Finally, the concept of crisis itself is being subjected to cross-cultural comparisons in order to understand the involvement of more than one decision system in the anticipation, avoidance, control, and termination of international crises.[30] These several developments suggest promising prospects for policy makers, political scientists, and diplomatic historians concerned with crisis behavior.

Crisis, Stress, and Decision Making: Some Evidence from Psychology

One of the more interesting bodies of theory on crisis behavior is that concentrating upon individual stress. This approach, as indicated previously, focuses upon the impact of crisis-induced stress on certain aspects of cognitive performance that are critical in decision making. In assessing the potential impact of crisis on cognitive performance, it is important to do so against realistic standards. Cognitive limits on rationality include, as suggested by evidence from psychology, limits on the individual's capacity to receive, process, and assimilate information about the situation; an inability to generate the entire set of policy alternatives; fragmentary knowledge about the consequences of each option; and an inability to order preferences for all possible consequences on a single utility scale.[31] Because these constraints exist in all but the most trivial decision-making situations, it is not instructive to assess the impact on crises against a standard of synoptic rationality. A more modest and useful set of criteria might include an individual's ability to do the following:

Identify adequately the objectives to be fulfilled;

Survey the major alternative courses of action;

Estimate the probable costs and risks, as well as the positive consequences, of various alternatives (and, as a corollary, distinguish the possible from the probable);

Search for new information relevant to assessment of the options;

Maintain an open mind to new information, even that which calls into question the validity of preferred courses of action (and as corollaries, discriminate between relevant and irrelevant information, resist premature cognitive closure, and tolerate ambiguity);

Assess the situation from the perspective of other parties;

Resist both defensive procrastination and premature decision;

Make adjustments to meet real changes in the situation (and, as a corollary, distinguish real from apparent changes).[32]

A vast body of theory and evidence suggests that intense and protracted crises tend to erode rather than enhance these cognitive abilities. Figure 1—a series of hypotheses linking the defining attributes of crisis, first to stress and then to selected aspects of cognitive and decision-making performance—is a variant of the individual stress model described earlier.[33] These propositions are presented not as iron laws but as an alternative to the view that crisis heightens propensities toward rational and calculated decision processes. The remainder of this section summarizes briefly some of the relevant psychological evidence.

An important aspect of crises is that they are characterized by high stress for the individuals and organizations involved. That a severe threat to important values is stress inducing requires little elaboration. The element of surprise is also a contributing factor; there is evidence that unanticipated and novel situations are generally viewed as more threatening.[34] Finally, crises are often marked by almost around-the-clock work schedules, owing to the severity of the situation (high threat), the absence of established routines for dealing with them (surprise), and the absence of extended decision time. Lack of rest and diversion, combined with excessively long working hours, are likely to magnify the stresses in the situation. Moreover, crisis decisions are rarely if

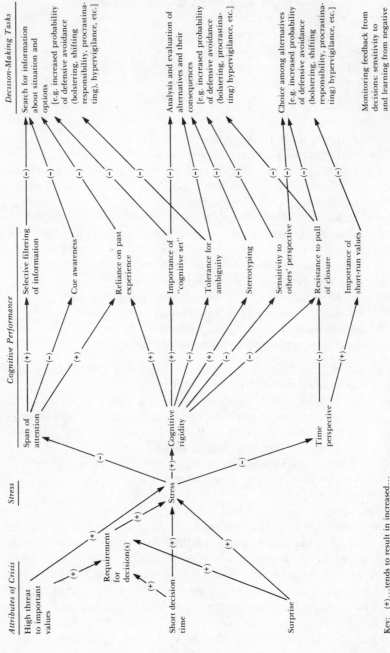

FIGURE 1.   Individual Decision Making in Crisis: Some Hypotheses

ever analogous to the familiar multiple-choice question, in which the full range of options is neatly outlined. The theoretical universe of choices usually exceeds by a substantial margin the number that can or will be considered. Especially in unanticipated situations for which there are no established SOPs (standard operating procedures) or decision rules, it is necessary to search out and perhaps create alternatives. Thus, the decision process itself may be a significant source of stress, arising, for example, from efforts to cope with cognitive constraints on rationality, role factors, small group dynamics, and bureaucratic politics.[35]

Some degree of stress is an integral and necessary precondition for individual or organizational problem solving; in its absence there is no motivation to act. Low levels of stress alert us to the existence of a situation requiring our attention, increase our vigilance and our preparedness to cope with it. Increasing stress to moderate levels may heighten our propensity and ability to find a satisfactory solution to the problem. Indeed, for some elementary tasks a rather high degree of stress may enhance performance, at least for limited periods of time. If the problem is qualitatively simple and performance is measured by quantitative criteria, stress can increase output. Our primary concern, however, is not with the effects of crisis on persons engaged in manual or routine tasks, but with its consequences on the performance of officials in leadership positions during major international crises. These are nearly always marked by complexity and ambiguity, and they usually demand responses which are judged by qualitative rather than quantitative criteria. It is precisely these qualitative aspects of performance that are most likely to suffer under high stress.[36]

Experimental findings generally indicate a curvilinear relationship, most easily described as an "inverted U," between stress and the performance of individuals and groups. A moderate level of anxiety can be beneficial, but at higher levels it disrupts decision processes.[37] Observational evidence from related field research (e.g., studies of natural disasters, or performance in combat and other dangerous circumstances) also suggests that intense and protracted stress often erodes rather than enhances the ability of individuals to cope with complex problems.[38] To summarize, in situations of high stress, "there is a narrowing of the cognitive organization at the moment; the individual loses broader perspective, he is no longer able to 'see' essential aspects of the situation and his behavior becomes, consequently, less adaptive."[39]

At this point we shall consider in more detail some potential consequences of stress for cognitive rigidity, span of attention, and time perspectives.

Cognitive rigidity. Charles Lindblom suggests that "a serious emergency or crisis often transforms a policy analyst's perceptions (and sometimes galvanizes his energies) with the result that he gets a new grasp on his problem."[40] But there is also evidence that the effects of stress on cognitive performance are often less benign. Persons experiencing intense stress tend to

107

suffer increased cognitive rigidity, and erosion of general cognitive abilities, including creativity and the ability to cope with complexity. As a consequence, the range of perceived policy options may be narrow. The decision maker is likely to establish a dominant percept through which to interpret information, and to maintain it tenaciously in the face of information that might seem to call for a reappraisal.[41] Often this percept is a familiar one transferred from previous situations (e.g., "lessons of history"), even though it may be inappropriate for the circumstances at hand,[42] and it is more likely to be characterized by stereotypes than by subtlety as the complexity of the psychological field is reduced.[43] To change one's beliefs and theories each time some discrepant information is received is neither possible nor wise, but it is at least useful to be aware that evidence about an unfolding situation may be consistent with more than a single explanation.[44] A finding of special relevance for crisis decision making is that tolerance for ambiguity is reduced when there is high stress. Under these conditions individuals made decisions before adequate information was available, with the result that they performed much less capably than persons working under normal conditions. The combination of stress and uncertainty leads some persons to feel that "the worst would be better than this."[45] Finally, caricatures of motivational structures may develop: the anxious become more anxious, the energetic become more energetic, the repressors become more repressive, and so on.[46] The effects of stress on perception has been summarized as follows:

> Perceptual behavior is disrupted, becomes less well controlled than under normal conditions, and hence is less adaptive. The major dimensions of perceptual function are affected: selection of percepts from a complex field becomes less adequate and sense is less well differentiated from nonsense; there is maladaptive accentuation in the direction of aggression and escape; untested hypotheses are fixated recklessly.[47]

As a result of these effects of stress, search for information and policy options may be adversely affected in several ways. Other actors and their motives are likely to be stereotyped, for example, and the situation itself may be defined in overly simple, one-dimensional terms—such as, that it is a zero-sum situation, or that everything is related to everything else.[48] The ability to invent nonobvious solutions to complex problems may also be impaired. Finally, complex problems are more likely to be defined by "what is already in" (the decision maker's beliefs, expectations, cognitive and emotional predispositions), and less by the "objective" attributes of the situation.[49]

The inception of a crisis usually results in a sharply increased pace of individual and bureaucratic activity and, concomitantly, an increasing volume of communication. Conversely, information overload in a decision-making situation may itself be a source of serious stress.[50] One way of coping with this phenomenon is to *narrow one's span of attention* to a few aspects of the decision-making task.[51] This may be a functional strategy if it permits the executive to eliminate trivial distractions, filter out irrelevant information, and develop an agenda of priorities. However, a number of costs may offset or even outweigh these benefits.

An experimental study of complex situations revealed that increased information loads resulted in fewer strategic integrated decisions and more unintegrated and simple retaliatory decisions.[52] As the volume of information directed at policy makers rises, the search for information within the communication system will tend to become less thorough, and selectivity in what is read, believed, and retained takes on increasing importance. In ambiguous situations or in circumstances of information overload, one may also be more likely to screen information and to respond in terms of personal predispositions.[53] Unpleasant information and that which does not support preferences and expectations may fall by the wayside, unless it is of such an unambiguous nature that it cannot be disregarded. "All Presidents, at least in modern times," writes Sorensen, "have complained about their reading pile, and few have been able to cope with it. There is a temptation, consequently, to cut out all that is unpleasant."[54] Thus, more communication may in fact result in less useful and valid information being available to policy makers.

Time perspectives are also likely to be affected by high stress. For example, the ability to judge time is impaired in situations which increase anxiety.[55] Thus, there appears to be a two-way relationship between time and stress. On the one hand, short decision time, a defining characteristic of crisis, is likely to increase the stress under which the executive must operate. On the other hand, increasing levels of stress tend to heighten the salience of time and to distort judgements about it. It has been found in "real life" crisis situations, as well as experimentally, that as danger increases there is a significant overestimation of how fast time is passing.[56]

Perceived time pressure may affect decision making in several ways. A number of studies indicate that some time pressure can enhance creativity as well as the rate of performance, but most of the evidence suggests that beyond a moderate level it has adverse effects. Because complex tasks requiring feats of memory and inference suffer more from time pressure,[57] its effects on the most important decisions—which are usually marked by complexity—are likely to be particularly harmful. In such situations there is a tendency to fix upon a single approach, to continue using it whether or not it proves effective, and to hang on to familiar solutions, applying them even to problems that may be substantially different.[58]

Experimental research has often shown a curvilinear relationship between time pressure and performance. Under severe time pressure, normal subjects produce errors similar to those committed by schizophrenics. Another study revealed that, although a moderate increase in time pressure can increase the productivity of groups, an increase from low to high pressure has an adverse effect. Increasing the number of decisions required in a given period of time by a factor of five led to a fifteenfold rise in decision errors. There is, in addition, evidence that time pressure increases the propensity to rely upon stereotypes, disrupts both individual and group problem solving, narrows the focus of attention, and impedes the use of available information. Finally, both experimental and historical evidence indicates that high stress tends to result in a shorter time perspective and, as consequence, a reduced resistance to premature closure.[59]

When decision time is short, the ability to estimate the range of possible consequences arising from a particular policy choice is likely to be impaired. Both experimental and field research indicate that severe stress is likely to give rise to a single-minded concern for the present and immediate future at the sacrifice of attention to longer range considerations.[60] The uncertainties attending severe crisis make it exceptionally difficult to follow outcomes from a sequence of actions and responses very far into the future. Increasing stress also tends to narrow the focus of attention, thereby further limiting perceptions of time to the more immediate future. During the Korean War, for instance, it was observed that combat troops "cannot exercise complex functions involving the scanning of a large number of factors or long-term foresight because the stress is too massive and time too short for anything but the immediately relevant."[61]

This brief overview of evidence is suggestive rather than exhaustive. Moreover, the emphasis has been on processes rather than on decision outputs and, just as we cannot assume that "good" processes will ensure high-quality decisions, we cannot assume that erratic processes will always result in low-quality decisions. But even if Figure 1 describes only some potential tendencies rather than unvarying responses to crisis, there is sufficient evidence to call into question the universal validity of the premise that we always rise to the occasion in crises, drawing if necessary upon hidden reservoirs of strength. The evidence cited here suggests that among the more probable casualties of crises and the accompanying high stress are the very abilities that distinguish men from other species: to establish logical links between present actions and future goals; to search effectively for relevant policy options; to create appropriate responses to unexpected events; to communicate complex ideas; to deal effectively with abstractions; to perceive not only blacks and whites, but also to distinguish them from the many subtle shades of gray that fall in between; to distinguish valid analogies from false ones, and sense from nonsense; and, perhaps most important of all, to enter into the frame of references of others. With respect to these precious cognitive abilities, the law of supply and demand seems to operate in a perverse manner; as crisis increases the need for them, it also appears to diminish the supply.

Suggestive as these models and theories of crisis decision making may be, they cannot substitute for evidence from actual foreign policy crises. Abstract and theoretical work must be examined and analyzed in terms of specific evidence—in this case, evidence from diplomatic history. Toward this end, the next two sections will utilize the "focused comparison" approach[62]—in which case studies aim not at a full historical description but at developing or testing explicit propositions of theoretical or policy relevance—and will explore several very specific aspects of individual stress in crisis decision making from the 1914 and Cuban missile crises.

Decision Making in the 1914 Crisis

The assassination of Archduke Franz Ferdinand on June 28, 1914, set off a chain of events that, within six weeks, brought all of the major powers of Europe into war. Soon after Prince von Bülow asked German Chancellor Bethmann Hollweg how the war had come about. "At last I said to him: 'Well, tell me, at least, how it all happened,' He raised his long, thin arms to heaven and answered in a dull exhausted voice: 'Oh—If I only knew.' " Another colleague wrote that "since the Russian mobilization the Chancellor gave one the impression of a drowning man."[63] Are these merely the self-serving recollections of war criminals or of fools whose incompetence visited upon the world a war of unparalleled devastation? If the answer is an affirmative one, the 1914 case is of little interest to the student of crisis, and the prescription is relatively simple—keep war criminals and fools out of high office.

But perhaps the answer to "how it all happened" is not quite so simple. The proposition to be explored in this section is that the individual stress model may help to explain the disastrous events of 1914. It should be made clear at the outset that what follows is an illustration and not an attempt at a full-scale explanation.[64] It does not deal with the state of military technology, European alliance commitments, the balance of power, contingency plans of foreign and war offices, historical enmities, economic competition, or imperial ambitions and rivalries. All of these were important in 1914 and nothing in the analysis that follows is intended to deny their relevance. Nevertheless, these were also important in 1911, in 1908, and in other years that featured confrontations among the major powers. But, unless we adopt a deterministic view—as is implied, for example, by the popular metaphor of the assassination as a lighted match thrown into a keg of powder—it is appropriate to consider not only the European context in 1914, but also the decision processes. The focus here is on two aspects of Figure 1—perceptions of time pressure and of policy options.

PERCEPTIONS OF TIME PRESSURE

To examine the effects of deepening crisis on perceptions of time pressure, techniques of content analysis were employed.[65] All documents written by

111

high-ranking foreign policy officials were coded for evidence of time pressure as a factor in policy decisions. The resulting 167 statements are classified according to date and nation and specific issue (Table 1). Statements of concern about decision time increased steadily (except in the case of Austria–Hungary), not only in absolute frequency, but even in relation to the total number of policy themes. Perceptions of time pressure were also associated with increasing stress, with correlations ranging from .16 to .82.

During the earliest period of the 1914 crisis approximately two-thirds of the references to time focused on the desirability or necessity of early action by Austria–Hungary against Serbia. Count Alexander Hoyos, Chief of the Cabinet of the Austro-Hungarian Foreign Ministry, for example, wrote on July 7 that "from a military standpoint . . . it would be much more favorable to start the war now than later since the balance of power would weigh against us in the future."[66] The view that time was working against the Dual Monarchy was supported, for Germany was exerting considerable pressure on its ally not to postpone, a showdown. Gottlieb von Jagow, German Foreign

TABLE 1. Perceptions of Time Pressure: The 1914 Crisis

Period	Total Themes	Austria–Hungary	Germany	Great Britain	France	Russia	Total	% Themes with Time Perceptions
June 27–July 20	1,031	13	9	0	0	0	22	2.1
July 21–28	1,658	3	11	18	13	8	53	3.2
July 29–August 2	1,910	0	35	12	13	3	63	3.3
August 3–4	479	0	14	12	3	0	29	6.1
June 27–August 4	5,078	16	69	42	29	11	167	3.3
Correlation (gamma) between stress and perceptions of time pressure		.16	.33	.61	.68	.82		

Period	A	B	C	D	E	Total
June 27–July 20	15	1	0	2	4	22
July 21–28	11	29	10	2	1	53
July 29–August 2	1	8	29	16	9	63
August 3–4	0	0	2	22	5	29
June 27–August 4	27	38	41	42	19	167

Codes for relevance of time:

A—As a factor in Austro-Hungarian action toward Serbia
B—As a factor in localization of conflict between Austria–Hungary and Serbia
C—As a factor in mobilization
D—As a factor in alliance and other political commitments
E—Other

112

Minister, wrote on July 15: "We are concerned at present with the pre-eminent political question, perhaps the last opportunity of giving the Greater-Serbia menace its death blow under comparatively favorable circumstances."[67] In contrast, the view in London, Paris, and St. Petersburg was initially one of relative lack of concern. There is no evidence that leaders in the capitals of the Entente nations felt themselves under any pressure of time to react to this latest episode of instability in the Balkans.

Time perceptions from July 21 through July 28 focused predominantly on the necessity of delaying the course of events in the Balkans. Once the content of the Austrian ultimatum became known, the forty-eight-hour time limit within which the Serbian government had to draft a reply became an immediate subject of concern. Some European officials recognized that the conflict in the Balkans might well engulf all Europe if existing alliance commitments were honored. Whereas both German and Austro–Hungarian leaders had frequently expressed the desirability of moving swiftly against Serbia, those in London, Paris, St. Petersburg, and Belgrade were especially concerned with the necessity of gaining the time which might be used to work out a peaceful settlement of Vienna's demands on Serbia. Although they were far from united on the details of policy, the single common theme in their proposals was the fear that precipitate action could lead only to war. Typical of diplomatic messages during this period was the assertion that "the immediate danger was that in a few hours Austria might march into Serbia and Russian Slav opinion demand that Russia should march to help Serbia; it would be very desirable to get Austria not to precipitate military action and so to gain more time."[68] By July 29 it was apparent that war between Austria-Hungary and Serbia could not be prevented. At the same time, it was increasingly evident that a chain reaction was in danger of being set off.

As late as August 1 many European leaders continued to express the belief that if time permitted the concert powers to be reconvened, general war might be avoided. British Foreign Secretary Grey wrote, for example: "I still believe that if only a little respite in time can be gained before any Great Power begins war it might be possible to secure peace."[69] By this time, however, the pressure of time had taken a different meaning for many decision makers. A major concern was that one's nation not be caught unprepared for the war which might break out.

The situation, as perceived by leaders in the major capitals of Europe, posed a terrible dilemma. It was widely recognized that more time would be required if a general European war were to be averted; above all, a moratorium on military operations was necessary. It was equally evident that military preparations could become the justification for similar actions by others. The German ambassador in St. Petersburg warned the Russian foreign minister that "the danger of every preparatory military measure lay in the counter measures of the other side."[70] But, increasingly, these considerations were overshadowed by the fear of disastrous consequences if a potential adversary gained even a momentary head start in mobilizing its armed forces. As early as July 24, the French minister of war, apprehensive about the outcome of the crisis in the Balkans, asserted that, for France, "first military precautions could not be delayed."[71] Although no *official* mobilization orders except those of Austria–Hungary and Serbia were issued until July 29, rumors and suspicions of undercover preparations were not wholly without foundation. On July 25 the Russian government decided to set into motion all of the preparations preliminary to mobilization. Despite a badly divided Cabinet, even the British were undertaking a number of important military preparations. Winston Churchill, First Lord of the Admiralty, for example, mobilized the British navy contrary to a decision of the Cabinet.

In the early hours of the morning of July 30, the Kaiser wrote on the margin of a message from the Czar: " . . . the Czar—as is openly admitted by him here—instituted 'mil[itary] measures which have *now come into force*' against Austria and us and as a matter of fact five days ago. Thus it is almost *a week ahead of us.* And these measures are for a *defense* against *Austria,* which is *in no way* attacking him!!! I can not agree to any more mediation, since the Czar who requested it has at the same time secretly mobilized behind my back. It is only a maneuver, in order to hold us back and to increase the start they have already got. My work is at an end!"[72] Later, the Kaiser added, "In view of the colossal war preparations of Russia now discovered, this is all too late, I fear. Begin! Now!"[73] On July 30, German Chancellor Bethmann Hollweg was also concerned with the disadvantages of delay: ". . . the military preparations of our neighbors, especially in the east, will force us to a speedy decision, unless we do not wish to expose ourselves to the danger of surprise."[74]

On the same day René Viviani, French premier, urged Russia to avoid provocative measures that might provide Germany with a pretext for a total or partial mobilization of its own forces. Nevertheless, the Russians decided in favor of general mobilization, German warnings notwithstanding. "In these conditions," according to Foreign Minister Sazonov, "Russia can only hasten its armaments and face the imminence of war and that it counts upon the assistance of its ally France; Russia considers it desirable that England join Russia and France without losing time."[75] In response to what was perceived as a mounting threat against its eastern frontiers, the German Empire proclaimed a "state of threatening danger of war" on July 31, dispatching a twelve-hour ultimatum to Russia demanding a cessation of military preparations along the border. Berlin then ordered mobilization on August 1. "We could not sit back quietly and wait to see whether a more commonsense view would gain the upper hand at Petersburg, while at the same time the Russian mobilization was proceeding at such speed, that, if the worst came, we should be left completely outstripped in a military sense."[76]

The French government simultaneously ordered general mobilization on August 1. General Joffre had earlier argued that "it is absolutely necessary that the government know that from this evening on, any delay of twenty-four hours applied to the calling up of reserves and to the sending of the telegram ordering covering troops will result in a backward movement of our troops, that is to say an initial abandonment of a part of our territory, either 15 or 20 kilometers every day of delay.''[77] Although official British naval mobilization was delayed until August 2, many officials in London had advocated such action considerably earlier. Winston Churchill was perhaps the most energetic proponent of early military preparations.[78] Others included Arthur Nicolson, Permanent Under Secretary for Foreign Affairs, who said on July 31: ''It seems to me most essential, whatever our future course may be in regard to intervention, that we should at once give orders for mobilization of the army. . . . Mobilization is a precautionary measure—and to my mind essential.'' Three days later he added that ''we ought to mobilize today so that our expeditionary force may be on its way during the next week. Should we waver now we shall rue the day later.''[79]

Thus, ten days after the full-scale mobilizations by Serbia and Austria–Hungary on July 25, each of the major European countries had called up its armed forces. As each mobilization was ordered, it was defended as a necessary reaction to a previous decision within the other coalition. And with each mobilization came assurances that it was a defensive measure, although in 1914 a decision to mobilize was commonly regarded as tantamount to an act of war. In the rush to mobilize no one wanted to be beaten to the draw, even though there was sometimes an awareness of the logical end of military measures and countermeasures.

In some cases the escalation of military actions and counteractions was sustained almost by accident, or by the failure to perceive the effects of one's own acts. The mobilization of the Russian Baltic fleet provides a good example. ''On 25 July, when the Czar looked over the minutes and resolutions of the Council of Ministers of the 24th, he not only approved them by adding 'agreed,' but, where it was the question of mobilizing the districts of Kiev, Moscow, Odessa and Kazan and the Black Sea fleet, he inserted in his own hand 'and Baltic' without any of his Ministers drawing his attention to the fact that the mobilization of the Baltic fleet constituted an act of hostility toward Germany.''[80] Although the Russian Baltic fleet was no match for the powerful German navy, the Kaiser apparently felt genuinely threatened. In response to Bethmann Hollweg's plea that the German fleet be left in Norway, he wrote: ''There is a Russian Fleet! In the Baltic there are now five Russian torpedo boat flotillas engaged in practice cruises, which as a whole or in part can be at the Belts within sixteen hours and close them. Port Arthur should be a lesson! My Fleet has orders to sail for Kiel, and to Kiel it is going to sail!''[81]

This inquiry into time pressures associated with the 1914 crisis supports the hypothesis that one reaction to decisional stress is hypervigilance. Concern for time increased as the crisis deepened, and it is also clear that time pressures were related to the central rather than peripheral issues in the crisis. When there was a conflict between the need to delay action in order to seek nonmilitary means of resolving the crisis and the perceived needs of military preparedness, the latter consideration prevailed, in large part because so many officials throughout Europe felt that the costs of falling behind the adversary's timetable would be catastrophic. Many decisions during the crisis were undertaken in great haste, and the processes by which they were made were at times highly erratic. For example, the initial Russian decision for a general mobilization was followed shortly by an order for only a partial callup of forces, and then by another reversal to the original decision. In the meanwhile, when it became clear that the conflict between Serbia and Austria–Hungary might lead to a general European war, a series of highly contradictory messages was dispatched from Berlin to Vienna. Demands for restraint in some of them were offset by a telegram from Moltke stating that Austria–Hungary should immediately mobilize against Russia, and that Germany would soon follow suit.

POLICY OPTIONS

One way of coping with decision stress is a form of bolstering, attributing to the adversary sole responsibility for choices and outcomes, while absolving oneself, owing to the absence of real alternatives. Data from the 1914 crisis provide some striking support for the proposition that, in a crisis situation, decision makers will tend to perceive the range of their own alternatives to be more restricted than those of their opponents. That is, they will perceive their own decision making to be characterized by *necessity* and *closed* options, whereas those of the adversary are characterized by *open* choices (Table 2).

The 1914 documents are filled with such words as "must," "compelled," "obliged," "unable," "driven," "impossible," and "helpless," but these rarely occur except when the author is referring to the policies of his own nation. To students of strategy the assertions of the Kaiser, the Czar, and others that they were helpless once they had set their military machines into motion may appear to be a "real life" application of the tactics of *commitment,* "a device to leave the last clear chance to decide the outcome with the other party, in a manner that he fully appreciates; it is to relinquish further initiative, having rigged the incentives so that the other party must choose in one's favor."[82] This explanation may be valid for messages that were intended for wide circulation among officials in allied or enemy countries. On the other hand, the most "private" documents—those intended only for circulation within the various foreign offices—do not differ materially from the entire set of documents in respect to the findings reported here. The clearest evidence in support of this assertion is to be found in the Kaiser's marginal notations and in the various minutes of Eyre Crowe, Assistant Under-Secretary of State, in the British Foreign Office.

TABLE 2. Perceptions of Alternatives (Choice, Necessity, Closed): Top-ranking Decision Makers During 1914 Crisis

	GERMANY *Own Nation*	*Allies*	*Opponents*
CHOICE	10	7	25
NECESSITY	110	20	2
CLOSED	20	2	0
% Choice	7.1%	24.1%	92.6%
	AUSTRIA–HUNGARY *Own Nation*	*Allies*	*Opponents*
CHOICE	13	1	1
NECESSITY	80	2	1
CLOSED	7	1	0
% Choice	13.0%	25.0%	50.0%
	GREAT BRITAIN *Own Nation*	*Allies*	*Opponents*
CHOICE	7	21	21
NECESSITY	20	8	2
CLOSED	23	2	0
% Choice	14.0%	67.7%	91.3%
	FRANCE *Own Nation*	*Allies*	*Opponents*
CHOICE	1	6	12
NECESSITY	13	4	2
CLOSED	5	2	2
% Choice	5.3%	50.0%	75.0%
	RUSSIA *Own Nation*	*Allies*	*Opponents*
CHOICE	7	4	6
NECESSITY	20	3	2
CLOSED	7	3	0
% Choice	20.6%	40.0%	75.0%

NOTE:
Choice: Decision maker perceives that more than one course of action is open.
Necessity: Decision maker perceives only one possible course of action in a given situation.
Closed: Decision maker perceives that some course of action is not possible.

Even a cursory survey of the diplomatic documents reveals that, with the exception of Austria–Hungary, European leaders consistently perceived fewer options open to themselves than to their adversaries. Edward Grey, for example, who took the most active role in seeking mediation, wrote on July 24 that "we can do nothing for moderation unless Germany is prepared *pari passu* to do the same."[83] Until the final hours of the crisis, leaders in Berlin were opposed to mediation of the local conflict, in part because previous conferences called to settle international crises (such as Algeciras in 1906) had, in the eyes of the Kaiser and others, denied them the diplomatic victories to which they were entitled. According to Bethmann Hollweg, "We cannot mediate in the conflict between Austria and Serbia but possibly later between

Austria and Russia."[84] Nor were the Russians inclined to mediation because, in the words of Sazonov, "we have assumed from the beginning a posture which we cannot change."[85]

But the same leaders who expressed varying degrees of inability to cope with the situation in the Balkans tended to perceive more freedom of action for members of the opposing alliance. After the outbreak of war between Serbia and Austria-Hungary, Grey wrote: "The whole idea of mediation or mediating influence was ready to be put into operation by any method that Germany could suggest if mine was not acceptable. In fact, mediation was ready to come into operation by any method that Germany thought possible if only Germany would 'press the button' in the interests of peace."[86]

The tendency to perceive one's own alternatives to be more restricted than those of the adversary is also evident in the reaction to the events leading up to general war. The reaction of German decision makers was typical. On the one hand, they asserted repeatedly that *they* had no choice but to take vigorous military measures against the threat to the east. "Then I must mobilize too! . . . He [Nicholas] expressly stated in his first telegram that he would be presumably forced to take measures that would lead to a European war. Thus he takes the responsibility upon himself."[87] On the other hand, they credited Russia with complete freedom to take the actions necessary to prevent war: "The responsibility for the disaster which is now threatening the whole civilized world will not be laid at my door. In this moment it still lies in your [Nicholas] power to avert it."[88] And Wilhelm, like the Czar, finally asserted that he had lost control of his own military and that only the actions of the adversary could stop further escalation: "On technical grounds my mobilization which had already been proclaimed this afternoon must proceed against two fronts, east and west as prepared. This cannot be countermanded because I am sorry your [George V] telegram came so late."[89] The same theme of a single option open to oneself, coupled with perceptions that the initiative for peace rested with the enemy, is evident in the French and Austrian statements regarding their own mobilizations.

An increasing sense of helplessness and resignation to the irresistible course of events is evident in many of the documents. On the day of the Serbian reply to the Austro-Hungarian ultimatum, Paul Cambon, French ambassador in London, stated that he saw "no way of halting the march of events."[90] In contrast to Edward Grey, who maintained the hope that the European powers would find a way to prevent a general war, Arthur Nicolson asserted on July 29, "I am of the opinion that the resources of diplomacy are, for the present, exhausted."[91] At the same time, in St. Petersburg, Sazonov wrote of the "inevitability of war" while in Berlin, the Kaiser, in one of the most vitriolic of his marginal notes, concluded that "we have proved ourselves helpless."[92]

Significantly contributing to the belief that options were severely restricted was the rigidity of the various mobilization plans. Austria–Hungary and Russia had more than one plan for mobilization, but once any one of them was set in motion, it could be altered only with great effort. The Russians could order either a general mobilization against both Germany and Austria–Hungary, or a partial one directed only at the latter. But, as Russian generals were to argue vehemently during the crucial days at the end of July, a partial mobilization would preclude a general one for months to come, leaving Russia completely at the mercy of Germany. According to General Dobrorolski, "The whole plan of mobilization is worked out ahead to its end in all its detail. When the moment has been chosen, one has only to press the button, and the whole state begins to function automatically with the precision of a clock's mechanism. . . . Once the moment has been fixed, everything is settled; there is no going back; it determines mechanically the beginning of war."[93]

France and Germany each had but a single plan for calling up their armed forces and, in the case of Germany, political leaders were ill informed about the rigidity of mobilization and war plans. The Kaiser's last-minute attempt to reverse the Schlieffen plan—to attack only in the East—shattered Moltke, Chief of the German General Staff, who replied: "That is impossible, Your Majesty. An army of a million cannot be improvised. It would be nothing but a rabble of undisciplined armed men, without a commissariat. . . .It is utterly impossible to advance except according to plan; strong in the west, weak in the east."[94]

Finally, all of the mobilization plans existed only on paper; except for the Russo-Japanese War, no major European power had mobilized since 1878. This fact rendered the plans all the more rigid and made military leaders responsible for carrying them out less likely to accept any last-minute modifications. It may also have added to the widely believed dictum that one did not mobilize for any purpose other than war.

Just as European leaders tended to perceive fewer alternatives open to themselves than to their adversaries, so they regarded their allies to be in a similar position vis-à-vis their enemies. On the one hand, German documents are replete with explanations that Austria was pursuing the *only* policy open to her and thus Germany could not play a moderating role in Vienna, although only four months earlier Wilhelm had stated that if Vienna gets into a war against the Slavs through "great stupidity," it would "leave us [Germany] quite cold."[95] On the other hand, the Kaiser appealed to England, apparently convinced that the latter could perform the very role which he felt was impossible for Germany—restraining the most belligerent member of the coalition. "Instead of making proposals for conferences, His Majesty the King should order France and Russia, frankly and plainly, at one and the same time—they were HIS ALLIES—to DESIST at once from the mobilization, remain NEUTRAL and await Austria's proposals, which I should immediately transmit as soon as I was informed of them. . . . I could do nothing more direct; it was for him to take hold now and prove the honesty of English love of peace.''[96] The assumption of British freedom to determine the policy of her allies, coupled with restrictions on German policy, is nowhere as clear as in one of the Kaiser's marginal notes: "He [Grey] knows perfectly well, that if he were to say one single serious sharp warning word at Paris and Petersburg, and were to warn them to remain neutral, both would become quiet at once. But he takes care not to speak the word, and threatens us instead! Common cur! England *alone* bears the responsibility for peace and war, and not we any longer.''[97]

This approach to the problem of allies was not confined to Berlin. Adducing arguments that were strikingly similar to those used by the Kaiser, British leaders denied their ability or willingness to dictate a policy of moderation in Paris or St. Petersburg. Nicolson wrote on July 29: "I do not think that Berlin quite understands that Russia cannot and will not stand quietly by while Austria administers a severe chastisement to Serbia. She does not consider that Serbia deserves it, and she could not, in view of that feeling and of her position in the Slav world, consent to it.''[98] Grey assessed the requirements of his French ally in similar terms: "France did not wish to join in the war that seemed about to break out, but she was obliged to join in it, because of her alliance.''[99] At the same time, however, he believed that Germany could constrain the cause of her ally: "But none of us could influence Austria in this direction unless Germany would propose and participate in such action in Vienna.''[100] On July 28 Nicholas had appealed to his counterpart in Berlin: "To try and avoid such a calamity as a European war, I beg you in the name of our old friendship to do what you can to *stop* your allies from *going too far.*''[101]

The few attempts made to restrain the militant members of each alliance were either halfhearted or too late. Typical was the advice of Sir Eyre Crowe, who had written on July 25: "The moment has passed when it might have been possible to enlist French support in an effort to hold back Russia. It is clear that France and Russia are decided to accept the challenge thrown to them." He expressed the opinion that it would be both impolitic and dangerous to try to change their minds.[102] Similarly, a last-minute German attempt to hold Austria in check failed. At 2:55 A.M., July 30, Bethmann Hollweg concluded a telegram to Vienna: "Under these circumstances we must urgently and impressively suggest to the consideration of the Vienna Cabinet that acceptance of mediation on the mentioned honorable conditions. The responsibility for the consequences that would otherwise follow would be an uncommonly heavy one both for Austria and for us.''[103] A few minutes later, however, Moltke sent a wire to Vienna urging immediate mobilization against Russia, promising Germany's full support for such an action—even if it led to general war.[104]

Decision Making During the Missile Crisis[105]

A single U-2 American surveillance plane took off on October 14, 1962, for a reconnaissance flight over Cuba. Immediately upon returning, its high-altitude cameras were unloaded. After intensive study of the developed films, intelligence analysts uncovered unmistakable evidence of two medium-range ballistic missile (MRBM) sites in areas previously photographed and found to be empty. Overflights three days later confirmed these reports and revealed nine sites—36 launch positions—six for the 1,100-mile MRBM and three for 2,200-mile intermediate-range ballistic missiles (IRBM) in various states of readiness. Thus began the most serious international crisis of the nuclear era, a confrontation during which President Kennedy estimated that the chances of a nuclear war between the United States and the Soviet Union were one in three.

The 1914 and Cuban situations were similar in a number of respects and differed in many others. The similarity of present interest is that both episodes conform to the definition of crisis used here. Despite widespread rumors of Soviet missile installations in Cuba, photographic evidence of their presence was a surprise to virtually all officials in Washington, including the President; the rate of construction on the missile sites made it evident that any decision to prevent their completion could not long be delayed; and, with the exception of Secretary of Defense Robert McNamara, all who joined the American decision group interpreted the Soviet move as a serious threat to national security. As one participant in these discussions put it: "Everyone round the table recognized that we were in a major crisis. We didn't know, that day, if the country would come through it with Washington intact."[106]

The most significant difference between these two events is that the 1914 crisis led to a world war, whereas the Cuban confrontation was resolved without recourse to violence. Thus, the situation that confronted national leaders in the two crises shared a number of attributes (surprise, high threat, short decision time), but the decisions they made led to significantly different results: peaceful settlement versus a world war. In an attempt to explain the different outcomes, the remainder of this section examines several aspects of the decision-making process in 1962, again with special attention to time pressure and the search for and appraisal of alternatives.

PERCEPTIONS OF TIME PRESSURE

Several sources of time pressure impinged on the President and his advisers during the missile crisis. Initially, there was the need to formulate a policy before the Soviets were alerted by the stepped-up U-2 flights to the fact that their launching installations had been discovered. Conversely, once developments in Cuba became public knowledge, there would be no further time for deliberation and debate on the proper response.

An overriding concern throughout the period was the knowledge that construction on the missile sites was continuing at a rapid pace. The first photographic evidence of construction activities in Cuba indicated that they would be operational within a week to ten days. American officials perceived that their task would become immeasurably more difficult once construction on the launching sites was completed: "For all of us knew that, once the missile sites under construction became operational, and capable of responding to any apparent threat or command with a nuclear volley, the President's options would be dramatically changed."[107] Thus, the situation did not compel a reflex-like response—at least, as it was defined by the President. But in relation to the task at hand decision time was indeed short, and all firsthand accounts of decision making during the Cuban crisis, especially that of Robert Kennedy, are replete with indications of time pressure.

Despite the sense of urgency created by these deadlines, the President and his advisers sought to reduce the probability that either side would respond by a "spasm reaction." Efforts were made to delay taking overt actions as long as the situation permitted. Equally important, discussions in Washington revealed a sensitivity for the time pressures under which the adversary was operating. There was a concern that Premier Khrushchev not be rushed into an irrevocable decision; it was agreed among members of the decision group that "we should slow down the escalation of the crisis to give Khrushchev time to consider his next move."[108] Measures designed to increase Soviet decision time included the President's management of the naval quarantine. He ordered American ships to delay intercepting Soviet vessels until the last possible moment, *and had the order transmitted in the clear.* The Soviets, who were certain to intercept the message, would thus learn that they had additional time in which to formulate a response to the blockade. This ploy also revealed a sophisticated understanding of the social psychology of communication; information from a distrusted source is more likely to be believed if it is obtained through the recipient's own efforts. The Soviet decision on October 25 to slow down the westward progress of their ships in mid-Atlantic can also be interpreted as an effort to lengthen decision time.

A comparison of the 1914 and 1962 crises points to the importance of a subjective rather than an objective definition of decision time. Owing to vast differences in military capabilities, time was objectively of far greater importance in 1962 than in 1914. Hence, Soviet and American leaders were no less aware of time pressures and of the potential costs of delaying action than were their counterparts in 1914. But they also perceived the dangers of acting in haste, and they were successful in mitigating the most severe dangers attending such pressures. They resisted the pressures for premature decisions and

122

took a number of actions which avoided putting their adversaries in a position of having to respond in haste. President Kennedy later acknowledged that the ability to delay a decision after receipt of the photographic evidence of missile sites was crucial to the *content* of American policy: "If we had had to act on Wednesday [October 17], in the first 24 hours, I don't think probably we would have chosen as prudently as we finally did, the quarantine against the use of offensive weapons."[109]

POLICY OPTIONS

During the missile crisis, the search for alternatives was intimately related to time pressures; in the words of Arthur Schlesinger, "The deadline defined the strategy."[110] Pressures of time notwithstanding, American policy makers made efforts to prevent premature foreclosure of options. McGeorge Bundy noted that upon receiving the first news of the photographic evidence, "his [Kennedy's] first reaction was that we must make sure, and were we making sure, and would there be evidence on which he could decide that this was in fact really the case."[111] As late as October 18, a series of alternatives was being considered pending more accurate information, and while the decision to institute a blockade was being hammered out, open discussion of the alternatives was encouraged. The President recalled that "though at the beginning there was a much sharper division . . . this was very valuable, because the people involved had particular responsibilities of their own."[112] Another participant in the crisis decision group asserted that President Kennedy, aware that discussion of alternatives in the National Security Council would be more frank in his absence, encouraged the group to hold preliminary meetings without him. Thus, the eventual decision was reached by relatively open and frank discussion.

Six alternative responses emerged from the initial discussions between the President's advisers. Ultimately, the choice narrowed down to the blockade and the air strike. Initially, the option of a sudden air strike against the missile sites had strong support among most of the conferees, including that of the President. An informal vote is reported to have revealed an 11-6 majority in favor of the blockade.[113] The United States Air Force could not guarantee, however, that an air strike would be 100 percent effective. The blockade did not necessarily guarantee success; on the other hand, it did not rule out further measures. After much shifting of positions, the blockade option was selected, partly on the reasoning that "the course we finally adopted had the advantage of permitting other steps, if this one was unsuccessful. In other words, we were starting, in a sense, at a minimum place."[114]

The desire to avoid killing Soviet troops also weighed heavily against the air strike option. The blockade shifted the immediate burden of decision concerning the use of violence to Premier Khrushchev and, should the blockade

123

have proved unsuccessful, it did not preclude later employment of a "much more massive action."[115] By adopting that strategy, no irrevocable decisions on the use of violence had been made and multiple options remained for possible future actions by the United States. At the same time, Soviet leaders were given the time and the opportunity to assess their own choices. Thus, unlike several of the key foreign policy officials in the 1914 crisis, those in October 1962 seemed to perceive a close relationship between their own actions and the options of their adversaries. According to Theodore Sorensen, "We discussed what the Soviet reaction would be to any possible move by the United States, what our reaction with them would have to be to that Soviet reaction, and so on, trying to follow each of those roads to their ultimate conclusion."[116]

American decision makers also displayed a sensitivity for the position and perspective of the adversary, trying to insure that a number of options other than total war or total surrender were available to Soviet leaders. An important advantage of the blockade over other strategies was that it appeared to avoid placing Soviet leaders in that situation. An air strike on the missile bases or invasion of the island would have left Soviet leaders only the alternatives of capitulating to the United States or of counterattacking. In that case, the latter might have seemed the less distasteful course. In disagreeing with General Curtis LeMay's optimistic assessment of the likely Soviet response to air raids on the missile installations, the President asserted, "They, no more than we, can let these things go by without doing something."[117] A blockade, on the other hand, gave the Soviet government a choice between turning back the weapons-bearing ships or running the blockade.

By October 26 it seemed clear that, Khrushchev's earlier threats to the contrary notwithstanding, Soviet ships would not challenge the blockade. Despite the advent of negotiations, however, it was far from certain that the Soviet missiles would be removed from Cuba; indeed, there was ample evidence of an accelerated pace of construction on the launching sites in Cuba that, it was then believed, would be completed by October 30. Thus, the question of further steps to be taken in case the blockade proved insufficient to force withdrawal of all offensive missiles again confronted American leaders. Among the options considered were: tightening the blockade to include all commodities other than food and medicine, increased low-level flights over Cuba for purposes of reconnaissance and harassment, action within Cuba, an air strike, and an invasion. In the meanwhile, the President's brother delivered an ultimatum to the Soviet ambassador, and both direct and indirect bargaining resulted in a settlement.[118] Just before "the most serious meeting ever to take place at the White House"[119] was to have started, Premier Khrushchev agreed to withdraw all offensive missiles from Cuba in exchange for President Kennedy's pledge not to invade Cuba.

Time pressure and the search for alternatives are key elements in crisis decision making. Data from 1914 indicate that these factors did in fact vary as crisis-induced stress increased, and these changes apparently had serious consequences for critical policy decisions. A more impressionistic analysis of the Cuban confrontation suggests that the ability of American decision makers to mitigate some of the adverse consequences of crisis contributed to its eventual peaceful resolution. In many respects, President Kennedy's behavior during the Cuban crisis appeared consciously designed to avert repetition of the 1914 disaster. Indeed, he frequently referred to the decision processes leading up to World War I as a source of negative lessons. Having read Barbara Tuchman's *The Guns of August,* for example, the President said: "I am not going to follow a course which will allow anyone to write a comparable book about this time, *The Missiles of October.* If anybody is around to write after this, they are going to understand that we made every effort to find peace and every effort to give our adversary room to move. I am not going to push the Russians an inch beyond what is necessary."[120] Even when discussing the Cuban missile crisis some weeks after its conclusion, he asserted, "Well now, if you look at the history of this century where World War I really came through a series of misjudgments of the intentions of others . . . it's very difficult to always make judgments here about what the effect will be of our decisions on other countries."[121] Yet the ability of American and Soviet leaders to avoid a nuclear Armageddon in October 1962, is not assurance that even great skill in crisis management will always yield a peaceful solution. As President Kennedy said some months later, referring to the missile crisis, "You can't have too many of those."[122]

Conclusion

The approach described here suffers from some clear limitations that should be addressed explicitly. Several objections might be raised about the relevance of the individual stress model of crisis decision making.[123] Does it adequately take into account the executive's prior experience in coping with crises? Will not experience, when combined with selective recruitment and promotion, weed out those who cannot stand "the heat in the kitchen" well before they reach top leadership positions? It is true that individuals differ in abilities to cope with crises and stress. The peak, breaking point and slope of the "inverted U" curve may vary not only according to the complexity of the task, but also across individuals. Thus, the point at which increasing stress begins to hamper cognitive performance, and the rate at which it does so, is not the same for all persons. But only the most optimistic will assume that the correlation between the importance of the executive's role and ability to cope with crisis-induced stress approaches unity. Richard Nixon's behavior during the Watergate episode is a grim reminder to the contrary. Perhaps even more sobering is Robert Kennedy's recollection of the Cuban missile crisis: "That kind of [crisis-induced] pressure does strange things to a human being, even to brilliant, self confident, experienced men. For some it brings out characteristics and strengths that perhaps they never knew they had, and for others the pressure is too overwhelming.''[124]

A second possible objection is that, whereas the emphasis here has been on the individual's cognitive performance under conditions of crisis-induced stress, foreign policy leaders rarely need to face crises alone. They can instead draw upon support and resources from both advisory groups and the larger organizations of which they are a part. This point is valid, but on further examination it is not wholly comforting. There is some evidence that during crises advisory groups may be vulnerable to such malfunctions as ''group-think.''[125] For various reasons, including preceived needs for secrecy, easier coordination, and the like, decision-making groups tend to become smaller during crises. There may be, moreover, a tendency to consult others less as the pressure of time increases, as well as to rely more heavily upon those who support the prevailing ''wisdom.''[126] Finally, leaders differ not only in their ''executive styles'' (note, for example, the strikingly different problem-solving styles exhibited by presidents Coolidge, Franklin Roosevelt, and Nixon), but also in their abilities to employ advisory groups effectively—that is, in ways that may help them to counteract some of the potentially adverse consequences of crisis. Even the same executive may demonstrate great skill during one crisis and equal ineptitude in another instance. John F. Kennedy's use of advisers during the missile crisis and the Bay of Pigs fiasco are illustrative in this respect.

Some more specific limitations can also be identified. Certainly, the two cases are not representative of all crises in any statistical sense. Thus, the results described here should be viewed as illustrative rather than definitive. Moreover, the analysis focused on very limited aspects of crises, to the exclusion of many other potentially fruitful comparisons. The results suggest that the individual stress model identifies some important elements of crises decision making, but the present analysis has not even fully explored the hypotheses identified in Figure 1. In any case, the rather different findings for the 1914 and 1962 crises raises a series of additional questions—about the necessary and sufficient conditions for avoiding decision-making malfunctions—that have barely been touched upon here. The individual stress model focuses on a few aspects of crisis and consciously excludes others. By posing some questions and not others, we have limited the range of answers. Every model or theoretical perspective does so, with some inevitable losses and, it is to be hoped, at least some commensurate gains. The proper question to ask, then, is not whether this approach serves as a complete model for all crises—the answer is unquestionably negative—but whether it directs our attention to important phenomena that might otherwise remain beyond our purview.

Variants of the individual stress model of crisis decision making have been employed in other studies and, not surprisingly, the pattern of findings is mixed. Lentner's study of State Department officials revealed that only about a third of the respondents felt a reduction in perceived alternatives as a result of crisis.[127] In their impressive study of a dozen international crises—including Fashoda (1898), Bosnia (1908–1909), Munich (1938), Iran (1945–1946), and Berlin (1948–1949)—Snyder and Diesing found no evidence of adverse consequences arising from high stress.[128] Yet they did report that misperception, miscalculation, and other cognitive malfunctions were common occurrences during the crises. Because their research was not designed to test for either the existence or consequences of crisis-induced stress, perhaps it is premature to count this study as definitive evidence against the propositions advanced here. On the other hand, drawing on his research on Israeli behavior during the crises of 1956, 1967, and 1970, Brecher found strong support for the hypotheses that time will be perceived as more salient, that decision makers will become more concerned with the immediate rather than the distant future, and that they will perceive the range of alternatives open to themselves to be narrow.[129] The individual stress model also received strong support in a study designed to test the effects of crisis-induced stress on information processing; in this respect, the convergence of findings from historical and experimental research adds an important element of confidence in the validity of the results and the underlying theory.[130]

These mixed results are not surprising, nor should they occasion premature conclusions about lack of significant research progress or the future of this approach for diplomatic history, theory, or even policy. Other studies could be cited in support of and against the individual stress model, but this does not appear to be the most fruitful way of proceeding. Sustained interest in the effects of crisis-induced stress does not depend on finding that *every* crisis from the historical past resulted in substandard decision-making performance, any more than concern for the consequences of smoking must await evidence that all smokers develop lung cancer. The much more interesting and important questions emerge precisely at the point of recognizing that the dangers and opportunities inherent in crises can give rise to various patterns of coping. At that point our attention is directed to a series of further questions—for example, what are the decision-making structures, personal attributes of leaders, strategies of crisis management, and other variables that are associated with more or less successful coping—that have barely been touched upon in this chapter. It is at this point that we can perhaps begin to appreciate the value of interdisciplinary approaches for the study of crises decision making.

Notes

1. Richard M. Nixon, *Six Crises* (New York: Doubleday, 1962), p. xvi.
2. Ibid., p. 105.

3. Herman Kahn, *On Escalation: Metaphors and Scenarios* (New York: Praeger, 1965), p. 38.

4. The literature on deterrence is enormous. Recent and indispensable are Alexander L. George and Richard Smoke, *Deterrence in American Foreign Policy: Theory and Practice* (New York: Columbia University Press, 1974); and Patrick M. Morgan, *Deterrence: A Conceptual Analysis* (Beverly Hills: Sage, 1977). For more discussion, see Paul Gordon Lauren's chapter in this book on bargaining theories.

5. Chris Argyris, *Some Causes of Organizational Ineffectiveness within the Department of State* (Washington, D. C.: Center for International Systems Research, Department of State Publication 8180, 1967), p. 42.

6. Richard E. Neustadt, *Alliance Politics* (New York: Columbia University Press, 1970), p. 116.

7. Charles A. McClelland, quoted in Michael Brecher, "Toward a Theory of International Crisis Behavior," *International Studies Quarterly* 21 (March 1977): 40.

8. Charles A. McClelland, quoted in Charles F. Hermann (ed.), *International Crises: Insights from Behavioral Research* (New York: Free Press, 1972), p. 6.

9. See Leo Hazelwood, John Hayes, and James Brownell, Jr., "Planning for Problems in Crisis Management," *International Studies Quarterly* 21 (March 1977): 78.

10. Charles F. Hermann, "Some Consequences of Crisis Which Limit the Viability of Organizations," *Administrative Science Quarterly* 8 (June 1963): 61-82. This definition has achieved moderately wide acceptance among students of foreign policy crises. For further discussions of the term, see Charles F. Hermann, *Crises in Foreign Policy: A Simulation Analysis* (Indianapolis: Bobbs-Merrill, 1969); Charles F. Hermann, "International Crisis as a Situational Variable," in James N. Rosenau (ed.), *International Politics and Foreign Policy* (New York: Free Press, 1969 ed.), pp. 409-421; James A. Robinson, "Crisis: An Appraisal of Concepts and Theories," in Hermann, *International Crises;* Kent Miller and Ira Iscoe, "The Concept of Crisis: Current Status and Mental Health Implications," *Human Organization* 22 (Fall 1963): 195-201; Glenn H. Snyder and Paul Diesing, *Conflict Among Nations: Bargaining, Decision Making and System Structure in International Crises* (Princeton: Princeton University Press, 1977); Richard W. Parker, "An Examination of Basic and Applied International Crisis Research," *International Studies Quarterly* 21 (March 1977): 225-246; Raymond Tanter, "Crisis Management: A Critical Review of Academic Literature," *Jerusalem Journal of International Relations* 2 (Fall 1975): 71-101; and Richard G. Head, Frisco W. Short, and Robert C. McFarlane, *Crisis Resolution: Presidential Decision Making in the Mayagüez and Korean Confrontations* (Boulder, Colo.: Westview Press, 1978).

11. Brecher, "Toward a Theory of International Crisis Behavior," pp. 42-44.

12. Snyder and Diesing, *Conflict Among Nations,* pp. 6-21.

13. Charles F. Hermann and Linda P. Brady, "Alternative Models of International Crisis Behavior," in Hermann, *International Crisis,* pp. 281-303. For another typology, see Parker, "An Examination of Basic and Applied International Crisis Research."

14. Irving Janis, *Victims of Groupthink: A Psychological Study of Foreign-Policy Decisions and Fiascoes* (Boston: Houghton Mifflin, 1972).

15. Sidney Verba, "Assumptions of Rationality and Non-rationality in Models of the International System," *World Politics* 14 (October 1961): 93–117.

16. H. O. Wilensky, *Organizational Intelligence* (New York: Basic Books, 1967).

17. See Samuel Williamson's chapter in this book, as well as Graham T. Allison, "Conceptual Models and Cuban Missile Crisis," *American Political Science Review* 63 (1969): 689–718; Graham T. Allison, *Essence of Decision: Explaining the Cuban Missile Crisis* (Boston: Little Brown, 1971); Graham T. Allison and Morton H. Halperin, "Bureaucratic Politics: A Paradigm and Some Policy Implications," *World Politics* 24 (1972, special supplement): 40–79; and Leon V. Sigal, "The 'Rational Policy' Model and the Formosa Straits Crises," *International Studies Quarterly* 14 (June 1970): 121–156.

18. See, for example, Dina A. Zinnes, Joseph L. Zinnes, and Robert D. McClure, "Hostility in Diplomatic Communication: A Study of the 1914 Crisis," in Hermann, *International Crises,* pp. 139–162; and David C. Schwartz, "Decision-Making in Historical and Simulated Crises," in Hermann, *International Crisis,* pp.167–184.

19. See, for example, Snyder and Diesing, *Conflict Among Nations;* Charles A. McClelland, "The Beginning, Duration and Abatement of International Crisis: Comparisons in Two Conflict Arenas," in Hermann, *International Crises,* pp. 83–105; and Glenn H. Snyder, "Crisis Bargaining," in Hermann, *International Crises,* pp. 217–256.

20. Quincy Wright, *A Study of War* (Chicago: University of Chicago Press, 1965 ed.), p. 1272; and Lewis F. Richardson, *Statistics of Deadly Quarrels* (Pittsburgh: Boxwood Press, 1960).

21. Charles A. McClelland, "The Acute International Crisis," *World Politics* 14 (October 1961); Kenneth Waltz, "The Stability of a Bipolar World," *Daedalus* 93 (Summer 1964): 883–884; and Coral Bell, *Conventions of Crisis: A Study in Diplomatic Management* (London: Oxford University Press, 1971), pp. 115–116.

22. Wright, *A Study of War,* p. 1272.

23. McClelland, "The Acute International Crisis," p. 199.

24. Ibid., p. 200. However, constant exposure to crises, especially simultaneous crises, may well result in a setting that is not conducive to rational decision making. On this point, see Wilensky, *Organizational Intelligence.*

25. Thomas C. Schelling, *The Strategy of Conflict* (New York: Oxford University Press, 1963), is a classic study. Less subtle and far more ideological are: Robert Strausz-Hupé et al., *Protracted Conflict* (New York: Harper and Brothers, 1959); as well as the many articles published in the journal *Orbis* by William Kintner, Stefan T. Possony, Chester C. Ward, and others.

26. See, for example, Morgan, *Deterrence;* Philip Green, *Deadly Logic* (Columbus: Ohio State University Press, 1966); Barry R. Schneider, "Danger and Opportunity," unpublished Ph.D. dissertation, Columbia University 1972; and Jack L. Snyder, "Rationality at the Brink: The Role of Cognitive Processes in Failures of Deterrence," *World Politics* 30 (April 1978): 345–365. Useful discussions of various views on these issues may be found in Aaron Wildavsky, "Practical Consequences of the Theoretical Study of Defence Policy," *Public Administration Review* 25 (March 1965): 90–103; Snyder and Diesing, *Conflict Among*

Nations, pp. 297–310; and Thomas C. Wiegele, "Models of Stress and Distur-bances in Elite Political Behaviors: Psychological Variables and Political Decision-Making," in Robert S. Robins (ed.), *Psychopathology and Political Leader-ship* (New Orleans: Tulane Studies in Political Science, 1977).

27. Allison, *Essence of Decision;* John D. Steinbruner, *The Cybernetic Theory of Decision* (Princeton: Princeton University Press, 1974); James M. McCormick, "Evaluating Models of Crisis Behavior: Some Evidence from the Middle East," *International Studies Quarterly* 19 (March 1975): 17–45; Raymond Tanter, *Modelling and Managing International Conflicts: The Berlin Crisis* (Beverly Hills: Sage, 1974); Janice Stein and Raymond Tanter, *Crisis Decision Making: Rationality and Israel's Choices* (forthcoming); and R. G. Trotter, "The Cuban Missile Crisis: An Analysis of Policy Formulation in Terms of Current Decision Making Theory," unpublished Ph.D. dissertation, University of Pennsylvania, 1971.

28. Alexander L. George, David Hall, and William Simons, *The Limits of Coercive Diplomacy* (Boston: Little, Brown, 1971); Head, Short, and McFarlane, *Crisis Resolution;* Richard Smoke, *War: Controlling Escalation* (Cambridge: Harvard University Press, 1977); Thomas Halper, *Foreign Policy Crises: Appearance and Reality In Decision-Making* (Columbus: Merrill, 1971); Holsti, *Crisis, Escalation, War* (Montreal: McGill–Queens University Press, 1972) Glenn D. Paige, "Comparative Case Analysis of Crisis Decisions: Korea and Cuba," in Her-mann, *International Crises,* pp. 41–55; Oran Young, *The Politics of Force: Bargaining During International Crises* (Princeton: Princeton University Press, 1968); Lawrence S. Falkowski, *Presidents, Secretaries of State, and Crises in U.S. Foreign Rela-tions: A Model and Predictive Analysis* (Boulder, Colo.: Westview Press, 1978); and Phil Williams, *Crisis Management* (New York: Wiley, 1977).

29. Snyder and Diesing, *Conflict Among Nations.* See also the major crisis research pro-ject directed by Michael Brecher, most recently described in his "Toward a Theory of International Crisis Behavior."

30. Davis B. Bobrow, Steve Chan, and John A. Kringen, "Understanding How Others Treat Crisis: A Mulitmethod Approach," *International Studies Quarterly* 21 (March 1977): 199–223. Assessments of how much progress has in fact been made in crisis research vary widely. Compare, in this respect, the optimistic ap-praisals of Charles A. McClelland, "The Anticipation of International Crises: Prospects for Theory and Research," *International Studies Quarterly* 21 (March 1977): 15–38, and Robert A. Young, "Perspectives on International Crisis: In-troduction," *International Studies Quarterly* 21 (March 1977): 3–14; with the much more critical views expressed in James A. Robinson, "Crises: An Appraisal of Concepts and Theories," in Hermann, *International Crises;* and Gerald W. Hop-ple and Paul J. Rossa, "International Crisis Analysis: An Assessment of Theory and Research," University of Maryland, Cross-National Crisis Indicators Proj-ect, Research Report No. 5, April 1978.

31. Herbert Simon, *Organizations* (New York: Wiley, 1958), p. 138.

32. Somewhat different lists appear in Morgan, *Deterrence,* pp. 102–103; and in Irving Janis and Leon Mann, *Decision-Making* (New York: Free Press, 1977).

33. Figure 1 is an expanded version of a diagram that initially appeared in Ole R. Holsti and Alexander L. George, "The Effects of Stress on the Performance of

Foreign Policy-Makers," in Cornelius P. Cotter (ed.), *Political Science Annual* (Indianapolis: Bobbs-Merrill, 1975), VI: 284.

34. Sheldon J. Korchin and Seymour Levine, "Anxiety and Verbal Learning," *Journal of Abnormal and Social Psychology* 54 (March 1957): 234–240.

35. For a further elaboration of this point, see Alexander L. George, *Toward A More Soundly Based Foreign Policy: Making Better Use of Information,* Appendix D, vol. 2, *Report of the Commission on the Organization of the Government for the Conduct of Foreign Policy* (Washington, D.C.: Government Printing Office, 1975), especially pp. 17–53.

36. Alfred Lowe, "Individual Differences in Reaction to Failure: Modes of Coping with Anxiety and Interference Proneness," *Journal of Abnormal and Social Psychology* 62 (May 1961): 303–308; and Sara B. Kiesler, "Stress, Affiliation and Performance," *Journal of Experimental Research in Personality* 1 (December 1966): 227–235.

37. Sheldon J. Korchin et al., "Visual Discrimination and the Decision process in Anxiety," *AMA Archive of Neurology and Psychiatry* 78 (1957): 424–438; Robert E. Murphy, "Effects of Threat of Shock, Distraction, and Task Design on Performance," *Journal of Experimental Psychology* 58 (August 1959): 134–141; Harold M. Schroeder, Michael J. Driver, and Siegfried Streufert, *Human Information Processing* (New York: Holt, Rinehart and Winston, 1967); and C. R. Anderson, "Coping Behavior as Intervening Mechanisms in the Inverted-U Stress-Performance Relationship," *Journal of Applied Psychology* 60 (February 1976): 30–34.

38. R. R. Grinker and J. P. Spiegel, *Men Under Stress* (New York: McGraw-Hill, 1945); E. Paul Torrance, "A Theory of Leadership and Interpersonal Behavior Under Stress," in Luigi Petrullo and Bernard M. Bass (eds.), *Leadership and Interpersonal Behavior* (New York: Holt, Rinehart, and Winston, 1961), pp. 100–117; George W. Baker and Dwight W. Chapman (eds.), *Man and Society in Disaster* (New York: Basic Books, 1962); and A. D. Baddeley, "Selective Attention and Performance in Dangerous Environments," *British Journal of Psychology* 63 (1972): 537–546.

39. Sheldon J. Korchin, "Anxiety and Cognition," in Constance Sheerer (ed.), *Cognition: Theory, Research, Promise* (New York: Harper and Row, 1964), p. 63.

40. Charles E. Lindblom, *The Policy-Making Process* (Englewood Cliffs, N.J.: Prentice-Hall, 1968), p. 22.

41. Fredric Bertram Nalven, "Defense Preference and Perceptual Decision-Making," Ph.D. dissertation, Boston University, Boston, 1961, abstracted in Paul Wasserman and Fred S. Silander, *Decision-Making: An Annotated Bibliography, Supplement, 1958–1963* (Ithaca, N.Y.: Cornell University Press, 1964), p. 78.

42. Melvin Manis, *Cognitive Processes* (Belmont, Calif.: Wadsworth, 1966), pp. 97–102; and F. P. Kilpatrick, "Problems of Perception in Extreme Situations," in Robert R. Evans (ed.), *Readings in Collective Behavior* (Chicago: Rand McNally, 1969), pp. 168, 171. For relevant historical evidence on this point, see Ernest R. May, *"Lessons" of the Past: The Use and Misuse of History in American Foreign Policy* (New York: Oxford University Press, 1973); and Robert Jervis, *Perception and Misperception in International Politics* (Princeton: Princeton University Press, 1976).

43. Ralph K. White and Ronald Lippitt, *Autocracy and Democracy: An Experimental Inquiry* (New York: Harper and Brothers, 1960), p. 171.

44. Robert Jervis, "Hypotheses on Misperception," *World Politics* 20 (April 1968): 454–479; and Robert Jervis, *Perception and Misperception.*

45. C. D. Smock, "The Influence of Psychological Stress on the 'Intolerance of Ambiguity,'" *Journal of Abnormal and Social Psychology* 50 (March 1955): 177–182.

46. Thomas Milburn, "The Management of Crisis," in Hermann, *International Crisis,* p. 265.

47. Leo Postman and Jerome S. Bruner, "Perception under Stress," *Psychological Review* 55 (1948): 322.

48. Milburn, "The Management of Crisis."

49. Jerome Bruner, cited in Louis C. Gawthrop, *Bureaucratic Behavior in the Executive Branch* (New York: Free Press, 1969), p. 113.

50. James G. Miller, "Information Input Overload and Psychopathology," *American Journal of Psychiatry* 116 (February 1960): 695–704; James G. Miller, "Information Input Overload," *Self Organizing Systems* (1962, n.p.); Harry B. Williams, "Some Functions of Communication in Crisis Behavior," *Human Organization* 16 (Summer 1957): 15–19; Charles F. Hermann, "Some Consequences of Crisis Which Limit the Viability of Organizations"; and Holsti, *Crisis, Escalation, War,* pp. 82–118.

51. Baddeley, "Selective Attention and Performance in Dangerous Environments."

52. George A. Miller, "The Magical Number Seven Plus or Minus Two: Some Limits on Our Capacity for Processing Information," *Psychological Review* 63 (March 1956): 81–97.

53. Karl. E. Weick, "Processes of Ramification Among Cognitive Links," in Robert P. Abelson et al. (eds.), *Theories of Cognitive Consistency* (Chicago: Rand McNally, 1968), pp. 516–517; and Jerome E. Singer, "Consistency as a Stimulus Processing Mechanism," in the same volume, pp. 337–342.

54. Theodore C. Sorensen, *Decision-Making in the White House* (New York: Columbia University Press, 1964), p. 38.

55. Samuel I. Cohen and A. G. Mezey, "The Effects of Anxiety on Time Judgment and Time Experience in Normal Persons," *Journal of Neurology, Neurosurgery and Psychiatry* 24 (August 1961): 266–268.

56. Harry B. Williams and Jeannette F. Rayner, "Emergency Medical Services in Disaster," *Medical Annals of the District of Columbia* 25 (1956); Jonas Langer, Seymour Wapner, and Heinz Werner, "The Effects of Danger Upon the Experience of Time," *American Journal of Psychology* 74 (March 1961): 94–97. See also John Cohen, "Psychological Time," *Scientific American* (November 1964): 116–124.

57. Jerome Bruner, Jacequeline J. Goodnow, and George A. Austin, *A Study of Thinking* (New York: Wiley, 1956), p. 147.

58. Abraham S. Luchins, "Mechanization in Problem-Solving," *Psychological Monographs* 54 (1942): whole no. 248; Steinbruner, *The Cybernetic Theory of Decision.*

59. George Usdansky and Loren J. Chapman, "Schizophrenic-like Response in Normal Subjects under Time Pressures," *Journal of Abnormal and Social Psychology* 60 (January 1960): 143–146; Pauline N. Pepinsky and William B. Pavlik, "The Effects of Task Complexity and Time Pressure Upon Team Productivity," *Jour-*

nal of Applied Psychology 44 (February 1960): 34–38; N. H. Mackworth and J. F. Mackworth, "Visual Search for Successive Decisions," *British Journal of Psychology* 49 (August 1958): 210–221; Herbert G. Birch, "Motivational Factors in Insightful Problem-Solving," *Journal of Comparative Psychology* 38 (October 1945): 295–317; Bruner et al., *A Study of Thinking;* Peter Dubno, "Decision Time Characteristics of Leaders and Group Problem Solving Behavior," *Journal of Social Psychology* 59 (April 1963): 259–282; F. E. Horvath, "Psychological Stress: A Review of Definitions and Experimental Research," *General Systems Yearbook* 4 (1959): 203–230; and Donald R. Hoffeld and S. Carolyn Kent, "Decision Time and Information Use in Choice Situations," *Psychological Reports* 12 (February 1963): 68–70.

60. Robert J. Albers, "Anxiety and Time Perspectives," *Dissertation Abstracts* 26 (February 1966): 4848; and James D. Thompson and Robert W. Hawkes, "Disaster, Community Organization, and Administrative Process," in George Baker and Dwight Chapman (eds.), *Man and Society in Disaster* (New York; Basic Books, 1962).

61. Korchin, "Anxiety and Cognition," p. 63.

62. See the discussion in Alexander L. George's chapter in this book; George and Smoke, *Deterrence in American Foreign Policy,* pp. 94–97; Sidney Verba, "Some Dilemmas in Comparative Research," *World Politics* 20 (October 1967): 111–127; Bruce M. Russett, "International Behavior Research: Case Studies and Cumulation," in Michael Haas and Henry Kariel (eds.), *Approaches to the Study of Political Science* (Scranton, Pa.: Chandler, 1970); Smoke, *War: Controlling Escalation;* James N. Rosenau, "Moral Fervor, Systematic Analysis, and Scientific Consciousness in Foreign Policy Research," in Austen Ranney (ed.), *Political Science and Public Policy* (Chicago: Markham, 1968); and Glenn D. Paige, *The Korean Decision: June 24–30, 1950* (New York: Free Press, 1968), pp. 3–18. The latter study is also an important contribution to the study of crisis decision making.

63. Prince Bernhard von Bülow, *Memoirs of Prince von Bülow,* 3 vols. (Boston: Little, Brown, 1932), III: 166; and Alfred von Tirpitz, *My Memoirs* (London: Hurst and Blackett, 1919), p. 280.

64. Further discussions of the 1914 crisis may be found in chapters by Robert Jervis and Samuel Williamson in this book.

65. A detailed discussion of the methods of content analysis used with the 1914 data has appeared in Holsti, *Crisis, Escalation, War,* and very briefly in Melvin Small's chapter in this book.

66. Quoted in Luigi Albertini, *Origins of the War of 1914,* 2 vols. (New York: Oxford University Press, 1953), II: 122.

67. Max Montgelas and Walter Schücking (eds.), *Outbreak of the World War, German Documents Collected by Karl Kautsky* (New York: Oxford University Press, 1924), #48. [Hereafter this source will be cited as Germany.]

68. Great Britain, Foreign Office, *British Documents on the Origins of the War, 1898–1914,* 11 vols., ed. G. P. Gooch and Harold Temperely, vol. 11, *Foreign Office Documents June 28th–August 4th, 1914,* collected by J. W. Headlam-Morely (London: His Majesty's Stationery Office,1926), #99. [Hereafter cited as Great Britain.]

69. Great Britain, #411.

70. Germany, #343.

71. France, Commission de Publication des documents relatifs aux origins de la guerre, 1914, *Documents Diplomatiques Français (1871-1914)*, 3rd series, vols. 10, 11 (Paris: Imprimerie nationale, 1936), #32. [Hereafter cited as France.]

72. Germany, #390.

73. Germany, #433.

74. Germany, #451.

75. France, #305.

76. Germany, #529.

77. France, #401.

78. Winston S. Churchill, *The World Crisis, 1911-1914* (New York: Scribner's, 1928), p. 211.

79. Great Britain, #368, 446.

80. Albertini, *Origins of the War in 1914,* II: 558.

81. Germany, #221.

82. Schelling, *The Strategy of Conflict,* pp. 137-138.

83. Great Britain, #103.

84. Germany, #247.

85. Russian, Komissiia po izdaiiu dokumentov epokhi imperializma, *Mezhdunarodnye otnosheniia v epokhe imperializma;* dokument 12 arkhivov tsarkogo i vremennogo pravitel'stv 1878-1917, gg. 3d series, vols. 4, 5, (Moscow and Leningrad: Gosudarstvennoe sotsial'no-ekonomicheskoe izdatal'stvo, 1931, 1934), #118. [Hereafter cited as Russia.]

86. Great Britain, #263.

87. Germany, #399.

88. Germany, #480.

89. Germany, #575.

90. France, #38.

91. Great Britain, #252.

92. Russia, #221; Germany, #401.

93. Quoted in Sidney B. Fay, *The Origins of the World War* (New York: Macmillan, 1930 ed.), II: 481.

94. Moltke, *Erinnerungen,* quoted in Virginia Cowles, *The Kaiser* (New York: Harper and Row, 1964), pp. 343-346.

95. Quoted in Fay, *The Origins of the World War,* II: 207.

96. Germany, #474.

97. Germany, #368.

98. Great Britain, #264.

99. Great Britain, #447.

100. Great Britain, #99.

101. Russia, #170.

102. Great Britain, #101.

103. Germany, #395.

104. Quoted in Fay, *The Origins of the World War*, II: 509.

105. The literature on the missile crisis is immense, including memoirs of participants, polemics, descriptive accounts, and explicitly comparative or theoretical studies. Of the latter genre, some of the most interesting are George, Hall, and Simons, *The Limits of Coercive Diplomacy;* George and Smoke, *Deterrence in American Foreign Policy;* Allison, *The Essence of Decision;* Roberta Wohlstetter, "Cuba and Pearl Harbor," *Foreign Affairs* 43 (July 1965): 691–707; Snyder and Diesing, *Conflict Among Nations;* Paige, "Comparative Case Analysis of Crisis Decision: Korea and Cuba"; Young, *The Politics of Force;* Snyder, "Rationality at the Brink"; and Albert and Roberta Wohlstetter, *Controlling the Risks in Cuba,* Adelphi Paper No. 17 (London: International Institute for Strategic Studies, 1965).

106. Douglas Dillon, quoted in Elie Abel, *The Missile Crisis* (Philadelphia: Lippincott, 1966), p. 48.

107. Theodore Soresen, *Decision-Making in the White House* (New York: Columbia University Press, 1963), p. 31.

108. National Broadcasting Company, "Cuba: The Missile Crisis" (mimeo. transcript, February 9, 1964), p. 12.

109. Columbia Broadcasting System, "Conversation with President Kennedy" (mimeo. transcript, December 17, 1963), pp. 2–3.

110. Arthur M. Schlesinger, Jr., *A Thousand Days* (New York: Houghton Mifflin, 1965), p. 804.

111. NBC, "Cuba," p. 14.

112. CBS, "Conversation with President Kennedy," p. 4.

113. Schlesinger, *A Thousand Days*, p. 808.

114. CBS, "Conversation with President Kennedy," p. 4.

115. Ibid.

116. NBC, "Cuba," p. 17.

117. Quoted in Snyder and Diesing, *Conflict Among Nations*, p. 301.

118. The important role of the ultimatum in settlement of the missile crisis is discussed in more detail by George, Hall, and Simons, *The Limits of Coercive Diplomacy.*

119. NBC, "Cuba," p. 42.

120. Robert F. Kennedy, *Thirteen Days* (New York: Norton, 1969), p. 127.

121. CBS, "Conversation with President Kennedy," p. 3.

122. Theodore Soresen, *Kennedy* (New York: Harper and Row, 1965), p. 726.

123. Interesting alternative explanations for the outcome in 1914, for example, may be found in Bruce M. Russett, "Cause, Surprise, and No Escape," *Journal of Politics* 24 (February 1962): 3–22; and Lancelot L. Farrar, Jr., "The Limits of Choice: July 1914 Reconsidered," *Journal of Conflict Resolution* 16 (March 1972): 1–24. Other approaches to crisis decision making that have not received attention here include those that emphasize aspects of personality; see, for example, Falkowski, *Presidents, Secretaries of State, and Crisis in U.S. Foreign Relations;* James David Barber, *The Presidential Character* (Englewood Cliffs, N.J.: Prentice-Hall,

1972); and Thomas M. Mongar, "Personality and Decision-Making: John F. Kennedy in Four Crisis Decisions," *Canadian Journal of Political Science* 2 (June 1962): 200–225. The psychobiological effects of crisis are discussed in Wiegele, "Models of Stress," and in the same author's "Decision Making in an International Crisis: Some Biological Factors," *International Studies Quarterly* 17 (September 1973): 295–335.

124. Robert F. Kennedy, "Thirteen Days: The Story About How the World Almost Ended," *McCall's* (November 1968): 148.

125. Janis, *Victims of Groupthink;* and Roland L. Frye and Thomas M. Stritch, "Effects of Timed vs. Non-timed Discussion Upon Measures of Influence and Change in Small Groups," *Journal of Social Psychology* 63 (June 1964): 139–143.

126. Dean G. Pruitt, "Problem Solving in the Department of State" (unpublished paper, Northwestern University, 1961).

127. Howard H. Lentner, "The Concept of Crisis as Viewed by the U.S. Department of State," in Hermann, *International Crisis,* pp. 112–135.

128. Snyder and Diesing, *Conflict Among Nations.*

129. Michael Brecher, "Research Findings and Theory-Building in Foreign Policy Behavior," in Patrick J. McGowan (ed.), *Sage International Yearbook of Foreign Policy Studies* (Beverly Hills: Sage, 1974), II: 71.

130. Peter Suedfeld and Philip Tetlock, "Integrative Complexity of Communications in International Crisis," *Journal of Conflict Resolution* 21 (March 1977): 169–186.

6
Theories of Organizational Process and Foreign Policy Outcomes

Samuel R. Williamson, Jr.

OLDER AND TRADITIONAL DIPLOMATIC HISTORIES frequently nodded in the direction of the organizational structures in which foreign policy decisions had been taken. Sometimes introductory comments, even a chapter, were devoted to such arrangements. Yet seldom did these obligatory remarks play any significant part in the subsequent explanation of policy outcomes.[1] The emphasis was instead upon documenting the course of policy discussions, seeking to account for them (especially from the information revealed in published diplomatic documents), and with the senior policy makers functioning almost as if aloof from the world of governmental machinery. And when the older studies did focus on the organization of the foreign ministries, they read like administrative history (which they were)—nice for reference, but dull and often unrewarding for an understanding of policy.[2] Only in isolated works, most notably *The Diplomats,* was the attention to organization and policy more definitive and less transient.[3]

With the expansion of diplomatic history in the 1950s and 1960s to include strategic and economic dimensions, these accounts necessarily touched upon the different organizational structures from which policy decisions emerged. But until the last decade and the appearance of a series of new studies, powerfully assisted by the work of Zara Steiner, the organizational aspects of policy—whether the Foreign Office, the Committee on Imperial Defence, the Wilhelmstrasse, or the State Department—were often treated by diplomatic historians as impedimenta to narration, analysis, and description.[4] Nor is this trend altogether abated. The growing emphasis on the domestic

Parts of this chapter have been given at Cambridge University, the London School of Economics, and the Historisches Institut, the University of Vienna. I am especially grateful for comments from F. H. Hinsley, James Joll, Jonathan Steinberg, Gerald Stourzh, Robert A. Kann, and the late Friedrich Engel-Janosì.

aspects of foreign policy, whether in the work of Fritz Fischer and the Hamburg school, or among some Cold War revisionists, has usually prompted no wider attention to decision-making structures. Rather, these works often appear to proceed on the assumption that if enough documentary evidence is advanced, then the problem of explaining how the evidence relates to the decisions and outcomes, to the policy makers, and to the overall governmental process is automatically answered.[5] This persistent inattention to organization has often left the diplomatic analyses incomplete, in some cases positively distorted the conclusions (here the Fischer school and some of the revisionists are comparable cases), and generally meant neglect of a point that constitutional historians have long asserted: that structure shapes process and that process often shapes policy decisions and government outcomes.[6]

If some historians have recently begun to worry about the organizational structure of foreign policy and especially the bureaucratic unit as a governmental actor, still more political scientists have done so in the last decade. Drawing from the writings of business scholars, sociologists, and economists, their works have applied concepts of organizational structure and organizational process to an analysis of diplomatic and security decisions and outcomes. In these works, usually linked to the school of "bureaucratic politics" and overshadowed by it, powerful arguments are advanced for considering the organization of a decision-making structure and the way it processes business as essential to understanding many—though certainly not all—diplomatic decisions and outcomes.[7]

Among conceptual tools now debated among and between political scientists and decision theorists—the cognitive model and problems of perception and misperception, the quantitative approach, and bureaucratic politics—the organizational process paradigm may be of more immediate use and value to historians.[8] It not only requires fewer methodological skills (or epistemological convictions) and a smaller data base, but it remains an essential first step in applying the bureaucratic politics approach or embarking upon the cognitive route. Moreover, the historian, unlike the political scientist, can be excused for being less excited about the bureaucratic politics paradigm, since it appears—at least for European diplomatic historians—simply to echo accounts of court and cabinet politics from an earlier age. By contrast, the concept of organizational process, of organizational complexity, and of how such units function is a less familiar world, one where insights from other disciplines offer a means of rethinking older puzzles and of tackling new challenges.

In this chapter a series of propositions about the organizational process paradigm are examined. Later, their utility will be shown in three examples drawn from the experience of the Austro–Hungarian monarchy on the eve of the Great War, examples not shopworn from their use by others who have directed their comments to Berlin's role in the July 1914 crisis.

The Organizational Process Paradigm

At the outset, it is imperative to distinguish between two aspects of the organizational process paradigm: organizational *structure* and organizational *process*. The former refers to the way a government, or indeed any sizable concern, is organized to conduct its business. Such a structure might, one could argue, cross state boundaries, as in the case of permanent alliance arrangements. The latter refers to the way the organizational unit or units and their chief actors behave within the organizational structure, how the units process business, how they are galvanized into action and to what effect, how they generate policy options, and how the stucture can influence the implementation of the decisions, once they are taken.

In the past diplomatic historians, even when they delineated the way a government was organized for the conduct of foreign policy, seldom made further distinctions. Too often there was a collapsing of the variegated parts into a single, monolithic structure (what Graham Allison calls the "rational" model) or a resort to explaining policy through the eyes of single actors, sequentially arranged.[9] And there was a willingness to assume that most of the decision makers in a country shared a common set of images of the world in which they operated. While the latter is doubtless true in many instances, it ignores the fact that organizational responsibilities often govern tactics, even positions, in the advocacy of policy options, and that these differences may be consequential. Above all, the first proposition of the organizatonal process paradigm is that structure is important and that the structured nature of the decision process is a crucial first distinction in assessing how policy outcomes occur.[10]

A second proposition, or really a set of them, are inherent in the pieces of the governmental structure itself. Institutions or bureaucratic units within a government develop missions and acquire capabilities for conducting those missions. They often come to possess a certain particular character (called "essence" by Morton Halperin). These units and their actors constantly seek influence while trying not to sacrifice their autonomy. Everywhere they help to legitimate governmental action.[11] Occasionally, they become units in a broader structural pattern such as an alliance (the North Atlantic Treaty Organization is the best example, but not the only one, as this chapter will show). An inadequate appreciation of the power of organizational missions and the capabilities to implement them not infrequently causes historians to despair at the competitive jealousy between units, at their unimaginative and lethargic pace, and to ask why governmental organizations cannot be as rational or as wise as latter-day historians in producing alternative policy options.[12] Such confusion about the major units of government—the monarchy

139

or presidency, the foreign service, the military and intelligence services—may extend to the subunits of the larger organizations. So that, to speak properly of the United States Air Force, one must know really which of three (some would say four) air forces you mean: the strategic or the tactical or the transport or the missile command.[13] Familiarity with organizational structure continuously reminds the analyst of the complexity of modern government and of the component units within it that may play a part in any decision process.

But these axioms, though not always used by diplomatic historians, will seem self-evident to many. Rather, it is in the definition and elucidation of the organizational process that the political scientists have rendered the more valuable and useful analytical insights. They ask how large governmental organizations, especially those concerned with diplomatic and strategic matters, process day-to-day business. They argue—and this is a key dimension of the organizational paradigm—that governmental decisions and outcomes are often the product of, or are dictated or constrained by organizational routines, rather than by independent and unfettered decision making. Organizations produce options, and in turn may dictate the options taken or shape the nature of a particular outcome. Policy makers must operate within, and with, the organizational "givens." And it is within these parameters that much of what is labeled "bureaucratic politics" takes place. Thus, decisions and outcomes often flow from the simple operation—or its failure to operate—of a piece or pieces of governmental machinery. Hence, the intelligence failure in the Pearl Harbor attack was less a command failure than the product of a set of organizational routines.[14]

The political scientists, again drawing from other disciplines, would advance two further propositions. First, a senior decision maker's ability to choose an option might well be restricted by routines and activities of the organization proposing the course of action or in line to implement it. Second, that dominant inference, that is the heavy weight of inertia, means that governmental behavior at "$t + 1$" will not be substantially different from that which took place at "t." If the behavior does differ or take an unexpected turn, then the task of explanation immediately becomes more significant and crucial.[15] Or, to put this in historical terms, what happened in the summer of 1914 to convince the Habsburg government to go to war when it had three times in the preceding twenty months avoided just that decision? Further, the organizational process model directs attention to the difficulties of coordinating and implementing governmental policy, reminding the observer to marvel when there is coordination and cooperation, not to despair when it is absent.

Within these parameters a variety of other insights spring from a study of the organizational process. What, for instance, sets the process in motion? Deadlines, changes in personnel, dramatic action by other states, unexpected or rapid technological changes, changes in shared images, even routine events: all can trigger the process of organizational response. Once triggered, the Standing Operating Procedures (SOPs) or planned programs and repertoires of the organization or organizations will often dictate or limit how units and their chief actors can respond. It is not that the policy maker is the puppet, only that he cannot do everything and must be dependent (and more dependent the higher he sits on the decision ladder) on the governmental machinery below him to assist in meeting many of this duties, be they budgetary allocations, routine promotions, a congressional deadline, or a major war–peace crisis. In these situations there is seldom time, and often little incentive, for innovation, only time to meet the problem at hand. Programmed responses may provide a first set of options, possibly to be modified later, and may at the very least enable complex governmental units to respond. Whether the senior decision maker can move beyond such constraints depends on many other variables, not least the amount of time available and whether or not a different option creates more problems of consensus and implementation than an apparently imperfect option taken from the shelf. Problemistic, satisfying behavior often characterizes the "government" response.[16] Not infrequently, the result will be to apply the solution for the last crisis—in apparently analogous situations—to a later crisis where the variables have in fact altered, possibly decisively. The "fighting the last war" cliché is not without a certain validity—and endurance.[17]

These insights will not revolutionize the way diplomatic historians explain the behavior of governmental units involved in diplomacy, strategic planning, alliance politics, or intergovernmental competition. But they will help to remind the practitioner that process, routine, the choice of modes of approach, or even the policy maker's expectation that an individual acting as a quasi-institution must be confronted (such as Admiral Hyman Rickover), will influence decisions and outcomes.[18] This paradigm can serve, moreover, as a prick to the historian's mindset, providing him with guides or a "laundry list" of things for consideration. When combined with other approaches (even the rational actor model), propositions from the organizational process paradigm may endow other types of explanations with more conviction and more completeness. Such analytical insights are imperative, furthermore, if the researcher is to have any hope of cutting through the thicket of both problems and overdocumentation that so characterizes the history of national security policies and of international relations since 1940.

Yet it is just because these insights may seem to many diplomatic historians and others to be so derivative of the Cold War experience, that it appears useful to suggest, even to demonstrate, their value for other periods and problems. Hence, the attention turns now to three examples drawn from the life of one of the most complex of all modern governmental organizations, the Austro–Hungarian monarchy before 1914. The three cases concern, first, the quasi-institutional role played by the Archduke Franz Ferdinand, the heir apparent, and the impact of his sudden disappearance upon the Habsburg decision makers in late June 1914; second, the subsequent decision to send Count Alexander Hoyos to Berlin in early July to seek acquiescence for a strong policy against Serbia; and, third, Vienna's failure to issue a prompt ultimatum and to move quickly against Serbia that same month. These episodes will, it is hoped, show uses of the organizational process paradigm in illuminating three puzzling, even troublesome, problems of modern diplomatic history.

Franz Ferdinand: The Individual as an Institution

The deaths of Archduke Franz Ferdinand and his wife Sophie at Sarajevo on June 28, 1914, unleashed the events that brought World War I. That much contemporary observers believed and historians have repeatedly affirmed. What was less noted was the impact that the heir apparent's disappearance had upon the structure of the Habsburg decision process. Not only was his death the pretext and the occasion for war, but it suddenly and dramatically altered the political structure in Vienna in ways that virtually insured military action against Serbia. Observers had long dreaded the possible impact of the death of the octogenarian Habsburg emperor, Franz Joseph, on the future of the Danubian monarchy and upon the European diplomatic scene.[19] What they had not, of course, anticipated were the ramifications of his nephew's abrupt demise. Indeed, this reversal of expectations may explain the ease with which the European powers (save for Berlin) had convinced themselves by mid-July that little would flow from the gunshots at Sarajevo save royal blood.[20]

Anyone studying the Habsburg monarchy before 1914 must of necessity examine the views and changes that might have come with a change of occupants on the Habsburg throne. Would the Dual Monarchy continue? Could the *Thronfolger,* or heir to the throne, contain his anti-Magyar prejudices? How would he handle the mounting challenge from the South Slavs? How strident were his military views and what control would he exert over his hand-picked chief of the General Staff, Conrad von Hötzendorf? Public and private concern over just these questions obscured for many contemporary observers a more fundamental organizational change already under way at the apex of the Habsburg political apparatus. (And it was just this change which the author's familiarity with the organizational process paradigm helped first to notice and then to identify.)[21]

In 1906 Franz Ferdinand was allowed to create (with Franz Joseph's tolerance and later recognition) a military chancellery of his own, headed by the talented political soldier, Major Alexander Brosch von Aarenau. Through this device the heir apparent sought to insert himself into the diplomatic, strategic, and political processes of the Dual Monarchy. Steadily his own chancellery acquired a staff, a place on the routing slips of all governmental memoranda, and the expectation that it would be regularly informed about major political and military *démarches*. Although never able to intrude effectively into Hungarian affairs, Franz Ferdinand had by mid-1912 become a substantial force, almost a quasi-institution, someone whose views had to be considered on diplomatic and strategic issues. Military figures, such as General Oskar Potiorek, the Governor-General of Bosnia–Herzegovina, would consult the archduke on returning to Vienna, and so did senior diplomatic and bureaucratic figures. The Ballhausplatz (the Habsburg foreign ministry) consulted him about new ambassadorships and the *Thronfolger* sought similar influence with the Austrian government on senior appointments. Belvedere, his official residence, became the focus for the ''government in waiting.'' As one Austrian politician quipped: ''We not only have two parliaments, we also have two emperors.''[22]

That remark was, of course, an exaggeration. Franz Joseph remained alert, diligent (though bouts of ill health were now more frequent), and the final, decisive figure on issues of peace or war.[23] But this should not obscure the fact that the archduke had real power and influence, especially on military issues. After 1906 one of the monarchy's two senior military posts—chief of the General Staff or minister of war—was chosen by Franz Ferdinand. And with the army as a foremost ''monarchical'' institution, this represented genuine power. Moreover, he was consulted on all military and naval budgets, participated in the selection of the top military commanders, and supervised the annual maneuvers. In 1913 Franz Joseph appointed him general inspector of all armed forces, giving him the right to deal directly on military matters with the two governments and to have access to all internal correspondence in the War Ministry and the General Staff. If war came, he would be the presumed commander of the military forces. The net result of these delegations of authority was to endow Franz Ferdinand with political power and institutional status.

Nor did Franz Ferdinand hesitate to venture into foreign affairs, though until Foreign Minister Aehrenthal's death in February 1912 he had little successful entrée with Ballhausplatz. The arrival of Leopold Berchtold altered things dramatically, for the new foreign minister regularly consulted with the archduke, briefed him on major issues, and exchanged personal letters.[24] If Count Berchtold never forgot that he worked for Franz Joseph, he also remembered that Franz Ferdinand in a twinkle could become emperor. And this fact, once the Balkan fighting began in October 1912, insured that the *Thronfolger* would be an active participant in the Habsburg decision process. In the succeeding crises, with one initial and isolated exception, the archduke was an advocate for caution and peace.

From December 1912 to October 1913, on three different occasions, the Habsburg monarchy faced genuine choices for peace or war: in each case another day, one more event, a different argument could have tilted the decision toward war rather than hesitation and peace.[25] During much of the time, moreover, over 600,000 troops were mobilized along both the Russian and Serbian borders.[26] In sum, Vienna appeared poised for war. In December

1912 Franz Ferdinand, fearful that the victorious Serbs would divert their troops from the Turkish campaign to a struggle with Austria–Hungary, accepted the "worst case" analysis presented by the military experts. He advocated a callup of the remaining reserves in the south and preventive action against Serbia. In fact, he even had the emperor reinstall Conrad as chief of the General Staff in the expectation that war was imminent. But Berlin's coolness toward any action, concern over not thwarting the soon-to-start peace talks in London, alarm about Russia's possible reaction, and dislike for a winter campaign, not to mention Franz Joseph's own aversion to war, kept the policy makers from taking the final plunge.[27] Never again during the remaining Balkan crises did the archduke press, as he had in December 1912, for a military solution or preventive action—against either Serbia or Montenegro.

In early May 1913, when tiny Montenegro refused to abandon Skutari to the newly created Albanian state, Vienna nearly launched the war plan drafted as "Case M[ontenegro]." Conrad pressed for action; Franz Joseph agreed; and even the Common Council and the Hungarians were resigned to action. Foreign Minister Berchtold disliked the prospect of war but saw no other option. This time, moreover, Berlin assented. But the *Thronfolger* never liked the idea, expressed continuing reservations about its necessity, and was delighted when King Nikita (after learning Vienna was not bluffing) capitulated on May 4. Further, once this crisis was over, the heir apparent pressured Berchtold to allow the reservists to return to their homes. This suggestion the foreign minister only partly accepted, so that many Habsburg reservists were still on active duty when the second Balkan war started in late June.[28]

Surprisingly, the second round of Balkan fighting brought no war–peace crisis in Vienna. Yet its aftermath (and that of the first war) did later in October. Again, the issue was the delimitation of Albania's border, only this time it was the Serbs, not the Montenegrins, who refused to abandon territory assigned by the London Conference of Ambassadors to the new state. Pressed hard by Conrad, by Leon Bilinski (the common finance minister who was responsible for Bosnia–Herzegovina), and by Stefan Tisza, the new Hungarian prime minister, Berchtold issued an eight-day ultimatum to Belgrade on October 18: abondon the territory or else. Franz Joseph agreed to this procedure, while Berlin received it as a virtual *fait accompli*. Franz Ferdinand disliked the step, and there is circumstantial evidence to suggest that he was deliberately not informed about its timing, possibly to prevent his intrusion.[29] In any event, the threat worked, Serbia withdrew its troops from the territory, and peace was preserved once more.

Thus, by late 1913, the archduke's caution and aversion to military action was well established. Because he was the heir apparent, the views of the *Thronfolger* could not be ignored, and they clearly served as a braking device on any dash to war on the South Slav issue. Furthermore, his separate links with Berlin and Kaiser Wilhelm, whose stance on any war–peace issue could be pivotal, were also recognized. Meanwhile, by 1914, Franz Ferdinand's chancellery was handling nearly a thousand documents a month and had become an accepted part of the governmental structure. The archduke had acquired, along with status and a set of delegated authorizations, actual power and influence seldom equaled—before or after—in any monarchical or cabinet or presidential system. The heir apparent was established as a part of the organizational structure, as a part of the organizational process of the monarchy, as a quasi-institution.

The assassination at Sarajevo abruptly altered everything. Changes were immediate. Indeed, the German ambassador reporting on July 2, spoke of the determination among senior officials never again to permit the creation of a "subsidiary government."[30] More important, and immediately, with the disappearance of the man and the institutional focus that he exerted, the political and organizational structure altered. Now there was no one to press Berchtold for caution or to support him when that was his own inclination. Nor was there support for Kaiser Franz Joseph should he also wish to defer or be cautious, and there was no one, no institution such as the archduke's military chancellery, to challenge the emperor's own chancellery (always more bellicose than its aging master). And, most important, there was no one with institutional responsibilites and privileges to interrogate Conrad about his war plans or to counter the military clique on the risks that war might entail.[31]

There were other ramifications as well. Those men who had been associated with Franz Ferdinand and who still held key posts were deliberately excluded from the policy making of July 1914. Ottokar Czernin, at one point the presumed foreign minister if the archduke came to power and now minister to Bucharest, was kept wholly uninformed about developments. Yet the Rumanians were a central piece of any chance for the war plans to succeed. Another leading member of Franz Ferdinand's circle, General Auffenberg, the former war minister and still a senior army commander, was also carefully excluded from participation in the July discussions.[32] No one who might pose counterarguments, or argue to go slow, or echo Franz Ferdinand's own fears had entrée to the crucial decisions. Perhaps more significant, the death of Franz Ferdinand eliminated the senior figure who most feared the Russians and what they might do if Austria–Hungary moved against Serbia. These fears the other policy makers (save Conrad) had shared in December 1912 and early 1913, yet progressively and dangerously less so thereafter.[33] But for the heir apparent, concern about Russia continued throughout 1913 and longer. Had Franz Ferdinand been present, Conrad's even Berchtold's, blasé attitude toward St. Petersburg would have been subject to scrutiny. As it was, the archduke's death was supposed to still St. Petersburg into inactivity on the grounds of monarchical solidarity. In July 1914 a major organizational actor and his institution were no longer present to argue for a policy of caution, even peace.

The impact of the change may be put more graphically if stated in this fashion. Had only General Potiorek, the *Landeschef* of Bosnia–Herzegovina, been the victim that day in Sarajevo (he was also riding in the car), the odds of a local Habsburg–Serbian war were, say, probably one in three. Had only Countess Sophie Chotek, Franz Ferdinand's wife, been the victim, the odds were two in five. Had the general and the countess been the victims, the odds would have been one in two. But with the heir apparent and his wife, the odds became four in five. Once Gavrilo Princip pulled the trigger in the Bosnian capital, the chance of other triggers being pulled was almost guaranteed. There were now few barriers, save possibly Berlin, that could block Vienna's rush to settle accounts with Belgrade.

This vignette emphasizes three important dimensions of the organizational process paradigm. First, on occasion individuals by their position and their staffs can become a part of an organizational structure. It is not merely the huge bureaucratic units or constitutionally acknowledged holders of power that form the structure. And once a part of the process, their mere presence vests them with legitimacy. Henry Kissinger's role in the early Nixon years is a further example of this phenomenon. Second, the organizational process paradigm reminds researchers that the sudden alteration of the process can often have a decisive effect. Patterns of consultation, calculation, or avoidance are radically changed. Too often this negative impact is overlooked. Presidential or ministerial transitions are a variation of this phenomenon, with John Kennedy's accession possibly the most spectacular illustration of the problem of gaining control and establishing command of an organizational process. Third, the organizational process paradigm reminds the analyst that separate residual centers of power and influence can exist, even in a well defined monarchical system, and that these may be acknowledged by all participants. Delegations of power occur, and with them political power and leverage. Hence Franz Joseph's designation of Franz Ferdinand first as *Thronfolger*, then his recognition of the military chancellery in 1908, and finally his appointment of the archduke as inspector general endowed the latter with an institutional base. This in turn brought the heir apparent into the policy process. In this Franz Ferdinand had his greatest role and his most secure demonstration that he was no mere archduke, but the *Thronfolger:* the heir apparent to the Habsburg dynasty.

Alliance Politics as Organizational Process: The Hoyos Mission

The murders that Sunday, June 28, 1914, galvanized the Vienna government to decisive steps. By July 2 the mood in the Habsburg capital was resolute and warlike: this time Belgrade had gone too far. This toughness of attitude, however, is not reflected in the Fischer school or in some of the other literature on the coming of the war of 1914. Instead, Vienna is often portrayed as hesitant and timid, uncertain and dependent on what Berlin would say or do or permit. The Austrians, therefore, sent Count Hoyos to Berlin and received an emphatic injunction to take action, and to take it quickly. From this point, the Fischer thesis suggests, Berlin dominated the Habsburg policy apparatus and exploited Austria–Hungary's willingness to act as the pretext for a German war. Or, put another way, Austria–Hungary was pressured to war and the responsibility for the war's origins is really Berlin's, not Vienna's. That explanation, while gratifying to many, is much exaggerated. In July 1914 it was Austria–Hungary that promoted a local war, determined its timing, and avoided any negotiated settlement. Berlin for its own reasons tolerated, abetted, and then regretted this development.[34]

In this drive to war the Hoyos mission was crucial. It can easily be seen as an example of "alliance politics" and thus addressed, as the author has addressed "entente politics" elsewhere, as a feature of transnational bureaucratic politics.[35] but it might be as profitably examined from the perspective of organizational structure, with the permanent Austro–German alliance the structure, and the relationship between the two capitals as part of the organizational process paradigm. Not only does this help to answer some questions not resolved by a traditional diplomatic or even bureaucratic analysis, but it may also serve to put into better perspective the relative roles of Vienna and Berlin.

Since its formation in 1879, the Austro–German alliance had survived repeated vicissitudes and crises. The Italian partner (1882) always remained a lesser light, though Berlin periodically sought to inflate Rome's role. Defensive in character and concerned chiefly with the strategic and political threat posed by Russia, the alliance only gained detailed military and naval dimensions after 1909—and then chiefly because of Conrad's insistence.[36] Even then its arrangements were less complex and complete than the Franco–Russian or Anglo–French ones. On diplomatic issues, the two capitals were often aligned (Vienna was the "brilliant second," so much so that the British Foreign Office often could not decide how much independence Vienna really possessed.)[37] But there were distinct differences between the Hohenzollern–Habsburg leaderships on issues, differences which the Balkan wars helped to aggravate. Berlin's *Weltpolitik* did not easily match with Vienna's *Balkanpolitik,* especially as German traders moved into the Balkans and Kaiser Wilhelm pursued an independent policy in Constantinople and Athens. There were also important differences in their assessment of Russia. Berlin inclined to accommodation and agreement, as in the Potsdam talks in 1910. Vienna regarded every Russian move with suspicion, especially after the 1908 crisis over Bosnia–Herzgovina. Russia's assistance in the formation of the Balkan League in 1912 and the latter's subsequent attack on Turkey did not, of course, reduce Habsburg apprehensions.[38]

The Balkan fighting and the subsequent war crises brought real tension to the Austro–German relationship. In November 1912 Wilhelm talked strongly of Habsburg action, only to have Chancellor Bethmann Hollweg and Foreign Secretary Kiderlen Wächter brusquely dampen the encouragement a few days later.[39] In January and February 1913, when the Russians still had an additional 370,000 troops on active duty and tensions were extremely high, Berlin through letters, direct admonitions, and special emissaries urged caution and flexibility on the Danubian capital.[40] In May 1913, however, there were indications that the German Kaiser would accept local action against Montenegro. Yet after the second Balkan war and Rumania's success, Wilhelm completely upset Berchtold's hope for a revision of the Treaty of Bucharest by proclaiming his support for it. And by the third crisis on October, Vienna's policy makers found themselves uncertain of Berlin's probable reaction to an eight-day ultimatum. Thus Berchtold was deliberately less than candid in advance about his intentions, informing Berlin of the delivery of the ultimatum only hours before it was actually handed over in Belgrade.[41]

Although the late fall also saw bellicose talk from the German Kaiser and apparent rapport between the Allies, the senior diplomatic and military policy makers in Vienna had their doubts. This uncertainty was buttressed, moreover, by German tolerance of Italian maneuvers in Albania, by Berlin's attitude toward belated Habsburg claims for a part of Asia Minor if Turkey collapsed, and by mutterings in Berlin about Vienna's worth as an ally. Further, there were serious differences on the eve of Sarajevo about how to handle an increasingly vexious Rumania and to prevent its defection from the camp of the Triple Alliance. When the July crisis came, Berchtold had real cause to be uncertain about Berlin's possible response to the prospect of firm action. Despite the alliance, the Ballhausplatz could wonder about its effective substance and whether the structure was as solid as it appeared on paper (a point he could, of course, ask even more insistently about Italy). The previous eigthteen months had revealed many promises, but scant performance, from the German capital.[42]

For the Habsburg foreign minister, the guarantee of German support (and therefore protection against the Russian threat) was imperative if Austria–Hungary attacked Serbia. But could he be sure that Berlin would not again change its mind? And when should he approach his ally—early or late in the crisis, in what detail, and at what level of the government? If he moved too early, the answer might be yes and then changed to no; if he moved too late, he might not only find the entire policy nullified, he might also suggest to Berlin the reverse of what he actually intended—to take decisive action. Berchtold's decision, when it was clear that Kaiser Wilhelm would not come to Vienna for Franz Ferdinand's funeral, was to sound out Berlin early and directly, but in broad and general terms. And, once the assurance was gained, to share few details with Berlin on the subsequent policy implementation. That Berlin for its own reasons might be anxious or willing for Austria–Hungary to proceed, could only be a matter for speculation and hope. Berchtold's chief concern was to get his ally's assent and then to prevent (or thwart) a change of mind if the war became larger than a local affair.[43]

But how to sound out Berlin, and through what mechanism? In answering this set of questions, the organizational structure of the alliance was important, conditioned heavily, to be sure, by the individuals who represented its organizational units. Among the possible avenues open to Berchtold were either the German embassy in Vienna or its Habsburg counterpart in Berlin, the chiefs of staff or the military attachés, a special aristocratic emissary (such as Prince Hohenlohe's journey to St. Petersburg in February 1913 to cool Austro–Russian relations), or a special, personal messenger from his own staff. To deal with Berlin through Ambassador Tschirschky (for whom Berchtold had no special fondness) was unpromising. Not only had the German emissary pointedly preached caution in the days following the assassination, but he had been less than helpful in the earlier crises. Any message through him, moreover, would be subject to reinterpretation, a point of great importance. On the other hand, to allow the aging Habsburg ambassador in Berlin, Count Szögyeny (already scheduled for replacement), to handle the issue had its risks. Not only had the Magyar diplomat preached caution before and faithfully represented German hesitance, but Szögyeny might also misunderstand his instructions. A second route, to use the chiefs of the general staff (or the attachés), as had been done with General Schemua in November 1912, had too many risks. It might occasion public comment and could, with bellicose General Conrad the agent, frighten the German leadership. A third, mode, to send a top-level, aristocratic delegate was never considered. The reasons for not doing so are obvious; the German Kaiser, unlike the Russian Czar, did not need to be impressed by aristocratic pedigree.

Berchtold decided to meld approaches and thus to exploit several dimensions of the alliance's organizational structure simultaneously. He repeated what he had done in January 1913 in dispatching Count Szápàry to Berlin: he selected a member of his immediate staff, Count Alexander von Hoyos (the *chef de cabinet*), to go to Berlin.[44] For one thing this insured that the emissary would be accurately informed of Ballhausplatz thinking and aware of the mood in Vienna. Moreover, Hoyos had drafted the letter for Franz Joseph to send to his German counterpart. But there were other, equally telling reasons. Hoyos had previously served in Berlin, was acquainted with most of the senior German leaders, and had personal ties with Dietrich, Bethmann Hollweg, the Chancellor's nephew, and a number of the embassy staff in Vienna. Equally important, Berlin knew that during the Balkan wars Hoyos had favored decisive action against Serbia and was a leading Ballhausplatz "hawk." And there was another, possibly symbolic reason. In the crucial days of October 1908, it had been Hoyos and Szögyeny who had visited Kaiser Wilhelm at his hunting lodge at Rominten, seeking and gaining the German monarch's backing in the Bosnian crisis. As Fritz Fellner writes,

"The identity of persons, words, and goals is striking; only the outcome, which directly reflected the intentions of the foreign ministers who defined Austro-Hungarian policy, differed in 1914 from 1908."[45]

There were two other reasons to choose Hoyos. He could be dispatched quickly and would be present to offset any doubts that the Magyar ambassador Szögyeny might inject. Given the opposition of Prime Minister Tisza to any military action, this consideration could not be ignored. Nor (and more important) could the usefulness of a German sanction in dealing with the recalcitrant Magyar leader be forgotten. Berchtold needed the German assurance early, not later, if he were to overcome Tisza'a resistance and reassert his own control over Habsburg foreign policy. A successful Hoyos trip would provide this possibility.[46]

Hoyos left for Berlin on July 4, carrying a long memorandum on foreign policy (drafted well before Sarajevo) and the "personal" letter he had penned for Franz Joseph. Although both documents talked in measured tones about a more aggressive diplomatic policy to isolate Serbia, two lines betrayed their real intent. In a postscript to the memorandum, there ran the sentence: "All the more imperative is the need for the Monarchy with a firm hand to sever the threads which its enemies seek to close into a net over its head." And, in the personal letter, the words "if Serbia, which at present forms the pivot of Pan-Slav policy, is eliminated as a political power factor in the Balkans" left no ambiguity about Vienna's real goal. Nor did Hoyos' verbal instructions allow any doubt, a point that his discussions of territorial partition naturally reinforced.[47]

On arrival in Berlin, Hoyos gave the documents to Ambassador Szögyeny. The aging envoy had lunch with Wilhelm on July 5 and received emphatic assurances of German support. These were reaffirmed to both Szögyeny and Hoyos the next day by Chancellor Bethmann Hollweg. A delighted Hoyos drafted cables each day, sent over the ambassador's signature, emphasizing the tenacity and solidity of German support. Vienna had truly obtained "a blank check" for action.[48] Or, as Sidney Fay once put it, the Kaiser and his advisers were "putting a noose around their necks; and handing the other end of the rope to a stupid and clumsy adventurer who now felt free to go as he liked."[49]

Throughout, it had been Vienna seeking assurances, timing the *démarche*, and framing it in just enough detail to make it plausible. The Hoyos mission could not have been more successful. Berchtold, now convinced of the need for action against Serbia, had selected an envoy whose very selection left no doubt about the course of action favored by Vienna. The Habsburg foreign minister had exploited the organizational machinery to get an outcome that he regarded as imperative.

This episode illustrates three important dimensions of the organizational process at work in alliance politics. First, the alliance relationship, unlike the adversarial, requires at least minimal consultation and agreement in advance if a partner is to ask for later support of a military operation (whether actively or only benevolently). The methods by which this occurs and their format are an essential operating problem for alliance management. Failure to heed this elementary aspect of alliance politics can, as Anthony Eden discovered in 1956 over Suez, have unfortunate consequences. Second, special missions often have a particular utility in prompting alliance agreements. Above all, they force the machinery of decision making to address the problem at hand. Quick arrivals, quick answers, and quick departures abort prolonged deliberations or the obscurantism that comes in framing and exchanging cables and dispatches. Third, in dependent alliance relationships (a not infrequent situation) the subordinate partner will—if it has decided to take military action—seek to evade or avoid a possible veto over its action. Either it tries to conceal the risks (as Vienna did in 1913 on the Montenegrin issue), or to deceive (as Vienna may have done in October 1913), or to win an early endorsement and then act without interference. In July 1914 Count Berchtold, by now quite familiar with Berlin's apparent fickleness, took no chances. Initially, he acted to minimize the veto. In this way he not only consolidated the organizational structure behind his course of action, but armed himself to deal with Tisza and the Hungarians. Now he could move to launch a military attack. But nearly three weeks went by. Why?

Explaining Vienna's Delay in July 1914: Organizational Routines and Options

A leitmotif of the historical and apologia literature on 1914 runs as follows: if Austria–Hungary had acted decisively, without delay or hesitation, it might have managed a local war against Serbia without also triggering a world war.[50] Three assumptions, some held at the time in Vienna and Berlin, buttress this generalization. First, that Berlin promised its help in the expectation that the Habsburgs would act quickly. Yet what did Berlin expect by prompt action? Recent experiences from the Balkan wars alone indicated that the Austro–Hungarian mobilization process was slow and cumbersome. At best, the monarchy needed fourteen to sixteen days to launch a military attack. Second, so one theme runs, had the Danubian monarchy moved rapidly, it might have caught the Triple Entente powers in a more sympathetic, understanding mood. In particular, Russia might have allowed feelings of monarchical solidarity to submerge its political and strategic interests.[51] Closely linked with this premise is a third: that the actual delay contributed to an overreaction by the Triple Entente. By deliberately misleading the other capitals and lulling them into complacency, only to spring the ultimatum on Belgrade, Vienna contributed to an expansion, not a localization, of the Balkan crisis.[52]

If these were the assumptions and some possible benefits from prompt action and if the pivotal German go-ahead had been received by July 6, what delayed Vienna's dispatch of the ultimatum until July 23? A number of explanations, or rationalizations, have been advanced for this seeming procrastination. One centers upon the delays caused by Tisza's opposition to a military showdown. His refusal to accede readily to his colleagues' (and Franz Joseph's) belief that war was a necessary, indeed the only, option upset the chances for quick action.[53] Moreover, Berchtold's need to convince the Magyar had another consequence: it forced Vienna to consider the long-scheduled French state visit to St. Petersburg.[54] Scheduled to leave France on July 15, President Poincaré and Premier Viviani would arrive by ship in St. Petersburg on July 20 and then depart on the twenty-third. Vienna's policy makers wanted no démarche while the French delegation was in the Russian capital. Yet this concern does not adequately explain why no ultimatum could be sent before their departure or while they were in transit (as would actually occur on their return voyage). Indeed, it can be argued that it would have been wiser to have moved hastily rather than allowing the two allies a further chance to exchange views. In any event, the impending visit posed a significant problem in timing the action against Serbia.

Another possible explanation for the delay focuses upon Vienna's need to establish Serbian complicity in the murders. Thus, while the senior Habsburg policy makers were fully prepared to act, they felt compelled to seek iron-clad evidence that would link the Serbian government with the murders. As part of this effort Friedrich von Wiesner, the legal counselor at the Ballhausplatz, was sent to Sarajevo on July 10 to cull the records of the local interrogations of Princip and his associates. Yet on July 13 he had to telegraph that no conclusive proof had emerged, while continuing to search for the kind of "smoking gun" evidence that would link Belgrade to the murders. But, while Wiesner's efforts took time and inevitably crossed the dates for the French state visit, they do not appear decisive in influencing the delivery of the ultimatum.[55]

A more prosaic explanation for the delay centers upon the need to gather the crops. Harvests were crucial to the agrarian economies of east European countries, more so, of course, than for the west European states with easier access to overseas foodstuffs. To collect the harvest before the campaigns began was, therefore, a consideration of more than passing importance, an instance of nature imposing its own organizational process (so to speak) on the decision process. And indeed it is the harvest issue which provides the best explanation of why Vienna took its time in July 1914 and why Berchtold abandoned his idea of a surprise attack on Serbia. It is an explanation, moreover, that unambiguously reflects the impact of organizational structure and process upon the availability of options for the policy makers.

The crux of the problem can be quickly stated. Early in his tenure as chief of the General Staff, General Conrad agreed to agrarian demands for the institution—on a routine basis—of a policy of harvest leaves. Such a procedure allowed troops on active duty to return home to help with the harvests and then rejoin their units for the usual summer maneuvers. At the completion of these exercises, the second-year troops were dismissed and the new recruits—in the early fall—brought on active duty. In this way, the agrarian interests were mollified, the crops were harvested, and the entire process was regularized throughout the army.[56] But this, of course, also meant that the machinery that permitted such leaves would operate on a regular, routine basis stopped or curtailed. And this Conrad discovered on July 6 when he received a status report on harvest leaves. For on that date half of the corps manpower at Agram, Innsbruck, Kaschau, Temesvár, Budapest, Pressburg, and Graz were away on harvest leave, scheduled to return to their posts between the dates of July 19 and July 25. This fact presented the military policy makers with a major dilemma. If the government wanted to act quickly (and that had been both Conrad's and Berchtold's initial plan), the troops on harvest leave would have to be recalled to their units immediately to avoid interference with mobilization. Yet to do this would not only disrupt the harvests and possibly confuse the mobilization, it would destroy any chance of a diplomatic and military surprise. Above all, the European powers would discover Habsburg intentions and have time to react and possibly block the prospect of action. Confronted with this set of organizational constraints, Conrad did what he could—he canceled the remaining leaves—and later decided to go on vacation in a deliberate ploy to deceive the other powers.[57]

With an awareness of the constraints imposed by the harvest leaves, the historian gains a new perspective into the delays that characterized Vienna's behavior in early July. Austria–Hungary could not move early or quickly without losing the element of surprise. When this proved impossible, the timing of the Russian state visit became important, actually coinciding with the completion of the leaves. All of this meant that Berchtold had time to deal leisurely with Tisza's opposition and to allow Wiesner to spend extra days in Sarajevo in the search for incriminating evidence. Blocked in their desire for immediate action, Berchtold and Conrad worked within the parameters of the available options bequeathed them by the organizational process. Earlier decisions and routines had produced the option of harvest leave; now that option foreclosed other options. Decisiveness and quickness gave way to waiting and impatience, and to the danger that other capitals would forget their dismay at the Sarajevo murders. And here lurked danger. For what had appeared in early July to be a calculated, acceptable risk—a local war with Serbia—would loom more dangerous and provocative two weeks later. This failure to recognize that a change of circumstances might bring new risks was one of Vienna's many errors of judgment that summer. For that, the problem of harvests played a key role, though not in the way usually imagined.

Two other points about this episode are worth stressing. First, that wherever large organizations exist, there also exist routines, processes, and patterns that at once facilitate and limit options. Military bureaucracies are the most conspicuous examples as disparate groups and elements have to be programmed and organized to do the simplest tasks—from harvest leaves to patterns for parking aircraft along runways. Second, routines continue un-molested once a crisis begins. Although they may contribute to a crisis, the established routines may pass unnoticed by those in charge. Someone has to cancel the orders, as Kennedy did for U-2 flights during the Cuban missile crisis (and, even then, one occurred). On the other hand, no one in that same crisis realized that depth-charging submarines was standard blockade pro-cedure, hence the dangerous episode with the Soviet submarine.[58] In a crisis, the senior policy makers can almost bet that there lurks some piece of the organizational process waiting to upset the calculated plans. The question is when and how.

Cautionary Injunctions for Historians and Policy Makers

Three vignettes from any historical era or country do not necessarily establish the case for the value of the organizational process paradigm and an enhanced historical explanation. A not unnatural retort at this point from a more traditional colleague might well be: any good diplomatic historian, working with abundant new evidence, would have reached similar conclu-sions. And in many senses that critique may be valid. But it is possibly less helpful if one remembers that often overfamiliarity with material can blind the observer or that often novitiate scholars do not yet possess that "intuitive sense" to grasp connections. Moreover, it minimizes the new problems caused by the sheer mass of documentation for the years of World War II and later, an overdocumentation that necessitates putting the policy apparatus into perspective and determining what did and did not contribute essentially to sets of outcomes.

For this paradigm, no less than the bureaucratic politics model or quan-titative practices, continually offers, moreover, a set of reminders to the historian to be alert to his assumptions. It provides a checklist that insists that the writer knows how a government is organized, how it functions, and how those functions may be disrupted or altered. From this there comes an awareness of how structure limits the range of options open to the policy maker and how the rush of business often allows structure and process to dic-tate choices and outcomes. It is not just that policy makers are often the prisoners of their own backgrounds, egos, and social classes (a point the Fischerites and Cold War revisionists never cease telling us), but that they are often prisoners within their own officialdom. Options are not unlimited, routines are necessary, and there is a sense of contraint and narrowness that has a "blinders" quality about it. Furthermore, governments do not operate in constant crisis situations. Even during the 1912–1914 crisis the Habsburg government had other, routine business to transact: budgets to prepare, ambassadors to appoint, war plans to revise. Interposed and mixed with momentous decisions were lesser ones, often with their own pressing deadlines. Finally, the paradigm reminds the analyst that to *make* a decision is not to *implement* it, that if the organizational process structures choice, it also—possibly more so—structures and conditions implementation. Here too structure is entangled with decision; here too it can distort outcomes. Throughout, the administrative-governmental structure exists to resolve issues, to recognize new ones, and to keep things manageable. An understanding of this process (which cannot be done apart from specific issues aggregated over time) is imperative for understanding when and why policy outcomes occur. With it, moreover, comes a sense of the larger context in which the pulling and tugging of bureaucratic or court or presidential politics takes place and a confidence that allows one to move more easily from one explanatory mode and task to another.

The organizational process model is, however, only a model and only a tool. To make it work effectively requires familiarity with constitutional, political, and budget arrangements, to go beyond administrative charts and rank lists, to the actual processing of issues. This is not easily done, can be misleading if only a few samples are selected, and will at times appear to lead the historian away from, not toward, the larger task of explanation. And even with this information and understanding of the organizational essence only a part of the historian's task is solved. He must still insert individual motives, ideology, and ambition into the matrix, while recognizing that crisis disrupts routines and injects new, unexpected variants.

Nor can one attempt too much with the paradigm. While it will offer new insights, it can also confuse. To try, for instance, to explain why General Conrad sent his troops in the wrong direction in early August 1914 would seem at first glance a problem almost tailor-made for the paradigm to explain: military movements, routines, mobilization timetables. It is just this type of explanation that has often been offered, even if not so labeled. Yet it would appear that a cybernetic or perceptual approach, coupled with some sense of the bureaucratic rivalries, may help to explain why Conrad so ignored the threat of Russia in his initial orders.[59] Another example, more contemporary, is also appropriate. The institution of the Berlin airlift in 1948 to overcome the Soviet land blockade appears a logical, almost natural response for the United States Air Force. Air power to the rescue! Yet the internal debates reveal that President Truman had to overcome stout air force resistance to the operation because they were afraid to wear out their precious cargo aircraft. Here a bureaucratic politics approach would tell the analyst far more.[60]

The exchange of ideas across disciplines remains difficult, often treacherous, not least for those that seem—like diplomatic history and international relations—so closely related and with so many mutual needs and interests. But it can be intensely rewarding, stimulating, and helpful. Nowhere, moreover, is the nexus so constant as between the theories of decision making (and the presence of the organizational process), on the one hand, and the explication of diplomatic history and strategic policy, on the other. The fusion between the operating elites and the large, often faceless institutions below them remains constant. Whether it be a small set of bureaucracies in a complex government, such as that of the Habsburgs, or organizational units in a large, western democracy, the problems of leadership, decision making, and effectiveness remain—at once a challenge, a threat, an abstract, an opportunity.

The organizational process ought to remind the historian and the contemporary observer that structure and routine do influence policy options, shape choices, and affect outcomes. Structures exist to facilitate, to restrain, to balance, while linking foreign with domestic politics. To bemoan the presence of structure is to ignore its benefits of option generation and implementation; to seek to erect universal structures for the conduct of diplomacy is to ignore the complexity of change in international relations.

It is the task of the historian to explain, yet occasionally he longs for the assurance that there will be something to explain. However gauged, the diplomatic historian and the scholar of international relations work in a substantive area of great promise—and greater danger. A decade or more ago the Habsburg monarchy would have appeared wholly unrelated to modern American life. Today, with governmental paralysis more systematic and ethnic differences shaping foreign policy in a more pronounced and constant fashion, there may indeed be lessons of instruction and caution in both the paradigm and the substance of this chapter.

Notes

1. Three recent examples of this tradition, in the area of European diplomatic history, suffice: F. R. Bridge, *From Sadowa to Sarajevo: The Foreign Policy of Austria-Hungary, 1866-1914* (London and Boston: Routledge and Kegan Paul, 1972); Briton Cooper Busch, *Mudros to Lausanne: Britain's Frontiers in West Asia, 1918-1923* (Albany, N.Y.: State University of New York Press, 1976); and Dwight E. Lee, *Europe's Crucial Decade: The Diplomatic Background of World War I, 1902-1914* (Hanover, N.H.: University Press of New England, 1974).

2. Even more recent efforts, such as Donald G. Bishop, *The Administration of British Foreign Relations* (Syracuse, N.Y.: Syracuse University Press, 1961), and Paul Seabury, *The Wilhelmstrasse* (Los Angeles: University of California Press, 1954), are not immune from this problem.

3. Gordon Craig and Felix Gilbert (eds.), *The Diplomats, 1919-1939* (Princeton: Princeton University Press, 1953).

4. Among those with a broader view are Zara Steiner, *The Foreign Office and British Foreign Policy, 1898-1914* (Cambridge, Eng.: Cambridge University Press, 1969), and her most recent study, *Britain and the Origins of the First World War* (London: Macmillan, 1977); Christopher Andrew, *Théophile Delcassé and the Making of the Entente Cordiale* (New York: St. Martin's Press, 1968); E. R. May, *"Lessons" of the Past: The Use and Misuse of History in American Foreign Policy* (New York: Oxford University Press, 1973); Nicholas d'Ombrain, *War Machinery and High Policy: Defence Administration in Peacetime Britain, 1902-1914* (London: Oxford University Press, 1973); Christopher Thorne, *Allies of a Kind: The United States, Britain, and the War Against Japan, 1941-1945* (New York: Oxford University Press, 1978); and possibly the author's *The Politics of Grand Strategy; Britain and France Prepare for War, 1904-1914* (Cambridge, Mass.: Harvard University Press, 1969). Two important new works that focus upon the structure or social character of foreign ministries are Lamar Cecil, *The German Diplomatic Service, 1871-1914* (Princeton: Princeton University Press, 1976), and Paul Gordon Lauren, *Diplomats and Bureaucrats: The First Institutional Response to Twentieth-Century Diplomacy in France and Germany* (Stanford: Hoover Institution Press, 1975); see also the monumental study by Hans-Adolf Jacobsen, *Nationalsozialistische Aussenpolitik, 1933-1938* (Frankfurt: Alfred Metzner Verlag, 1968).

5. Fritz Fischer, *Krieg der Illusionen: Die deutsche Politik von 1911 bis 1914* (Düsseldorf: Droste Verlag, 1969) [*War of Illusions: German Policies from 1911 to 1914,* trans. Marian Jackson (New York: Norton, 1975)]; Immanuel Geiss, *German Foreign Policy, 1871-1914* (London and Boston: Routledge and Kegan Paul, 1976); Gabriel and Joyce Kolko, *The Limits of Power: The World and United States Foreign Policy, 1945-1954* (New York: Knopf, 1972). For a revisionist study that does grapple with structure, see R. J. Barnet, *The Roots of War* (New York: Atheneum, 1972).

6. Among the many works on this problem, those of Charles Black are noteworthy: see, for example, *Perspectives in Constitutional Law* (Englewood Cliffs, N.J.: Prentice-Hall, 1963) and (with Bob Eckhardt) *The Tides of Power: Conversations on The American Constitution* (New Haven: Yale University Press, 1976).

7. Among these are Graham T. Allison, *The Essence of Decision: Explaining The Cuban Missile Crisis* (Boston: Little Brown, 1971); Morton Halperin, *Bureaucratic Politics and Foreign Policy* (Washington, D.C.: Brookings Institution, 1974) Graham T. Allison and Morton H. Halperin, "Bureaucratic Politics: A Paradigm and Some Policy Implications," in Raymond Tanter and Richard Ullman (eds.), *Theory and Policy in International Relations* (Princeton: Princeton University Press, 1972). For some of the underlying works on which the above draw heavily, see James G. March and Herbert A. Simon, *Organizations* (New York: Wiley, 1958); Richard Cyert and James G. March, *A Behavioral Theory of the Firm* (Englewood Cliffs, N.J.: Prentice-Hall, 1963); and T. S. Kuhn, *The Structure of Scientific Revolutions* (Chicago: University of Chicago Press, 1962).

8. On cognitive models, see John Steinbruner, *The Cybernetic Theory of Decision* (Princeton: Princeton University Press, 1974); Robert Jervis, *Perception and Misperception in International Politics* (Princeton: Princeton University Press, 1976); and Robert Axelrod (ed.), *Structure of Decision: The Cognitive Maps of Political Elites*

(Princeton: Princeton University Press, 1976); on the quantitative, see as examples that deal with pre-1914 Europe, Nazli Choucri and Robert C. North, *Nations in Conflict: Domestic Growth and International Violence* (San Fransisco: Freeman, 1975); Richard Rosecrance, *Power, Balance of Power and Status in Nineteenth Century International Relations* (Beverly Hills, Calif.: Sage, 1975); and an important critique of this school by Paul Schroeder, "Quantitative Studies in the Balance of Power: An Historian's Reaction," *Journal of Conflict Resolution* 21 (March 1977): 3-21.

9. Even two of the century's giants did this occasionally: A. J. P. Taylor in *The Struggle for Mastery in Europe, 1848-1918* (Oxford: Oxford University Press, 1954) talked as if governments were monolithic, while William Langer—in exhaustive detail—often allowed the sequential account by the main participants to dominate, especially in *The Diplomacy of Imperialism* (New York: Knopf, 1956 ed.).

10. Allison, *Essence of Decision,* Chapter 3, *passim,* and pp. 255-257.

11. Halperin, *Bureaucratic Politics,* Chapter 3, *passim.*

12. Two recent studies that occasionally betray this attitude are Barton J. Berstein, "Roosevelt, Truman, and the Atomic bomb, 1941-1945: A Reinterpretation," *Political Science Quarterly* 90 (Spring 1975): 23-69; Martin J. Sherwin, *A World Destroyed: The Atomic Bomb and the Grand Alliance* (New York: Knopf, 1975).

13. See, for example, Edmund Beard, *Developing the ICBM: A Study in Bureaucratic Politics* (New York: Columbia University Press, 1976).

14. Roberta Wohlstetter's brilliant analysis is replete with examples of the organizational process paradigm at work: *Pearl Harbor: Warning and Decision* (Stanford: Stanford University Press, 1962).

15. Allison, *Essence of Decision,* pp. 89-95.

16. Ibid., pp. 70-78.

17. Michael S. Sherry, *Preparing for the Next War: American Plans for Postwar Defense, 1941-1945* (New Haven: Yale University Press, 1977).

18. On Rickover, see Richard G. Hewlett and Francis Duncan, *Nuclear Navy: 1946-1962* (Chicago: University of Chicago Press, 1974). Two pre-1914 naval figures, Admiral von Tirpitz and Lord Fisher, enjoyed comparable sway as quasi-institutions; see Jonathan Steinberg, *Yesterday's Deterrent: Tirpitz and the Birth of the German Battle Fleet* (London: Macdonald, 1965); Volker Berghahn, *Der Tirpitz Plan: Genesis und Verfall einer innenpolitischen Krisenstrategie unter Wilhelm II* (Düsseldorf: Droste Verlag, 1971); Ruddock F. Mackay, *Fisher of Kilverstone* (Oxford: Clarendon Press, 1973).

19. Joachim Remak, "The Healthy Invalid: How Doomed the Habsburg Empire," *Journal of Modern History* 41 (June 1969): 127-143.

20. On the European reactions, see Luigi Albertini, *The Origins of the War of 1914,* trans. and ed. by Isabella Massey, 3 vols. (London: Oxford University Press, 1952-1957), II, chapters 5-6; see also Steiner, *Britain and the Origins of the First World War,* Chapter 9.

21. Samuel R. Williamson, Jr., "Influence, Power, and the Policy Process: The Case of Franz Ferdinand, 1906-1914," *Historical Journal* 17 (1974): 417-434. See also Robert A. Kann, *Erzherzog Franz Ferdinand Studien* (Vienna: Verlag für Geschichte und Politik, 1976), pp. 15-25.

22. Quoted in Maurice Muret, *L'archiduc François-Ferdinand* (Paris: Éditions Bernard Grasset, 1932), p. 172.

23. See, for example, Robert A. Kann, *Kaiser Franz Joseph und der Ausbruch des Weltkrieges* (Vienna: Hermann Böhlaus Nachf., 1971).

24. See Robert A. Kann, "Erzherzog Franz Ferdinand und Graf Berchtold als Aussenminister, 1912–1914," *Mitteilungen des österreichischen Staatsarchivs* 22 (1969): 246–278, reprinted in Kann, *Franz Ferdinand Studien*, pp. 206–240. See also Hugo Hantsch, "Erzherzog Thronfolger Franz Ferdinand und Graf Leopold Berchtold," *Historica* (Vienna: Herder, 1965), pp. 175–198.

25. The best study of the Balkan wars remains E. C. Helmreich, *The Diplomacy of the Balkan Wars, 1912–1913* (Cambridge: Harvard University Press, 1938); see also Albertini, *Origins*, I: 365–578.

26. The normal, peacetime strength of the army was just over 400,000. For a summary of the measures, see Helmreich, *Diplomacy*, pp. 461–462.

27. Williamson, "Franz Ferdinand," pp. 427–429. Conrad had been ousted by Franz Joseph in November 1911. for his recall in December 1912 the archduke paid a price: General Auffenberg, the war minister and a "nonfavorite" of the emperor, was ousted. On Berlin's views in December 1912, see the important new article by John C. G. Röhl, "An der Schwelle zum Weltkrieg: Eine Dokumentation über den 'Kriegsrat' vom 8. Dezember 1912," *Militärgeschichtliche Mitteilungen* 1 (1977): 77–134.

28. On Franz Ferdinand's views, see the diary entries for May 2 and 5, 1912, in the Berchtold diary, Memoiren des Grafen Leopold Berchtold, Politisches Archiv I/carton 524 b, Haus-, Hof-, und Staatsarchiv, Vienna [hereafter cited as P.A.I.]. On the demobilization issue, see Wilhelm Deutschman, "Die militärischen Massnahmen in Österreich-Ungarn während der Balkankrieg, 1912–13," unpublished Ph.D. dissertation, University of Vienna, 1965, pp. 207ff.

29. Diary entries, October 11–12, 1913, Berchtold diary, P.A.I./carton 524a; Kann, *Franz Ferdinand*, pp. 231–232.

30. Tschirschky to Bethmann Hollweg, July 2, 1914, reprinted in Imanuel Geiss (ed.), *Julikrise und Kriegsausbruch 1914*, 2 vols. (Hannover: Verlag für Literatur und Zeitgeschehen, 1963), I: 65–66.

31. Franz Ferdinand had by late 1913 come to distrust Conrad's judgment and loyalty. Both men expected Conrad to be replaced as chief of the General Staff during 1914.

32. Schiessl (head of Franz Joseph's cabinet chancellery) to Berchtold, July 16, 1914, Kabinetts Archiv: Direktionsakten/carton 19, haus-, Hof-, und Staatsarchiv; also in *Österreich-Ungarns Aussenpolitik von der bosnichen Krise 1908 bis zum Kriegsausbruch: 1914*, ed. by Ludwig Bittner and Hans Uebersberger, 9 vols. (Vienna: Österreichischer Bundesverlag, 1930), VIII, No. 10317 [hereafter cited as Ö.U.A.]. See also Moritz Auffenburg-Komarów, *Aus Österreichs Höhe und Niedergang* (Munich: Drei Masken Verlag, 1921), pp. 256–259.

33. The failure of the policy apparatus in Vienna to assess the Russian danger with care and caution, especially after the experience in 1912, remains a continuing mystery. It is possibly a nearly classic case of misperception—or self-delusion. For two recent works on Russia and views of Russia, see Risto Ropponen, *Die Kraft*

Russlands (Helsinki: Edidit Societas Historica Finlandiae, 1968); and Andrew Rossos, "Russia and the Balkans, 1909-1914," unpublished Ph.D. dissertation, Stanford University, 1971.

34. Fischer, *Krieg der Illusionen,* pp. 684-699. See also his *Germany's Aims in the First World War* (New York: Norton, 1967), pp. 50-92; Imanuel Geiss (ed.), *July 1914: The Outbreak of the First World War: Selected Documents* (New York: Scribner's 1967), pp. 54-76, 89-101; Albertini, *Origins,* II: 124-137. Cf. Sidney B. Fay, *The Origins of the World War,* 2 vols, (New York: Macmillan, 1930 ed.), II: 183-223.

35. See, for example, the Anglo-French discussions during July 1914, in Williamson, *Politics,* pp. 343-367. For an influential study of alliance politics after 1945 see Richard E. Neustadt, *Alliance Politics* (New York: Columbia University Press, 1970).

36. Norman Stone, "Moltke-Conrad: Relations between the Austro-Hungarian and German General Staffs, 1909-14," *Historical Journal* 9 (1966): 201-228; Horst Brettner-Messler, "Die militärischen Absprachen zwischen den Generalstäben Österreich-Ungarns und Italiens vom Dezember 1912 bis June 1914," *Mitteilungen des österreichischen Staatsarchivs* 22 (1970): 225-249; and Paul G. Halpern, *The Mediterranean Naval Situation, 1908-1914* (Cambridge: Harvard University Press, 1971), Chapter 8.

37. See F. R. Bridge, *Great Britain and Austria-Hungary, 1906-1914: A Diplomatic History* (London: Weidenfeld and Nicolson, 1972).

38. On Austro-German rivalry in the Balkans, see Dörte Löding, "Deutschlands und Österreich-Ungarns Balkanpolitik vom 1912-1914 unter besonderer Berucksichtigung ihrer Wirtschaftsinteressen," unpublished Ph.D. dissertation, University of Hamburg, 1969; on Austro-Russian relations, see Bridge, *From Sadowa,* Chapter 7.

39. Fischer, *Krieg der Illusionen,* pp. 226-241; Helmreich, *Balkan Wars,* pp. 236-248.

40. For one example of the pressure, see Moltke to Conrad, February 10, 1913, in Conrad von Hötzendorf, *Aus Meiner Dienstzeit,* 5 vols. (Vienna: Rikola Verlag, 1921-1925), II: 144-147.

41. Berlin knew of the ultimatum only hours before its delivery, Stolberg to Auswärtiges Amt. (tel.), October 17, 1913, Johannes Lepsius et al (eds.), *Die grosse Politik der europäischen Kabinette, 1871-1914,* 40 vols. (Berlin: Deutsche Verlagsgesellschaft für Politik, 1922-1927), XXXVI (pt. 1), No. 14170. The ultimatum was telegraphed to the Habsburg minister, Stephan von Ugron. late on the seventeenth, Ö.U.A., VII, No. 8850.

42. On Austro-German relations, see Bridge, *From Sadowa,* pp. 360-368; see also his "*Tarde venientibus ossa:* Austro-Hungarian Colonial Aspirations in Asia Minor, 1913-14," *Middle Eastern Studies* 6 (October 1970): 319-330; Erwin Hölzle, *Die Selbstentmachtung Europas* (Frankfurt: Musterschmidt Göttingen, 1975), pp. 269-278; and Hugo Hantsch, *Leopold Graf Berchtold: Grandseigneur und Staatsman,* 2 vols. (Graz: Verlag Stryria, 1963), II: 520-539.

43. Hantsch, *Berchtold,* II: 557-569; Kann, *Franz Joseph,* p. 16.

44. No files on the Szápàry trip have yet been located. On its origins, see Berchtold to Franz Ferdinand, January 13-14, 1913, Nachlass Franz Ferndinand, carton 9,

Haus-, Hof-, und Staatsarchiv; Conrad to Berschtold, January 10, 1913, P.A.I./carton 493; and Conrad, *Aus meiner Dienstzeit,* III: 77–79.

45. Fritz Fellner, "Die 'Mission Hoyos,'" in *Recueil des travaux aux Assises scientifiques internationales: Les grandes puissances et la Serbie à la veille de la Première guerre mondiale* (Belgrade: Assie scientifiques de l'académie serba des sciences et des arts, 1976), p. 392.

46. Berchtold and Tisza had carried on a steady, if covert, struggle over the control of foreign policy since August 1913. It had, however, grown more noticeable in the months before Sarajevo; see Hantsch, *Berchtold,* II: 549–569. Their contest provides an interesting, still unexplored example of "bureaucratic politics."

47. The revised memorandum, dated July 1, 1914, and the letter, dated July 2, 1914, are reprinted in *Ö.U.A.,* VIII, No. 9984.

48. Albertini gives a complete summary, *Origins,* II: 133–150. See also Hoyos's own account, reprinted in Fellner, "Die 'Hoyos Mission,'" pp. 411–418.

49. Fay, *Origins,* II: 223.

50. E.g., Taylor, *Struggle for Mastery,* pp. 522–523.

51. Lee, *Europe's Crucial Years,* pp. 382–386; Albertini, *Origins,* II: 159–160.

52. Bernadotte E. Schmitt, *The Coming of the War 1914,* 2 vols. (New York; Scribner's 1930), I: 393.

53. On the problem of convincing Tisza, see Norman Stone, "Hungary and the Crisis of July 1914," in Walter Laquer and George Mosse (eds.), *1914: The Coming of the First World War* (New York: Harper and Row, 1966), pp. 147–164; see also Schmitt, *Coming of the War,* I: 345–355.

54. For example, Tschirschky to Bethmann Hollweg, July 14, 1914, reprinted in Geiss, *July 1914,* pp. 114–116; and Berchtold to Szögyeny (tel.) July 15, 1914, ibid, pp. 116–117.

55. Albertini, *Origins,* II: 170–175. On the consipiracy itself, the most recent work is Friedrich Würthle, *Die Spur Führt nach Belgrad: Die Hintergrunde des Dramas von Sarajevo 1914* (Vienna: Verlag Fritz Molden, 1975).

56. No systematic study on this policy exists, but it is briefly discussed in "Die Ernteurlaube," *Streffleurs Österreichische Militärische Zeitschrift* 1 (1909): 685–686.

57. See the General Staff memorandum, "Vorbereitende Massnahmen," n.d., but seen by Conrad, July 6, 1914, Generalstab: Operations Bureau, Faszikel 43, Kriegsarchiv, Vienna. On Conrad's general activities in early July, see his *Aus meiner Dienstzeit,* IV: 13–87. I am indebted to Dr. Kurt Peball of the Kriegsarchiv for generous assistance on this and other research matters.

58. Allison, *Essence of Decision,* pp. 138, 141.

59. The most recent summary of explanations for Conrad's actions are in Norman Stone, "Die Mobilmachung der österreichisch-ungarischen Armee 1914," *Militärgeschichtliche Mitteilungen* 2 (1974):67–95.

60. Truman's memoirs, based on the National Security Council papers, give the best account: *Memoirs by Harry S. Truman,* 2 vols. (Garden City, N.Y.: Doubleday, 1955–1956), II: 124–126.

7
Theories of Escalation

Richard Smoke

ESCALATION IS A TOPIC VAST IN SCOPE AND COMPLEXITY: so much so, indeed, as almost to rival in these qualities the very fields, diplomacy and war, from which it derives. In the general sense in which it is commonly used, escalation (and deescalation) represent a basic dimension of both fields, and apply, actually or potentially, to virtually every real or hypothetical event that war can suggest, and to most that diplomacy can suggest. Any war, any diplomatic crisis, almost any situation, even of low level or potential conflict among nations, can be, and often is, discussed from the viewpoint of whether it could escalate. In the entire domain of international relations, in fact, the sole area in which people do not commonly discuss escalation is that class of relations that involves only cooperative endeavor. As soon as present or potential conflict enters a situation, so does the actuality or possibility of escalation.[1]

The breadth and omnipresence of this subject has made it a difficult one to study systematically; and indeed, until fairly recently, it would hardly have occurred to anyone to do so. The topic automatically took place so central in the arts of diplomacy and war that no one tried to separate it out for independent study. The classical military writers, such as Jomini and von Clausewitz, touch upon it everwhere and nowhere. It is part of the very stuff of their subject matter. If possible, the same has been even more true in the field of diplomacy (which, anyway, tended to be handed down more in the form of vicarious experience than of theorization or doctrine). Intensifying or mitigating diplomatic conflict, or setting the stage to do so by way of forming or modifying *de facto* or formal alliances, was simply what diplomacy was all about. Traditional thinking in both diplomacy and war saw no reason to isolate something as pervasive as escalation.

What changed things, evidently, was the enormous elevation in the level of possible destruction which came with nuclear weapons. The spectrum of possible escalation—the potential escalation "ladder," as it came to be called—was frightfully extended by Hiroshima and Nagasaki, and perhaps even more terribly extended by the invention of the hydrogen (fusion) bomb.

162

After the latter invention particularly, it became possible, even easy, to visualize the wholesale destruction of an entire society, perhaps of all of civilization.[2]

The extreme to which the escalation dimension of warfare had suddenly gone drew attention to it. And the imperative necessity of preventing this kind of annihilation compelled theorists to disinguish clearly between *escalation* in war, which in its more severe forms simply could not be permitted, and war itself, which inevitably would recur time and again.

This at least seems the likely explanation why escalation, never really isolated for study previously, was now identified and received attention as a problem in its own right. In any case it is a historical fact that the term "escalation" was first used, not just by military theorists in the post–World War II era, but by that special class of *civilian* military theorists, or "national security specialists," as they came to be called, who made it their business to study the novel properties and conditions of war in the nuclear era. Virtually all the important early work in escalation theorizing (to be reviewed momentarily) focused either on nuclear war itself, or on lower level conflict between the nuclear superpowers or their immediate proxies which might develop into a nuclear confrontation.

This work appeared in the late 1950s—at which time the term "escalation" was coined—and early 1960s. The Cuban missile crisis of October 1962, which was indeed a confrontation between the nuclear superpowers, made the word part of nearly everyone's vocabulary. Even before this, however, the term was being rapidly generalized to apply to any kind of warfare, however remote from nuclear confrontation, a usage universalized during the long, slow intensification of the Vietnam War. As used now for years by specialists and public alike, escalation may occur during intense diplomatic crises as well as in war; indeed, in almost any kind of conflict. To a significant degree, however, the way specialists in military and international affairs have thought about escalation has continued to be influenced by the fact that the first theorizing on the subject sprang from the danger of nuclear war. Let us explore the sources and context of escalation theory a little more deeply.

The Development of Escalation Theory

The roots of contemporary theorizing about escalation, at least in English, spring from the American experience in the Korean War. In the years immediately following World War II, it had been taken for granted in the United States that "the next war" would be even larger and more devastating. Presuming some sort of Soviet attack on Western Europe, war plans called for atomic bombing of the Soviet industrial plant and other war-making capabilities, followed by a grand remobilization and reliberation of

163

Europe on the World War II model. So strong was this presupposition that when South Korea was first attacked, in June 1950, and even for some days and weeks thereafter, the dominant perception in Washington was that this was probably a Soviet feint, and a principal response was to reinforce *Europe* against the expected main attack there.[3] When this did not happen, and when Korea remained a "small," localized war and did not trigger a much larger conflict even after sizable quantities of first American, and subsequently Chinese, troops were committed, American specialists found themselves faced with a kind of war which their previous thinking had not encompassed. Coping with its implications, as well as with the implications of an unexpectedly early Soviet A-bomb test the previous year, led to the first major theorizing about escalation, as well as about deterrence and other major topics in "national security affairs," during the decade following.

I have highlighted this genesis of escalation theorizing, because it illuminates the great emphasis that this theorizing was to give to the novelty of escalation, deterrence, etc. under Cold War conditions. It also illuminates the abstract, *ahistorical* character of the theorizing itself. To the diplomatic historian, for instance, it is not necessarily obvious why the Korean War should be seen as such a novel and unique occurrence. There have been plenty of other examples of Great Powers engaging less than their full capabilities against each other, in a geographically localized theater, sometimes with one or more other nearby Great Powers diplomatically but not militarily engaged. It would be entirely natural, from this perspective, to see the Korean War as another of a number of instances of this kind of conflict, every one of which (not just Korea) had had its own unique features. If, in addition, one is interested in going on to theorize about actual or potential escalation in this kind of situation, one presumably would want to note similarities and comparisons among a number of such cases.

But this is definitely not the way that theorization about escalation actually developed. Although such cases had occurred before, they had not occurred in *American* diplomatic and military history; nor during the lifetimes or personal experience of the theorists.[4] In living memory the American experience had been one either of grand conflict with other Great Powers for grand objectives (viz., the two worlds wars) or of minor actions to get rid of nuisances (e.g., Mexicans in 1916). Korea was nothing like these. Korea turned out to be surprisingly costly, painful, and long lasting; yet for all the effort expended, it proved frustrating, unproductive in its results, and dangerous to some unknown degree. How close had we really come to a world war with Russia? To nuclear war? Why hadn't these things happened? Would they happen the next time a war like Korea broke out? Or was there something about this kind of conflict that kept it "controlled," or at any rate controllable if one tried? How large can a "little" war get before restraints are dropped? How does one know if a war is in imminent danger of "going nuclear''? These, and not comparisons to other wars in other eras, were the questions that were asked as the 1950s proceeded, the Korean experience sank in, and the Russian atomic stockpile grew.

The result was the development of a literature on what was soon called "limited war." Some theory, or at any rate some concepts, emerged, as specialists understandably focused on what Korea could teach us about keeping limited wars limited in the nuclear age. *Limits on war,* their source, nature, and strengthening, became the principal topic on the intellectual agenda as we moved into an era in which likely enemies had nuclear weapons.[5]

The concepts of a war "arena" and of geographic sanctuaries, as two devices to keep a war confined, readily suggested themselves from the Korean experience. Fighting had been held to the peninsula and its immediate air and sea environs, and had not been allowed to extend itself to, for instance, the Formosa Straits, across which the Chinese Communists wished to complete, and the Nationalists to reverse, the revolution so recently accomplished on the mainland. Japan had remained a sanctuary for the United Nations, and Manchuria for the Communists, despite the enormous value and relative vulnerability of each to the enemy. The Yalu River had been strictly respected by the United Nations as a limit to its operations, even in the air, despite the repeated appeals of its own military in the field to be allowed more flexibility.

Such appeals, and in particular the publicly voiced demand by General MacArthur to carry the war into China, suggested to theorists the importance of firm civilian control in a limited war. Strictly military considerations should not be permitted to determine the basic strategic decisions that helped determine the scope of such a war. The determination of what geographic limits might be politically feasible for the enemy, as well as oneself, required a diplomatic judgement that transcended military factors. (We will return to this issue later.)

Similarly, some kinds of strategic decisions regarding the tempo of operations, weapons used and not used, and other such matters might also have to be made with an eye to their impact on the enemy's political perceptions. Theorists suggested the idea that some form of visible moderation in *methods* could reinforce verbal declarations of moderate *objectives.* Conversely, military steps that could seem highly threatening to the enemy might undercut diplomatic protestations of moderate objectives and encourage him to enlarge the war. Just this, some argued, had probably occurred in the wake of the Inchon landing in the fall of 1950. MacArthur's powerful drive northward could have appeared to the enemy to be aimed at utterly vanquishing the North Koreans as a fighting force, suggesting that the real American objective was not to repel the invasion of the South, as publicly stated, but the conquest and reunification of the peninsula under a single, anticommunist regime. This objective was, very probably, intolerable to the Chinese. To the extent that they

165

interpreted MacArthur's aggressive deployments and tactics as indicating that this was the real U.S. goal, his decisions may have been a principal cause of their massive intervention in November.[6]

Besides concepts of arena, of sanctuary, of civilian "political" planning and control of scope and methods, and of moderation in means as a way of communicating moderation in objectives, limited war theorists of the 1950s also concluded (in part from the Korean experience and in part from more general considerations) that the only way of preventing, with any confidence, a non-nuclear conflict from spiraling into an all-out nuclear war was for no nuclear weapons to be used at all. This was by no means as obvious an idea at the time as it appears to us now. In the 1950s the United States enjoyed a great superiority over the USSR in both numbers of, and ability to deliver, atomic weapons—as well as considerable superiority in many other categories of military power, except sheer numbers of men in uniform. Many argued that American use of "a few" nuclear weapons in a Korea-sized war could demonstrate to the Kremlin (widely assumed to be master of all communist aggression) that the United States "meant business," whereupon the Soviets and their proxies would back down. The 1950s, furthermore, was the time at which "tactical nuclear weapons" were first being developed. Before the end of the decade, atomic arms packaged for use in the field were entering the U.S. inventory in quantity, some of them not much larger in explosive yield than the largest conventional bombs and shells. The argument was put forward that this continuity in explosive force between the high end of the conventional spectrum and the low end of the nuclear, meant that nuclear arms were becoming "just another weapon." The United States, it followed, should exploit its superiority in this technology to prevail quickly in a limited war rather than let the war drag on painfully as in Korea.

Against this, the limited war theorists had to argue vigorously the escalation danger of any use of nuclear weapons. U.S. technical superiority in this field would decline, they predicted, as the Soviets strove rapidly to develop their own weapons and means of delivery, for battlefield and theater nuclear warfare. (In fact, this did occur.) Even at the moment, American superiority was far from absolute. The USSR did possess bombs, and bombers for delivering them, both locally around its periphery and against Western Europe, Japan, or the United States itself, in retaliation. Furthermore, atomic weapons were felt by most people to be indisputably very different in their strangeness and horror from conventional arms. Hence, politically they *were* different, however moderate in explosive power some of them might be. Once the "firebreak" between conventional war and nuclear war was breached, the conflict would become extremely dangerous and extremely unpredictable. No one could really know what a war would be like in which atomic weapons were exploding and each side had more to use. Perhaps it could "get out of control" and erupt into all-out strategic nuclear strikes at the superpowers' homelands. The danger was too great to take a chance.

As the 1950s faded into the 1960s this point of view, probably the most important contribution of early escalation theorizing, largely prevailed in American strategic thinking. The frightening experience of the Cuban missile crisis in 1962 and the relentless growth in Soviet military power year by year reduced the earlier plausibility of nuclear operations and encouraged a consensus around the orginally controversial firebreak concept. Even now, though, the desirability of "tactical nuclear war," at least in some situations, has its proponents and attracts another flurry of interest when new technical advances appear, such as the class of weapons sometimes called "mini-nukes" developed in the 1970s.[7]

Meanwhile, an important advance in the pure theory of limited war and escalation had been made in a series of articles by Thomas C. Schelling that appeared at the end of the 1950s.[8] Schelling, an economist by training, was a specialist in the field of mathematics called game theory, and pioneered a new branch of the field, the theory of "non-zero-sum games." Such a game (also called a "mixed motive game") occurs when two players find themselves partially in cooperation with each other. The application was directed to limited war, where the adversaries desire to defeat each other, yet to cooperate tacitly in holding their competition within constraints. Since there is almost never communication or explicit negotiation between the two sides over the "ground rules" of a war, Schelling pointed out, the bargaining is tacit—by the moves each side makes. Each wants ground rules that will be advantageous to itself, or at least not disadvantageous, but each also wants rules that *both* sides can find acceptable, or else the war will not remain limited for long. The problem, as Schelling defined it, is one of "coordinating expectations" of the two sides about feasible limits. "The best choice for either depends on what he expects the other to do, knowing that the other is similarly guided."[9]

Using mathematics and close reasoning, plus some laboratory experimental gaming reminiscent of research in gestalt psychology, Schelling demonstrated that stable solutions to the problem of coordinating expectations depend upon finding or creating what he termed "saliencies" in the situation. A saliency is a unique or special element that is objective enough and noticeable enough that both sides will notice it and can use it as a focus for their expectations. In one of Schelling's well known games, for instance, two opposing commanders are each ordered to seize as much as possible of a territory while avoiding contact with each other's forces. Prominent among the geographical features of the territory is a river that approximately but not exactly bisects it. Schelling was able to show that in the majority of cases the two commanders seized opposite sides of the river and avoided a clash, even though this left one of them in a somewhat inferior position.[10]

Geography provides many of the best saliencies, so long as the belligerents' behavior highlights and thus reinforces them. In Korea, for instance, the Yalu became a sharp limit because the United Nations respected it scrupulously, even in air operations. Had UN air forces engaged in no air battles north of the Yalu except with enemy aircraft of wingspan greater than forty feet, or even none except with enemy aircraft capable of carrying atomic bombs, the limit being "offered" might or might not have registered clearly with the communists. But *no* air operations north of the Yalu *at all* signaled an intention that could hardly be misunderstood. The most effective saliencies are simple. "There is little room [says Schelling] for fine print."[11] Again, in its air operations over North Vietnam, fifteen years later, the United States strictly forbade its pilots to fly over the Chinese border, and to make sure they did not do so even accidentally, also ordered a ten-mile strip of North Vietnamese territory next to the border off limits to American warplanes. The North Vietnamese quickly took advantage of this safety zone to store war matériel, but even so Washington denied requests from the field to make air strikes there, because it was more important to make sure that no incident might occur that could cause the Chinese to misread American intentions regarding the war's limits.

Saliencies do not have to be geographic. Thus, no gas was used on the battlefields of World War II, not even by Hitler, because each side feared that crossing the simple saliency "no gas" with even a few relatively mild gas attacks might leave no clear barrier against use of the far worse gases, including nerve gases, that both sides knew the other possessed.

The concept of saliencies, in essence a more elaborate and refined version of the "firebreak" idea, has proved to be the most important contribution to date to limited war and escalation theory. It has also proved to be a useful starting point for additional theorization. In most wars, the situation will provide not one but a number of possible geographic and other saliencies. A more violent war, proceeding within "wider" or "roomier" saliencies, might still be limited compared to all-out nuclear warfare, and might be preferred by one belligerent who might believe, for instance, that his forces would enjoy a relative advantage at a higher level of violence, or that his society could better bear the cost.

Here we arrive at escalation proper, as opposed simply to limited war. Saliencies are not only limits. They are also thresholds in the process of escalation. Unless one belligerent chooses suddenly to breach all the conflict's limits and launch an all-out attack, the escalation of the war proceeds by steps—unilateral steps taken one after another by one side, or more likely counterescalating steps taken back and forth by both sides against each other. Typically, each step is taken partly in the hope that it will be the last: that the war will restabilize at that level. (Else, why stop there?) The same logic of finding or creating a saliency upon which both sides can coordinate expectations applies to the new step just as to the conflict's original limits. Saliencies are not only potential stopping points, but also potential thresholds. They are at once barriers and steppingstones.

This plausible conception, also pioneered by Schelling, has come to dominate escalation theory, so prevasively indeed that it often is not articulated. Today the implicit model of escalation most common in discussions of the subject assumes that any given war possesses, in addition to whatever is the currently ongoing level of conflict, a series of more or less discrete levels of larger, more violent potential conflicts, each of which defines a limit to the war before it is reached and an escalatory step when it *is* reached. These levels of potential conflict may be visualized as a ladder up which the conflict climbs rung by rung, or as a set of concentric spheres each of which holds the flames of war for a while, until they burn it through and expand to the next sphere. Of course, some rungs or spheres can be skipped—sometimes called "preemptive escalation."

This conception reached its fullest elaboration in Herman Kahn's book, *On Escalation: Metaphors and Scenarios* (1965).[12] In this, the best known book to date devoted entirely to escalation (as Schelling's are not), the conception is set forth as a formal, general model. Kahn, originally a physicist, presents an escalation "ladder" stretching from a preconflict, background tension or "Cold War" situation at its base, up to all-out "spasm war" at the top in which the superpowers mindlessly fling all available atomic weapons at each other's homelands. Kahn defines six major thresholds along the way, of which one is the vital firebreak between nonuse and first use of nuclear weapons. Each of these thresholds, in turn, is broken down into some half-dozen or more smaller steps that Kahn asserts would be identifiable and potentially useful in most of the relevant situations. Thus his escalation ladder has a total of 44 rungs, and most of the book is devoted to discussing in some detail the properties and potential significance of each of these rungs. The great majority of them, 30 in all, concern some kind or other of nuclear warfare between the superpowers, and hence can be discussed only hypothetically.[13]

Recent Escalation Theorizing

We have moved a long way from diplomatic history. Yet the sequence of thought presented so summarily here roughly reproduces the main trend of escalation theorizing in the contemporary period up to the mid-1960s. Beginning with a predisposition to see the Korean War as *sui generis* and to see nuclear weapons opening an entirely new historical era, specialists proceeded into the realms of escalation with the approach of theoreticians, not historians.[14] Extracting what "lessons" they could from Korea, they turned mainly to abstract reasoning, mathematics, and the description and structuring of hypothetical situations—not the real past of diplomatic and military relations among nations—to build escalation theory. The two major contributors to the theory, whose influence still dominates it, hailed from disciplines far removed from history and used historical instances rarely

(Kahn) or "as illustrations, not evidence" (Schelling).[15] The inevitable result is a body of escalation theory that is mainly abstract, deductivistic, a priori, and ahistorical.

To some extent this was unavoidable and even, in a sense, desirable—at least at first. Since Hiroshima and Nagasaki can tell us relatively little, history does not have much to offer (except by questionable analogies) to the specialists who is concerned with the special properties and problems of nuclear war. And it was not unreasonable for the first generation of theorists to concentrate their attention on nuclear war, the supreme danger at all times, especially during the tense years of the Cold War. Theorists then did not know, as we do now, that nuclear weapons would not be used again for decades at least. And it was probably thanks in part to their efforts that the weapons have not been used (especially their effort to identify the prerequisites of a stable nuclear deterrent balance).

By the middle of the 1960s the main bulk of this important work had been accomplished. Some of the first generation of theorists (including both Schelling and Kahn) departed national security to work in other fields. Other specialists, especially those who were more involved with practical United States policy making, were drawn into the interminable and imponderable morass of Vietnam, or later, into the almost equally interminable and imponderable morass of SALT. The momentum of the main trend in escalation theory faded, and little more of the same kind has been done in the years since.[16]

Instead, a modest countertrend began developing in the 1960s, as yet not nearly as widely influential, but quite distinguishable. Concluding that most of what could be done on the basis of pure theorization had probably been done, some political scientists and other specialists who were receptive to the values of the past began to explore what diplomatic and military history could offer. This was also the time when the starkly bipolar Cold War, to which two-person game theory logic seemed most applicable, was dissolving into a more complicated multipolar world, in which local political factors and other theoretically messy details played a larger role. These scholars wished to test, refine, extend, and as necessary modify the accepted theoretical ideas by examining them somewhat systematically in the light of past realities; they also wished to develop new ideas via an approach not yet much used—empirical *inductive* research. This countertrend is discernible across the whole field of national security studies from the mid-1960s to the present. In the area of escalation theory, it took the form of examining how escalation had occurred in major wars of the fairly recent past.

Both George Quester, in several chapters of his book *Deterrence Before Hiroshima* (1966), and Fritz Sallagar, in his book *The Road to Total War* (1975), studied the gradual escalation of strategic air strikes by Britain and Germany against each other's homelands in the opening years of World War II.[17] On the basis of empirical analysis both ended up emphasizing, not the distinctness of the "rungs" of the escalation ladder, but just the reverse—the gradualness of the war's expansion, the ease with which intellectually clear limits could be smudged in practice, and the realistic possibility that policy makers could enlarge the conflict without their fully realizing what they were doing. Both authors also emphasized the importance of the political context of any given escalation decision; that is, the perceived meaning of a step in terms of the circumstances, perceptions, and preconceptions of each side at that moment, as opposed to the logical relationship of multiple steps across time. However, the use of an escalatory move as a means of signaling motivation or intentions, another major theme of the earlier literature, did receive some confirmation in these World War II studies.

Communications and decision making during the crisis that led to World War I were studied by Ole Holsti. In his book *Crisis Escalation War* (1972), Holsti used mathematical techniques to assess the quantities, and some of the attributes, of messages flowing into the main capitals at different times during the prewar crisis.[18] Correlating these with decision makers' perceptions of hostility, as measured by their own messages and other behavior, he was able to show that as the amount of incoming information grew, the decision makers were less and less able to cope with it. In particular they tended, under stress and time pressure, to single out threats from the spectrum of incoming information, and to deemphasize or overlook indications of conciliation or other possibilities than escalation and war. Holsti also drew comparisons with the Cuban missile crisis of 1962, suggesting that the relatively few messages and considerable time available during this crisis were helpful in keeping it controlled.

Holsti's study of the 1914 case is unusually apropos for contemporary escalation theory in that its theme, although drawn from well before the nuclear era, is peculiarly relevant to nuclear confrontation or war. Specialists presume that the "typical" intense nuclear crisis (unlike the Cuban missile crisis) would move very rapidly. Only a very days, perhaps only hours, might pass between the onset of acute crisis and its threatened escalation to nuclear warfare. Under conditions of even greater stress and time pressure than occurred in the summer of 1914, wouldn't decision makers be likely to perform at least as poorly? In this instance, the "irrelevance" so often claimed for prenuclear history is upended: a serious problem in earlier times must be presumed to be potentially even more worrisome now. As Holsti points out, the policy implication seem clear that decision makers would do well both to slow down crises as much as possible, and to do all they can in advance to improve their crisis information-handling and decision-making procedures.[19]

These examples suggest that historical studies of escalation may be most useful when they avoid direct comparison of the technical military or diplomatic aspects of past crises with real or hypothetical present ones, and instead concentrate on decision making and some kinds of political analysis. It is hard to argue convincingly that we will learn much from the German 1917 escalation to unrestricted submarine warfare that will help us to deter or counter the Soviet submarine fleet in a Persian Gulf crisis in 1983. It is easier to show the similarity over time of factors in the logic or psychologic of decision and decision-making processes, or of various *types* of political influences. Having shown this, one can also go on to study how *variations* in these factors from one case to another may suggest analytic conclusions that may be relevant to all situations where these factors appear.

The scope of this chapter does not permit an analysis of the latter kind. Comparisons among historical case studies which have been structured to bring out significant yet manageable variance in interesting variables is a relatively advanced technique—which is discussed by Alexander L. George in his contribution in this volume. In a topic area as complicated as escalation, a large body of information must be presented and analyzed before one can arrive at anything very interesting. The scope of this chapter does, however, permit a demonstration of an interesting similarity between a nineteenth- and a twentieth-century case. It concerns one of the traditional issues in escalation theory—namely, the relation between "political" and "military" factors—as they appear both in the logic of escalation decisions and in the decision-making processes that typically occur within governments. The remainder of this chapter is devoted to sketching two cases from diplomatic history in sufficient detail to try to demonstrate the significance and some of the implications of the issue.[20]

Bismarck and the Franco–Prussian War

When the Franco–Prussian War broke out in July 1870, Otto von Bismarck, the chancellor of the German confederation, took pains to see that other Great Powers would remain uninvolved.[21] During the weeks immediately following, there was little threat of this, but after the great German victory in the battle of Sedan early in September, Bismarck became concerned about the danger of foreign intervention. This would most likely have taken the form, in the first instance, of offers of mediation by one or more Great Powers, but these could have been backed at some point with a threat of armed intervention if the offers were declined. And it was unlikely that peace terms out forward by mediating powers would much resemble Bismarck's war objectives.

Meanwhile, the German General Staff had not forgotten Bismarck's "interference," as they had perceived it, during the Austro–Prussian War four years earlier. They were determined that this time he not be allowed to interject himself into what they regarded as purely military decisions regarding the details of strategy and tactics. To protect themselves, the generals began to try to draw a definite line between what they believed were "military" matters and what they saw as "political" affairs. They excluded Bismarck from the General Staff's daily planning session when the basic operational decisions were made, and they also consistently refused his requests for current information about German and enemy force deployments and German operations in progress, among other important matters.

Bismarck could not accept the validity of this position. He insisted, as did Clausewitz, that war was an instrument of civilian policy. Bismarck maintained that chance events, or the nonmilitary implications of a battle lost or won, or the acceleration of deceleration of military operations, or other things, might change perceptions and incentives in ways of which the General Staff might be unaware. Infuriated at his being excluded from military decision making, he quarreled constantly with the generals, including the Chief of Staff, von Moltke. But the generals' policy did not change. For much of the autumn and early winter, the foreign minister and his staff were reduced to trying to get the information they needed from contacts among lower ranking officers and news correspondents, and from reading the brief and out-of-date military communiques in the German newspapers.[22]

In opposition to the staff's attempt to draw a sharp dividing line between military and political affairs, Bismarck argued that no identification of "the purely military" was possible. Among other things, he pointed out that the General Staff was not qualified by itself "to judge whether and with what motives the neutral powers might be inclined to assist the adversary, in the first instance diplomatically and eventually by armed force." He argued that judgments about how the international context surrounding the war might alter to one's detriment, as well as judgments about war objectives, and everything involved with making peace, belonged preeminently to the "responsible political minister."[23]

A specific instance of a policy error resulting from the generals' attempt to draw a clear dividing line soon came to light. Emperor Napoleon III, who had been personally leading the largest French army, surrendered after the disastrous battle of Sedan on September 2. Another French army was besieged in the fortress of Metz and did not surrender until October 27. During the intervening seven weeks, Bismarck tried to find ways of combining the surrender of the fortress with a possible capitulation by France as a whole. The Imperial army bottled up in Metz was still bound by its oath of loyalty to Napoleon, and would not necessarily follow the orders of the new Government of National Defense that had been formed in Paris to replace the Imperial regime. Bismarck hoped to secure agreement to give up the provinces of Alsace and Lorraine from the Empress Eugenie, who had fled to England and could act as the Imperial government-in-exile. In return for this, the Germans would end the war immediately, free the army at Metz, and allow it to march on Paris under Eugenie's command to reestablish the Imperial government. In the end these negotiations came to nothing. But while they were under way the German General Staff placed various obstacles in Bismarck's path, of which the most striking was a very long delay, ostensibly on "military" grounds, in granting a safe-conduct pass to a subordinate French general at Metz who had gone to London to see Eugenie, so that he could return to the fortress. The staff wanted Bismarck's negotiations to fail, substantially because they intended to give Germany complete military security for several years to come by capturing or annihilating all organized French forces. The idea of letting a large French army go free did not square with their conception of military security.

Bismarck was furious. On the one hand, he was seriously worried about the short-term danger of a wider war and wanted to end the conflict quickly; on the other, he was thinking farther ahead than several years and wanted an Imperial government in Paris because he thought it would necessarily be a weak one. He was unable to persuade the General Staff that these considerations outweighed the ones they were emphasizing. He also did not think he should have to convince them, for his considerations turned on the kind of diplomatic and political judgments which he and his ministry, not they, existed in the government to make.[24]

However, Bismarck did not take the position during the ongoing conflict with the General Staff that political and military aspects of events and problems during warfare are mutually inseparable and intermingling. Instead he took the position, in effect, that whenever military and political considerations clashed, the political must always outweigh the military. In a sense, then, he accepted the generals' attempt to draw a line between military and political affairs, and differed with them only by placing political consideration above—superior to or subsuming—military ones. This doctrine also led, a little later in the fall, to a specific policy error. In November, the Russians took advantage of the turmoil in Western Europe to announce their unilateral abrogation of the "Black Sea Clauses" of the treaty that had ended the Crimean War some fifteen years before. These clauses, essentially forbidding Russian naval activity on the Black Sea, had been imposed mainly at British insistence, and now the outcry in England, including demand for military action, was tremendous.

Bismarck's anxiety about the danger of a general European war mounted still higher. To try to end the war in France as quickly as possible, he demanded that the German forces, which now surrounded and were besieging Paris, start to bombard the city and its protective forts with artillery fire. Unanimously, except for von Roon, the German generals opposed this strongly. An intense argument went on at headquarters for weeks over the bombardment question. The General Staff believed that the operation would be costly, but Bismarck was so anxious by now that he volunteered to pay for it out of chancellery funds so it would not appear in the military budget.[25] The generals pointed out, though, that costs in casualties and in destroyed artillery from the French counterfire could not be made up so easily. In addition, the staff estimated that under the circumstances a bombardment would probably be ineffective in military terms: conditions were such that it would be likely to do only modest damage to the enemy's military capabilities. Nor did they believe it would be any more coercive to the Parisian populace than approaching starvation was already. For all these reasons the generals flatly refused the foreign minister's demands. "Against this obstructionism [writes one historian] Bismarck mobilized the resources of public opinion, and soon German newspapers were demanding an attack on Paris and popular songs were composed to encourage Moltke to begin the shelling of the city."[26] Finally, King Wilhelm overruled the General Staff and the bombardent began on December 27. But the Parisians surrendered a month later, not because of damage to the city or to its forts, but because of hunger. The General Staff had been correct.[27]

The doctrine of the supremacy of political over military factors which Bismarck advocated was almost as simplistic as the military's effort to draw a sharp dividing line between them, and to define an inviolate "military sphere." Apparently Bismarck did not appreciate that however desirable a quicker end to the war might be, his policy argument logically depended also upon an estimate of the effectiveness of the specific measures that could be taken: if the concrete means at hand were inadequate, then the priority to be attached to the desired end became academic. And while the psychological effect upon the Parisians might at least have been arguable, the probable level of damage to be expected from the bombardment was something that the General Staff was best equipped to estimate.

Nor may one conclude that if only the estimated effectiveness of the strategy had been higher, or at least more uncertain, that *then* Bismarck's rule of the supremacy of political factors could have applied. For there was still the question of balancing the estimated costs to Prussia, in casualties and destroyed artillery, as well as in financial expenditures, against the possible benefits of—perhaps—shortening the war by a few weeks. The true calculus facing the German policy makers at this point was one in which political and military factors were married in such a way that they could not be simply divided, or judged by a single "decision rule" such as Bismarck's. On the one hand, the Germans needed to make an estimate of the danger of escalation implicit in a slightly longer war, combined with an estimate of the probability of shortening it by these means. On the other hand, they needed to make an estimate of the various costs of shortening it, plus an estimate of the probability that this action might itself inspire the sort of involvement by outside nations that Bismarck was trying to avoid. There were difficult and necessarily uncertain political and military factors on both sides of the scales.

Kennedy, McNamara, and the Cuban Missile Crisis

In recent times many governments, agencies, and decision makers have developed a greater awareness of the need for coordinating political and military perspectives. A large number of coordinating committees, interdepartmental groups, and other formal devices to link military and civilian agencies exist in the American and most other governments. Official manuals, and not just scholars' analyses, use "politicomilitary" as a single word. Even so, some deep divisions remain.

An episode that occurred during the tense days of the Cuban missile crisis illustrates this.[28] The American government discovered that Soviet missiles were being emplaced in Cuba on Wednesday, October 16, 1962. Shortly thereafter President Kennedy formed an Executive Committee of the National Security Council, generally called "the ExCom," to determine what the American response should be. By the following Sunday the President had decided upon a naval blockade of Cuba rather than the major alternative, air strikes against the missile sites and related targets on the island. On Monday evening, this was announced publicly, and the blockade went into effect Wednesday morning, the twenty-fourth.

The previous evening, the twenty-third, the British ambassador attended an ExCom meeting and put forward the suggestion that the blockade line be moved closer to Cuba. As currently planned, he pointed out, it was so far from the island (about 500 miles) that Soviet ships en route to Cuba and possibly carrying missiles or other proscribed matériel would meet U.S. warships very soon. By bringing the blockade closer to the island, the Americans could give the Kremlin more time to decide what it was going to do. President Kennedy, who had recently read Barbara Tuchman's book *The Guns of August* about the outbreak of World War I and who was trying in various ways to increase the time available to both sides, agreed instantly and issued the appropriate orders, over navy objections.

The following day, Wednesday, as the blockade was going into effect, Secretary of Defense Robert McNamara realized that not just the location of the line, but also many other details of how the operation would be carried out, could have an impact on Soviet behavior or perceptions. The action of boarding Soviet vessels, for instance, could appear belligerent or relatively restrained, depending on how it was done. Navy officials had given a general briefing to the ExCom on how the blockade would be put into effect, but McNamara wanted to know more. For example: Would each of the intercepting United States vessels have a Russian-speaking officer on board? What exactly would be said, and done, if a Soviet captain permitted his vessel to be boarded but refused to allow its hold to be inspected?

With questions like these in his mind and with his deputy in tow, McNamara visited the navy *sanctum sanctorum,* the Flag Plot (command room), in the depths of the Pentagon. He promptly put a long series of very detailed questions to the Chief of Naval Operations, Admiral George Anderson, in front of other officers. Admiral Anderson was upset by this, and the conversation became heated. At one point the Admiral picked up a copy of the *Manual of Naval Regulations* and shouted, "It's all in there." At another point, McNamara lectured the Admiral on the President's intentions in ordering the blockade: the primary object was not to prevent Soviet ships from reaching Cuba but to communicate a message to the Kremlin. Finally the conversation ended, with McNamara only partially satisfied in his questions, and with the Admiral remarking while saying goodbye, "Now Mr. Secretary, if you and your deputy will go back to your offices the Navy will run the blockade."[29]

Even so, the civilians who were trying to manage the crisis exercised an unprecedented degree of control over the operation. Maps in the White House basement Situation Room tracked the location and movements of Soviet ships approaching Cuba. The members of the ExCom knew the ships by name and debated which ones should be stopped, and when. There is indirect evidence that some were allowed through the blockade without public comment. Certainly the White House was cutting through the normal chain of command and the principle of local commanders' autonomy, to direct the operation on a ship-by-ship basis.[30]

At the same time, the political decision makers never did gain the degree of control over U.S. military operations in the crisis that they wanted. Graham Allison has pointed out that the President's order to pull the blockade line in closer to Cuba was not promptly carried out. The Soviet-chartered ship *Marcula,* for instance, was stopped by American destroyers and boarded, along the original blockade line, 500 miles out from Cuba.[31] To be sure, the *Marcula* was the first ship to be boarded. But this event did not occur until around 8:00 A.M. Friday morning, almost 60 hours after the President had given the pullback order. Although verifying details are mostly classified, it is clear that in this and other respects the spirit and to some extent the letter of the ExCom's instructions were not carried out. To what extent this was due to practical infeasibility, such as the navy simply not being able to reposition its blockading destroyers fast enough, and to what extent it was due to the military commanders being unused to receiving detailed operational orders from the highest political levels (and to some extent unwilling to do so), will be impossible to ascertain until the military archives are opened.

On the basis of available evidence, however, it seems likely that some of the delays and some of the military's inability to carry out the original wishes of the political decision makers resulted from ignorance among the latter concerning military necessities and procedures. No reasonable number of questions addressed to officers could provide the policy makers with enough information to "fine-tune" the operation as totally as they might wish, or as escalation theory might recommend. Inevitably, the thousands of men and scores of far-flung ships and other units involved acted, and had to act, in accordance with the Manual (that is, with standard naval procedures and routines for this kind of operation). The orders from the White House came like a series of rapier thrusts plunging down into this vast and well drilled body of doctrine and procedure, and the contradictions had to be worked out by lower- and middle-ranking officers as best they could. Except in the most blatant cases, time pressure and overworked communications channels prevented these officers from sending explanations of the necessities, and requests for revised orders, back up to the political decision makers—and some orders were probably disobeyed.

In short, political and military considerations in managing the crisis became inextricably intertwined, with neither the military fully comprehending the political motives (such as "signaling" correctly to the Russians) behind the ExCom's "interference" in the blockade operation, nor the political decision makers fully comprehending the military necessities, if the operation was to go forward successfully at all. Fortunately, sufficient time was available and sufficiently few real blunders were made, that the enormous threat of escalation was avoided.

Comparing the Cases

Not too much should be expected from any comparison of the two simple cases reviewed here. The negotiations with Empress Eugenie and the argument over the bombardment of Paris in 1870–1871, and the argument with Admiral Anderson and some retention in practice of the 500-mile blockade line in 1962, appear from the diplomatic historian's viewpoint as relatively minor episodes in their respective dramas, which had little effect on the outcomes. But if things had been a little different, perhaps they could have had more effect. The negotiations with Eugenie might have developed; the first ship to be boarded at the 500-mile line might have been boarded too soon, before the Soviets had worked out a moderate response to American policy. In any case, of interest to the escalation theorist are any suggestive similarities in the dynamics of these cases' development, not the role of any particular event in determining outcomes.

Diplomatic historians might be interested in these similarities as well. The roles of Bismarck and McNamara in the two cases, for example, closely resemble each other. They acted from the same motive, a desire to prevent potentially dangerous, self-defeating escalation. And they faced the same difficulty in securing cooperation and information from ranking officers of the military, who failed to understand what this motive implied in practice. Probably the two men entertained very similar frustrations about "the military mind," yet the analyst, working with the advantage of hindsight, must conclude that in both cases something substantial must also be said for the military point of view.

Other interesting similarities between two cases so different in their circumstances and so far apart in time suggest, for the escalation theorist, some ideas about the relationship of political and military considerations. On the basis of two sketchy summaries these could hardly be called "conclusions," but they might become "hypotheses" for some more extensive study.

One, mentioned already, is that these factors tend to be intertwined in complicated ways, so that they cannot adequately be separated by means of organizational divisions within governments. Another is that the integration and synthesis of these factors into a single workable policy may be even harder to do in the midst of a full-fledged, intense crisis or during a critical, rapidly shifting phase of a war than one would expect normally. Third, the amount of time available is likely to be crucial. And finally, in the absence of a real integration of political and military considerations, a rough, somewhat jumbled mix of the two will probably result from the almost completely *ad hoc* processes that take over during intense crises.

None of these ideas is especially new to theorists of escalation or "crisis management." Yet comparisons of recent instances where these problems appeared with historical instances may provide new perspectives of value. For instance, the General Staff proving partially correct in its disputes with Bismarck could remind analysts to reexamine what military viewpoints may be too readily discounted today. The problematical effects of quite necessary navy standard procedures could remind historians of the importance of such mundane matters in past crises. And at a minimum, the striking similarity of two instances, presented even as sketchily as here, gives us a strong indication that the familiar problems of integrating political and military elements in the contemporary era are not an artifact of contemporary conditions, but are deeply imbedded in the nature of government and the dynamics of conflict. When two episodes nearly a century apart resemble each other so markedly, one may conclude that the problems involved are fundamental.

Notes

1. The first portion of this chapter draws heavily upon my recent book, *War: Controlling Escalation* (Cambridge: Harvard University Press, 1977), especially Chapter 1. Some of the issues and arguments considered briefly here are treated in more detail there.

2. It would be more difficult to do this using Hiroshima-sized fission weapons than nonspecialists commonly believe. But with fusion weapons of a hundred to a thou-

sand times the power, the popular image of the "end of civilization" becomes entirely plausible.

3. There is an extensive literature, analytical as well as historical, on the Korean War. Bibliographies listing most of the important works appear following chapters 6 and 7 of Alexander L. George and Richard Smoke, *Deterrence in American Foreign Policy: Theory and Practice* (New York: Columbia University Press, 1974).

4. An exception might be the Spanish Civil War, where military forces of several Great Powers did engage each other in a geographically localized theater, without triggering a world war. But the forces involved had been small, far smaller than in Korea, and had not included opposing infantry.

5. An exhaustive listing of this sizable literature is not feasible; a valuable annotated bibliography to that which appeared prior to 1963 is given in Morton H. Halperin, *Limited War in the Nuclear Age* (New York: Wiley, 1963), itself an important contribution. Any listing of the most influential works (prior to the contributions of Thomas Schelling, which we will take up momentarily) would certainly include the following: Bernard Brodie, "Unlimited Weapons and Limited War," *Reporter* (November 18, 1954): 16-21; "More About Limited War," *World Politics* 10 (October 1957): 112-122, and *Strategy in the Missile Age* (Princeton: Princeton University Press, 1959), Chapter 9; William W. Kaufmann, "Limited Warfare," in William W. Kaufmann (ed.), *Military Policy and National Security* (Princeton: Princeton University Press, 1956), and "The Crisis in Military Affairs," *World Politics* 10 (July 1958): 579-603; and Robert E. Osgood, *Limited War* (Chicago: University of Chicago Press, 1957).

6. Perhaps the best-developed version of the argument that political control of military means could reassure an opponent and help limit the war, appears in William W. Kaufmann's article "Limited Warfare." This is not to say that moderate objectives always lead to moderate means; since one or both sides commit very great resources and employ quite violent means, for fairly modest objectives. See, for instance, William W. Kaufmann's article "The Crisis in Military Affairs." This review article of Kissinger's *Nuclear Weapons and Foreign Policy* was the first widely influential statement to point out that limited objectives need *not* correlate with limited means or scope in war. Kissinger's book, asserting that limited objectives were the basic means of restraining escalation, repeated in this respect the conventional wisdom of the period, to be found in many other treatments of limited war during the 1950s. Kissinger's 1960 sequel, *The Necessity for Choice* (New York: Harper and Brothers, 1960), reflected development of the theory to include the recognition that this is not true. An assessment of plausible Chinese perceptions and calculations in the period just prior to their intervention in the Korean War appears in Chapter 7 of George and Smoke, *Deterrence in American Foreign Policy*.

7. "Mini-nukes" are nuclear weapons of low yield, often less than the largest conventional bombs. They are packaged to be not much larger or more difficult to handle than ordinary conventional bombs and warheads, and in some cases the explosive power ("yield") can be determined ("dialed") just before use.

8. The articles were gathered together into a well known book, *The Strategy of Conflict* (New York: Oxford University Press, 1963), and the ideas enlarged upon in a subsequent book, *Arms and Influence* (New Haven: Yale University Press, 1966).

9. Schelling, *Strategy of Conflict,* p. 87.

10. Ibid., p. 62.

11. Schelling, *Arms and Influence,* p. 137.

12. Herman Kahn, *On Escalation: Metaphors and Scenarios* (New York: Praeger, 1965).

13. The reader will have noticed that the evocation of a relatively large number of saliencies potentially undercuts the "simplicity" notion that was part of Schelling's original concept. It would be consistent with Kahn's approach, for instance, to count the difference between non-nerve gases and nerve gases as a "rung." To the extent that this distinction is introduced, it tends to vitiate the simplicity and power of "no gas" as a saliency. In any concrete case, knowing how finely differentiated one may safely become in one's tacit "offer" of war limits is largely a matter of knowing the opponent's military doctrine, decision-making presuppositions, and strategic style.

    The five other main thresholds described by Kahn are: "don't rock the boat" and "nuclear war is unthinkable" thresholds below "no nuclear use"; and "central sanctuary" (i.e., homelands), "general war," and "city targetting" thresholds above.

14. To be sure, there were important exceptions. Robert E. Osgood devoted a sizable part of his book, *Limited War,* to such wars in past centuries and an assessment of how conditions had changed in the nuclear era. To give a second example, William W. Kaufmann, who made important contributions to limited war theory in the 1950s, had been originally trained as a diplomatic historian. Despite these and other significant influences, I believe the argument presented here fairly summarizes the main trend.

15. Schelling, *Arms and Influence,* Preface, p. vii. This second book of Schelling's is relatively rich in historical material, but as the author says, mainly used illustratively.

16. Robert E. Osgood's "Reappraisal of Limited War," *Problems of Modern Strategy,* pt. 1, Adelphi Paper No. 54 (London: International Institute of Strategic Studies, 1969): 41–54, is an assessment of the strengths and weaknesses of contemporary understanding of this topic. Although his paper was published in 1969, the literature on limited war has developed so little since that time that it is almost equally relevant today.

17. George Quester, *Deterrence Before Hiroshima* (New York: Wiley, 1966); and Frederick M. Sallagar, *The Road to Total War* (New York: Van Nostrand Reinhold, 1975).

18. Ole Holsti, *Crisis, Escalation, War* (Montreal: McGill-Queen's University Press, 1972).

19. There is a rather large literature devoted to impediments to sound decision-making processes, and means of mitigating them. A substantial bibliography can be found in Alexander L. George (ed.), *Toward A More Soundly Based Foreign Policy: Making Better Use of Information,* Appendix D, vol. 2, *Report of the Commission on the Organization of the Government for the Conduct of Foreign Policy* (Washington, D.C.: Government Printing Office, 1975).

20. This concludes our survey of escalation theory. A few other works which deal fairly directly with escalation and contain at least some theory are touched upon in

Chapter 1 and Appendix 2 of Smoke, *War: Controlling Escalation*. Depending on how far one wishes to extend the borders of "escalation theory" the body of literature devoted thereto could, of course, be enlarged greatly. As discussed at the outset of this chapter, escalation is a pervasive phenemenon in war and most diplomacy, and a great deal of the literature in these vast fields could be considered relevant in one sense or another. In this chapter, though, I have preferred to confine the discussion to theory that deals directly and centrally with escalation, and to limited war theory, its almost indistinguishable, immediate precursor.

In *War: Controlling Escalation,* I have tried to undertake the analysis of bodies of information sufficiently large to permit the derivation of potentially interesting conclusions by the structured-comparison method.

21. My interest in the Franco–Prussian War derives in part from my use of that case as a chapter in *War: Controlling Escalation,* but the episodes and analysis presented here are not drawn from that chapter. A bibliography for that case is given in that work, pp. 371-373. The sources most used for information given here are: Gordon Craig, *The Politics of the Prussian Army, 1640-1945* (New York; Oxford University Press, 1955), pp. 204-216; Otto Pflanze, *Bismarck and the Development of Germany* (Princeton: Princeton University Press, 1963), pp. 462-468; and C. Grant Robertson, *Bismarck* (New York: Holt, 1919), pp. 282-286.

22. Craig, *Politics,* p. 205; Pflanze, *Bismarck,* p. 463. See also Otto von Bismarck, *Memoirs,* trans. by A. J. Butler, 2 vols. (London: Remington, 1887), II: 104-108.

23. Bismarck, *Memoirs,* II: 104-108.

24. Craig, *Politics,* pp. 206-208.

25. Bismarck, *memoirs,* II: 122-126.

26. Craig, *Politics,* p. 211.

27. I have somewhat oversimplified both this argument and the one about the surrender of Metz in order to emphasize my theme. Von Moltke's refusal to begin the bombardment, for instance, was also based in part upon his expectation that the fall of Paris would not be the end of the war; Bismarck correctly thought that at this point the French would surrender. In the Metz dispute, another factor was the German commander's apparent belief that Bismarck wished to deprive him of the glory of receiving the French commander's surrender.

28. The Cuban missile crisis is the most studied crisis of the contemporary era, and has accumulated a large literature. For a bibliography current through 1973, consult Chapter 15 of George and Smoke, *Deterrence in American Foreign Policy.*

29. This story is told by Elie Abel in his book *The Missile Crisis* (Philadelphia: Lippincott, 1966), pp. 154-156. It is repeated with amplifying contextual detail by Graham Allison in *Essence of Decision* (Boston: Little, Brown, 1971), pp. 129-132.

30. Allison, *Essence of Decision,* pp. 128, 130.

31. Ibid., p. 130.

8
Theories of Bargaining with Threats of Force: Deterrence and Coercive Diplomacy

Paul Gordon Lauren

BARGAINING WITH THREATS OF FORCE in international politics has occupied the thoughts of concerned scholars, philosophers, generals, and statesmen for centuries. Men and women have recognized that in a world where military power is always present, it is essential to understand both how to control and how to contain armed force. They learned long ago that, although highly dangerous, the attempt to gain objectives by threatening—rather than actually using—violence could save time, money, and precious human lives. For this reason, the history of relations between city-states, empires, and nations has been characterized by innumerable instances of threats designed either to deter or to coerce opponents. Since World War II the occurrence of such threats linked with nuclear weapons has led many observers to contend that today the main purpose of military power is not to be employed in war, but rather to be threatened and manipulated in peace.

As diplomatic historians, we have long known that these threats of force presented a common phenomena in international relations of the past. We know that in bargaining situations during crises states have threatened violence upon other states. They have insisted that unless their opponent agreed to stop encroaching or to give them what they wanted, they would resort to force. In any traditional textbook or monograph on diplomatic history we could find the simple facts of these historical cases. Here we could find descriptions of who made what demands upon whom, what actions were threatened, and what actually happened. This approach of the past, however, was largely descriptive rather than analytical. It is for this reason that we cannot find answers in most traditional works to some of the essential and fascinating issues which are also important to diplomacy, such as: What exactly is the nature of bargaining with threats of force? What is deterrence, and what are its various features? In coercion, does it make any difference what types of demands are placed upon an opponent? Are there certain aspects of threats that either facilitate or inhibit success? In general, these kinds of queries have not only remained unanswered by diplomatic historians but, even worse, they have not been asked.

In an effort to provide some answers to these questions, and to fill this gap, a number of contemporary theorists from the social sciences are analyzing the nature of bargaining rather than simply describing its effects. Together, they are helping to explain how states use threats of force to influence the calculations and behavior of others in international politics. The results suggest exciting new possibilities for diplomatic historians, theorists, and policy makers.

The Practice and Theories of Bargaining

Threatening to use force as a means of bargaining is as old as the arts of diplomacy and warfare themselves. Thucydides, writing his *Peloponnesian War* four hundred years before the birth of Christ, provides many examples of Athens and Sparta threatening to use their power as a means of influence. Any number of times, troops were mobilized and fleets were stationed in order to make others "think twice before attacking," thus deterring them from aggression.[1] Potential opponents were sternly warned in advance that if they launched a war, then they would be fiercely met "in any and every field of action" and thus incur considerable losses.[2] In a classic example of coercion, the powerful Athenians issued demands upon the weaker Melians, and threatened that failure to comply would result in complete devastation:

> You, by giving in, would save yourself from disaster . . . your actual resources are too scanty to give you a chance of survival against the forces that are opposed to you at this moment. You will therefore be showing an extraordinary lack of common sense if . . . you still fail to reach a conclusion wiser than anything you have mentioned so far. . . . Think it over again . . . and let this be a point that constantly recurs to your minds—that you are discussing the fate of your country, that you have only one country, and its future for good or ill depends on this one single decision which you are going to make.[3]

Similar examples could be found in the techniques used by Charlemagne, Richelieu, Palmerston, or Bismarck. As Frederick the Great once said: "Diplomacy without arms is music without instruments."[4]

In the past a number of writers and philosophers attempted to discover general principles of statecraft and to explore the role of threats of force. One of the earliest and most brilliant of these was Niccolò Machiavelli, whose own personal experiences in the realm of diplomatic negotiation always impressed upon him the intimate relationship between political and military factors. The classic pages of his *Art of War* (1521) and *The Prince* (1532) continually stressed that successful bargaining requires a thorough understanding of how armed force can be utilized as an instrument of policy.[5] Thomas Hobbes in *Leviathan*

(1651) emphasized the importance of the power of the sword in deterring aggression by "a Feare of the consequences"[6] and in providing "some coercive Power to compel men equally to the performance of their Covenants by the terror of some punishment greater than the benefit they expect by breach of their Covenant."[7] Similar ideas were discussed by Montesquieu in his *L'Esprit des lois* (1748).[8] Even the refined and restrained François de Callières who insisted that diplomats should be Christian men of peace rather than of war, maintained in *De la manière de négocier avec les Souverains* (1716) that every negotiator must "inform himself exactly of the state of the military forces both on land and sea" in order to understand the significance of pressure and thus be effective in persuasion.[9]

Beyond these general propositions of statecraft, however, there was little systematic theorizing about the nature of bargaining in international politics. The practice of coercion and deterrence was not accompanied by any explicit theory or elaborate conceptual framework. Statesmen and generals in the past simply based their actions on accepted conduct and common sense. They understood that if they were strong enough, they frequently could use threats instead of actual armed force to persuade opponents to modify behavior. This rather simplistic bargaining approach was reinforced by at least two factors. In the first place, if threats proved to be insufficient and tense relations unexpectedly escalated into violence, war was considered to be a perfectly legitimate instrument of foreign policy with limited costs. As one author writes, prior to 1914 war was "a part of the natural order of events" and was accepted "as both inevitable and expedient":

> By war, danger was averted, empire extended, and prestige enhanced. By war, reputation was maintained. Nor was this process considered a particularly ugly one. Armies were small, the devastation they caused was mostly limited to a narrow line of march and to battlefields which one man could survey at a glance. . . .
> [S]ociety, which provided the politicians and filled the salons with chatter, was hardly touched. . . . War was something that affected armies, not peoples: it was a political exercise, not a social and psychological catastrophe.[10]

Second, it was difficult to elaborate a sophisticated theory of employing threats of force when restricted technological capabilities prevented any sharp distinction from being made between the power to hurt and the power to destroy. From the time of the ancients to the first half of the twentieth century, it was essentially impossible to hurt an enemy seriously—to burn cities, ruin crops, seize property, and inflict pain—without first having defeated his military forces.[11]

This situation changed with the advent of strategic bombing. Military technology made it possible for the first time to hurt an opponent terribly before—or even without—destroying his armed forces. With the development of this possibility, the *threat* to hurt him could be separated—in fact, and therefore in theory—from the threat to engage and destroy his military capability.[12] This particular distinction, when coupled with the distinction between the threat and the use of armed force, appeared all the more important with the emergence of nuclear weapons and sophisticated delivery systems. The new extent of potential devastation convinced many strategists that war no longer could be considered a rational policy option as it had been throughout human history. A prescient book entitled *The Absolute Weapon* confirmed this attitude as early as 1946. In the words of its editor, Bernard Brodie:

> Thus far the chief purpose of our military establishment has been to win wars. From now on its chief purpose must be to avert them. It can have almost no other useful purpose.[13]

Thus, to avert nuclear war and yet maintain security in the context of the Cold War became a matter of vital concern to policy makers and scholars alike. The result has been an imposing body of theory created primarily by Americans and focusing primarily upon bargaining with threats of force.

Some of the first writers on the subject of bargaining utilized many of the concepts of game theory to analyze how interdependent actors in a highly decentralized international setting bargain with each other.[14] One of the most influential of these was Thomas Schelling, who wrote a pioneering work entitled *The Strategy of Conflict* (1960). This study revolved around the theme that "most conflict situations are essentially *bargaining* situations" and that a strategy for dealing with these should be concerned not "with the efficient *application* of force but with the *exploitation of potential force.*"[15] This thesis received fur*u*er amplification in Schelling's *Arms and Influence* (1966), in which he discussed how nations use threats of their capacity for violence as bargaining power. "To inflict suffering," he maintained,

> gains nothing and saves nothing directly; it can only make people behave to avoid it. The only purpose, unless sport or revenge, must be to influence somebody's behavior, to coerce his decision or choice. To be coercive, violence has to be anticipated. And it has to be avoidable by accommodation. The power to hurt is bargaining power.[16]

Additional work by Fred Charles Iklé in *How Nations Negotiate* (1964), Herman Kahn in *On Escalation* (1965), Klaus Knorr in *On the Uses of Military Power in the Nuclear Age* (1966) and *Military Power and Potential* (1970), and Oran Young in *The Politics of Force* (1968) and *Bargaining* (1975) elaborated even further on this use of potential power to influence behavior.[17] The most recent and ambitious study of bargaining is that written by Glenn H. Snyder and Paul Diesing entitled *Conflict Among Nations* (1977), which views bargaining as "the central element" of international behavior between sovereign states.[18] Collectively, attention in this area focuses upon various features of bargaining with threats of force, including the strategies and tactics of such bargaining, the importance of rational calculations among adversaries, communication (or signaling), the asymmetries of power and motivation, the deliberate manipulation of danger (or "risk taking"), and credibility to actually do what one threatens.

This concern about bargaining threats rather than the use of violence has been accompanied by a strong emphasis upon deterrence. Given the destructive capabilities and the "unacceptable costs" of nuclear weapons, many theorists and practitioners believed—and still do believe—that the first task of diplomacy and strategy should be to prevent rather than to wage war. Official American foreign policy designed to deter possible Soviet and/or communist aggression reinforced this particular attitude even further. For these reasons, a massive amount of literature resulted on the subject of deterrence. Early writings by Sir John Slessor (1953, 1955), William Kaufman in *Military Policy and National Security* (1956), Henry Kissinger in *Nuclear Weapons and Foreign Policy* (1957), Oskar Morgenstern (1959), Bernard Brodie in *Strategy in the Missile Age* (1959), and Albert Wohlstetter (1959) initially opened the field with strategical considerations and policy recommendations.[19] These were soon followed by more critical and theoretical work by Daniel Ellsberg (1960), Herman Kahn in his provocative *On Thermonuclear War* (1961), Glenn H. Snyder (1961), J. David Singer in *Deterrence, Arms Control, and Disarmament* (1962), Bruce Russett (1963, 1967), and Stephen Maxwell (1968).[20] The most recent and sophisticated studies include *Deterrence in American Foreign Policy: Theory and Practice* (1974) by Alexander L. George and Richard Smoke and *Deterrence: A Conceptual Analysis* (1977) by Patrick Morgan.[21] These scholars collectively address the issue of how states attempt to persuade opponents to refrain from initiating particular courses of action. This is done by threatening in advance that the costs of certain behavior might far outweigh any possible benefits.

Theories of bargaining with threats of force have also been employed to understand the nature of coercion. Building upon the earlier work of Schelling and Young in particular, scholars have concentrated upon states employing coercive bargaining tactics in order to resolve a conflict of interests. One of the most articulate and imaginative studies in this area is that of Alexander George and his colleagues entitled *The Limits of Coercive Diplomacy* (1971).[22] It is supplemented by the works of Daniel Ellsberg (1959), Glenn H. Snyder (1972), Robert Jervis (1972), Paul Gordon Lauren (1972, 1975), and most recently the book by Phil Williams, *Crisis Management: Confrontation and Diplomacy in the Nuclear Age* (1976).[23] These authors observe that, as a bargaining method, coercion relies upon the threat of inflicting harm to convince an opponent to revise his calculations and agree to a mutually acceptable termination of a dispute. "Coercive diplomacy," as described by George, "seeks to persuade the opponent to do something, instead of bludgeoning him into doing it, or physically preventing him from doing it."[24] Although much more dangerous than deterrence, because of its increased risks and greater demands, successful coercion still relies upon threats rather than the use of military force to achieve one's objectives. As Schelling succinctly states:

> There is a difference between taking what you want and making someone give it to you. . . . It is the difference . . . between action and threats.[25]

These very recent and valuable theoretical contributions have greatly expanded our understanding of the nature of bargaining in international politics. They have advanced our awareness of the role and limitations of threats of force, encouraged the analytical study of human behavior, and fostered the development of prescriptive recommendations for the actual formulation of policy. If only used by historians, it is possible that they may also contribute to an enriched and more sophisticated writing of diplomatic history. This may be seen with reference to historical cases first of deterrence and then of coercion.

Deterrence

Theories of deterrence stress the importance of bargaining with threats of force as a means of preventing a serious crisis. Deterrence attempts to persuade an opponent to refrain from initiating certain action, such as an armed attack,[26] that is viewed as highly dangerous by making him fear the consequences of such behavior. It tries to convince an adversary that the costs and risks of a given course of action that he might undertake will far outweigh any possible benefits. "To deter," observe Robert Art and Kenneth Waltz,

> literally means to stop someone from doing something by frightening him . . . dissuasion by deterrence operates by frightening a state out of attacking, not because of the difficulty of launching an attack and carrying it home, but because the expected reaction of the opponent will result in one's own severe punishment.[27]

In this kind of persuasion, the relationship between the protagonists is clearly psychological rather than physical. Deterrence tries not to destroy an opponent or to physically restrain him, but to affect his motivation or *will*. The strategy attempts to persuade him that his interests would be served best by not embarking upon a particular course of action.

By directing threats of force toward an opponent's will, therefore, deterrence attempts to influence his future behavior. The adversary is warned in advance that if he initiates action contrary to the wishes of the state practicing deterrence, he will suffer unacceptable consequences. In this situation of shared risk, the opponent is thus told that any pain or suffering is contingent upon *his* behavior, and that *he* is the one who must make the agonizing decision to proceed toward a clash. If he acts, then the threats will be carried out. If he does nothing, then he can avoid the threatened punishment indefinitely.

Schelling describes this strategy somewhat colloquially by having one state bargain with threats of force in the following words:

> If you cross the line we shoot in self-defense, or the mines explode. . . . If *you* cross it, *then* is when the threat is fulfilled, either automatically, if we've rigged it so, or by obligation that immediately becomes due. But we can wait—preferably forever; that's our purpose.[28]

In the language of the theorists, the deterring state must convince the opponent that it has both the will and the ability to inflict considerable damage upon something that the opponent values more than the possible benefits to be gained from initiating certain action, and thereby to persuade the opponent to refrain from such action against the deterring state.

The first problem of operationalizing this bargaining strategy, therefore, is to convince an opponent of one's determination and strength to enforce threats and thus to deter a particular course of action. In this process communication is of essential importance. Indeed, Oran Young describes communication as "the basis of all bargaining."[29] Some states attempting deterrence may prefer to communicate by essentially nonverbal means. This might include reliance upon past relations or historical traditions of self-defense, the existence of alliances for mutual protection, troops stationed along a border, ships deployed in nearby waters, or general strategic superiority in weaponry. Such actions may speak louder than words.[30] Nevertheless, there also may be certain disadvantages in permitting the politicomilitary context or structure of a particular situation alone to suffice for accurate communication. As Robert Jervis observes, many factors (rational or otherwise) influence perceptions and the images of adversaries in bargaining.[31] Thus, a state seeking to avoid these risks of misperception and ambiguity may reinforce actions with more precise and explicit verbal statements. This might include public speeches, formal diplomatic messages, or even personal letters between heads of state.

An understanding of these features of communication between states may help diplomatic historians to explain the nature and purpose of deliberate deterrent actions and words in the past. As a means of physically conveying resolve and strength, naval squadrons have been used frequently in history. Fearing another Russian encroachment in the eastern Mediterranean in 1853, for example, the British and the French sent a combined fleet to the Dardanelles specifically to communicate a threat and thus to deter anticipated military attack by Russia upon the Ottoman Empire.[32] Nearly one hundred years later and with the beginning of the Korean War, President Truman ordered the American Seventh Fleet to the Taiwan Straits in order to convey to the Communist Chinese that any aggression against the island of Taiwan would be met by force and thereby "prevent the conflict from spreading to that area."[33] Much more frequently, such actions have been preceded or accompanied by explicit verbal communication. With the approaching outbreak of the Franco–Prussian War of 1870–1871, Otto von Bismarck attempted to deter Austria–Hungary from supporting France by informing them that such behavior would result in 300,000 Russian troops on their eastern borders.[34] During the course of the Anglo–German naval race, the zealous and out-spoken British Admiral Sir John Fisher delivered a public speech explicitly stating his country's policy of deterrence:

> My sole objective is PEACE in doing all this! Because if you rub it in both at home and abroad that you are ready for instant war with every unit of your strength in the first line and intend to be "first in" and hit your enemy in the belly and kick him when he's down and boil your prisoners in oil (if you take any!) and torture his women and children, then people will stay clear of you.[35]

In order to be effective, of course, such communicated threats must have credibility. Deterrence requires that a state genuinely convince its adversary in advance that it does in fact have both the ability and the will to inflict con-siderable harm and/or to prevent the adversary from accomplishing his opera-tion by an effective defense. When the potential power to hurt is used as bargaining power, the threat will deter an aggressor only if it is believable and does not sound like mere bluster. Some threats are inherently credible, others must be made persuasive, and some are bound to appear like bluffs.[36] States possessing large amounts of military strength or those protecting their own national borders against invasion frequently can issue highly credible threats. The problem in achieving credibility for them is usually that of convincing the opponent that they have the motivation and will to use the ample capabilities and that they deem these capabilities appropriate for that kind of conflict. Weak states or those threatening to project their military force over other countries in defense of other objectives have a more difficult time in creating such credibility. They often have to emphasize their strong motivation to use their available capabilities and their willingness to pay a high price to protect their interests.

An awareness of the importance of credible threats may assist us in under-standing cases of deterrence in history. In terms of the *ability* of states to carry out their threats, a number of examples are available. Following the upheaval of the Napoleonic wars, Prince Metternich spent years as the Austrian foreign minister carefully trying to orchestrate the collective strength of the Concert of Europe in order to protect the balance of power and maintain the peace. The purpose of creating this "strong union of States," he wrote, was to deter "the storm" of possible aggression or revolution against the status quo.[37] Few doubted the physical strength of Austria or the other Great Powers. Indeed, it was that criterion that allowed them to use the designation of "great" in the first place. This matter of possessing enough power to enforce deterrent threats was recognized as well in Premier Nikita Khrushchev's famous 1960 speech to the Supreme Soviet. Emphasizing the importance of being able to deter an aggressor, he declared:

> The Soviet Army today possesses such combat means and such firepower as no ar-my has ever had before. I stress once again that we already have enough nuclear

weapons—atomic and hydrogen—and enough rockets to deliver them to the territory of a possible aggressor, and that if some madman should cause an attack on our state or on other socialist states, we could literally wipe the country or countries that attack us off the face of the earth.[38]

More recently, the members of the North Atlantic Treaty Organization debated this same issue in 1977 and 1978 with reference to the enhanced radiation weapon, or the "neutron bomb." Proponents argued that the weapon's instantaneous burst of intense radiation which destroyed people rather than buildings would make it less dangerous than existing tactical atomic warheads to friendly forces, and at the same time ideal for stopping a massive communist tank invasion against Western Europe. Such capabilities, in the words of one observer, would thus provide the ability to be "more credible as a deterrent to aggression."[39]

In addition to capabilities, credibility is a function of *will,* or intentions. A state attempting deterrence may have considerable physical power (which it is willing to threaten), but may be unwilling to use it. The employment of armed force escalates a crisis well beyond its verbal stages and may entail considerable costs.[40] When this becomes evident, it may erode the motivation of a state to enforce deterrent threats, and thus reduce credibility. Since the inception of NATO, for example, Europeans have worried over the question of whether or not the Americans would be willing to risk nuclear holocaust by defending territory thousands of miles from their own shores. Much of the discussion about obtaining independent capabilities for Britain and France, in fact, derived "from doubts about the readiness of the United States Government and the American citizens to risk the destruction of their cities on behalf of Europe."[41] This question of commitment continued to plague credibility and eventually prompted Defense Secretary Robert NcNamara, among others, to recognize the crucial importance of combining both strength and determination in deterrent threats. As he asserted during his 1968 "posture statement" to Congress:

> [It is] the clear and present ability to destroy the attacker as a viable 20th Century nation and an unwavering will to use these ["assured destruction"] forces in retaliation to a nuclear attack upon ourselves or our allies that provides the deterrent.[42]

Finally, any analysis of deterrence must also take into account what is demanded of (or, more appropriately, denied) an opponent and how this influences his motivation to refrain from initiating action. A deterrence posture may seek to deny an opponent something that he considers extremely important. This might include strategic strongholds, territory for expansion, oil wells, or wealth. A state strongly motivated to obtain such things by changing the existing order may calculate that to be denied these objectives is, for whatever reason, too high a price to pay. The threat against it may be well communicated and highly credible but, at the same time, insufficient to deter. An aggressor may calculate that, although the costs of launching a campaign might be high relative to the prospective benefits, they are acceptable. This concept is of crucial significance to deterrence theory, for as George and Smoke observe, it is the initiator's "utility calculation"—not that of the defender—that determines whether or not a challenge will be made against the status quo.[43]

Diplomatic historians may find these theoretical considerations of an initiator's calculations valuable in understanding certain attempts at deterrence in the past. In examining the potential costs and benefits of launching the Seven Weeks War, for instance, Bismarck valued the potential gains of eventual German unification more than the probable losses to be suffered at the hands of the Austrians. He certainly was not deterred from initiating his military campaign in 1866 despite troop mobilizations against him, and had spent months preparing for it in advance. Indeed, as Emperor Franz Joseph is reported to have said in frustration once he realized that his threats were insufficient: "How can one avoid war when the other side wants it?"[44] During the next century, the case of the Japanese attack on Pearl Harbor, in the words of Bruce Russett, "represents one of the most conspicuous and costly failures of deterrence in history."[45] Here again, the leaders of Japan valued the prospective benefits of empire more than the possible losses to be inflicted by the Americans. They were acutely aware that the United States had forged strong commitments to defend Southeast Asia from attack. Moreover, they knew that in terms of its military–industrial potential and its Pacific fleet, the United States possessed a very powerful deterrent capable of inflicting great harm. Nevertheless, the credible threat was not sufficient to deter when compared with the motivation to gain the objective. The Japanese calculated that to be denied vital strategic raw materials from Malaya and the Dutch East Indies would mean the end of their expansionist dreams and perhaps "national suicide." In this context, the costs of being deterred were deemed completely unacceptable, and Japan launched its attack.

Thus, the risks of bargaining with threats of force may be considerable. Unequivocal communication, determination, and capabilities do not provide guaranteed success. To threaten harm and punishment against another state may produce a preemptive strike or some other form of retaliation. These dangers exist not only in deterrence, but in coercive diplomacy as well.

Coercive Diplomacy

Theories of coercion also analyze how states bargain with threats of force. Unlike deterrence, however, which tries to convince an opponent not to initiate any harmful actions at all, coercion deals with action that is taking, or has taken, place. Deterrence tries to dissuade or *inhibit* behavior through fear. To deter, a state incurs an obligation to defend or digs in and waits—in the interest of inaction. Coercive diplomacy, by contrast, tries to *initiate* behavior by fear. To coerce, a state puts in motion a policy to make the other move—in the interest of action. It is the opponent who must act in order to avoid a collision.[46]

Another distinction between deterrence and coercion lies in the difference of purpose. Although each attempts to influence behavior, deterrence is a defensive strategy while coercive diplomacy can be either defensive or offensive in nature. Defensive coercion may be attempted, for example, to persuade an opponent to stop or undo an encroachment viewed as highly dangerous to peace. Its purpose clearly is to maintain the status quo. Offensive coercion, on the other hand, may be attempted to blackmail an adversary in an effort to make him give up something that he already possesses simply because it is easier to take it peacefully rather than by using force. It is important to make this distinction.[47]

Regardless of its particular purpose, successful coercive diplomacy re-quires that one state create in an adversary the expectation of unacceptable costs that will erode his motivation to continue whatever he is doing. Once again, coercion—like deterrence—tries to use threats not to harm an adversary physically or negate his capabilities, but to affect his will. It attempts to convince and to persuade. In this sense, coercion is in keeping with de Callières' advice years ago that

> every Christian prince must take as his chief maxim not to employ arms to support or vindicate his rights until he has employed and exhausted the way of reason and persuasion.[48]

This bargaining strategy attempts to persuade an opponent that his interests would be served best by changing the direction of his behavior. In the language of the theorists, the coercing state must convince the opponent that it has both the will and the ability to inflict considerable damage upon something that the opponent values more than the object of dispute, and thereby to persuade the opponent to take the kind of action desired by the coercing state. To operationalize this bargaining strategy, therefore, a state must begin by convincing the opponent of its determination and strength. This is the problem of credibility in intimidation. The aim is to communicate to the adversary the message that there is an asymmetry of motivation; that, for whatever reason, one's own propensity for creating and tolerating risks is by far the higher of the two. The potential power to hurt is used as bargaining power, as a means of making people behave to avoid it. Once again, the behavior of one is contingent upon the behavior of the other. Since neither side wants the conflict to end in disaster—and both sides are acutely aware of this fact—the coercing power must convince the opponent that *he* must be the one to turn aside if catastrophe is to be avoided. The adversary must be made to believe not only that one is unwilling to give way at the present level of conflict, but that one is ready and able to go even further if necessary.[49]

An awareness of this feature of coercive diplomacy may help diplomatic

193

historians to explain why some cases of coercion have succeeded and why others have failed in the past. In 1850, powerful and confident Great Britain attempted to coerce the much weaker state of Greece. The spirited Lord Palmerston demanded in ultimatum form that the Greek government settle certain damage claims within twenty-four hours or else face "coercive measures." He threatened that in the event of noncompliance "the Commander-in-Chief of Her Majesty's Naval Forces in the Mediterranean will have no other alternative (however painful the necessity might be to him) than to act at once."[50] The Greeks clearly understood that Britain had both the will and the ability to carry through on their threats and complied with the demands. Later, in 1939, Hitler successfully employed the same kind of coercion in connection with the invasion of Czechoslovakia. He summoned Czech President Hacha to Berlin and personally informed him that German troops had been given the order to march into Czechoslovakia. "The military operation," he said, "was not a trifling one, but had been planned on a most generous scale."[51] Prague would probably be destroyed and many Czechs would be killed. Hitler threatened that the only way to avert this catastrophe would be for Czechoslovakia to revoke its plans for armed resistance and deliberately permit the Germans to march in unopposed. An observer at the meeting recorded: "The Führer says that his decision is irrevocable. Everyone knows what a decision by the Führer means."[52] Hacha also possessed few illusions about the credibility of either Hitler's willingness or his ability to use armed force ruthlessly and, after initially fainting, capitulated.

Historical cases of failures of coercion demonstrate entirely different features of credibility. At perhaps the height of European colonialism, relatively weak South Africa attempted coercive diplomacy against Great Britain in 1899. Fearing the concentration of British forces along his borders, President Kruger of the Transvaal demanded that London take action to regulate all points of dispute by amicable means. In the event of noncompliance, he threatened a declaration of war and said that he could not be held responsible for the consequences. Britain ignored these threats and refused to modify its position. Coercion failed not because the Cabinet believed that the feisty Kruger lacked the determination to fight, but because it believed that he did not possess the strength to harm them.[53] By way of contrast, the Soviet Union attempted to coerce the West on several occasions from 1956 to 1958 with threats of newly obtained nuclear weapons. Each time Premier Khrushchev demanded that the Western powers pull back from their positions or reduce their stated commitments. In these instances, Khrushchev threatened to use his Medium Range Ballistic Missiles to knock NATO countries "out of commission" and emphasized that if war broke out between the superpowers, West Germany would have "no chance of survival."[54] These efforts of coercion seldom succeeded, in part because few people believed that the Soviet Union actually possessed the will to risk nuclear war and its own possible destruction over relatively peripheral issues.[55] The threat, in short, lacked credibility.

In coercive diplomacy, there is also the problem of persuading or compelling an opponent to do what one wants him to do. With the defensive variant of this strategy there are essentially two types of demands that can be made of an opponent. He can either (1) be asked to *stop* what he is doing, or (2) be asked to *undo* what has been done or to reverse what has already been accomplished. This distinction is, as Alexander George observes,[56] of considerable importance for the theory and practice of coercion. The reason should be obvious: the demand requiring an opponent to stop what he is doing asks appreciably less of him than a demand requiring him to undo whatever he has already gained at the cost of time, money, and perhaps even lives. Thus, the willingness—or the motivation—to comply with the demands in a particular case or coercive diplomacy can be considered in part a function of what is demanded.

This theoretical analysis may assist diplomatic historians to understand why, for example, the British coercion of the Soviet Union was so successful in 1923. Greatly disturbed by the continued and deliberate spread of communist literature in his country, Lord Curzon demanded that Moscow stop all of its propaganda activities or face a formal break in diplomatic relations. This demand asked very little of the Soviets and, within a matter of days, they complied.[57] An entirely different case occurred when Britain and France attempted to coerce Nazi Germany in 1939. After the invasion of Poland, they demanded that the territorial occupation of that country by Hitler's forces be undone and that all the German gains be renounced immediately. This price (when coupled with the problem of credibility on the part of the appeasers) was considered to be much too high for the ambitions of the Third Reich. Adolf Hitler therefore refused to comply, and the attempt at coercive bargaining failed.[58]

Persuading an opponent in coercion, note a number of theorists, may also be enhanced by combining certain incentives with the threats—or a classic "carrot-and-stick" approach.[59] A regrettable emphasis in the past upon demands and punishments in bargaining should not allow us to continue ignoring the essential fact that the presence of concessions is often a fundamental requirement for the management and resolution of conflicts. As one scholar clearly observes, "making threats is not enough."[60] In addition to limiting one's demands on an opponent, the inclusion of positive inducements may significantly encourage a settlement by reducing an opponent's disinclination to comply with what is demanded of him. There is, of course, an inherent incentive in that both the coercing and the coerced parties generally would prefer to avoid the mutually unpleasant consequences of an enforced threat. This particular inducement may not always suffice, however, and the very feasibility of coercive diplomacy may be dependent upon the inclusion of genuine concessions. According to Glenn Synder: "Accommodating gestures made concurrently with coercive tactics may defuse a confrontation of much of its emotional overtones of hostility, duress, and engagements of 'face.'"[61] During the tense Cuban missile crisis of 1962, for instance, the United States provided incentives to the Soviet Union in conjunction with its considerable threats. In a formal letter to Khrushchev, President Kennedy offered a *quid pro quo* in the promise that compliance with the demand for removing the missile bases would be rewarded by terminating the naval quarantine then in effect and with a guarantee against an armed invasion of Cuba by American forces.[62] Such an offer surely facilitated a peaceful resolution to the conflict. Few examples of these positive incentives in coercive diplomacy can be found, however, and this may help to explain why so many attempts at coercion have failed.

An Assessment of Theory and a Conclusion for Policy

These theories of deterrence and coercive diplomacy are able to teach us a great deal about bargaining with threats of force. They help us to understand how potential military strength has been—and still is—threatened in international bargaining either to prevent an attack or to resolve a serious dispute. With these theories we can become much more sensitive to the importance of containing and controlling violence, the significance of communication and credibility, the effect of threats and demands upon an opponent's will, and perhaps some of those elements that either facilitate or retard successful bargaining. An appreciation of these considerable contributions of theory, however, should not blind us to a number of serious hazards.

One of the problems with abstract and formal bargaining theory, for example, is its assumption of "rationality" in decision making. Theories of deterrence and coercion conceptualize an international contest between two hostile players, each of which tries to maximize its gains and minimize its losses by careful and rational calculation. This requires that the decision makers be capable of making correct and measurable calculations on the basis of a complex matrix of payoffs.[63] They must perceive, evaluate, and then assign relative weight to a large number of possible consequences that might follow from either their action or inaction. In this sense, successful bargaining with threats of force depends upon an opponent capable of rationally calculating that the threat is credible and that any possible benefits to be derived from an attack (in the case of deterrence) or from maintaining a particular position (in the case of coercion) will be far outweighed by the costs. Such a model of rationality provides a useful tool for deductive analysis and theory building, and certainly has the greatest acceptance within our particular culture.[64]

Nevertheless, a model of completely rational decision making remains highly abstract and divorced from the real world of human events. Historical experience, as well as recent scientific investigations into the subtleties and complexities of behavior, indicate that men and women do not always act in mechanical or logically consistent patterns like computerized circuitry. Indeed, when dealing with the stress of international crisis, threats of war, or imminent attack, decision makers may be highly susceptible to cognitive rigidity, shortened attention span, and limited perspectives of time.[65] Clausewitz, writing early in the nineteenth century, cautioned that abstract theory is always subject to those "modifications of practice" of real life. "No other human activity," he asserted with specific reference to war and violence, "is so continually or universally bound up with chance."[66] Bismarck similarly warned of the need for statesmen to appreciate the unforeseen and the incalculable, or what he called the "imponderabilia," of diplomacy.[67] What he and others recognized is that people have physical and psychological limits on their ability to think, to obtain accurate information, to recall detailed facts, to analyze, and to calculate. Decision makers are subject, individually and collectively, to impulses, emotions, misperceptions, pressures, competing demands, and highly subjective values and goals that cannot easily be placed in sterile cells on a neat matrix of possible outcomes. This problem has been recognized, in fact, by a number of theorists;[68] and has prompted one to state that, even after all of the analytical treatment, we still must remember that

> uncertainty exists. Not everybody is always in his right mind. Not all the frontiers and thresholds are precisely defined, fully reliable, and known to be so beyond the least temptation to test them out, to explore for loopholes, or to take a chance. . . . Violence, especially war, is a confused and uncertain activity, highly unpredictable, depending upon decisions made by fallible human beings organized into imperfect governments, depending on fallible communications and warning systems and on the untested performance of people and equipment. It is furthermore a hotheaded activity, in which commitments and reputations can develop a momentum of their own.[69]

Living in this kind of world, policy makers can achieve only a rough approximation of the requirements of abstract theory.[70]

This issue of rationality is related to another problem in theories of deterrence and coercive diplomacy: namely, the assumption that each side is a unitary player. Bargaining theories consistently adhere to the view that to deter or to coerce is to influence the decision making of a foreign government by means of threatening to use potential force. To understand and appreciate how threats actually influence behavior, therefore, it is necessary to know how such governments reach a decision in the first place. This is not an easy matter at all, for it is often extremely difficult to determine the precise manner by which a government makes decisions during international crises. Theories of bargaining, however, as George and Smoke observe, largely ignore this difficulty and simply presume that a nation can be compressed into a single, or unitary, decision maker.[71] "The player" perceives a situation, issues or receives threats that are interpreted on the basis of "the" national interest, purposefully calculates "his" possible gains or losses, and then selects a strategy that will maximize "the" government's payoffs.

Such a simplification does violence to reality as we know it. Historical accounts, as well as contemporary analytical treatments of decision making, demonstrate that a modern nation-state is certainly no monolithic or unitary actor. Instead, and as demonstrated particularly well by Graham Allison and Morton Halperin,[72] it is comprised of multiple actors representing many individual officials with their own bureaucratic positions or political careers to protect and many organizations or groups with different interpretations of "the" national interest in given situations. Consequently, foreign policy should be seen not as a unified decision, but rather as a "product of political bargaining among different groups and individuals with different interests, values, and objectives."[73] Decision making during international bargaining, therefore, should be analyzed from a variety of perspectives. At the individual level of analysis, one would examine the particular decision makers themselves, concentrating upon their abilities, weaknesses, perceptions, personalities, and "operational codes."[74] As the experience of the 1930s indicates, the failure of deterrence at that time hardly can be understood without reference to the personality of Adolf Hitler and the image that he held of himself and his opponents. At the group level of analysis, one would explore bureaucratic politics or the organizational process.[75] The coercive diplomacy of the United States against the Soviet Union during the Cuban missile crisis, as Allison demonstrates in his imaginative study, must be seen in the context of the influence of established bureaucratic routine and of the context of the political maneuvering of officials with diverse interests and unequal influence.[76] This task of analyzing the making of decisions is as important as it is difficult, for as Morgan perceptively observes, different conceptions of how governments make decisions, aimed at different levels of analysis, produce different images of bargaining, how it works, and what its chances are of success.[77]

Another problem with much bargaining theory is an almost exclusive emphasis upon conflict. Theories of deterrence and coercion view international politics as a fiercely competitive endeavor in which rival states struggle against each other in order to maintain their independence or extend their influence. Thus, bargaining is seen as a contest in which each side attempts to maximize its own gains at the expense of the other (or, in the expression of game theory, as a zero-sum situation in which the benefits accruing to one side automatically mean a loss for the opponent). The objectives are seen as manipulating or influencing an enemy's behavior by threats of superior military force, making him back down or capitulate, gaining concessions, and thereby furthering one's own ambitions in the international arena. With this

Hobbesian perspective of a world of "continual fear and danger of violent death,"[78] there is little conception of common interests uniting the protagonists, only of the conflicting issues that divide them.

Such an attitude represents a very limited view of the nature of international bargaining. Cases from diplomatic history and works by several political scientists show that any attempt to bargain entails elements of *both* conflict and cooperation. It is the conflicting issues that precipitate a clash, but it is the cooperative interests that encourage each side to bargain. "Without common interest there is nothing to negotiate for," observers Iklé, "without conflict nothing to negotiate about."[79] During most bargaining situations, this creates a kind of "adverse partnership"[80] in which each side tries to uphold essential national interests while at the same time experiencing a *shared* risk, a *mutual* desire to avoid the consequences of an enforced threat, and *common* interest (certainly in the nuclear area) to escape the disaster of war.[81] In this regard, future theories of deterrence and coercion might do well to investigate the importance of incentives or inducements in facilitating the bargaining process.[82] As Holsti suggests, if the purpose of threats

> is to convince the opponent that certain options are unacceptable and that he cannot improve his bargaining position by escalation, the role of diplomacy is to create a situation in which there are acceptable alternatives, and to persuade him that these are more compatible with his self interest.[83]

Attention to this matter clearly would be in keeping with the wisdom of de Callières, who advised that "the great secret of negotiation is to bring out prominently the common advantage to both parties" of a dispute, and who warned that any bargain which does not satisfy this condition "is apt to contain the seeds of its own dissolution."[84]

Perhaps this emphasis upon conflict rather than cooperation or inducements in most theories of bargaining explains why so much attention is devoted to threats of strictly military action at the expense of other possibilities. The literature on deterrence and coercion, as has been discussed, invarariably focuses upon the political or bargaining value of armed strength and physical power. The potential to hurt is seen in terms of military might, the cost in terms of physical punishment, and the final consequence in terms of war or peace. Hence, Schelling's popular and widely accepted expressions of "*arms* and influence" and "the diplomacy of *violence*."[85] Attention at one time might be upon the bargaining value of the *Dreadnought* battleship or numbers of ground forces, at another of the B-52 aircraft, or at still another of the American cruise missile or the Soviet Backfire bomber. In any ultimate contest of wills or strength, these weapons or others like them may have decisive influence and, in that sense, may warrant the attention bestowed upon them.

Nevertheless, as the richness of diplomatic history demonstrates, bargaining situations have occurred—and continue to occur—at a wide range of levels, not simply at the intense level of strategic conflict. Disputes arise over many different and complex issues, but most of these never approach the threshold of war. In fact, military attack does not appear to be a plausible contingency in very many cases.[86] Much more likely are instances of limited challenges, political probes, or controversies which have nothing to do with military considerations at all. For this reason, theorists and policy makers alike might be well advised to explore the possibilities of nonmilitary threats short of armed force. Diplomatic, economic, and psychological measures, for instance, can be threatened in varying combinations and sequences with differing degrees of intensity. In order to influence adversaries and yet avoid the clash of arms, statesmen of classical diplomacy utilized threats to withdraw from negotiations, to terminate commercial agreements, to break diplomatic relations, to establish an embargo, or to launch a propaganda campaign, among other sanctions.[87] More recently, the Organization of Petroleum-Exporting Countries has demonstrated the effects of threatening economic sanctions against the industrialized nations of the world. A recognition of these gradual and differentiated measures may encourage more sophisticated theories of deterrence and coercion to consider the possibilities of a more flexible, careful, and specific tailoring of threats to fit the unique configurations of each bargaining situation, rather than an automatic and exclusive reliance upon military might. Such refined distinctions may become increasingly important, for as armed force becomes less and less usable, other kinds of threatened sanctions become all the more critical.

Finally, an assessment of bargaining theories must also consider the potential dangers for policy. By making the assumptions and simplifications just described, some theories of deterrence and coercive diplomacy may lead policy makers into believing that they in fact readily and fully understand how theats can be made to work. If this occurs, and if officials take comfort in prepackaged analyses, as Harold Wilensky writes, there may be serious hazards:

> T. S. Eliot once spoke of a world that ends "not with a bang but a whimper." What we have to fear is that the bang will come, preceded by the whimper—a faint rustle of paper as some self-convinced chief of state, reviewing a secret memo full of comfortable rationalizations just repeated at the final conference, fails to muster the necessary intelligence and wit and miscalculates the power and the intent of his adversaries.[88]

This problem exists with the application of any theory, but it appears to be particularly acute with the beguiling and seductive features of deterrence and coercion. When compared with military strategies, bargaining with threats is understandably attractive. Threats are infinitely more palatable than the actual use of force. If successful, they achieve policy objectives with much less money, less bloodshed, fewer psychological and political costs, and less risk than strategies that rely directly and exclusively upon using force to influence behavior.

These favorable and encouraging features, however, should not be allowed to distract us from the inherent limitations and very serious dangers of bargaining with threats of force. The intimidation of threats tends to clash easily with the restraints imposed by domestic traditions and procedures, crisis management and foreign opinion, moral principles, and (however frail and rudimentary) the precepts of international law.[89] Bargaining is a highly competitive and dangerous process with threats, manipulations, and counterthreats. Each side has certain objectives for which it is willing not only to tolerate, but also to create, risks of possible war. These risks produce uncertainties that often cannot be entirely controlled by the protagonists. Threats may provoke anger, frustration, pride, suspicion, or a desire for revenge which, in turn, may lead to highly emotional rather than calculated behavior. The threats of one side may be regarded with contempt and thus not treated with the seriousness they deserve. Or, one state might overestimate its own ability to persuade and dangerously underestimate the opponent's disinclination to yield. The seriousness of these risks can certainly be seen in the careening outbreak of World War I, as the diplomats stumbled and the troop trains rolled, and clearly were recognized by Khrushchev when he wrote in fear to Kennedy during the intense bargaining over the missiles in Cuba. "The more the two of us pull the tighter the knot will be tied," he said. "And a moment may come when that knot will be tied so tight that even he who tied it will not have the strength to untie it."[90]

A closely related problem is that of possible escalation when bargaining with threats of force.[91] Although threats may make an adversary more accommodating, as is their purpose, this is far from a foregone conclusion. Threats, by their very nature, excite rather than inhibit tensions. Thus, they may easily boomerang or precipitate a chain reaction. One side can prevail by increasing its threats only if the opponent does not do the same. If, on the other hand, each protagonist matches any threat by the opponent with an equivalent or even greater threat of its own, serious complications arise. As described by Clausewitz long ago: "Each side, therefore, compels its opponent to follow suit; a reciprocal action is started which must lead, in theory, to extremes."[92] Each increase up the escalation ladder dangerously heightens the level of tension and inexorably raises the stakes for both sides. "Finally," in the words of Williams,

> they may reach a point where each side's commitment of prestige and resources becomes so great that it calculates that it cannot afford to back down. The expectation that the adversary will capitulate is replaced by the decision that the adversary must capitulate.[93]

When this occurs, control and flexibility in bargaining are significantly diminished, if not reduced completely.[94]

These several dangers become all the more acute when one considers the problems of achieving the necessary preconditions for success and of actually

201

operationalizing the strategies of deterrence or coercive diplomacy.[95] Successful deterrence requires some combination of the following: that an aggressor view a defender's commitment as credible, believe that his risks are incalculable and his options are not controllable, and perceive that the defender possesses adequate capabilities and sufficient motivation to employ them. Similarly, successful coercion requires that the state being coerced be made to believe that there is an asymmetry of motivation favoring the coercing state, clarity of objectives, usable military options, and sufficient fear of unacceptable costs on the part of the opponent, among many other conditions. To determine whether these appropriate conditions exist, and to measure accurately the calculations, motivations, or fears of each side in an international dispute, however, is an extremely difficult—if not impossible—task. Historical research can barely approach this problem after the fact, and for statesmen involved at the time the problem is even worse.

All these factors might suggest to historians concerned with the past why so many cases of deterrence and coercive diplomacy have failed. These failures of the past, in turn, might suggest to theorists and policy makers concerned with the future that there will probably be few cases in which bargaining exclusively with threats of force will constitute a feasible or successful strategy at all. Together, these conclusions may lead us all, in the words of one observer, "to reconsider our willingness to continue entrusting our fate to our capacities for violence."[96]

This two-way research strategy of examining the past with theories of deterrence and coercion and analyzing the theories with historical evidence suggests a conclusion. That is, that diplomatic historians and contemporary bargaining theorists may be able to learn a great deal from each other. The interdisciplinary interchange between their distinctive perspectives and skills, in addition to their common interests, should be considered for its potential contribution to the work of each scholar and to the study of diplomacy.[97]

Diplomatic history, for example, could become much more sophisticated and enriched by drawing upon theory, methodological experimentation, systematic analysis of phenomena, sharper identification of variables, and explicit definitions of problems and concepts. A knowledge of theories of deterrence and coercion can help us understand the nature of bargaining with threats of force, the significance of credibility, and the importance of motivation and calculation in international behavior. Bargaining theory, in turn, could become much more extended, qualified, differentiated, and highly enlivened from its abstract conceptualization by drawing upon the empirical evidence of history. A knowledge of historical cases and the actual behavior of governments and individuals can help theorists understand the importance of human actors, the multiple determinants of policy, and the mistakes and miscalculations that can be made to cause deterrence and coercion to fail. At present, according to Morgan, contemporary bargaining theory does not do this, and thus is dangerous for policy:

> By encouraging attempts to engage in carefully rational decision making in a crisis, measuring and weighing costs and benefits as if they were precise measures and exact scales, it can heighten the risks of war by upping the confidence of leaders that they know what they are doing and can control the situation. In oversimplifying the nature of the decision making involved, it develops insufficiently subtle models of the impact of threats on international relationships.[98]

New approaches in interdisciplinary study may help alleviate this problem, and in the process may even lead to improvements in policy.

Notes

1. Thucydides, *The Peloponnesian War*, Introduction by M.I. Finley (New York: Penguin Books, 1972 ed.), Book I, p. 57.

2. Ibid., p. 82.

3. Ibid., Book V, pp. 402, 406–407.

4. Frederick the Great, as cited in Robert Heinl, Jr., *Dictionary of Military and Naval Quotations* (Annapolis: United States Naval Institute, 1966), p. 88.

5. Niccolò Machiavelli, *Art of War*, Introduction by Neal Wood (New York: Bobbs-Merrill, 1965 ed.), Book I, p. 30, Book VII, pp. 210–212; and *The Prince*, Introduction by Christian Gauss (New York; New American Library, 1952 ed.), Chapter 13, p. 80, Chapter 14, p. 81, Chapter 24, p. 118. See also Felix Gilbert's insightful "Machiavelli: The Renaissance of the Art of War," in Edward Mead Earle (ed.), *Makers of Modern Strategy* (New York: Atheneum, 1969 ed.), pp. 3–25.

6. Thomas Hobbes, *Leviathan*, Introduction by Francis B. Randall (New York: Washington Square Press, 1964 ed.), Chapter 14, p. 96.

7. Ibid., Chapter 15, p. 98.

8. Baron de Montesquieu, *Oeuvres complètes*, Preface by Georges Vedel (Paris: Editions du Sueil, 1964 ed.), Book IX, pp. 577–579; Book X, pp. 579–585.

9. François de Callières, in translation under *On the Manner of Negotiating with Princes* (Notre Dame; University of Notre Dame Press, 1963), p. 117. See also pp. 7, 41, 55. Another classic writer on the intimate relationship between politics and armed force is, of course, Carl von Clausewitz, *On War*, trans. and ed. by Michael Howard and Peter Paret (Princeton: Princeton University Press, 1976 ed.), especially Book I, Chapter 1, pp. 75–89.

10. Martin Gilbert, *The Roots of Appeasement* (New York: New American Library, 1966), p. 1. See also Richard Preston and Sydney Wise, *Men in Arms: A History of Warfare and Its Interrelationships with Western Society* (New York: Praeger, 1970 ed.), especially pp. 1–149.

11. See Glenn Snyder, *Deterrence and Defense: Toward a Theory of National Defense* (Princeton: Princeton University Press, 1961), pp. 8–9. See also the discussion in

George Quester, *Deterrence Before Hiroshima: The Airpower Background of Modern Strategy* (New York: Wiley, 1966).

12. Alexander L. George and Richard Smoke, *Deterrence in American Foreign Policy: Theory and Practice* (New York: Columbia University Press, 1974), p. 21.

13. Bernard Brodie, *The Absolute Weapon: Atomic Power and World Order* (New York: Harcourt, Brace, 1946), p. 76. See also Walter Millis, *The Abolition of War* (New York: Macmillan, 1963); Hans Morgenthau, "The Four Paradoxes of Nuclear Strategy," *American Political Science Review* 58 (March 1964): 23–35; and J. Baylis, K. Booth, J. Garnett, and P. Williams, *Contemporary Strategy: Theories and Policies* (London; Croom-Helm, 1975), p. 59.

14. "Game theory" is the general term applied to formal conceptions of bargaining behavior that can be expressed as a mathematical model. In these abstract models, there are two or more rational players who have deductively logical choices to make, unitary preference functions regarding possible outcomes (which can be visually displayed as cells on a two-dimensional matrix), and some knowledge of the choices available to each other. The essence of the game is that it involves players whose choices and fates are intertwined. Although such games may deal with diplomats involved in international bargaining (and hence mentioned here), their applicability to decision making is much wider and may entail generals engaged in battle, politicians attempting to form legislative coalitions, labor unions striking against firms, or members of a cartel negotiating market shares. These formal models provide a structure or framework for analysis rather than a set of theorems or conclusions and, in this sense, the word "theory" is somewhat of a misnomer, at least for social scientists who find "game theory" more useful as a methodological tool. See Thomas Schelling, "What Is Game Theory?", and Martin Shubik, "The Uses of Game Theory," both in James C. Charlesworth (ed.), *Contemporary Political Analysis* (New York: Free Press, 1967), pp. 212–272. The best and most recent summary and evaluation of these models can be found in Glenn H. Snyder and Paul Diesing, *Conflict Among Nations: Bargaining, Decision Making, and System Structure in International Crisis* (Princeton: Princeton Univeristy Press, 1977), pp. 33–182.

15. Thomas C. Schelling, *The Strategy of Conflict* (New York: Oxford University Press, 1960), p. 5.

16. Thomas C. Schelling, *Arms and Influence* (New Haven: Yale University Press, 1966), p. 2.

17. Fred Charles Iklé, *How Nations Negotiate* (New York: Praeger, 1964); Herman Kahn, *On Escalation: Metaphors and Scenarios* (New York: Praeger, 1965); Klaus Knorr, *On the Uses of Military Power in the Nuclear Age* (Princeton: Princeton University Press, 1966); Klaus Knorr, *Military Power and Potential* (Lexington, Mass.: Heath, 1970); Oran Young, *The Politics of Force: Bargaining During International Crises* (Princeton: Princeton University Press, 1968); and Oran Young (ed.), *Bargaining: Formal Theories of Negotiation* (Urbana: University of Illinois Press, 1975). See also Ole Holsti, *Crisis, Escalation, War* (Montreal: McGill–Queen's University Press, 1972); Robert Jervis, *The Logic of Images in International Relations* (Princeton: Princeton University Press, 1968); Michael Howard, *Studies in War and Peace* (New York: Viking, 1971); Hans Speier, *Force and Folly* (Cambridge: MIT Press, 1969); Stanley Hoffman, Laurence Martin, and Ian Smart, *Force in Modern Societies: Its*

Place in International Politics, Adelphi Paper No. 102 (London: International Institute for Strategic Studies, 1973); B. Byeley et al., *Marxism-Leninism on War and Army* (Moscow: Progress Publishers, 1972); Anatol Rapoport, *Fights, Games, and Debates* (Ann Arbor: University of Michigan Press, 1960); and F. S. Northedge (ed.), *The Use of Force in International Relations* (New York: Free Press, 1974).

18. Snyder and Diesing, *Conflict Among Nations,* p. 22. This impressive study undertakes a synthesis and evaluation of bargaining theory, decision-making theory, and systems theory in analyzing international relations.

19. Sir John Slessor, "The Place of the Bomber in British Policy," an address to the Royal Institute of International Affairs, March 1953, and "The Policy of Deterrence," a lecture at Oxford University, April 1955, both reproduced in *The Great Deterrent* (New York: Praeger, 1957), pp. 121-129, 180-199; William Kaufmann, *Military Policy and National Security* (Princeton: Princeton University Press, 1956); Henry Kissinger, *Nuclear Weapons and Foreign Policy* (New York: Harper and Brothers, 1957); Oskar Morgenstern, *The Question of National Defense* (New York: Random House, 1959); Bernard Brodie, *Strategy in the Missile Age* (Princeton: Princeton University Press, 1959); and Albert Wohlstetter, "The Delicate Balance of Terror," *Foreign Affairs* 37 (January 1959):211-234.

20. Daniel Ellsberg, "The Crude Analysis of Strategic Choices," P-2183, The RAND Corporation, December 15, 1960, reproduced in abbreviated form in *American Economic Review* 51 (May 1961): 472-478; Herman Kahn, *On Thermonuclear War* (Princeton: Princeton University Press, 1961); Snyder, *Deterrence and Defense;* J. David Singer, *Deterrence, Arms Controls, and Disarmament* (Columbus: Ohio State University Press, 1962); Bruce M. Russett, "The Calculus of Deterrence," *Journal of Conflict Resolution* 7 (June 1963): 97-109, and "Pearl Harbor: Deterrence Theory and Decision Theory," *Journal of Peace Research* 4 (1967): 89-106; and Stephen Maxwell, *Rationality in Deterrence,* Adelphi Paper No. 50 (London; International Institute for Strategic Studies, 1968). See also Thomas Milburn, "The Concept of Deterrence: Some Logical and Psychological Considerations," *Journal of Social Issues* 17 (1961): 3-11; Richard Brody, "Deterrence Strategies: An Annotated Bibliography," *Journal of Conflict Resolution* 4 (December 1960): 163-178; Douglas Hunter, *Aspects of Mathematical Deterrence Theory* (Los Angeles: Security Studies Project, UCLA, 1971); and Raoul Naroll et al., *Military Deterrence in History: A Pilot Cross-Historical Survey* (Albany: State University of New York, 1974).

21. George and Smoke, *Deterrence in American Foreign Policy;* and Patrick M. Morgan, *Deterrence: A Conceptual Analysis* (Beverly Hills: Sage, 1977). Robert Jervis, *Perception and Misperception in International Politics* (Princeton: Princeton University Press, 1976) also must be included in this category. In the January 1979 issue of *World Politics,* Robert Jervis will be discussing the different "waves" of deterrence literature in his article entitled "Deterrence Theory Revisited."

22. Alexander L. George, David Hall, and William Simons, *The Limits of Coercive Diplomacy: Laos, Cuba, Vietnam* (Boston: Little, Brown, 1971).

23. Daniel Ellsberg, "The Theory and Practice of Blackmail," a lecture delivered at the Lowell Institute in 1959 and reproduced in U.S. Senate, Subcommittee on National Security and International Operations of the Committee on Governmental Operations, "Negotiation and Statecraft: A Selection of Readings," 91st Con-

gress, 2nd Session (Washington, D.C.: Government Printing Office, 1971): 39–43; Glenn Snyder, "Crisis Bargaining," in Charles Hermann (ed.), *International Crisis: Insights from Behavioral Research* (New York: Free Press, 1972), pp. 217–256; Robert Jervis, "Bargaining and Bargaining Tactics," in J. Roland Pennock and John Chapman (eds.), *Coercion, NOMOS XIV* (Chicago: Aldine, 1972), pp. 272–288, Paul Gordon Lauren, "Ultimata and Coercive Diplomacy," *International Studies Quarterly* 16 (June 1972): 131–165, and "Coercive Diplomacy: Cases from Modern European History," a paper presented at the annual meeting American Historical Association, December 1975; and Phil Williams, *Crisis Management: Confrontation and Diplomacy in the Nuclear Age* (New York: Wiley, 1976). See also Myres S. McDougal and Florentino Feliciano, *Law and Minimum World Public Order: Legal Regulations of International Coercion* (New Haven: Yale University Press, 1961). Snyder and Diesing, *Conflict Among Nations,* could be listed under this category as well.

24. George, Hall, and Simons, *The Limits of Coercive Diplomacy,* pp. 18–19.

25. Schelling, *Arms and Influence,* p. 2.

26. Some theorists of deterrence define the problem in terms of a wide variety of possible courses of action that a state might wish to deter. A notable recent exception to this is Morgan, *Deterrence,* pp. 25–45, who maintains that an "immediate" or "pure" deterrence relates only to a situation where one state is seriously considering an imminent military attack upon another.

27. Robert Art and Kenneth Waltz (eds.), *The Use of Force: International Politics and Foreign Policy* (Boston: Little, Brown, 1971), p. 6.

28. Schelling, *Arms and Influence,* p. 72.

29. Young, *The Politics of Force,* p. 40. For more discussion of communication, see Roberta Wohlstetter, *Pearl Harbor: Warning and Decision* (Stanford: Stanford University Press, 1962); and Jervis, *The Logic of Images.*

30. For more discussion on this point, see Schelling, *Arms and Influence,* p. 150.

31. See the insightful comments in Jervis, *The Logic of Images* and *Perception and Misperception,* passim.

32. Paul W. Schroeder, *Austria, Great Britain, and the Crimean War* (Ithaca, N.Y.: Cornell University Press, 1972), p. 33.

33. Harry S. Truman, *Memoirs: Years of Trial and Hope* (New York: New American Library, 1956), p. 380.

34. See Telegramm an Werthern-München, W.6b, 389 Nr. 1652, Berlin, July 17, 1870, in Otto von Bismarck, *Werke in Auswahl,* ed. by Gustav Rein et al. 8 vols. (Stuttgart: Kohlhammer, 1968), IV: 487; and W. E. Mosse, *The European Powers and the German Question, 1848–1871* (Cambridge, Eng.: Cambridge University Press, 1958), pp. 306–308.

35. Sir John Fisher in a speech during the 1904 fleet redistribution debate, as cited in Leonard Wainstein, "The Dreadnought Gap," *U.S. Naval Institute Proceedings* 92 (September 1966):90.

36. See Schelling, *Arms and Influence,* p. 36.

37. Prince Metternich, *Mémoirs: documents et écrits divers,* ed. by Alfons von Klinkowström, 8 vols. (Paris: Plon, 1881–1886), III: 445. For one of the most

stimulating accounts of Metternich's philosophy and policy in English, see Henry A. Kissinger, *A World Restored* (Boston: Houghton Mifflin, 1973 ed.).

38. Nikita Khrushchev, "Khrushchev's Supreme Soviet Report," *The Current Digest of the Soviet Press* 12 (February 10, 1960): 10. For a discussion of this matter in a larger context, see Ken Booth, *The Military Instrument in Soviet Foreign Policy, 1917–1972* (London: Royal United Services Institute, 1973).

39. "Furor Over the Neutron Bomb," *Newsweek,* April 17, 1978, p. 35. See also U.S. Congress, Senate, 95th Congress, 1st Session, July 13, 1977, *Congressional Record* (Washington, D.C.: Government Printing Office, 1977), 123: 11741–11788; "Nicht humaner als Giftgas," *Der Spiegel,* April 10, 1978, pp. 36–41, among other articles in this issue; and V. Amelchenko, "A Barbarous Weapon," *Soviet Military Review* 11 (November 1977): 51–52.

40. For more discussion of escalation, see Richard Smoke's chapter in this book entitled "Theories of Escalation"; Richard Smoke, *War: Controlling Escalation* (Cambridge: Harvard University Press, 1977); Holsti, *Crisis, Escalation, War;* and Kahn, *On Escalation.*

41. The words are those of Hugh Gaitskell on March 1, 1960, in Great Britain, House of Commons, *Parliamentary Debates,* 5th Series (London: Her Majesty's Stationery Office, 1960), 618: 1136–1137. See also Wolf Mendl, *Deterrence and Persuasion: French Nuclear Armament in the Context of National Policy, 1945–1969* (New York: Praeger, 1970).

42. Robert S. McNamara, *Statement of Secretary of Defense Robert S. McNamara Before the Senate Armed Services Committee on the Fiscal Year 1969–73 Defense Program and 1969 Defense Budget* (Washington, D.C.: Government Printing Office, 1968), p. 47 See also pp. 30–31.

43. George and Smoke, *Deterrence in American Foreign Policy,* pp. 519–532, for a discussion of "initiation theory." See also Snyder, *Deterrence and Defense,* pp. 12–14.

44. Franz Joseph, as cited in Gordon A. Craig, *Europe Since 1815* (New York: Holt, Rinehart, and Winston, 1971 ed.), p. 212. Only in a strictly technical sense did Austria launch the war. As A. J. P. Taylor observes in *The Struggle for Mastery in Europe* (Oxford: Clarendon Press, 1954), p. 166, Austria, the conservative power standing on the defensive, was "baited beyond endurance" by Bismarck. She declared war against Prussia on June 17, 1866, and Prussia reciprocated on the following day.

45. Russett, "Pearl Harbor," p. 91. This section on the Japanese attack draws heavily from Russett's article.

46. See Schelling, *Arms and Influence,* pp. 69–72. I prefer to use the terms "deterrence" and "coercion" to describe these different characteristics of bargaining with threats of force rather than combining them and making no distinction (as some authors do) or than using the terms "deterrence" and "compellence" as Schelling does.

47. Schelling's "compellence" does not distinguish between offensive and defensive uses. The distinction is important, however, because of the moral and political implications of making effective use of coercive diplomacy. I am indebted to Alexander George for helping me understand the significance of this matter.

48. De Callières, *On the Manner of Negotiating with Princes,* p. 7.

49. See the excellent discussion in Williams, *Crisis Management,* p. 141.

50. "Further correspondence respecting the demands made upon the Greek government," in Great Britain, House of Commons, *Sessional Papers, 1850* (London: Her Majesty's Stationery Office, 1850), LVI: 3, 6, 9.

51. Document 2798-PS, Conference Between the Führer and President Hacha, March 15, 1939, Minutes by Hewel, in United States, War Department, Office of Chief Counsel for Prosecution of Axis Criminality, *Nazi Conspiracy and Aggression,* 7 vols. (Washington, D.C.: Government Printing Office, 1946), V: 438.

52. Ibid., p. 439. See also Ellsberg, "The Theory and Practice of Blackmail," pp. 39-43.

53. See United States, Naval War College, *International Law Topics and Discussions, 1913* (Washington, D.C.: Government Printing Office, 1914), pp. 60-61.

54. Khrushchev, as cited in Walter LaFeber, *America, Russia, and the Cold War, 1945-1971* (New York: Wiley, 1972 ed.), p. 208.

55. For this interpretation, see Adam Ulam, *Expansion and Coexistence: Soviet Foreign Policy, 1917-73* (New York: Praeger, 1974 ed.), p. 620.

56. George, Hall, and Simons, *The Limits of Coercive Diplomacy,* pp. 22-25.

57. Great Britain, House of Commons, *Sessional Papers, 1923,* Command Paper No. 1858 (London: His Majesty's Stationery Office, 1923), XXV: 5-13.

58. Great Britain, House of Commons, *Sessional Papers, 1938-39,* Command Paper No. 6106 (London: His Majesty's Stationery Office, 1939), XXVII: 175. See also A. Alexandroff and R. Rosecrance, "Deterrence in 1939," *World Politics* 29 (April 1977): 404-424.

59. This is emphasized and elaborated especially well in George, Hall, and Simons, *The Limits of Coercive Diplomacy,* pp. 18, 25-26, 101, 243-244. See also Schelling, *The Strategy of Conflict,* p. 40; Lauren, "Ultimata and Coercive Diplomacy,; pp. 142-143; and Snyder and Diesing, *Conflict Among Nations,* pp. 195-198, 209.

60. Roger Fisher, *International Conflict for Beginners* (New York: Harper and Row, 1969), p. 27.

61. Snyder, "Crisis Bargaining," p. 255.

62. Robert Kennedy, *Thirteen Days: A Memoir of the Cuban Missile Crisis* (New York: Norton, 1969), pp. 103-108.

63. Schelling, "What Is Game Theory?", pp. 236-237. This problem, as well as others, will also be discussed in Jervis, "Deterrence Theory Revisited."

64. See the discussions of this problem in George and Smoke, *Deterrence in American Foreign Policy,* pp. 72-76; Morgan, *Deterrence,* pp. 70-100; John Steinbruner, "Beyond Rational Deterrence," *World Politics* 28 (January 1976): 223-245; Maxwell, *Rationality in Deterrence;* and Jack Snyder, "Rationality at the Brink: The Role of Cognitive Process in Failures of Deterrence," *World Politics* 30 (April 1978): 345-365.

65. See Ole Holsti's chapter in this book entitled "Theories of Crisis Decision Making."

66. Clausewitz, *On War,* p. 85.

67. See Gordon A. Craig, *From Bismarck to Adenauer: Aspects of German Statecraft* (New York: Harper and Row, 1965 ed.), p. 18.

68. The best work is Jervis' *Perception and Misperception,* which pulls together much relevant psychological literature on this subject and provides evidence of its applicability to many historical cases. See also Carl Friedrich (ed.), *Rational Decision, NOMOS VII* (New York: Atherton, 1964); Stan Kaplowitz, "An Experimental Test of a Rationalistic Theory of Deterrence," *Journal of Conflict Resolution* 17 (September 1973): 535–572; Singer, *Deterrence, Arms Control, and Disarmament,* pp. 9, 24–25; Snyder, *Deterrence and Defense,* pp. 27–30; and Snyder and Diesing, *Conflict Among Nations,* pp. 75, 80–82, 333–336, 340–348.

69. Schelling, *Arms and Influence,* p. 93. See also Klaus Knorr (ed.), *Historical Dimensions of National Security Problems* (Lawrence: University Press of Kansas, 1976), pp. 78–119. Although this citation is taken from Schelling, it should be stated that the bulk of his work ignores the thrust of this point, and suffers thereby. He dangerously suggests, for instance, that it may be useful for policy makers to deliberately lose control of decisions, to become reckless, or to create a risk that leaves something to chance. See, for example, the incisive critique by Karl W. Deutsch, *The Nerves of Government* (New York: Free Press, 1966 ed.), pp. 68–69.

70. Some possible alternatives to the strictly "rational decision making" model are suggested by Morgan, *Deterrence,* pp. 101–124, who argues for "sensible decision making"; and John Steinbruner, *The Cybernetic Theory of Decision* (Princeton: Princeton University Press, 1974), who argues for a "cybernetic theory" of decision making.

71. George and Smoke, *Deterrence in American Foreign Policy,* p. 72.

72. Graham T. Allison, *The Essence of Decision: Explaining the Cuban Missile Crisis* (Boston: Little, Brown, 1971); Morton H. Halperin, *Bureaucratic Politics and Foreign Policy* (Washington, D.C.: Brookings Institution, 1974); and Graham T. Allison and Morton H. Halperin, "Bureaucratic Politics: A Paradigm and Some Policy Implications;" in Raymond Tanter and Richard H. Ullman (eds.), *Theory and Policy in International Relations* (Princeton: Princeton University Press, 1972).

73. The words are those of Williams, *Crisis Management,* p. 64.

74. The "operational code" is a technique for analyzing the presuppositions, attitudes, and characteristic modes of behavior, as described by Nathan Leites, *The Operational Code of the Politburo* (New York: McGraw-Hill, 1951); and Alexander L. George, "The 'Operational Code': A Neglected Approach to the Study of Political Leaders and Decision-Making," *International Studies Quarterly* 13 (June 1969): 190–222. See also Lloyd S. Etheredge, "Personality Effects on American Foreign Policy, 1898–1968: A Test of Interpersonal Generalization Theory," *American Political Science Review* 72 (June 1978): 434–451.

75. See Samuel Williamson's chapter in this book entitled "Theories of Organizational Process and Foreign Policy Outcomes." See also, for example, Zara Steiner, *The Foreign Office and Foreign Policy, 1898–1914* (Cambridge, Eng.: Cambridge University Press, 1969); and, to a lesser extent, Paul Gordon Lauren, *Diplomats and Bureaucrats* (Stanford: Hoover Institution Press, 1976).

76. Allison, *Essence of Decision.*

77. Morgan, *Deterrence,* p. 49. Morgan's analysis of this whole problem of the connection between deterrence and decision-making theory is excellent.

78. Hobbes, *Leviathan,* Chapter 13, p. 85.

79. Iklé, *How Nations Negotiate,* p. 2.

80. The expression comes from Coral Bell, *The Conventions of Crisis: A Study in Diplomatic Management* (London: Oxford University Press, 1971), p. 50.

81. In addition to Iklé and Bell, see Williams, *Crisis Management,* pp. 27–31; Snyder, "Crisis Bargaining," pp. 240–241, 251–255; and Kenneth Boulding, *Conflict and Defense* (New York: Harper and Row, 1962), p. 314.

82. George and Smoke, *Deterrence in American Foreign Policy,* pp. 604–610, for example, call for the development of "inducement theory" to supplement deterrence theory.

83. Holsti, *Crisis, Escalation, War,* p. 224.

84. De Callières, *On the Manner of Negotiating with Princes,* p. 110. In this regard, it is interesting to note that mathematical decision theory recently has been applied to integrative bargaining techniques as a means of rating the value that each side attaches to various points of issue and then arriving at a solution that is better for both sides than would have resulted from single-issue bargains. This was done in practice by American policy makers during the recent Panama Canal and Philippine bases negotiations. See Scott Barclay and Cameron R. Peterson, "Multi-Attribute Utility Models for Negotiations," Decisions and Designs, Inc., Technical Report No. 76-i, prepared for the Defense Advanced Research Projects Agency, March 1976. I am indebted to Ernest R. May of Harvard University for bringing this matter to my attention.

85. Schelling, *Arms and Influence,* pp. 1–34 (my emphasis). More recently, Morgan, *Deterrence,* pp. 21, 27, 31–45, emphasizes military factors; as does Richard Pipes, "Why the Soviet Union Thinks It Could Fight and Win a Nuclear War," *Air Force Magazine* (September 1977): 54–66, appearing originally in *Commentary* (July 1977).

86. See George and Smoke, *Deterrence in American Foreign Policy,* p. 79. They observe (pp. 38–47) that attention to the strategic level has been due to the locus of the most salient threat to the United States from the Soviet Union and the image of a sharply bipolar world during the Cold War.

87. For more discussion of this point, as well as specific historical examples from diplomacy, see Lauren, "Ultimata and Coercive Diplomacy," especially pp. 144–148. See also Bruce Russett, *Power and Community in World Politics* (San Francisco: Freeman, 1974), Chapter 15, "The Instruments of Influence and the Limits of Power," pp. 255–281.

88. Harold Wilensky, *Organizational Intelligence* (New York: Basic Books, 1967), p. 191.

89. Under the United Nations Charter, for example, coercive threats of war and force are legal only if in self-defense or in collective defense of the Charter. More recently, the Final Act of the Conference on Security and Cooperation in Europe, signed in 1975, commits the signatories to refrain "from the threat or use of force against the territorial integrity or political independence of any State....No consideration may be invoked to serve to warrant resort to the threat or use of force in contravention of this principle." "No such threat or use of force," the Act continues, "will be employed as a means of settling disputes, or questions likely to give rise to disputes." See Konferenz über Sicherheit und Zusammenarbeit in Europa, *Schlussakte* (Lausanne: Imprimeries Réunies, 1975), p. 9.

90. Khruschev, as cited in Kennedy, *Thirteen Days,* p. 89. See also Charles Lockhart, *The Efficacy of Threats in International Interaction Strategies* (Beverly Hills: Sage, 1973).

91. For more discussion on this subject, see Richard Smoke's chapter in this book entitled "Theories of Escalation".

92. Clausewitz, *On War,* p. 77.

93. Williams, *Crisis Management,* p. 149. See also the stimulating discussion in Jervis, *Perception and Misperception,* especially Chapter 3, "Deterrence, the Spiral Model, and Intentions of the Adversary," pp. 58–113.

94. Another problem may arise when the use of threats produces a deceptive short-term gain, but actually results in a long-term loss if an opponent vows that "the next time" he will fight rather than capitulate. I have benefited from discussions on this matter with James Austin of Yale University.

95. The best treatment of these necessary preconditions are to be found in George and Smoke, *Deterrence in American Foreign Policy,* pp. 522–532; and George, Hall, and Simons, *The Limits of Coercive Diplomacy,* pp. 211–253.

96. Morgan, *Deterrence,* p. 15.

97. For more discussion of this theme, see the author's introductory chapter and Samuel Wells' concluding chapter in this book.

98. Morgan, *Deterrence,* p. 15. See also p. 207.

9
Systems Theories and Diplomatic History

Robert Jervis

MOST STUDIES THAT WE CALL "INTERNATIONAL RELATIONS" are really studies of foreign policies, analyzing as they do the causes of an individual state's actions. There is nothing wrong with this, but focusing upon the international system and patterns of interaction can be equally illuminating. I want to explore this by examining some of the important insights of systems theories.[1]

What Is a System?

The term, "international system," is usually used very loosely, as little more than a synonym for the environment in which states operate. I think that the term more usefully applies when two conditions are met: first, one cannot infer the outcomes from the attributes and behavior of the actors and, second, interconnections are present with the result that changes in some parts of the system produce changes in other parts. These conditions lead to a major characteristic of systems: the consequences of behavior are often not expected or intended by the actors.

WHOLE DIFFERENT FROM THE SUM OF THE PARTS

In a system the whole is different from the sum of the parts, not in any metaphysical sense, "but in the more important pragmatic sense that given the properties of the parts and the laws of their interaction, it is not a trivial matter to infer the properties of the whole."[2] It is often claimed that the whole is greater than the sum of the parts, but while this way of putting it is more dramatic, it is also less accurate because there is a lot in the parts that is omit-

I would like to thank Robert Art, Robert Dallek, Alexander George, Ole Holsti, Paul Gordon Lauren, and Samuel Williamson for comments and the UCLA Committee on Research of the UCLA Academic Senate for financial support.

ted from a consideration of the system. The important point is that even complete knowledge of the actors, their characteristics, their goals, and their intentions does not allow us to understand the system. "The whole might be symmetric in spite of its parts being asymmetric, a whole might be unstable in spite of its parts being stable in themselves. . . . Properties of a social group, such as its organization, its stability, its goals, are something different from the organization, the stability, and the goals of the individuals in it."[3] A system can be bipolar or multipolar; actors cannot be. And while we may talk about the stability of actors and the stability of the international system, the meaning of the concepts is not exactly the same.

A system cannot be described by adding up the policies of the individual states or summing their bilateral relations. Adding up the aggressiveness of each state cannot tell us how violent the system will be. For example, it is a gross misunderstanding to argue that "a system of merely growth-seeking actors will obviously be unstable; there would be no provision for balancing or restraint."[4] If this kind of additive operation were possible, then we could dispense with the concept of a system. In fact, the central idea of a balance of power system is that each state's expansion works to contain that of others, just as in the free market the interaction of each person's greed keeps profits low and advances the interests of the wider society. The other side of the coin is that a major war can occur even if all members of the system are following moderate foreign policies. World War I is an example. Even if the Germany of the Kaiser was expansionist, her goals, while perhaps too ambitious for the good of Europe or her own good, were not like those of Nazi Germany. If we were to add up each state's expansionism in this period, we would expect a moderate international system.

INTERCONNECTEDNESS

The second characteristic of a system is what Ashby calls conditionality.[5] The relations between two actors depend in part on the relations between each of those actors and other actors in the system. This means that whether actors ally with or oppose each other is influenced by factors outside of their bilateral relationship. Thus, Lenin argued in 1920 that "an independent Poland is very dangerous to Soviet Russia: it is an evil, however [that] also has its redeeming feature; for while it exists we may safely count on Germany because the Germans hate Poland and will at any time make common cause with us in order to strangle Poland."[6] As one Japanese leader put it in November 1941: "We have come to where we are [in our relations with the United States] because of the war between Germany and Great Britain."[7] A few years earlier, Japan had signed a treaty with Germany in the expectation that such a tie would discourage the United States from opposing Japan's efforts to dominate China. In fact, American opposition increased as it saw Japan linked to the power that was menacing Britain. More recently, Sadat's visit to Jerusalem led the Syrians into closer cooperation with the Palestine Liberation Organization because they both opposed conciliation of Israel, and this led to greater conflict between the Syrian and Christian forces in Lebanon, which in turn strengthened the bonds between the Christians and Israel.[8]

A system, then, is interconnected. Events in one area influence other areas. Changes in the relations between two states lead to alterations in the relations between other states. One minor example can stand for many: British relations with Persia in the nineteenth and early twentieth century depended in part on British relations with Russia, which in turn were influenced by Britain's relations with France. During the Napoleonic wars, France was Britain's main enemy, Russia therefore had to be courted, and Russian encroachments on Persia—which would threaten India—had to be ignored. When relations with France improved, relations with Russia deteriorated, and Britain came to Persia's support.[9] With the beginning of the twentieth century Germany became Britain's chief concern, giving England a major incentive to establish good relations with Russia. To this end, she first agreed to divide Persia into spheres of influence and then tolerated Russian violations of the agreement.

In a system, policies and events have ramifications that extend through distant periods of time, areas of the globe, and states involved. For example, Paul Schroeder argues that it was not Germany that was most injured by the French takeover of Morocco in 1911. The more important consequences were less direct: "What the French protectorate in Morocco actually did was to pave the way for Italy to attack Turkey over Tripoli and to spread the war into the eastern Mediterranean to encourage Russia to advance her plans for the Straits, and to promote the assault of the Balkan states upon Turkey, thus raising life-and-death questions for Austria."[10]

Statesmen are often aware of this interconnectedness and diplomatic history is full of instances in which a decision is made because of the expected indirect consequences. Thus, Schroeder continues: "This is not merely what happened in the event; it was what sensible leaders foresaw and planned for, what was in good part provided for in written agreements."[11] In 1889, when Bismarck proposed to England a treaty of mutual guarantee against attack by France, he argued that the British would gain not only security from France, but also from Russia and the United States, since these states would contemplate war with England only if they thought France would assist them. Neutralizing the threat from France would then induce other states to be more cautious.[12] In other cases, observers see important ramifications that are missed by the statesman taking the action. The former's greater objectivity and distance from the details may allow them to grasp the essentials. Thus, although the British did not think that the signing of the naval treaty with Germany in 1935 presaged any basic shift in policy, some observers realized that because Britain would need to keep more of her ships in the North Sea she would be unable to keep her pledge to send her main fleet to Singapore in the event of a war with Japan, and so the Japanese would therefore feel fewer restraints.[13] Similarly, in the 1920s and early 1930s, Japan did not think that her China policy would strongly influence her relations with other countries, especially the United States. "From the Japanese point of view, China and America were separate problems."[14] Many observers saw the links that would create such problems for Japan in the coming years.

Systems vary in how interconnected they are. As one student of systems theories has put it: "Everything is connected, but some things are more connected than others. The world is a large matrix of interactions in which most of the entries are very close to zero."[15] A change in relations between Argentina and Chile, for instance, has little effect on Pakistan. Some points of elaboration can be noted. First, almost by definition, a great power is more tightly connected to larger numbers of other states than is a small power. Because it has involvements all over the world, a great power is at least slightly affected by most changes in relations of other states. Growing conflict or growing cooperation between Argentina and Chile would not affect Pakistan, but it would affect America and American policy toward those states, and American policy toward other South American countries. Second, many interconnections are not direct, but involve links through regional or great powers. Although most states had no direct concerns in Vietnam, they were affected by what happened there because of the changes in U.S. policy that the war produced. Many of the effects went beyond the bilateral relations between each of these states and the United States and extended to their relations with each other. To the extent that Vietnam led the United States to pull back from being a world policeman, it took the lid off local conflicts and encouraged regional powers to play a greater role.

The belief that the world is tightly interconnected supports the theory and practice of deterrence. The notion of commitment—a state staking its reputation on responding strongly if its adversary should take a proscribed action even though such a response would not have been in the state's interest had it not given the pledge—rests on the belief that a default in one instance will lead others to expect further defaults. If this is the case, states will see very high costs in capitulation.[16] Even in the absence of a commitment, one retreat can have widespread impact if others believe it shows that the state is likely to back down on other issues in the future. But such dynamics will not operate if the world is not tightly interconnected. To the extent that states are strongly influenced by internally established goals and the configuration of the specific situation, their appetites will not grow with the eating. Local conditions will be of most importance and neither the state's past behavior nor the outcomes of previous disputes in other areas will strongly influence the course of later conflicts. This was Halifax's point in March 1938: "Much of the argument for the need of a deterrent rested on the assumption that when Germany secured the hegemony over Central Europe, she would pick a quarrel with

215

France and ourselves. He did not agree." That he was incorrect should not blind us to the validity of this position in many other cases.[17]

Interconnectedness can exist between two actors over time. One state's behavior toward another can so strongly influence the other's behavior, which in turn so strongly influences the first state's later behavior, that understanding is not well served by trying to deal with each action separately. Rather, the actors must be seen as forming a system, and it is the system that we must seek to understand. The characteristics and idiosyncrasies of the individual states do not matter and their behavior is insensitive to a wide range of variation in their goals. Some of the best known examples are spirals of arms and hostility, called "Richardson processes" after the scholar who performed the path-breaking investigations of them. In arguing that mathematical equations can portray state behavior, Richardson admits that they describe "how people would behave if they did not stop to think."[18] But, he claims, this does not do injustice to the process because the states are responding to each other almost automatically.

UNINTENDED CONSEQUENCES

Because the behavior of states is interconnected, their goals conflict, and none of them is strong enough to control all the others, states' actions often produce unintended consequences.[19] Behavior frequently yields results that are opposite from, or at a tangent to, those sought and predicted, thus leading to what are often called ironies of history. In 1938 representatives of British bicyclists argued that if bicycles were required to have rear lamps "the mortality among cyclists would immediately go up enormously" because motorists would drive faster, expecting to be able to see all bicycles, and would run over those whose lights had burned out.[20] One of the reasons why the United States annexed Texas was the fear that if the latter remained independent she would fall under the sway of European powers, especially England. Indeed, because the slavery issue was so divisive, this was the most powerful appeal that could be made to all sections of the American polity. Britain wanted to prevent annexation in order to curb American power, and she developed several diplomatic maneuvers to this end. But their main effect was to increase American incentives to take Texas into the Union.[21]

Unexpected and unintended results can also be produced through longer and more complex chains of interconnections. For example, at the same time that Britain was trying to form the first coalition against Napoleon, Russia and Prussia were excluding Austria from the second partition of Poland. Britain's need for Russian support against France gave Russia much of the leverage she needed to carry out this maneuver. But the result of this anti-Austrian move was to embitter Russo–Austrian relations to the point where no coalition was possible.[22] Thus, Britain's strong incentives to rally other states to the alliance encouraged others to follow policies that undermined her own efforts. A more recent, although debatable, example is provided by Liddell Hart in discussing

> what would have happened in Europe if we had not committed ourselves to the Polish Guarantee [in 1939]. How would our restraint have affected the strategic balance? If we had not given that delusory guarantee, Poland would have been forced to accept Russia's help, as the only chance of withstanding German pressure. And Russia would have been forced to give Poland such support, because of her then existing value as a buffer-State, and as an auxiliary army. In these circumstances, it would have been much less likely that Germany would have attacked Poland than it was when an isolated Poland depended merely on an illusory promise of help from the Western Powers, and Russia had been temporarily bought off.[23]

At times the result will be desired by the state but the steps intervening between its actions and the outcome will be very different from those it expected. The existence of many powerful actors pulling in different directions means that sometimes their moves will cancel each other out. For example, once they recovered from their surprise, most American decision makers welcomed Sadat's visit to Jerusalem in 1977. It is probable that American policy helped bring about this outcome, but not in the way that President Carter expected. By pushing for a comprehensive settlement which included a large role for the Soviets and Palestinians, the United States menaced Sadat. The latter apparently saw that the only way to regain control of the situation was to take a dramatic initiative. He was trying to counteract American policy, but in doing so he was also moving toward a goal that America sought.

More often, the unintended consequences are undesired. Perhaps the most common examples are the operation of a balance of power, mentioned earlier, and arms races in which states end up worse off than they were before the interaction started. The latter dynamic can be seen in terms of the security dilemma, one of the foundations of international politics.[24] Because of the lack of an international sovereign, states must be prepared to protect themselves. But the means chosen to reach this end—for example, armed forces or alliances—usually decrease the security of others. The state may not seek this objective. It may have no aggressive designs, and may even want to see the other secure. But the other cannot know that the state is peaceful or be sure that, even if it is, it will remain so. The other must regard the state's arms as threatening and act accordingly. This means that two states which want only security and wish to maintain the status quo can get into conflicts with each other. The compatibility of their goals does not insure cooperation. To look at this process from another perspective, the existence of wars does not prove that men and states are evil or greedy or misunderstand each other.[25] Conflict is created by the anarchic system and resulting security dilemma.

217

The problem is most acute when offensive military strategies are more effective than defensive ones—that is, when it is highly advantageous to strike first. Both long- and short-run problems are thereby created. In the short run, there are strong pressures to attack in a crisis. Even a state that prefers the maintenance of the status quo to launching a war will attack if the alternative to striking is not the status quo, but being defeated by an adversary that gets in the first blow. This is part of the explanation for the immediate outbreak of World War I. Because each side thought that moving first gave great military advantages, the mobilization races were particularly difficult to stop. The situation was unstable because measures taken to protect the state if war broke out made war more likely. Long-run dynamics also magnified the security dilemma. It is not clear that either side could have increased its security without endangering the other side. One scholar poses the common question about the origins of the war by asking: "Did Germany unleash the war deliberately to become a world power or did she support Austria merely to defend a weakening ally?"[26] This implies that it was possible for Germany to have just maintained her position—to have neither lost power nor to have expanded. But, could Germany have been able to gain a good measure of security without gravely menacing several of the other powers? The title of one of Fritz Fischer's books—"world power or decline"—may catch the nature of the situation more accurately than Fischer's argument.[27] That this phrase was orginally the title of a book by a German expansionist should not lead us to conclude that this view was nothing more than a rationalization for aggression. Even if it is not driven by unreasonable ambitions, deep internal conflicts, or unstable leaders, a state may choose expansionism rather than accept decline if the status quo cannot be maintained.

Unintended consequences are also common in domestic politics when there are many independent actors whose behavior affects each other in complicated ways. Jay Forrester argues that for this reason urban policies usually produce outcomes opposite from those that are sought. Most official attempts to increase employment and the supply of housing reduce these commodities. Straightforward policies fail because the environment in which they operate is a complex one, with large numbers of strong and obscure connections among its elements. A move that initially increases the supply of low-cost housing will have lots of side effects—for example, making a whole area of its city more valuable—and these, in turn, have unforeseen consequences—such as attracting more people into the area and reducing the land available for employment-generating industry—which will defeat the purposes of the policy.[28]

An implication of this analysis is that in politics, as in military endeavors, the indirect approach is often best. To pursue a policy that heads straight for your goal may be to insure that you will not reach it. You must instead head off on a tangent, or even in the opposite direction. Thus, during the first stages of the Berlin blockade, allied authorities feared a water shortage because much of the water had been supplied by the East. West Berliners knew this and started to fill their tubs as insurance, thus dangerously depleting the water supply. The authorities reacted not by urging people to use less water, but by assuring them that the supplies were ample and that they could use all the water they wanted. As a result, the demand for water quickly dropped to manageable levels.[29]

Policy makers, too, must use the forces generated by the effects that their policies have on other states. One definition of a skillful diplomat would be one who can do this, who can see the interconnections in the system, understand how others see their interests, predict their reactions, and take advantage of the complexities rather than work against them. The policies adopted then will not be the obvious ones and the links between them and the statesman's goals will be obscure to many at home (raising problems for democracies) and abroad (raising a question discussed below). For example, one way in which Germany reduced French resistance to British entry into the Common Market was by advocating monetary policies that France and Britain opposed. The former could then reason that the latter's participation in the EEC would bring it a needed ally on this important issue. Similarly, in the first decade of the twentieth century, some of the British officials in South Africa advocated a paradoxical policy for insuring consolidation of British power over the Boers. They called for

> the immediate consolidation of the various areas of British South Africa into one nation. Although unification would at first place Boers in authority over all of South Africa, it would, they believed, ironically cause their eventual political decline. No matter which group stepped into power, unification would create conditions of economic prosperity and political security which had been lacking ever since the war. With prosperity and security would come British immigrants in greater and greater numbers. Assuming a condition containing equitable franchise and constituency provisions, the result, they insisted, would be an eventual transfer of political power from the Boer population to the British.[30]

More recently, the main gains to the United States of its opening to China were not improved Sino–American relations—since these are of little importance—but the changes in Soviet–American relations.

These examples raise the question alluded to above: Can policy makers learn to take advantage of these processes when others with conflicting interests are also trying to do so? The systems we are dealing with are composed not of inanimate objects, but of people—goal-seeking actors who are trying to manipulate each other. If they all realize that straightforward policies are not likely to reach the desired goals, how will they react to each other? If the others are expecting indirect policies of the type outlined above, will those policies then fail? I have no good answers to these questions except to note that in some cases others lack sufficient freedom of maneuver to be able to take advantage of an understanding of the system. Some strategic positions make a state vulnerable and rob a person of the ability to turn the tables on his adversaries even if he knows what they are up to.

Systems Effects

What kinds of effects are produced by the dynamics that we have discussed? We cannot give anything like an exhaustive list, nor, more important, can we specify the detailed conditions under which each will occur. But we can at least make a start.

First, we should note that the concepts of positive and negative feedback help clarify two well known processes and theories. *Positive feedback* leads to instability and can be defined as being present when a change that pushes a variable in one direction calls up reinforcing changes that move the variable even further in that direction. *Negative feedback* occurs when a change that pushes a variable in one direction calls up counterbalancing forces that restore the variable to something approximating its original position. Therefore, it makes the system stable.[31] In most systems theories, in realms other than international politics, negative feedback is a way in which the actor protects himself from changes in the environment. If a cold-blooded animal begins to overheat, it will move into the shade or turn its body so that less of it is exposed to the sunlight. In international politics, negative feedback is displayed in the ways in which the members of the system control a disturbing actor. The most obvious and important illustration is the operation of the balance of power. If one actor grows powerful enough to threaten domination, others will submerge their differences and unite against him. If they are successful (and success is neither automatic nor easy), the power of the offending state will be curbed, and the basic characteristics of the system will be maintained.

Positive feedback occurs when accretions of power to one actor, far from calling up counteracting forces, lead to further gains. Hitler's victories in the spring of 1940 led Mussolini to join him. Just as delegates in a presidential convention rush to get on the bandwagon of a winning candidate, so many states will side with a power that is gaining the ascendancy. And the more states that do so, the more others will follow suit. Some go more willingly than others; some may go out of fear and others out of the hope to get a share of the spoils; some may go because of changes in internal politics. But the result is that more and more states fall under the sway of the leading power. A variant of this process is described by the domino theory, which stresses the importance of perceptions of the major powers' resolve. In defending the Truman Doctrine, an administration spokesman argued: "Anything that happens in Greece and Turkey inevitably has an effect on the rest of the Middle East, on western Europe, and clear around into the Pacific, because all these people are watching what the United States is doing. . . . [I]f the countries of the world lose confidence in us they may in effect pass under the Iron Curtain."[32] Similarly, President Nixon defended his refusal to compromise on U.S. control of the Panama Canal by arguing: "If the United States retreats one inch in this respect, we will have raised serious doubts about our bases throughout the world.''[33] In pushing for aid to Vietnam in the spring of 1975, Kissinger argued: ''We cannot pursue a policy of selective reliability. We cannot abandon friends in one part of the world without jeopardizing the security of friends everywhere.'' He felt a heightened sense of urgency because at this time negotiations in the Middle East were resuming and he believed that both Egypt and Israel would not place much faith in American pledges to them if the United States did not do all it could in Southeast Asia.[34]

Of course other inferences and ramifications are possible. Other states might be less influenced by the fact that the United States finally ''abandoned'' Vietnam than by the fact that it spent tens of thousands of lives and billions of dollars to try to save it. Or, they might conclude that once America was no longer tied down in Vietnam she would be able to concentrate on areas of greater importance, such as Europe and the Middle East. If others accepted either of these chains of reasoning, they would place more, rather than less, faith in America's other commitments.

Furthermore, the domino theory neglects or denies an important counteracting dynamic. A power may react to a defeat by becoming more resolute in the next conflict in order to avoid the very effects described above. Here is a possible situation where the actors' anticipation of the system's dynamics can lead them to alter their behavior to avoid the ''natural'' outcome. This is not an uncommon pattern. One reason why Britain felt she had to support Russia in 1914 was that she had failed to do so in the previous Balkan crisis and feared a Russian defection from the entente if Russia were disappointed too often. And the United States followed this logic when she jumped at the chance to use force in the Mayaguez incident to demonstrate that her defeats in Vietnam and Cambodia did not mean, as she had been predicting, that her resolve would henceforth be eroded. (Of course, it will be dangerous if the state that retreats once feels compelled to stand firm the next time, but its adversary expects the retreat to be repeated.)

In the kinds of cases described by both the domino theory and the balance of power theory, the behavior of the major power produce changes throughout the system. But the content of the changes is very different, and the obvious question is under what conditions each kind of feedback occurs. Negative feedback is likely to occur when decision makers believe that the gains of opposing the potential hegemonic state are greater than those of failing to do so. This calculation is determined by estimates of the value of controlling the hegemon, the value of siding with it, the costs of opposition (which will vary, depending on whether or not the hegemon is brought down), and the perceived probability that the hegemon will fail (which, in turn, is influenced by what each state, including the decision maker's own state, does). While some of these estimates are influenced by nonsystemic factors and thus require detailed examination of each state and each decision maker, one important factor involves the international system. When each state wants to see the hegemon controlled, but believes that participating in the opposition is costly and dangerous, we have an example of what is called a public or collective goods problem.[35] *Collective goods* are those that, if acquired, benefit everyone whether or not he has contributed to their acquisition. National defense, for example, is a collective good. If the nation is defended, everyone in it is defended, whether or not he has paid his taxes. If the hegemon is defeated, all states benefit, whether or not they participated in the coalition. Since joining the coalition is costly, the state's first choice would be to have the hegemon defeated without having to join in the opposition. In other words, the state would like to be the "free rider," taking advantage of the efforts of others. But since this is true of each of the states, there is a danger that no one will oppose the hegemon, even though all want it stopped. Indeed, all would join a coalition if the only choices were doing so or being dominated by the hegemon. Furthermore, if the state thinks that the hegemon will win even if the state opposes it, joining is pointless. Since the participation of small states makes less of a difference in the outcome than does the participation of larger states, we would expect them to follow balance-of-power prescriptions less frequently and to be more subject to domino dynamics than are larger powers. Systems composed of many small powers will therefore be more subject to positive feedback and instability than will a system that contains several powers large enough to believe that their action could tip the balance.

Other interactions involve dynamics more complex than positive and negative feedback and can best be seen in relations among three states. Unfortunately, many of the limits apparent in our earlier discussion reappear; we cannot always determine which pattern will occur, partly because many of the influences at work involve not the system but the decision makers' values, beliefs, and calculations. Nevertheless, we can isolate a number of recurring patterns.

When a state is faced with two possible adversaries, for example, it usually seeks to insure that they do not collaborate against it. At best, the state may be able to "divide and conquer" the other two. But even if it cannot, it can at least try to avoid the worst contingency. The Anglo–French dispute over Egypt gave Bismarck greater freedom of maneuver because it made it unlikely that these two powers could cooperate and increased their need for German support, thereby enabling Germany to take actions which could harm either of them. One scholar argues that this conflict "is probably the main reason why Bismarck was soon quarrelling with England over colonial rivalry in Africa."[36] When two of the state's potential adversaries do not of their own accord oppose each other, the state may sow discord between them. Thus, after a war, the winner may change borders to create conflict among those who might seek revenge. Philip of Macedon made Thebes cede a border territory to Athens so that the latter could not afford to alienate him,[37] and in 1945 Russia insisted on moving Poland a hundred miles to the west, not only gaining land for herself, but also increasing Poland's need for Soviet support against Germany.

Alternatively, the state may conciliate another to patch up a quarrel which is making either of them dependent on a third party. In the 1880s, Giers, the Russian foreign minister, wanted to curb his country's expansion in Central Asia, which was threatening British India and thus limiting Russia's diplomatic flexibility. As long as war with England was a real possibility, Russia's bargaining power with others was reduced because her need for allies was so great.[38] In other cases the third party can, even without knowing it, open the way to conflict between two others by decreasing its pressure on one or both of them. It has been argued that the "U.S. self-limitation on use of its military power against China [in the mid and late 1950s] . . . first reduced, and then eliminated Chinese dependence on the military power of the Soviet Union to ward off attack from the United States. Without this tacit American reassurance to the Chinese, the breach between the Soviet Union and China might never have taken place."[39] And to the extent that China feared the possibility of a Soviet–American common front, the Vietnam War was a blessing to her, for it allowed her to work against the interests of either or both those powers in relative safety.

Of course, refraining from behavior that would bring potential adversaries together may be at some cost to the state if it means not stopping others from reaching goals which are not in the state's interest. Thus, Britain might have been able to split the Axis by granting Mussolini a free hand in the Mediterranean, but the international and domestic price might not have been worth paying. At least in the short run, it is cheaper to break up a potentially hostile coalition by creating and playing on divisions among its members than to make concessions to one of them. But even when the former alternative is available, it carries a longer run cost: if the conflict between two of the others is not only sufficient to prevent them from allying, but also high enough to create a risk of war between them, the state may have avoided one danger only to have created others. Although it may be able to take advantage of these tensions, it may also find itself drawn into them. It may face pressures to join one or the other of the disputing pair. Or one of the others may find that the best way to attract allies is to promise opposition to the state. These, of course, were some of the dangers in Bismarck's policies toward Russia and Austria after the Franco–Prussian War. Bismarck and his colleagues argued that "because of her weak geographical location Germany had no interest in a lasting peace in the Near East; she was hated by her neighbours who would probably unite against her as soon as they had their hands free."[40] However, for a power to encourage conflict between her neighbors not as a temporary expedient to tide her over a particularly vulnerable period, but as the basis for long-term security, is to court multiple dangers.

In dealing with relations among three states, one obvious question is whether two will form a firm alliance against one. For this to happen requires either that one issue dominates the states' concerns or that all the issues divide the states in the same way. When issues cross-cut, on the other hand, countries that are adversaries on one issue are allies on another, thus giving each state incentives to find solutions to each conflict that are relatively satisfactory to all concerned. There may even be competition in reasonableness as states that are nominally working together on an issue vie with each other to get in the good graces of the adversary whose help they will need later. This condition of multiple cross-cutting conflicts is most likely to arise when security threats are diffuse. (Of course, states can unite against another in the hope of making positive gains, but offensive coalitions are hard to maintain because the benefits are often uncertain, mutual rivalries and suspicions are great, and the incentives for the victim to split the coalition by buying off one of its members are high.)

A state must calculate whether pursuing quarrels with several others will unite them against it or whether the conflicts among the others are so strong that they cannot cooperate. If the others cannot unite, then the state is free to exert pressure on each of them. Indeed, at least some of the others may be compelled to seek the state's support if they cannot find allies elsewhere. This was the expectation that underlay Germany's policy toward England in the late nineteenth and early twentieth centuries. Most of the powers had grievances against England, and it was the fear of facing a united front on which Bismarck successfully played during the Balkan crisis of 1887 in order to gain British support for the coalition that he built to stalemate Russia in the Balkans.

As the previous example shows, a state's bargaining power is determined largely by the availability of alternatives rather than by its economic and military resources or its contributions to the common cause. A state which has no choice but to ally itself with another cannot exact much of a price for its commitment. The easier it is for the state to defect, the more it can compel its partners to conform to its wishes. The threat to defect is credible if there are other policies nearly as attractive as the alliance. This can be the case either because the alliance is failing to meet the state's needs or because joining with others has positive attractions. The pull can come from having relatively few direct conflicts with the other side (and in the first years of this century Britain had few direct conflicts with Germany and probably could have exploited this in her bargaining with France more effectively than she did) and from wanting things that the other side can grant relatively easily, such as the territory of a former ally. The push can be generated by the belief that the current alliance will not last or by the state's need for assistance that its allies cannot or will not supply.

Since statesmen understand the advantages to be derived from the ability to change sides, they often exaggerate both their dissatisfaction with their current alliance and the attractiveness of the other side. In the mid-1920s Germany played up the possibility of ties with Russia in order to try to extract concessions from the West.[41] Similarly, in May 1972 Russia argued that the American mining of Haiphong was increasing the pressure on her to draw closer to China. The Sino–Soviet split was not irreconcilable, Russia implied, and there were limits to the indignities she would endure in cooperating with the United States.[42] The same logic was at work in the summer of 1977 when Chinese leaders, angered at President Carter's unwillingness to make the concessions that would lead to normalization of relations, argued that Russia threatened the West more than she did China. "[I]f you compare the two sides, Europe and China, in terms of which part is of greater interest to the Soviet Union, I think it is Europe." Dismissing the significance of the Soviet-American détente, the Chinese spokesman said: "If one poses the question as to which will be the first to be bitten by the polar bear, it is not necessarily China. Perhaps it will be Europe."[43] If the Chinese leaders believed this, they had less need for American support.

The other side of this coin is that the state which benefits greatly from an alliance or which can defect to the other side only at great cost will have to make concessions to its present partners. To admit one's need for the alliance and one's lack of alternatives is to invite depredation. For this reason, Thomas Sanderson, the British permanent undersecretary at the Foreign Office, in 1905 wrote the ambassador in Berlin: "I wish we could make the lunatics here who denounce Germany in such unmeasured terms and howl for an agreement with Russia understand that the natural effect is to drive Germany into the Russian camp and encourage the Russians to believe that they can get all they want at our expense and without coming to any agreement with us."[44]

A state that is trying to rally others to a coalition against what it perceives to be a grave menace faces a dilemma. In order to persuade others to join, the state will want to stress the danger that the adversary constitutes to them all and its commitment to the common defense. But to do this is to acknowledge that it believes it imperative to form an alliance, thus allowing others who are, or pretend to be, less alarmed to exact a higher price for their cooperation.

These factors help to explain the relations within and between the Triple Alliance and the Triple Entente. Britain was in a weak position vis-à-vis her partners because she could not be sure that they would not defect. In 1911 Grey denied that Germany's annexation of Alsace-Lorraine "has made a combination between France and Germany against us impossible,"[45] and therefore took great care not to offend France. He also doubted whether they could rely upon Russia. Russian leaders realized this and understood that it gave them the freedom to disregard British interests in areas like Persia. Since Britain felt that one reason why her partners might desert the Entente was the fear that the coalition was not strong and resolute enough to contain the Triple Alliance, she had to reassure France and Russia. For if they thought the Entente was failing, they would rush to strike a bargain with Germany; signs of weakness in the Entente could set off positive feedback that would destroy it. The very vulnerability of France and, to a lesser extent, Russia made them more likely than England to cut their losses if the Entente could not provide for their security. As Grey put it as early as 1905, "The weak point is that [France] might some day have a scare that we intend to change [our policy of supporting her]. . . . If . . . by some misfortune or blunder our Entente were to be broken up, France will have to make her own terms with Germany."[46] So in the next nine years France had few causes for complaint on this score. Britain even decided against sending a military band to Germany on the grounds that it might unduly disturb her ally. More significant, one of the reasons why she did not try to restrain her allies in 1914 was the fear that the attempt to do so would break up the Entente, leaving her at Germany's mercy.

This analysis indicates that the common claim that the rigidity of the alliances was a major power cause of the war is misleading. Although no major power had shifted sides during the ten years preceding the war, Britain, and to a lesser extent Germany,[47] feared such shifts and so made concessions to partners. Had the alliances been rigid—or had Britain and Germany thought they were—the distribution of power within them would have been different and the outcome of the disputes between the two sides might have been different. A second point follows: Even if it is true that this configuration contributed to the war, one cannot claim that the same logic makes the bipolarity of the Cold War also unstable. The two kinds of systems are very different, although both are often labeled bipolar.[48] In the earlier period each camp was composed of states of relatively equal strength. Therefore, the defection of any one of them could tip the balance. This produced the internal bargaining situation described above. The post–World War II bipolarity is different. Here each camp is dominated by a single state. The others contribute relatively little. When France threatened to virtually withdraw from the North Atlantic Treaty Organization, the United States did not offer major concessions to dissuade her, and when she acted on her threat the effects were hardly noticeable. Thus, in the current system, small allies cannot drag their mentors into conflicts in the way that they could before World War I. (It should also be noted that the pre–World War I configuration is not automatically conducive to war. Allies could use their greater bargaining power to restrain their partners.)

Balance Theory—"The Enemy of My Enemy Is My Friend"

One kind of interaction dynamic merits special attention. Although there are many exceptions to the rule, it can be thought of as providing a baseline that represents what would happen if the main forces in the situation were the only things at work. It neglects blunders, exceptional skill, and idiosyncratic choices.

Known as balance or consistency theory, this view echoes the old Arab proverbs: "The friend of my friend is my friend; the enemy of my friend is my enemy; the enemy of my enemy is my friend." Actors who are friendly with each other share mutual friendships and enmities. A configuration which is described by these proverbs is balanced or consistent.[49] Consistency develops through interconnections. Two states with no direct bilateral conflicts can become enemies if one supports and the other opposes a third state. States can cooperate not because their direct interests coincide, but because they are linked through support of or opposition to a third power. Often the relations between two states are determined by the relations between each of them and others in the system. Thus, a state that wants to form an alliance with another may become hostile to the other's adversary. In 1914, for example, several British leaders argued that "the best method of persuading the Balkan States to join the Allies would be in alliance against their common and traditional enemy, the Turk."[50]

Although many configurations are not perfectly balanced, a topic to which we will return, the reasons for balance are fairly obvious. Two states which have a quarrel with a third can benefit from working together. It is hard to imagine that China and the United States would have maintained indefinitely a high level of hostility in the face of Soviet conflicts with both of them. A state which opposes another will usually develop bad relations with a third state that supports the other because this support will have the effect, even if it does not have the intent, of harming the first state. Finally, two states which have good relations with a third state are likely to gain by working together. In many instances, the same considerations that lead each of them to cooperate with the third state will lead each to cooperate with each other. In other instances, the links that each country has to the third will earn them a common enemy. And the third state may seek to bring its two allies together. Doing so will sacrifice the benefit of being indispensable to two others who must rely on the state because they cannot cooperate with each other, but this advantage is hard to gain when there are fourth states around that can bid for the friendship of either of the other two. If a state's two allies have serious conflicts with each other, the obvious danger is that the one the state fails to support will gravitate to the state's enemies. Developing good relations among all three states will help maintain the alliance and so will bolster the state's position. Therefore, it is not surprising that the German ambassador to Japan in 1941 argued that his instructions to encourage German-Japanese-Russian cooperation justified his pledge that Germany would "do everything within her power to promote a friendly understanding" between Russia and Japan.[51] And in 1906 the French prime minister told the Russian foreign minister that France was "anxious that Russia and England should come to agreements, that France meant to remain the Ally of Russia and the friend of England and would not drop either one or the other."[52]

In consistent international systems the states are divided into two camps. Each state has friendly relations with all other members of its alliance and hostile relations with all members of the opposite camp. No states are cross-pressured by supporting or opposing only one of two allied states, or by supporting or opposing two states which are at odds with each other. Systems are likely to be most consistent when there is a dominant conflict around which all states orient themselves. There is, then, only a single question that a state asks another: Is it aiding the state or supporting the main adversary? Thus, Churchill's defense of aiding the Soviet Union in June 1941: "I have only one purpose, the destruction of Hitler, and my life is much simplified thereby. If Hitler invaded Hell I would make at least a favourable reference to the Devil in the House of Commons."[53] The same thought was put less graphically by George Canning in 1808 when he described the basic principle of his foreign policy: "Any nation of Europe that starts up with a determination to oppose a power which . . . is the common enemy of all nations, whatever may be the existing political relations of that nation and Great Britain, becomes instantly our essential ally."[54] In the tense atmosphere of 1948, General Eisenhower similarly defined a friendly country as one that opposed the Soviet Union.[55]

In such cases the major powers, and many minor ones, feel that the conflict is the most important cleavage in the system. For states big enough to be able to influence the outcome significantly, doing so is worth the use of a large proportion of their resources. The gains that might accrue from maintaining good relations with both sides are less than the value of helping to determine the shape of the postwar world. Great pressure will be put on smaller states for them to take a stand too, as each side strives for every possible advantage. So most states will feel both pushes and pulls toward alignment. Few significant states wanted and were able to stay neutral in world wars I and II. As the French ambassador to Moscow reported before World War II, the question was not "whether the U.S.S.R. will, or will not, be with us, but *with whom* they will be."[56]

If two great powers feel their relations are characterized by overriding conflict, but the smaller states are more concerned with local conflicts, then the pressures for balance lead to negative feedback. The gains for a great power lead, not to dominoes falling, but to compensating gains for the other side, because the power that wins the support of a local state will find itself opposed by the state's enemies. Thus, the British plans for getting all the Balkan states on their side in World War I foundered on the rock of local conflicts. Bulgaria would not fight on the same side as Rumania and Greece. Recent events in the Horn of Africa show the same dynamics. A leftist revolution led Ethiopia to switch allegiance from the United States to the USSR. But

228

Ethiopia was engaged in serious quarrels with its neighbors, some of whom also had close ties to the Soviet Union. These states reacted with hostility to Ethiopia's new patron and with friendship to her enemy. The Sudan's movement away from the Soviet Union was accelerated and Somalia closed the Soviet base at Berbera, expelled all Soviet and Cuban personnel, and broke diplomatic relations with those states. Furthermore, even though the United States was trying to decrease arms sales to the Third World, it was willing to sell arms to the Sudan, and it might well have sold them to Somalia had that country not attacked Ethiopia. So if the pressures toward balance are strong, a state that seeks to win over several countries in an area must encourage good relations among them. This strategy is risky because it entails the danger that they all will turn against the state, but it may be the only route to a major diplomatic victory.

If the existence of conflicts among the small states limits the damage suffered by a great power which falls out of favor with one of them, the friction between two great powers gives the smaller states freedom of action.[57] The small power that becomes the target of hostility from a larger state is likely to receive the support of the latter's rivals. Most of us have had the experience of angering a powerful person and finding that, instead of being an isolated, one had gained the support of those who disliked or opposed the person. The same effect occurs with political alignments. Russian support for India was solidified by the Sino–Indian War. Egypt's break with Russia in 1972 made it possible for that country to obtain aid from the United States, just as the American refusal to help build the Aswan dam paved the way for closer relations between Egypt and Russia.

Because countries are likely to develop conflicts with their neighbors, balance often leads to a checkerboard pattern. Kautilya, the ancient Indian student of international politics, noted that states on either side of a third state become allies, and states on either side of those two join with each other and the state in the middle.[58] Of course, few situations actually conform to all details of this ideal, but many show traces of it as the underlying dynamics make themselves felt.

Although there are always pressures toward balance, they do not always prevail. Some of the special circumstances that produced imbalance in the pre–World War I era will be discussed later. Here we want to stress the tensions created when a balanced configuration is not in the interest of one of the actors. Obeying one of the Arab proverbs—the enemy of my friend is my enemy—is often costly to the state. As we noted earlier, to increase its bargaining power, a state may try to make itself indispensable to two others which are in conflict with each other rather than joining either side. The point of balance theory, however, is that this will be hard to do and there will be a tendency either for the two other states to overcome their antipathy and work together against the third, or for the state to become the enemy of one of them.

A state is also not likely to obey the rules of balance in its behavior toward another which is providing limited assistance to the state's adversary if it thinks that a conciliatory policy can woo the other to its side. Balance theory says that if relations between the United States and Russia are bad, Russia should respond to a Sino-American reapproachment by becoming hostile, or more hostile, to China. But if the Russian leaders believe that China's support for the United States is not permanent, they could offer concessions in the expectation of winning her over. The predictions of balance theory will hold, however, once the state has concluded that the third power is irrevocably tied to its enemy.

Another balanced pattern that is not in the interest of some of the states is one in which a single state faces a more powerful coalition. This was the situation toward the end of the struggles against Napoleon and Hitler. Since this is not a situation that the weaker party desires, it will make great efforts to avoid it, and, with a modicum of resources and skill, should be able to do so. Napoleon and Hitler became isolated because of their great ambitions. At the beginning of the conflicts they thought they had sufficient power to win. By the time they realized that this was not true, they could not buy off any of the members of the opposing coalitions because the latter were convinced both that victory was in sight and that it was necessary to maintain the coalition in order to contain the aggressor who would remain a threat even after the war. But in the more common peacetime case, the problem facing an isolated state is usually not as great. The ties among the other states, not having been through the forge of wartime collaboration, are weaker, and the degree of hostility between the state and each of the others is lower and less uniform.

The more isolated the state is, the more it will be willing to sacrifice to better its position. Unless the state is so weak as to be an obvious candidate for dismemberment (Poland in the late eighteenth and early nineteenth centuries), or has been so reckless as to convince all the others that it is such a menace that it must be stopped by force, it should be able to offer sufficient inducements to win over at least one ally. Even if it cannot succeed quickly, an isolated state will rarely accept its vulnerability. In the Balkan crisis of 1887, Bismarck was able to threaten to unite all the continental powers against England unless she joined with Austria and Italy to contain Russia in the Balkans—a coalition in which Bismarck himself could not participate without sacrificing his good relations with Russia. This threat was potent because the others had grievances against England. So unless England were to accept dependence on Germany she had to change this situation. To do so was costly, and for years it appeared that working with Germany might be the best course. But the dangers of isolation and dependence were great enough so that Britain could not rest easy with this configuration, and so sought to reduce the grievances others had against her and to generate alternative sources of support. The fact that a system in which all were united against England would be balanced did not thereby make it a likely outcome.

Britain was less successful in the interwar period. As early as the first defense reviews of the 1930s, British leaders realized that even with the support of France she could not simultaneously oppose Germany, Italy, and Japan:

> We consider it to be a cardinal requirement of our national and imperial security that our foreign policy should be so conducted as to avoid the possible development of a situation in which we might be confronted simultaneously with the hostility, open or veiled, of Japan in the Far East, Germany in the West, and any Power on the main line of communication between the two.[59]

That her efforts failed is largely explained by nonsystemic factors. Public opinion made it difficult for England to buy off Italy. American policy, based to a large extent on considerations of morality and public opinion, made conciliation of Japan very costly. The view that Chamberlain expressed in 1934 was a common one: "I have *no* doubt we could easily make an agreement with [the Japanese] if the U.S.A. were out of the picture. It is the Americans who are the difficulty and I don't know how we can get over it."[60] And British statesmanship in the period was deficient. So the bonds among Germany, Italy, and Japan tightened. But even though she did not succeed in doing so, preventing this was one of England's prime objectives.

The utility of balance theory can best be demonstrated by taking a period of history and showing how the kinds of propositions we have been discussing can bring together disparate phenomena, shed new light on familiar incidents, locate previously unnoticed patterns, and provide satisfactory explanations for puzzling behavior. These are the tasks of the next section.

Balance Theory and Pre–World War I Diplomacy

The broad outlines of pre–World War I diplomacy conform to much of balance theory. One of the striking things about this war is that many states seem to be on the wrong side. If we look at the bilateral conflicts, it is not surprising that France fought Germany and Russia fought Austria. But Austria and France had no quarrels and Russia and France had few common interests. Even more strikingly, Germany and England seemed like natural allies, as many German statesmen and not a Few Englishmen noted throughout this period. By contrast, the far-flung British Empire was directly threatened by Russia and France. British and French colonies touched each other at many points, and the French outrage at the British occupation of Egypt created constant friction from 1886 to 1904. Russia was even more of a threat. Her expansion in Central Asia brought the two countries close to war and even her defeat by Japan and the revision of the Anglo–Japanese Alliance in 1905 that insured Japanese support in the event of a war with Russia did not totally set England's mind at rest. The Russian desire for Constantinople

231

was another source of tension, one that diminished but did not disappear when Britain decided that the northeastern Mediterranean could not be defended and that she had to rely on her Egyptian bases.

Many of the conflicts that developed in this period can be understood only in terms of the dynamics of balance. States developed enemies and allies out of their relations with others. To concentrate on the main features, we will ignore Italy and Japan and postpone treatment of England. Of the relations among the other four major powers—Germany, Austria, France, and Russia—the main line of conflict was between Germany and France and a secondary line was between Russia and Austria. Even had France become reconciled to the loss of Alsace-Lorraine, geography would have made France and Germany rivals if not enemies. The clash between Austria and Russia was not quite as deep. Although controlling if not suppressing Balkan nationalism was a vital interest for Austria, the Russian stake in the Balkans was not immutable. There were other outlets from Russian expansionism and the depth of Pan-Slav feeling was much less in some Russian factions and leaders than in others. But as long as the Russians did sponsor Balkan nationalism, she would menace Austria–Hungary's international standing and domestic stability. If Russia and Austria were enemies, balance theory predicts that Germany cannot be friends with both. Thus, during the Balkan crisis of 1875–1878, "Any marked improvement in friendship with Russia would have to be purchased with a deterioration in relations with her rivals."[61] Of course, Bismarck did maintain good relations with both adversaries, which is testimony both to special circumstances and to his great skill—neither of which, however, might have lasted out the century.

Even if the system becomes balanced, the theory cannot tell us how it will be balanced—that is, whether Germany will side with Russia or Austria. On this point other systems dynamics are relevant, although not completely determining. German statesmen believed that Austria, being the weaker of the two, would more surely be forced into alliance with France if she were deserted by Germany. Russia was strong enough to stand by herself. Furthermore, the reactionary nature of Russia's regime inhibited cooperation with France and conflict over Central Asia and Constantinople made a link between Russia and England unlikely. Russia was then strong but isolated and, even without a tie to Germany, might not be able to afford bad relations with her or establish good relations with her enemies. Thus, part of the reason why German decision makers chose Austria was that they underestimated the strength of the forces impelling the system toward balance. They thought that the antipathy between France and Russia was great enough to prevent their allying even if both had grievances against Germany.

Once Germany's choice was made, however, balance theory does offer a firm prediction. If Germany had allied with Russia, the theory says that Austria and France would have worked together. Austria was the enemy of Russia, and since Russia and Germany were allies, would become the enemy of Germany too. Since France was also Germany's enemy, they would become friends. Another positive bond would have been the shared enmity toward Russia. In Austria's case, this was a direct relationship; in France's case, mediated by the ties between Russia and Germany. If England became involved, the theory says that she would have either developed friendly relations with Germany and Russia, coupled with hostile relations with France and Austria, or else allied with the latter two powers and opposed the former two. Again, it cannot say which of these patterns would have occurred, but it does say that England would not have allied with Germany and against Russia or with France and against Austria. Of course, Germany did not choose Russia as a partner, and so we cannot say whether the theory's predictions would have been borne out. But I think they are plausible. So did German statesmen, who feared that abandoning Austria would lead that country to turn to France.

Before turning our attention to England, we should discuss the obvious and important exception to our generalization—the period from the Franco-Prussian War to 1890 (excepting 1878–1881), in which Germany maintained good relations with both Russia and Austria. Bismarck's skill was a necessary ingredient. By its nature, skill is difficult to generalize about, and all we can do here is note Bismarck's ability to empathize with others, to alter forms of inducements and pressures as the situation changed, and to construct intricate arrangements that were hard for his contemporaries—and later scholars—to fully understand, let alone combat. Because his alliance systems were not balanced, he had to walk a number of delicate lines. "It was necessary to support Russia just enough to convince her of the advantages of German goodwill, but not enough to make her believe this could be got for nothing, and not enough to estrange England or irritate Austria. On the other hand, he had to support England and Austria enough to maintain good relations . . . as well as to preserve the atmosphere of suspicion between England and Russia. Too much support here, or the appearance of it, might, however, antagonize the Russians."[62] Whether this skill was put to the best uses and whether a less devious policy would have better served the cause of peace and the long-run interests of Germany is beyond the scope of this chapter, but the virtuosity of his performance is not to be doubted.

Even Bismarck's skill might have been to no avail had it not been for propitious circumstances. His primary goal was to isolate France. To reach both this end and to make secondary gains, he sought to make Germany indispensable to all the others and insure that they could not get what they wanted without his brokerage. French weakness in the years immediately following the Franco-Prussian War helped reduce her value as an ally. Colonial expansion, encouraged by Bismarck, both distracted France from continental issues and created conflicts with England, thus increasing both states' need for German diplomatic assistance. Britain, although stronger, was potentially vulnerable, as her leaders fully realized by the turn of the century. Her decision not to intervene in the war for Schleswig–Holstein despite her previous pledge,[63] her weakness on the issue of the Belgian railroads in 1869, which raised doubts about her willingness to run risks even for Belgian independence,[64] the sorry state of her navy in the period before the 1890s,[65] all diminished her diplomatic weight. Her widespread empire, furthermore, brought her many enemies. Germany, which cared less for new territory could afford to help Britain. And she could extract a price for such cooperation because she could also afford to remain neutral in England's disputes or even rally the others against her. Even after the signing of the Anglo-Japanese Alliance in 1902 eased Britain's position, she was still partly dependent on German goodwill because of her severe conflicts with France and Russia.

Germany's policy in the post-Bismarckian era relied on these conflicts for its success. Because England could not ally with France and Russia, German leaders believed that she would have to turn for support to the Triple Alliance. So it was safe, indeed wise, to antagonize England and to threaten her interests in order to show her that failing to support Germany would be very costly. Of course, the fatal errors were the linked ones of overestimating the strengths of the conflicts dividing England from Russia and France and failing to see that German pressure was leading England to see Germany as an unreasonable and greedy state that was not a fit alliance partner. But this should not obscure the point that England's alternatives *were* sharply limited, especially before Fashoda and the Russo–Japanese War.

The isolation of England and France helps to explain why Bismarck was able to construct a system that violated balance theory. Although Russia was unhappy with the German support for Austria, she could not leave the coalition because she had no alternative allies. To make a Franco–Russian pact even more difficult, Bismarck tried to maintain good relations with France, thereby putting Germany in a position to grant or withhold assistance to her. Bismarck also made sure that Russia received something from her ties with Germany so that severing them would be a loss. The main gain for Russia was a moderation of German support for Austria. To break with Germany could easily lead to greater Austrian influence over Germany, which Russia could ill afford. Thus, the Russians were forced to reestablish the Dreikaiserbund after having broken it in the wake of the Balkan crisis of 1877. The Russians had recognized "the facts of life: lofty treatment of Germany did not mix well with fear of English attack and Austrian intrigues,"[66] Crucial here, as in the case of relations with England, was Germany's indispensability. Only if Germany could insure that Russia could not ally with France or England would even great skill permit the maintenance of this unbalanced system. Although Bismarck's successors ended this ambitious policy, it is doubtful whether even he could have maintained it indefinitely. Many of the important factors in Russia's isolation were beyond his control (e.g., the French recovery after her defeat in 1871) and even Bismarck made some errors—such as freezing Russia out of the Berlin money market, with the result that Russia turned to Paris.

If unusual circumstances and skill account for the one major and lasting deviation from balance theory, blunders and nonstrategic factors can also produce similar results. Thus, the Kaiser sometimes supported Austria's enemies and did so not because of complex calculations, but because of ties of personal loyalty. Similarly, strong ideological preferences can interfere with the operation of balance dynamics, as they delayed the ties between France and Russia in the 1890s and China and the United States in the 1960s.

The pressures which brought England into alignment with France and Russia and into opposition to the Triple Alliance are similar to those discussed earlier, but with the significant difference that the process was gradual and that English statesmen were not entirely aware of why events were unfolding as they were. Furthermore, if these leaders had been able to foresee the consequences of their initial policies, they might have chosen differently. They did not want to join a continental alliance and strongly resisted the German blandishments to do so. Overt French approaches might not have been any more successful. It can be objected that the ties with France were not necessary to turn Britain into Germany's enemy. Since Germany was the strongest state on the continent, England had to oppose her. She would win any war in which England was neutral, and the result would be to gravely menace British security. In retrospect, this may be correct. But British statesmen did not see it this way and did not automatically line up against the potentially dominating German power.

The Anglo–Japanese Alliance of 1902 alleviated, but did not solve, England's problem of isolation. To solve it by reaching a general understanding with Germany would be to increase French and Russian grievances against England and to divide Europe into two hostile alliances. The obvious alternative was to try to deal with the specific issues on which England clashed with France and Russia and which made England's isolation so dangerous. This led to negotiations for a colonial entente in which France ended her two decades of opposition to British rule in Egypt in return for England's acquiescence in French control of Morocco. British leaders gave little thought to the implications of such an agreement for continental politics—or, rather, they did not think there were any. Indeed, there might have been no such implications if Cromer and Balfour had not insisted that France not only vote with England and Egyptian matters, but also provide active diplomatic support to help overcome the opposition of other powers. The French resisted, but finally offered to concede in return for a reciprocal grant of British support for the French efforts in Morocco. Lansdowne, who had not cared about the British demand in the first place, ''immediately accepted, without realizing how far this clause threatened to lead him. In his view, it was merely a question of 'moral support.''"[67] Most British statesmen believed that this stance was compatible with the maintenance of good relations with Germany.

As one leader said when denying that the entente was a menace to the Triple Alliance, "Our earnest wish is to be friends with both [France and Germany], and not only them, but with other countries also."[68]

Even during the first Moroccan crisis, England did not consider that she had permanently aligned herself with France, as Grey made clear in his report of a conversation with the German ambassador in early 1906: "Count Metternich said that, if England was to use the French *entente* always to side with France against Germany, of course Germany would come to look on England as her enemy, I said there had been no question of always siding with France against Germany. Since the *entente* was framed there had been one point of difference—the subject of Morocco—which happened to be one of the very subjects covered by a definite agreement between England and France. . . . I could again assure him that, were the Morocco difficulty satisfactorily settled, it was our desire to show that the *entente* was not to be used in a sense hostile to Germany."[69]

But Grey was not able to act on his desire. The problem was twofold. First, the Germans misinterpreted the degree of British support for France. On the one hand, they overestimated the initial British commitment and thought that unless they reacted strongly a pattern of cooperation would be set. On the other hand, they thought that strong opposition to the French claims on Morocco would break up the entente. German pressure nearly worked, and might have done so had she not overplayed her hand. But the pressure was probably not needed. The colonial agreement would not have automatically led to continued and close Anglo–French cooperation. In 1890 Britain and Germany signed an agreement similar to the entente in which Germany limited her claims in East Africa in return for Britain's ceding Helgoland. But this agreement had no ramifications because the two states could carry it out by themselves. They did not earn the enmity of any other state; there was no opposition to cause the two states to work more closely together. Had there been no opposition in Morocco, the entente might have been similarly short lived. The second problem was that Britain did not understand the legitimacy of German grievances. Although the German claims of economic interests in Morocco were patently false, her wider argument had more validity. France had provided compensation to England and Italy, so why should Germany not claim her reward? Was Germany not a world power like England which had to be consulted on all changes of the status quo? Furthermore, England was at least potentially menacing Germany by even temporarily joining with France.

Partly because she did not see the degree of justification for Germany's demand for compensation and hostility toward England, English statesmen were greatly alarmed by Germany's behavior. First, they thought that Germany's attempt to bully France indicated that Germany would not tolerate an equal power on the Continent. Then, as German hostility became aimed as much toward England as toward France, British leaders saw a direct threat to

·their own security. Since they believed that the German behavior was not a reasonable response to anything they had done, they concluded that her hostility was gratuitous and showed that she was a danger, being exceptionally greedy and believing that others could be bullied into doing her bidding. A twofold response was needed: France had to be supported lest she give way and allow Germany full sway over the Continent, and England herself had to oppose Germany. Eyre Crowe put the British perception well: initially, the entente "had been but a friendly settlement of particular outstanding differences, giving hope for future harmonious relations between two neighbouring countries that had got into the habit of looking at one another askance; now there had emerged an element of common resistance to outside dictation and aggression, a unity of special interests tending to develop into active cooperation against a third power. It is essential to bear in mind that this new feature of the *entente* was the direct effect produced by Germany's effort to break it up, and that, failing the active or threatening hostility of Germany, such anti-German bias as the *entente* must be admitted to have at one time assumed, would certainly not exist at present, nor probably survive in the future."[70]

Of course, there were other sources of conflict between England and Germany, especially the German naval building program. By itself this would have been a powerful impetus to close ties with France (although the German policy was initially predicated on the belief that England could never ally with France and Russia). But, in the absence of the dynamics discussed above, the chances for a negotiated settlement of the naval race would have been greater. And even without one, British hostility would have been significantly less. England still would have viewed the German navy with alarm, both because it constituted a threat to her power and because it indicated that German intentions were hostile. But the German actions were perceived as especially dangerous because they were seen in the context of suspicion growing out of the German reaction to the entente. The navy greatly contributed to the British decision makers' fears of Germany, but would their reaction have been as strong had they not been already predisposed to believe the worst?

Ironically, the presence of specific disputes with France and Russia, and the absence of such disputes with Germany, help explain Britain's alignment with the former.[71] Crowe's argument on this point has a good deal of merit: with France and Russia there were "ancient and real sources of conflict, springing from imperfectly patched-up differences of past centuries, the inelastic stipulations of antiquated treaties, or the troubles incidental to unsettled colonial frontiers."[72] These required special efforts if they were not to lead to a rupture. Thus, "The Anglo-French *entente* had a very material basis and tangible object—namely, the adjustment of a number of actually—existing serious differences. The efforts now [January 1907] being made by England to arrive at an understanding with Russia are justified by a very similar situation. But for an Anglo–German understanding on the same lines

237

there is no room since none could be built up on the same foundation. . . . [T]here are no questions of any importance now at issue between
the two countries. Any understanding must therefore be entirely different in
object and scope.''[73] The resulting problem was described in a minute by
Crowe six months earlier: "With Germany we have no differences whatever.
An understanding which does not consist in the removal of differences can
only mean a plan of cooperation in political transactions, whether offensive,
defensive, or for the maintenance of neutrality. It is difficult to see on what
point such cooperation between England and Germany is at this moment appropriate.''[74] Grey agreed: "There was nothing out of which [an Anglo–Ger-
man] *entente* might be made. At present, there was nothing to discuss between the two Governments. . . . I regarded the relations between England
and Germany as being now normal, and I saw no reason for saying anything
about them.''[75]

Around the turn of the century, England rejected several German over-
tures, largely on the ground that she did not want to enter into a general
agreement that would link her to the continental alignments. Instead she
opted for limited ententes which, she believed, would have fewer implications
and leave her with fewer obligations. But the effect of this course of action was
the same as that of the rejected alternative. In reply to a parliamentary question as to whether the negotiations with Russia involved "general political
relationships," Grey said:

> The direct object of the negotiations is to prevent conflict and difficulties between
> the two Powers and in the part of Asia which affects the Indian frontier and the
> Russian frontiers in that region. If these negotiations result in an agreement, it will
> deal only with these questions. What the indirect result will be as regard general
> political relationships must depend on how such an agreement works in practice
> and what effect it has on public opinion in both countries.[76]

As we have seen, the crucial "indirect results" of the ententes depended
in part on the British statesmen's failure to anticipate the effects of their
policy, their lack of empathy with the German position, and the alarming inferences they drew from German behavior. This raises the question of
whether this outcome would have occurred in the absence of these
peculiarities of British statesmen and decision making. To reply in the
negative is to stress the importance of factors that are, from the standpoint of
the system, accidental. Obviously a definitive answer is impossible, but two
points indicate that the British response was, at least in part, the product of
the dynamics of the system. First, the British interpretation of and reaction to
German behavior, although questionable in light of evidence available to later
scholars, was not strikingly unusual. Statesmen often fail to understand how
others see their own state's actions and underestimate the degree to which
their behavior harms others.[77] Second, even had the British perceptions been
more accurate, the initial decision to support France in the face of German
opposition did align England with the former. Given the competition between

the Triple Alliance and its adversaries, it is not at all clear that England could have maintained good relations with both sides. A better British understanding of the situation might have led them to react a bit less sharply to the German hostility, but would not have altered the basic dilemma that to support France was to incur the wrath of France's enemies. Irrespective of the special problems of British decision making, there were strong pressures operating that made it likely that the system would be balanced.

Conclusion

This chapter has tried to demonstrate that focusing on the international system and the patterns of interaction within it illuminates a great deal of international politics. Much of the complexity of international affairs and many of the problems of foreign policy making arise from the fact that policies operate in an interconnected environment in which the actors have diverse and conflicting goals. Thus, small issues can have great significance and minor acts can have major consequences. Often the results are not those expected by any of the statesmen. The interconnections are difficult to detect and susceptible to the divergent pressures of independent actors. Nevertheless, scholars can identify a number of common kinds of systems effects and specify some of the conditions under which they are likely to occur. Such analysis is both limited and useful. Useful because it is highly parsimonious. Because systems theory starts with the most important factors, it allows us to grasp a great deal of what is happening by looking at only a few causes or independent variables. It often gives us a baseline of expected behavior which both predicts and explains a lot of state action and also calls our attention to deviations that call for special analysis. The principles that provide the dynamics of the systems are fairly simple; and this makes the theories we have discussed manageable. But the ways that the dynamics work themselves out in any situation are usually complicated; and this is why it is so useful to employ the theories. Without them it is easy to get lost in a mass of confusing detail and miss the essentials.

But systems theories of the kind I have presented are also limited because they ignore domestic politics, personalities, and accidents. Even when the external pressures are strong, they may be resisted. For example, to explain the British behavior in the last week of July 1914, one must understand not only the international system but also the internal conflict. Although those who had been most active in setting British foreign policy in the previous years wanted to stand by the entente, others in the Cabinet disagreed, and the policy adopted had to satisfy both groups. In other cases, characteristics of individual decision makers matter. Some statesmen are skilled; some are blunderers. Some are very timid; others will run risks that any sensible person would avoid. Sometimes the aberrant behavior has little long-run effect because it is counteracted by others. But, even when this is the case, the short-run impact—and the cost in resources and human lives—can be very high. And in other cases the behavior can produce ramifying changes whose effects will be felt for generations. Starting with a systems perspective helps us to see the patterns that stay the same as personalities and domestic politics change; but it is clear that these patterns are not always present, and so we must also be alert to the role of chance and contingency.

Notes

1. The best-know applications of systems theory to international relations are Morton Kaplan, *System and Process in International Politics* (New York: Wiley, 1957); Stanley Hoffmann, "International Systems and International Law," in Klaus Knorr and Sidney Verba (eds.), *The International System* (Princeton: Princeton University Press, 1961), pp. 205–237; and Richard Rosecrance, *Action and Reaction in World Politics* (Boston: Little, Brown, 1963). For an excellent critique and the development of much better arguments, see Kenneth Waltz, *A Theory of International Politics* (Reading, Mass.: Addison-Wesley, 1979). For discussions of systems theory as a general approach, see Walter Buckley (ed.), *Modern Systems Research for the Behavioral Scientist* (Chicago: Aldine, 1968); Howard Pattee (ed.), *Hierarchy Theory: The Challenge of Complex Systems* (New York: Braziller, 1973); John Sutherland, *A General Systems Philosophy for the Social and Behavioral Sciences* (New York: Braziller, 1973); Siegfried Nadel, *The Theory of Social Structure* (London: Cohen and West, 1957); C. H. Waddington, *Tools for Thought* (London: Jonathan Cape, 1977); and W. Ross Ashby, *Design for a Brain* (New York: Wiley, 1952).

2. Herbert Simon, *The Sciences of the Artificial* (Cambridge: MIT Press, 1969), p. 86.

3. Kurt Lewin, *Resolving Social Conflicts* (New York: Harper and Brothers, 1948), p. 73.

4. Donald Reinken, "Computer Explorations of the 'Balance of Power,' " in Morton Kaplan (ed.), *New Approaches to International Relations* (New York: St. Martin's Press, 1968), p. 469.

5. W. Ross Ashby, *Introduction to Cybernetics* (New York: Barnes and Noble, 1968).

6. Herbert Molly Mason, Jr., *The Rise of the Luftwaffe, 1918–1940* (New York: Dial Press, 1973), pp. 99–109.

7. Nobutaka Ike (ed.), *Japan's Decision for War* (Stanford: Stanford University Press, 1967), p. 237.

8. For a good discussion, see Marvine Howe, "Showdown in Lebanon, Again," *New York Times,* July 12, 1978.

9. Edward Ingram, "An Aspiring Buffer State: Anglo–Persian Relations in the Third Coalition, 1804–1807," *Historical Journal* 16 (September 1973): 509–533.

10. Paul Schroeder, "World War I as Galloping Gertie," *Journal of Modern History* 44 (September 1972): 337–338.

11. Ibid.

12. E. T. S. Dugdale (ed.), *German Diplomatic Documents, 1871-1914*, vol 1, *The Bismarck Period* (New York: Barnes and Noble, 1969), pp. 369-372.

13. Historical Office, Department of State, *Foreign Relations of the United States: Diplomatic Papers 1935*, vol 1, *General, the Near East and Africa* (Washington, D.C.: Government Printing Office, 1953), p. 168.

14. Akira Iriye, "The Role of the United States Embassy in Tokyo," in Dorothy Borg and Shumpei Ikamoto (eds.), *Pearl Harbor as History* (New York: Columbia University Press, 1973), p. 126.

15. Pattee, *Hierarchy Theory*, p. 23.

16. For a further discussion, see my "Deterrence Theory Revisited," *World Politics* 31 (January 1979): 314-322. For an additional treatment of deterrence, see Paul Gordon Lauren's chapter in this book on bargaining.

17. Quoted in Keith Middlemas, *The Strategy of Appeasement* (Chicago: Quadrangle, 1972), pp. 190-191. Debate on this point is usually at the heart of discussions on how to respond to aggression.

18. Lewis Richardson, *Statistics of Deadly Quarrels* (Pittsburgh: Boxwood Press, Chicago: Quadrangle, 1960), p. xxiv.

19. Waltz, *Theory of International Relations*, Chapter 4.

20. William Plowden, *The Motor Car and Politics, 1896-1970* (London: Bodley Head, 1971), p. 241.

21. David Pletcher, *The Diplomacy of Annexation* (Columbia: University of Missouri Press, 1973), pp. 113-207.

22. John Sherwig, *Guineas and Gunpowder* (Cambridge: Harvard University Press, 1969), pp. 21-23.

23. Basil Liddell Hart, *Why Don't We Learn From History?* (London: Allen and Unwin, 1944), p. 39.

24. For an extended discussion, see my "Cooperation Under the Security Dilemma," *World Politics* 30 (January 1978): 167-214.

25. Kenneth Waltz, *Man, the State, and War* (New York: Columbia University Press, 1959).

26. Konrad Jarausch, "The Illusion of Limited War: Chancellor Bethmann Hollweg's Calculated Risk, July 1914," *Central European History* 2 (March 1969): 50. For more discussion of the outbreak of World War I, see the chapters by Ole Holsti and Samuel Williamson in this book.

27. Fischer, *World Power or Decline*, trans. by Lancelot Farrar, Robert Kimber, and Rita Kimber (New York: Norton, 1974). Fischer's main argument can be found in *War of Illusions*, trans. by Marian Jackson (New York: Norton, 1975).

28. Jay Forrester, *Urban Dynamics* (Cambridge: MIT Press, 1969).

29. Frank Howley, *Berlin Command* (New York: Putnam's, 1950), pp. 202-203.

30. Walter Nimocks, *Milner's Young Men* (Durham, N.C.: Duke University Press, 1968), pp. 75-81.

31. This usage stretches the technical definitions of feedback, which applies only in

hierarchical systems, but I think the meaning is close enough to merit my employment of the term.

32. U.S. Senate, Committee on Foreign Relations, *Legislative Origins of the Truman Doctrine,* Hearings Held in Executive Session, Historical Series (executive hearings held in 1947 and made public in 1973), 80th Congress, 1st Session (Washington, D.C.: Government Printing Office, 1973), p. 160.

33. Quoted in Stephen Rosenfeld, "The Panama Negotiations—A Close-Run Thing," *Foreign Affairs* 54 (October 1975): 2.

34. Frank Snepp, *Decent Interval* (New York: Random House, 1977), pp. 175–176, 143–144, 237–238.

35. The basic discussion of the problem is in Mancur Olson, *The Logic of Collective Action* (Cambridge: Harvard University Press, 1965).

36. Kenneth Bourne, *The Foreign Policy of Victorian England, 1830–1902* (Oxford: Clarendon Press, 1970), p. 140.

37. Andrew Burn, *Alexander the Great* (London: Hodder and Stoughton, 1947), p. 45.

38. W. N. Medlicott, "Bismarck and the Three Emperors' Alliance, 1881–87," *Transactions of the Royal Historical Society,* 4th series, 27 (1945): 67–68.

39. Herbert Dinerstein, "The Soviet Outlook: America, Europe, and China," in Robert Osgood et al., *Retreat from Empire?* (Baltimore: Johns Hopkins University Press, 1973), p. 125. Of course, this was not America's intention. Indeed, a major reason for American restraint vis-à-vis China was the fear that the use of force against her would trigger Soviet involvement.

40. Bruce Waller, *Bismarck at the Crossroads* (London: Athlone, 1974), p. 44.

41. Kurt Rosenbaum, *Community of Fate* (Syracuse, N. Y.: Syracuse University Press, 1965), pp. 129, 145, 241.

42. Hedrick Smith, "Soviet Hints Mining Fosters Cooperation with China to Aid Hanoi," *New York Times,* May 18, 1972.

43. Harrison Salisbury, "China 'Quite Unhappy' with Carter over Taiwan, a Top Leader Says," *New York Times,* August 30, 1977.

44. George Monger, *The End of Isolation* (London: Nelson, 1963), pp. 177–178. For more discussion of alliances in general, see Roger Dingman's chapter in this book.

45. Quoted in C. J. Lowe and M. L. Dockrill, *The Mirage of Power,* vol. 1, *British Foreign Policy, 1902–14* (London: Routledge and Kegan Paul, 1972), p. 25.

46. Ibid.

47. Germany feared Austria's disintegration more than her defection. But the effect was the same.

48. Kenneth Waltz, "The Stability of a Bipolar World," *Daedalus* 93 (Summer 1964): 900–902; Glenn Snyder and Paul Diesing, *Conflict Among Nations* (Princeton: Princeton University Press, 1977), pp. 429–450.

49. There is a large literature on consistency in psychology. For a summary see Robert Zajonc, "Cognitive Theories in Social Psychology," in Gardner Lindzey and Elliott Aronson (eds.), *The Handbook of Social Psychology* (Reading, Mass.: Addison-Wesley, 1968 ed.), I: 345–353. A good discussion of consistency in small groups is in Howard Taylor, *Balance in Small Groups* (New York: Van Nostrand Reinhold,

1970). Applications to international politics are presented by Frank Harary, "A Structural Analysis of the Situation in the Middle East in 1956," *Journal of Conflict Resolution* 5 (June 1961): 167–178, and Brian Healy and Arthur Stein, "The Balance of Power in International History," *Journal of Conflict Resolution* 17 (March 1973): 33–62.

50. Martin Gilbert, *Winston Churchill*, vol. 3, *1914–1916, The Challenge of War* (Boston: Houghton Mifflin, 1971), p. 200. The problem, however, was that the Balkans were rife with local conflicts and so, as we will discuss below, it was unlikely that all these states would fight on the same side.

51. James Morley, "Introduction," in James Morley (ed.), *Deterrent Diplomacy* (New York: Columbia University Press, 1976), p. 188.

52. Great Britain, Foreign Office, *British Documents on the Origins of the War, 1898–1914,* 11 vols., ed. by G. P. Gooch and Harold Temperley, vol. 4, *The Anglo-Russian Rapprochement, 1903–7* (London: His Majesty's Stationery Office, 1929), p. 245. [Hereafter cited as Britain, *British Documents on the Origins of the War.*]

53. Winston Churchill, *The Second World War*, vol. 3, *The Grand Alliance* (Boston: Houghton Mifflin, 1950), p. 370.

54. Sherwig, *Guineas and Gunpowder,* p. 197.

55. Charles Maier, "Introduction," in George Kistiakowsky, *A Scientist in the White House* (Cambridge: Harvard University Press, 1976), p. xxi.

56. Quoted in Lewis Namier, *In the Nazi Era* (London: Macmillan, 1952), p. 171.

57. This analysis also holds if all states are of relatively equal power, in which case the line between gaining freedom of action and limiting losses disappears.

58. George Modelski, "Kautilya," *American Political Science Review* 58 (September 1964): 554–557.

59. Quoted in Peter Dennis, *Decision by Default* (Durham, N.C.: Duke University Press, 1972), p. 58.

60. Quoted in N. H. Gibbs, *Grand Strategy*, vol. 1, *Rearmament Policy* (London: Her Majesty's Stationery Office, 1976), pp. 394–395.

61. Waller, *Bismarck at the Crossroads,* p. 23.

62. Ibid,. p. 202. See also p. 133.

63. Keith Sandiford, *Great Britain and the Schleswig–Holstein Question* (Toronto: Toronto University Press, 1975).

64. Gordon Craig, *War, Politics, and Diplomacy* (New York: Praeger, 1966), pp. 153–178.

65. Arthur Marder, *The Anatomy of British Sea Power* (New York: Knopf, 1940).

66. Waller, *Bismarck at the Crossroads,* p. 242. Again, the short-run success of Bismarck's policy may have been outweighed by the long-term results. "Russo–German relations," Waller states, "were strained and the hand of those most suspicious of Germany was strengthened....The price paid for an Austro–German united front against Russia in the armaments question was increased, or at least sustained, Austrian suspicion of Germany and her eastern neighbour."

67. Pierre Guillen, "The Entente of 1904 as a Colonial Settlement," in Prosser Gif-

ford and William Roger Lewis (eds.), *France and Britain in Africa* (New Haven: Yale University Press, 1971), p. 365. See also Monger, *The End of Isolation,* pp. 158–159.

68. Quoted in A. J. Anthony Morris, *Radicalism Against War, 1906–1914* (London: Longmans, 1972), p. 46.

69. Britain, *British Documents on the Origins of the War,* vol. 3, *The Testing of the Entente, 1904–06* (London: His Majesty's Stationery Office, 1928), p. 263.

70. "Memorandum on the Present State of British Relations with France and Germany," January 1, 1907, printed in ibid., p. 402.

71. Most Anglo-German disputes were viewed by both sides as aspects and indicators of the general state of their relations, and not as problems that could be fruitfully dealt with in isolation.

72. Britain, *British Documents on the Origins of the War,* vol 3, *The Testing of the Entente, 1904–06,* p. 408.

73. Ibid., p. 418.

74. Ibid., p. 358.

75. Ibid., p. 361.

76. Quoted in Morris, *Radicalism Against War,* p. 65.

77. Robert Jervis, *Perception and Misperception in International Politics* (Princeton: Princeton University Press, 1976), pp. 70–74, 354–355.

10
Theories of, and Approaches to, Alliance Politics

Roger V. Dingman

THE QUESTION OF HOW TO STUDY ALLIANCES does not lend itself to an easy answer. Although I have spent some years in doing so, I cannot provide a checklist of what one should do in analyzing either alliances in general or a particular alliance. Instead, I propose to offer in this chapter some reflections, based on my own experience, which may be of use to other scholars. My thoughts concern three broad issues: the limitations of much of the existing literature on the theory of alliance; the historian's need for a working conceptual understanding of alliances; and the relative utility of various methods, new and old, for analyzing alliances.

Theories, Approaches, and Their Limitations

Perhaps I can best begin by recalling an incident that occurred at Stanford University several years ago. In giving a talk on the 1951 alliance between Japan and the United States, I proposed a definition of alliance, and then analyzed the formation of this particular one. When I had finished speaking, a distinguished philosopher in the audience offered some advice. "Drop that definition," he counseled, "and just proceed with your story." When I asked why, he responded with a paradox. "Everyone," he said, "knows what an alliance is; but no two scholars or editors can agree on a definition. Yours might well prejudice those who must pass on the merits of your work against it."

At the time I thought such advice politically wise but somehow intellectually unsound. But after examining relatively recent works of historians and international relations theorists, I came to the conclusion that my philosopher friend had spoken a truth of sorts. Rare, indeed, was the historian who attempted to define an alliance. One of the most distinguished European diplomatic historians, William L. Langer, produced a classic study of alliance diplomacy. Yet he never bothered to distinguish between the two terms in his title, *European Alliances and Alignments* (1964 ed.). Writers of international relations textbooks seem to have followed a similar course. When I examined five of the most frequently used among them, I discovered a startling lack of clarity about alliances. None made any effort to define them. Nor did any distinguish alliances from coalitions, ententes, or alignments—words frequently misused as synonyms.[1]

Dismayed, I thought of looking for enlightenment and perhaps more intellectual honesty elsewhere. What about the classic writings of historians, political philosophers, and statesmen on alliances? When I examined their works, I found that they were, for the most part, protagonists in an ongoing debate. Time and again, they posed the same questions: Why do states form alliances? Do they gain greater security, and hence more freedom of action, from alliances? Or do commitments formalized in an alliance limit the choices before decision makers? Do alliances genuinely help preserve peace—or contribute to its destruction? The authors I read gave highly subjective and experiential responses to these questions. The sixteenth-century Italian historian Francesco Guicciardini, for example, saw alliances as products of human passion. Princes moved by "mutual jealousy" formed pacts which were limited in time and glued together by fear. Through them, other rulers' efforts to increase their "dominion or prestige" could be upset.[2] Sir Edmund Burke took precisely the opposite view. Alliances were positive combinations which reflected a "correspondence in laws, customs, manners, and habits of life" among states.[3] The former view made sense in the world of Italian city-states; the latter suited the temper of an ideological crusader against Napoleon.

Similarly subjective judgments ran through the classic writings on the consequences of alliance. It was quite reasonable for Sir Robert Walpole, who lived through a series of coalition wars against Louis XIV, to praise alliances as the means by which "the equipoise of power is maintained."[4] One could understand how Rousseau, familiar with the life and government of the Swiss confederation, could regard alliances as "fragile mitigating devices" by which numerous "good societies" might forge themselves into a warless world.[5] That Leopold von Ranke, the German historian, in 1833 wrote that the states of Europe would combine naturally against any one which sought hegemony came as no surprise.[6] Nor could I, when reading Lord Bryce's passionate denunciation of alliances, divorce his judgments from the experience of his generation. Well might those who had suffered so much yet gained so little from World War I conclude that alliances spewed "jealousies, rivalries, and suspicions" among nations and thus destroyed their leaders' freedom of choice. In an alliance-filled world, it was only natural that statesmen would be predisposed to choose war over peace.[7]

My search might well have proven fruitless had I not read Thucydides.

His treatment of alliances in *The Peloponnesian War,* even if not completely free of subjective judgments, was extraordinarily rich in insight. In presenting the arguments of Corcyra and Corinth for and against the former's bid for alliance with Athens, Thucydides showed how alliances were born from an unstable combination of both passion and reason. Fear—not simply fear of war or of a greater power, but fear of the consequences of violating national or individual honor pledged in their making—held alliances together. Where but in Thucydides' account of changing alliance relationships in war could one find a better demonstration of how alliance obligations are eternally open to dispute and reinterpretation? Thucydides also seemed to offer the wisest counsel on the problem of alliance effects. His account of the Athenians' effort to limit the risks of a defensive pact with Corcyra showed how unpredictable the consequences of alliance may be.[8]

Unfortunately, there is no Thucydides among contemporary theorists who have written about alliances. Their work, whether in article or book form, is not extensive. Only twenty-eight books in Western languages are listed under the subject heading "Alliances" in the published Library of Congress catalogue for the 1950–1977 period. While these works provide useful information and analysis about contemporary alliances (the North Atlantic Treaty Organization, in particular), they offer little in the way of definition or theory that would be of use to the working historian.

These works do not define alliance clearly. In a manner not unlike that Felix Gilbert ascribes to the leaders of the American Revolution,[9] contemporary theorists seem to have understood the term in a variety of ways. Some treated alliance as a special type of alignment; others termed it a subspecies of coalition. One definition seemed attractive at first glance. It termed alliance a collaboration among states concerning "a mutually perceived problem." Such cooperation involved aggregation of capabilities, joint or parallel pursuit of national interests, and the probability of mutual assistance.[10] But after a few moments' reflection, one could think of several alliances which lacked such characteristics. Another definition, which described alliance as "a formal agreement between two or more nations to collaborate on national security issues," was technically correct[11] but from the historian's point of view overly static. Edwin H. Fedder provided a more dynamic definition. An alliance was a set of states "acting in X time regarding the mutual enhancement of . . . military security."[12] but even this improvement said nothing about the form of alliances.

I found much contemporary writing about alliances marked by the authors' fascination with the new techniques of quantitative analysis. But although these analysts' methods were new, their questions were old. Like classic writers, contemporary theorists debated the origins and impact of alliances on the international system. They dealt with alliances in two ways. At the bilateral level, they tried to quantify the closeness or distance between states. Bruce Russett, for example, measured the number of formal

247

agreements, size of embassy staffs, amount of editorial space devoted to bilateral relations, and volume of trade and mail between America and Britain in an effort to uncover the broader pattern of their twentieth-century relationship.[13] While information of this sort might be useful, it seems only secondarily important. Closeness or distance between alliance partners is in the eye of the beholder, in the thoughts and perceptions of statesmen rather than in raw statistics.

On another level, contemporary theorists wrestled with the old problem of the relationship between alliances and the international system. They addressed themselves to the formation, termination, purposes, and performance of alliances. Then they posed correlative questions: Did alliances correlate to war? Were there recurrent patterns of alliance distribution in the international system? Was alliance formation random and ahistorical, or did preferred combinations recur? In trying to answer these questions, quantitative theorists made use of ever more sophisticated statistical and mathematical models. But the fruits of their labors were only marginally helpful for the diplomatic historian. Their level of analysis was too general for one interested in particular alliances. Moreover, these theorists sidestepped the complex issues of causation to deal only with correlations. They also seemed confused about the very subject of their study, some arguing that alliances were a primary variable, others seeing them as a secondary manifestation of the risk-taking proclivities of statesmen.[14]

One quantitatively based study proved useful. *Unity and Disintegration in International Alliances* (1973) tested the validity of various traditional maxims about alliance behavior and found that many of them did not stand up to careful scrutiny. Ideological similarity among allies was not especially important, nor was the domestic political stability of alliance partners. Clarity of purpose seemed to correlate negatively to longevity; the more ambiguous the terms of an alliance, the better its chances for survival. This study also showed that conflict between blocs of allies was neither a necessary nor a sufficient condition for their cohesion within a bloc.[15] Negative findings of this sort were helpful, for at the very least they reinforced my skepticism about any and all generalizations concerning alliances.

The Necessity for Meaningful Conceptualization

The foregoing limitations of both contemporary and classic treatments of alliances brought me to an uncomfortable realization: If the diplomatic historian is to analyze a particular alliance, he needs to develop a working conceptual understanding of alliances, however imperfect it may be in both definitional and theoretical terms.

It is relatively easy to clear away much of the verbal confusion that surrounds alliances. An alliance is a particular form of international political cooperation which is quite distinct from alignment, coalition, or entente. The term *alliance* is not synonymous with any of the latter three words. *Alignment* is the most general term among them. The dictionary defines it simply as an arraying of states or individuals for or against a cause. *Coalition,* a more specific term borrowed from the language of domestic politics, signifies a temporary coming together of parties in pursuit of one or more aims. Historians have tended to use it to refer to combinations formed to prosecute a war. *Entente* carries a meaning still more specific. It defines an understanding or agreement among states which is based on conventions or declarations. In contrast to an alliance, an entente is not written; nor does it have a specified duration. Some theorists argue that the word connotes a relationship less firm, and hence less constraining, of decision makers' freedom of choice, than an alliance between states.[16] Alliance, then, must at the very least be understood as a specific form of international relationship. The word refers to a written, formal agreement among two or more states which is designed to serve, for a specified term, the interests of those states, or of their statesmen and bureaucrats, in regard to national security.

With the terminology of alliance more clearly in mind, it is possible for the diplomatic historian to think of them in more creative conceptual terms. It is useful to envisage an alliance metaphorically. One can imagine it to be an organism. That organism is compounded of complex linkages. It exists in a multilayered environment which itself changes over time. The historian, much like a physician or biologist, is interested both in the external movements and behavior of the organism and in the internal processes which give it life.

One can, for instance, imagine the linkages which make up an alliance as bonds of two sorts. At one level, they can be seen as ties between various parts of complex entities called governments. These constantly shifting linkages can be ordered in terms of their level of existence *within* governments. In eighteenth-century Europe, for example, alliances were ties that bound monarchs or heads of state; personal relationships among rulers were critical factors in determining the health of any alliance relationship. In more complex governments, alliances might take shape at *different levels.* Ian Nish describes the Anglo–Japanese Alliance of 1902–1922 as an "alliance of secretariats." It was a bond shaped and sustained by particular elements in the foreign and navy ministries of each government to serve their particular interests.[17] The United States' Cold War alliances reveal another pattern of linkages. Washington's mutual defense agreements with Franco's Spain and Chiang Kai-shek's Taiwan were created by and for *particular interests* within the armed services and powerful legislators on Capitol Hill. At still another level, an alliance can be an emotional bond between *peoples.* The Anglo–American relationship during and immediately after World War II might stand as an example of this sort. While shaped by heads of government, and while useful to various elements in their respective bureaucracies, this alliance grew out of the broad emotional and experiential ties that crisscrossed the Atlantic.

An alliance is also a series of linkages between *nations* that concerns *issues*. Analysts want to know which among them constitutes the core, the quintessential bonding element. They are also concerned with how and why the relationship between core and peripheral issues change over time. Sometimes the terms of an alliance clearly express such a relationship. More often than not, what is quintessential will be obscured in mists created by other related issues whose importance may not be at all clear.

The linkages at both the structural and issue levels of an alliance are constantly changing. Their movement in one sense belies the accuracy of the organic metaphor. A human or animal body has a definite skeletal structure; it has a central nervous system, with a brain that directs the actions of the individual. The biologist or physician, once he knows something about the norms and patterns of each, can begin to explain changes or disorders in the organism. But an alliance has neither a skeletal framework nor a centrally directed nervous system. The linkages which comprise it shift and reshape themselves so as to present a myriad of patterns to the historian–observer.

His analytical task might be impossible if the sources of change in alliances were infinite in number. Theoretically, they may be so. In fact, they can logically be reduced to but three. The *bonding elements* that make up an alliance may themselves be one such source. At the macroscopic level, changes in the relative strength and cohesion of the nations that are parties to an alliance may alter its very nature. Their rise to the status of economic superpowers, for example, might be said to have transformed the alliance ties of West Germany and Japan with the United States. At the microscopic level, changes in the bonding elements of an alliance may in fact be changes of personalities. Historians agree that Bismarck was the *sine qua non* of late nineteenth-century Germany's alliance system.[18] More than a few observers on both sides of the Atlantic have concluded that John Foster Dulles' replacing Dean Acheson as Secretary of State fundamentally altered Anglo-American alliance relationships.[9]

The *domestic political climate* of nations that are parties to an alliance is a second major source of change. Something shifts at home, or is perceived by a nation's leaders to have changed, in such a way as to modify the value or domestic political saliency of an alliance. Neither historians nor international relations theorists have succeeded in conceptualizing this sort of change, but there are examples which provide evidence of how it occurs. The Japanese origins of the Tripartite Pact of 1940 are a case in point. For years Japanese naval leaders had strongly opposed conclusion of an alliance with Berlin and Rome. But in the late summer of 1940, Navy Minister Oikawa Koshirō changed his service's position. He did not acquiesce in concluding a pact which many naval leaders still thought useless, if not dangerous, because he or they reached new conclusions about Germany's strength or value as a potential partner. Rather, his position changed, because Oikawa realized that continued opposition to those within the government and in the press who clamored for such a pact would hurt the navy's bureaucratic political position. To obtain other "goods," he had to accept the "evil" of an alliance with Berlin.[20]

Changes in alliance relationships can also originate in real or perceived shifts in the *international political environment*. Classical political theorists conceptualized this notion by talking about the balance of power. In their view, states constantly combined and recombined in alliances so as to maintain an acceptable distribution of power in the international political system. Contemporary theorists dispute the validity of a balance-of-power analytical framework,[21] but they accept the proposition that there are various states or stages of the international political environment which can and do affect alliance behavior. It is useful to think of these as points along a spectrum, ranging from Clausewitz's ideal state of total war to the equally unattainable condition of perfect peace. As the international environment stabilizes at various intermediate points, the strength and patterns of interconnection of the linkages constituting an alliance must adapt to suit new circumstances.

The changes that occur in an alliance may originate in any one or a combination of these three sources. They do not happen purely at random, but take place within what might be termed the life cycle of an alliance. Again, the biological metaphor is useful for understanding that process of change. Just as there are certain phases in the life of an organism within which particular developments or crises occur, so, too, are there identifiable stages in the life cycle of an alliance. Within each—gestation, growth and adaptation, and termination—alliance managers face definite decision-making problems. While they vary in form and intensity with each individual case, these problems have certain structural similarities with which the diplomatic historian should be familiar.

The foregoing considerations suggest that those who make an alliance must fashion answers to a series of difficult questions. The first is why: Why should an exciting or desired international relationship be formalized as an alliance? In thinking about that problem, alliance makers have to consider what its constituent elements or linkages are to be. Should the proposed pact involve two—or more—nations? What governmental units should serve as bonding elements? Should an alliance involve political cooperation only, and thus engage principally the energies and attention of heads of governments, secretaries of state, and ambassadors? Those who form an alliance must also consider whether or nor it is to contain definite military commitments, and thus involve professional soldiers in varying degree. They must also ask themselves if economic linkages, which would engage still other interest groups and issues, are essential to the life of the proposed pact.

A third question that presents itself during the formative stage of an alliance's life is how: How can the linkage of governmental units or issues be brought about? The alliance makers must determine whether or not there are present in the domestic or international political environment elements which will, as Burke claimed, "naturally" assure a pact's cohesion. If he concludes that they are absent, then the alliance architect faces a series of difficult choices. He may think it necessary to create ongoing bureaucratic and structural linkages. The fathers of NATO, for example, came to believe that their alliance needed a complex bureaucratic structure of its own to achieve deterrence in peace and success in war. In so doing, they derogated no small amount of their freedom of choice to the professional soldiers who would have no redesign strategic plans, demand bigger budgets, and coordinate weapons acquisition programs. The alliance maker might, on the contrary, see it purely as an instrument of psychological warfare. The Eisenhower administration regarded the Southeast Asia Treaty Organization in this light.[22] Finally, in creating an alliance, its makers must provide for its adaptation and survival. They must set the term of its life span and agree upon provisions for its revision.

But the diplomatic historian must beware of such provisions. They can alert him to the fact that the middle phase of an alliance's life cycle is a series of transitions. Only rarely, however, do explicit provisions for alliance extension or revision provide clues as to its inner dynamics of change. The Anglo-Japanese Alliance, when revised in 1911, was concluded for a ten-year term. Yet in 1921, for a congeries of reasons which grew out of his immediate domestic political needs, his relations with fellow prime ministers at the Imperial Conference, and his difficulties in dealing with Washington, British Prime Minister David Lloyd George obfuscated the alliance's provisions for revision. He used the lord chancellor's legal opinions to set, in effect, the stage for termination of the pact with Tokyo.[23] In this case, as in many others, the historian simply cannot be satisfied with terms for revision as an explanation for alliance managers' actions.

Diplomatic historians and theorists alike can usefully regard the middle phase of an alliance's life cycle as a series of transitions. As changes in its environment take place, the human, institutional, and issue relationships within an alliance must adapt. If alliance decision makers take the right steps, the organism will survive; if their decisions are otherwise, it will decline and die. The most dramatic and challenging of these choices are forced upon alliance managers as the international environment moves from a condition of peace to war and back again. As crises become more frequent and serious, the parties to an alliance must decide whether or not to increase the number and intensity of their connections. This was the problem that London and Paris faced from 1911 onward. They resolved it, as Samuel Williamson has shown, by transforming their entente into a *de facto* alliance replete with joint military plans.[24] Once war has broken out, alliance managers face still more difficult decisions. At the political level, they must resolve civil–military problems at home and establish an effective system of command and control for their forces in the field. And they must discuss and resolve economic burden-sharing questions if their alliance is to be welded into a coalition capable of bringing victory.[25] One can see classic evidence of this sort of adaptive decision making in the efforts of Franklin D. Roosevelt and Winston Churchill between 1939 and 1941 to meet the challenge of global war.[26]

As the international environment shifts back toward peace, yet another series of decisions must be made. Leaders must not only reexamine and clarify their long-range war aims, but they also have to reassess the utility of an alliance in achieving them. Such scrutiny can produce *de facto* sundering of alliance ties, such as occurred in 1783 when American negotiators, despite commitments to France to the countrary, made a separate peace with Great Britain. It can lead to a reevaluation of the ends to be gained by continuation of a wartime partnership in peace. In 1918, for example, Woodrow Wilson and David Lloyd George came by very different routes to the conclusion that more was to be gained than lost by preserving their collaboration.[27] Once that choice has been made, alliance leaders have to determine anew how to structure their network of relationships. In 1815 Castlereagh and Metternich concluded that periodic reassemblages of principal statesmen would suffice to preserve their alliance and the peace of Europe. A century and more later, Roosevelt, Churchill, and Stalin tried to establish a much more complex system of alliance-sustaining relationships, ranging from shared power in the United Nations Security Council through periodic meetings of their foreign ministers down to coordination of occupation efforts in Germany. Yet they let their economic ties lapse, a failure which some historians have seen as a principal cause for the disintegration of their alliance.[28]

As it enters the terminal phase of its life cycle, an alliance presents decision makers with another set of questions. Theoretically, they are the obverse of those raised at the time of its conception: Why end a formal relationship? Which ties should be broken? How should the severance process be managed? Logic would suggest that alliance leaders address the first question first; but more often the latter issues take precedence. This is because alliance managers face so many constraints in dealing with the bonds that link their nations together. It may seem far easier and less momentous to make small incremental choices about alliance bonds than to denounce a pact in its entirety. That fact can blind both contemporaries and historians to the process of alliance decay. Americans continued during World War II to think of Germany and Japan as Axis partners long after their pact had withered into a "hollow alliance."[29] We made the same mistake in assessing the Sino–Soviet Alliance of 1950, which Peking now seems ready to denounce. We debate the expediency, morality, and effect on other allies of ending our 1954 mutual defense treaty with Taiwan when, in fact, presidents have made or allowed their subordinates to make decisions which have stripped this particular alliance of all but its bones. The processes of alliance decay, then, would seem to be, like those of an organism, as critical and yet less obvious than the mechanisms of growth.

Metaphorical thinking of the sort just presented may lack the grace and precision of a formal theory of alliance. But it is useful for at least three reasons. In the first instance, it enables one to think and write in comparative terms. One need not burden his account of one alliance with numerous references to others. But whether dealing with the whole life cycle of an alliance or with only one of its phases, the historian will produce a better analysis if he identifies his subject as one example of a general phenomenon. As Alexander George points out elsewhere in this volume, such an approach sharpens the historian's focus. He can see and single out for special attention what is unique about the particular alliance he is studying. He can draw on the richness of his predecesors' accounts of other alliances. And the historian is less likely to bury himself and his readers in an abyss of detail if he takes a comparative analytical view of the alliance he is studying.

The metaphor of alliance as organism is also useful because it rivets one's attention on the historian's preeminent concern: the processes of change. He is not, in the manner of the political scientist, looking for structures, patterns, or variables worthy of study in their own right. On the contrary, the historian probes the movement of life over time. He needs more than an X-ray of the organism that is an alliance. He cannot be satisfied with a schematic diagram of its linkages at any one moment in time. Instead, the historian must create a whole series of X-rays and motion pictures of an alliance if he is to present a coherent explanation for all or parts of its life.

Conceptualizing an alliance as an organism is useful in a third way. Doing so, as the foregoing discussion suggests, puts the questions that alliance managers face before the historian. It gives him a strategy of inquiry, one which forces him to ask why they make the choices they do. That approach is the one most likely to lead historians toward the deepest insights into alliances. By its very nature, such an approach reminds the historian of the essence of his craft: explaining change. If properly used, the decision-making approach can also help the historian to structure his analysis so as to make it a coherent and indeed compelling account for his readers.

It is important for the diplomatic historian to be familiar with the strengths and limitations of classic and contemporary theoretical discussions of alliances. It is also true that conceptual clarity, whether in the form of an organic metaphor, as discussed above, or in a different one of the historian's own making, is essential to sound thinking about alliances. But how should the diplomatic historian go about writing of them? Can he gain fresh insights by using the methodologies described elsewhere in this book? And which of them is likely to be of the greatest use to him?

There is no single, general answer to any of those questions. The best one can offer is a conditional answer based on experience: It depends. In the first instance, it is necessary to look not only at the state of the international environment but also at the structure of the governments which comprise it. If one is going to explain how an alliance takes shape, for example, one has to know whether the bonding units that form it are relatively singular elements or extremely pluralistic ones. The historian also has to assess the utility of methodology in terms of the particular issue with which he is concerned. He must ask himself if his is the kind of question which lends itself to multiple levels of analysis. Perhaps the utility of alternative analytical approaches can best be shown by examining a particular alliance-related puzzle. The case of Japan and the United States in 1951 is especially fascinating, in that it deals with a logical anomaly and with the transformation of bonding elements in an alliance.

Washington and Tokyo, 1951

On September 8, 1951, representatives of the United States and Japan signed a treaty of alliance at San Francisco. It was but one element of a peace settlement designed to restore Japanese sovereignty, assuage other Asian and Pacific nations' fears of Japan, and assure Tokyo's voluntary alignment with Washington in the Cold War. The treaty was burdened with a clause in its first article which seemed to contradict those aims. It provided for the stationing of U.S. forces in Japan, not simply to provide for her security and the peace of the Far East, but also to give aid "at the express request of the Japanese Government" in putting down major internal riots or disturbances "caused through instigation or intervention by an outside Power or Powers."[30] These words transformed the nature of the alliance. What had been envisaged as a spontaneous accord between peoples and governments became a pact sponsored by the military and attacked by their opponents. For a decade, revision of the treaty text to excise the offending words disturbed relations between Washington and Tokyo. The treaty was modified in 1960, but only at the cost of riots, political chaos in Japan, and the career of the prime minister who renegotiated it.[31]

We know who put these critical words in the treaty: U.S. Special Ambassador John Foster Dulles and Japanese Prime Minister Yoshida Shigeru. They found their way into the text sometime between January 12 and February 9, 1951. On the first date, Dulles indicated his intention to put them there; on the latter, American and Japanese negotiators initialed a draft treaty containing them. Documents in the *Foreign Relations of the United States* volume on East Asia for 1950 show how State and Defense Department officials quarreled earlier over draft language which would either expressly permit or even more clearly prohibit American interference in Japanese internal affairs. Records of the Dulles–Yoshida negotiations of January and February 1951 also reveal that it was the American who inserted the words authorizing the intervention of U.S. forces to put down domestic disorders and the Japanese who, after protesting that Tokyo could manage its own internal security affairs, suggested the "compromise" qualifying phrase that permitted intervention when trouble was fomented from without.[32]

This explains much of the when and the how. But why? Why did two men, both of whom wanted voluntary association between their nations on the freest and most nearly equal terms possible, write such unequalizing provisions into their treaty of alliance? Such questions presume that there must be a logical explanation for so seemingly irrational an action. One is drawn, almost without thinking, into what Graham Allison has termed the "rational actor" mode of analysis.[33] One assumes that Dulles and Yoshida, as principal negotiators for their respective governments, went through a calculating process, which the historian can replicate, which led them to choose to act as they did. The decisions were made by design, not default.

That seems clearest on the Japanese side. Yoshida Shigeru was a skilled diplomat, a professional who had served as vice minister of foreign affairs and as ambassador to England. He knew he was in a difficult position, speaking for a defeated and occupied nation that wanted desperately to recover its full independence. He faced a formidable adversary. Reportedly, Dulles in the flesh so overawed Yoshida that the prime minister paled and was at a loss for words in his presence. The Americans knew what they wanted: base rights in Japan and Japanese rearmament. But Yoshida had qualms about the latter. Its consitutionality was debatable, it would be costly and it touched deep-seated fears about the role professional military men might play in Japanese political life. Yet the Americans harped time and again on the fact that Tokyo lacked forces adequate to maintain domestic security. Should Yoshida run all the risks associated with their development, or would it be better to stave off American pressures for rearmament by giving them interventionary rights?[34]

The latter alternative might seem eminently reasonable, even if distasteful, in Tokyo. But the Americans' behavior cannot be explained in terms of cold logic. That they were staunchly anticommunist there can be no doubt. Dulles had written extensively on the evils emanating from Moscow, and in October 1950 he went so far as to lecture Soviet United Nations Ambassador Yakov Malik on why Americans justifiably feared communism. His principal assistants had sound anticommunist credentials. John Allison had advocated chastising the Reds for their invasion of South Korea, and Robert Fearey was sufficiently anti-Soviet to survive the McCarthyite purges that struck terror in Foggy Bottom. But none of these men thought a communist uprising in Japan probable. General MacArthur's staff pointed out that the Soviets had the capability, but not the intent, to mount an invasion. Dulles echoed that view. Moreover, it is hard to imagine that he, a subtle, rigorously logical, and usually cautious man, contemplated actual American intervention in Japanese affairs. He came to Tokyo armed with instructions which would not even allow firm commitment to a mutual defense agreement. If President Truman and Secretary of State Acheson would not go that far, how could Dulles be certain that they would pledge action against internal subversion? It is also hard to explain Dulles' insertion of interventionary language as an act of rhetorical deterrence. When he proposed it, the special ambassador was not yet certain whether it would appear in a treaty or in a quiet executive agreement.[35]

These unresolved puzzles suggest the need for other, less "rational" explanations for both American and Japanese behavior. The diplomatic historian may find some through using a mode of analysis conceptualized in John Steinbruner's *The Cybernetic Theory of Decision* (1974). Steinbruner argues that the individual makes decisions under complex conditions through inference more often than by calculation or abstract reasoning. Decision makers seek to preserve preexisting systems of belief. They scan the past for pertinent images or analogies, they engage in wishful thinking, or they dredge up "reasons" that make it impossible for them to accept one or more alternatives. In this analytical mode, the historian does not attempt to replicate a reasoning process; he re-creates a series of inferential attempts at choice. His task is to describe the decision maker's structure of beliefs and to locate those analogies which are used to preserve and protect them.[36]

It is not hard to test such theories in the case of John Foster Dulles. There can be little doubt that he thought of post–World War II peacemaking in terms of the "lessons" of the post–World War I era. Having played a small part in negotiating the Versailles settlement, he was determined not to repeat its errors. From this source sprang his oft-repeated insistence on the need for a peace of mutual acceptance. From this source, too, came his determination to be certain that a strong bipartisan consensus backed any and all agreements made. This conviction was as valid for Tokyo as for Washington. While in Japan, Dulles insisted on meeting with nongovernment party leaders in an effort to gain their support for the treaties being negotiated. He was convinced that post-treaty Japan must not be wracked by the kind of internal dissidence and turmoil that eventually destroyed Weimar Germany.[37] To that end he repeatedly fought off efforts to impose limitations on Japanese sovereignty that emanated from London, Canberra, and Wellington. But another train of thought born of the analogy to Weimar may have given birth to Dulles' contradictory insistence on rights of intervention. He may have thought of them as a "backup" solution, efficient in precluding a renewed drift toward totalitarianism in Japan in a way that the few, feeble allied forces remaining in Germany during the 1920s had never been.

One can imagine similar kinds of thoughts running through Yoshida's mind. Although he, too, had had a small part in shaping the Versailles peace settlement,[38] two other seemingly analogous instances may have occurred to him. One was the triple intervention of 1895, by which France, Russia, and

257

Germany snatched the Manchurian fruits of victory from Japan. Tokyo swallowed that bitter pill, only to retake and retain the territory in question a decade later. Perhaps Yoshida thought that what was lost in his negotiations might, in similar fashion, be recovered in later years. More probable and perhaps more vivid in his thoughts were the events of the 1930s. Then the forces of order in Japan had lost control of the police power. Radical groups within the army seized it and attempted coups. In one of them, Yoshida's father-in-law narrowly escaped assassination.[39] Such turmoil first threatened the solidarity of the state, then plunged it into a disastrous war. In 1951 Yoshida may have thought that all of this might never have occurred had there been a *deus ex machina,* an external force such as that the Americans might provide in the future, to protect reason and order.

Inferences of this sort are plausible in both the Japanese and American cases. They may even seem probable. They can lift the historian up to a wholly different plane of reconstructive effort and greatly enrich the complexity of his narrative. But, one must hasten to add, such inferential reconstructions remain speculative and forever unprovable. Even if the historian were to summon up the shades of Dulles and Yoshida, subjecting both to the most rigorous sort of questioning, he could never be certain beyond all doubt that such inferences were the ones that guided their actions early in 1951.

There is another, radically different new approach to the analysis of decisions that might offer more certainty about the formative events of 1951 in the history of the United States–Japanese Alliance. It assumes that organizations rather than individuals are the proper subject of study. Organizations are presumed to have interests of their own which they protect or advance by employing certain "standard operating procedures." The latter are routines which need not be "rational" in some abstract objective sense, but which may well appear to be so to those individuals who live and work within the organization.[40] Can one explain the presence of the internal intervention clause in the 1951 alliance as a result of organizational needs and behavior?

Insofar as Tokyo is concerned, I doubt it. The internal climate and mood of the Foreign Ministry worked against rather than for interventionary rights. Treaty specialists at Kasumigaseki had been studying precedents in other treaties between victors and vanquished from 1946 onward. Their preparations revealed determination to fashion peace treaty language which would in no way impair Japan's sovereignty.[41] Moreover, the pattern of negotiating behavior in 1951 contradicted norms of the past.[42] The Japanese did not cling tenaciously to a position until forced to give way, but quite uncharacteristically put forward compromising language. Finally, neither the foreign nor the finance ministries had yet grown into organizations powerful or wily enough to constrain Yoshida. In short, the evidence points almost overwhelmingly against an organizationally grounded explanation for Japanese behavior.

The organizational approach, however, does provide clues which can help explain American behavior. There can be little doubt that the original impulse for an intervention clause came from United States Army sources. Even before the Korean War made the question of securing the rear of U.S. forces critical, army spokesmen had worried about possible post-treaty internal security problems in Japan. Responding to such fears, Major General Carter B. Magruder in August 1950 wrote provisions for U.S. intervention in Japanese internal affairs into a draft security agreement. But in December 1950 he gave way before State Department demands for removal of the offensive language. At the most bitter moments of the Korean conflict, however, the issue resurfaced with MacArthur's request for four more divisions to protect the Japanese bases of his embattled troops in Korea. The Joint Chiefs of Staff responded by arguing that the ultimate solution to his problem lay in the expansion and "heavying up" of the Japanese National Police Reserve.[43] Their position, rooted in the organizational need to assure successful performance of mission, ironically coincided with that of the most nationalistically minded Japanese treaty experts.

John Foster Dulles may have exaggerated and catered to fears running through the "military mind." He knew of past Pentagon objections to proceeding with a Japanese peace settlement and had to get a presidential decision to override them. He was well aware of the fact that the Joint Chiefs thought it unwise to conclude a peace while a war was on.[44] Dulles may have felt that a "gift," in the form of interventionary language, was necessary to secure the Pentagon's cooperation in further efforts for peace and alliance. If this was the case, Dulles possessed extraordinary prescience and insight into organizational behavior. Records of the Joint Chiefs of Staff reveal that as late as July 1951 the Defense Department committee reviewing the proposed security treaty objected to the interventionary language of its first article as too *restrictive* of American military action.[45]

Richard Neustadt has developed in practice, and Graham Allison has conceptualized, yet another, extremely fruitful analytical paradigm. This "bureaucratic politics" approach contends that external policies are the results of internal bargaining among officials who seek to maximize personal power or the favor of presidents and prime ministers. To understand why Dulles put interventionary language in the alliance, and to grasp why Yoshida accepted it with modifications, one must first uncover "the fine detail of structure, of positions, channels, stakes and state of play" in their respective intragovernmental games.[46] Might this approach yield deeper insights into their actions?

To answer that question, one must look first at the structure of the politics of peace and alliance making in both capital cities. The situation in Washington was paradoxical. Everyone recognized the need for a Japanese peace settlement and for an alliance which would secure American bases. All could perceive benefits—personal, organizational, and diplomatic—which might flow from treaties of peace and alliance. But no Democrat of stature within the Truman administration stood ready to take domestic political risks to achieve either. The administration was still smarting from charges that it had "lost" China. The Korean War became more costly and more controversial with each passing day. Little wonder, then, that the administration, over and above President Truman's personal distaste for the man, had given John Foster Dulles the negotiating job. At the worst, this Republican might serve as a rod to attract the lighting of partisan and bureaucratic attacks on adminstration policies. At best, he might help restore shattered bipartisanship on East Asian matters.[47] Under these circumstances the silence of Dean Acheson, Dean Rusk, and Philip Jessup—liberals who might have opposed intervention in the internal affairs of an ally as a matter of principle—becomes quite comprehensible.

But Dulles' conduct remains to be explained. He, too, was in an anomalous situation. On the one hand, he had the opportunity to demonstrate that he had qualities of mind and negotiating skills requisite to the office he coveted, the secretaryship of state. He could demonstrate that he could avoid the shoals in talks with Japanese, Britons, and Australians and, at the same time, pass safely between the rocks on Capitol Hill and those on the Pentagon side of the Potomac. But, on the other hand, Dulles was on trial. He had to do the job: he had to do it smoothly and well.[48] Under these conditions, caution no less than daring was essential.

Dulles thus may have given higher priority to the imperatives of his own domestic political situation than to the principles of a liberal peace and equitable alliance with Japan. His reinsertion of language permitting American interference in Japanese internal affairs may have seemed a kind of insurance against future troubles—at home. Through these words, Pentagon fears over the timing of a Japanese settlement and the inadequacies of Tokyo's internal security forces might be assuaged. Dulles may also have been trying to deal with anticipated questions from Republican prima donnas on Capitol Hill. The intervention clause may have been meant to fend off their questions about the safety of American boys in alien Japan. If Dulles' words were so intended, they succeeded. Nowhere in the records of the special ambassador's conversations with ranking congressional leaders can one find questions about the matter.

This same mode of analysis can also shed a different light on Yoshida's behavior. "Considerable politics," as Ambassador William Sebald understated it, surrounded the peace and security treaties under discussion between Tokyo and Washington.[49] Both promised considerable changes in Japanese political life. In his brighter moments, Yoshida may have hoped to emerge as the symbol of a new era, as the popular hero who negotiated Japan's return to full independence and sovereignty. Success in negotiations with the Americans might give the lie to those Cassandras who foretold the demise of his regime once the treaties were signed and ratified. But at darker moments Yoshida had to acknowledge that the end of the Occupation would mean the return to domestic political activity of men purged by the Americans. These professional politicians, strengthened by local organizations and fattened with funds from industrialists, might force him from office. And they might use supposed imperfections in the treaties of peace and alliance to do so.

Facing such prospects, Yoshida had to think of the texts of both as a shield. If they were not to become his domestic political Achilles' heel, he had to show that he had done everything possible to achieve the most favorable terms. Yoshida had long since fallen into a defensive mood; he argued, for example, that an imperfect peace treaty was better than none at all.[50] Similarly, if the record of his secret talks with Dulles were ever leaked, he might claim that he had done everything possible on the matter of American rights of intervention. That document would show that Tokyo had opposed them to no avail. Even more significant, the record would reveal that Yoshida had inserted qualifying language which both diminished the scope of such rights and hinted that the Soviet Union and Communist China were the probable instigators of domestic unrest. How then could the more probably potent of his critics—staunch anticommunists on the right—attack him? When considered in this light, the interventionary language in the alliance text makes sense. It was as much a hedge against future domestic political troubles for Yoshida as it was for Dulles.

Some might contend that the foregoing offers many answers, but no solution, to the puzzle of why Dulles inserted, and Yoshida accepted, interventionary language in the 1951 alliance treaty. Such a conclusion might well be justified if the diplomatic historian were simply to construct different hypotheses and test alternative methodologies. His obligations go beyond that, for in the end he must offer judgments—however tentative—that can provide a coherent explanation.

In this particular case, both the facts available and the insights drawn from the use of various methodologies point toward an essentially political explanation for the behavior of the two men in question. Dulles put those words into the draft treaty for reasons which seem to be rooted more in inferential thinking by analogy, domestic political considerations, and perhaps even misperception than in conscious design. He was not using words to fend off a real threat of Red subversion in Japan so much as he was insuring himself against domestic and bureaucratic political eventualities only dimly perceived. Yoshida, by contrast, seems to have had much more straightforward reasons for acting as he did. It was sensible to accept the limits of his negotiating position and to acquiesce in what Dulles appeared to want. It was also wise to offer a "yes-able proposition"[51] in the form of the qualifying clause; such a positive proposal would express his willingness to cooperate in order to achieve an alliance agreement. Behavior of this sort would be especially useful if Yoshida hoped to wheedle concessions on other, more significant issues out of the Americans. Yoshida also had every reason to put his own mark on the language of the intervention clause if he expected to succeed in managing its domestic political consequences.

Conclusion

The foregoing episode from the history of the formation of the United States–Japanese Alliance of 1951 may suggest to some that new approaches lead simply to old conclusions. In this instance they reaffirm a truth that diplomatic historians have known for centuries: namely, that external negotiators are constrained and guided by the circumstances of their domestic politics. But the utility of new theories and methodologies ought not to be judged solely in terms of whether or not they produce "new" conclusions. Indeed, the more one studies the history of alliances, the more hauntingly forceful those famous words of Thucydides become: "The events which happened in the past . . . (human nature being what it is) will, at some time or other, in much the same ways, be repeated in the future."[52] It is extremely difficult, and perhaps even unnecessary, for the historian of an alliance to argue that what he has to say is completely new and different.

On the contrary, new approaches to the study of diplomatic history in general and alliances in particular, which have emerged from and continue to be born in the social sciences, are valuable for quite different reasons. They can sensitize the historian to levels and patterns of intellectual and political interaction within governments that he might otherwise miss. Few would deny that the cybernetic approach's concept of how the human mind works, or the bureaucratic political vision of the nature of domestic politics, far exceed in complexity the paradigms of political psychologists or organizational sociologists of a generation ago. If he is aware of them, new approaches of the sort discussed in this chapter can help the diplomatic historian to fashion much more sophisticated and realistic explanations for the events he places before his readers.

New approaches are also a valuable means by which the historian can form and test the validity of various hypotheses. They can serve as a check on the natural and often subliminal tendency of the historian to judge men and events of the past in terms of the subjective standards of his own time and experience. The use of various theories and methodologies can, indeed, strengthen the force of the diplomatic historian's conclusions. The latter will be all the more convincing if, whether implicitly or explicitly they have been weighed against alternative explanations generated and brought into focus by different theoretical and methodological premises.

Finally, the knowledge and use of new social science approaches ought to reinforce the historian's natural pragmatism. In his search for an understanding of alliances, he must judge the utility of any particular tool in relation to the task before him. One needs the old, the attempted rational reconstruction of decision makers' thought processes. One also requires the new. But an analytical approach which yields insights in one instance may fail in another. If he is to understand and explain to others the intricacies of alliances, then, the historian must be open-minded. He needs a breadth of vision that will recognize both the advantages and the limitations in theories of the past. He must develop conceptual clarity in defining the subject of his study. And he needs to be familiar with a variety of analytical techniques. If he has all of this, the odds are good that he will write an interesting, insightful, and useful history of an alliance.

Notes

1. James Rosenau et al., "Of Syllabi, Texts, Students and Scholarship in International Relations," *World Politics 29* (January 1977): 263–340. The texts I surveyed were: William D. Coplin, *Introduction to International Politics* (Chicago: Rand McNally, 1974 ed.); Hans J. Morgenthau, *Politics among the Nations* (New York: Knopf, 1973 ed); John W. Spanier, *Games Nations Play Analyzing International Politics* (New York: Praeger, 1972); Karl Deutsch, *The Analysis of International Relations* (Englewood Cliffs, N.J.: Prentice-Hall, 1968); and K. J. Holsti, *International Politics* (Englewood Cliffs, N.J.: Prentice-Hall, 1977 ed.).

2. Francesco Guicciardini, *Storia d'Italia,* Book I, Chapter 1, cited in Herbert Butterfield and Martin Wight, *Diplomatic Investigations* (Cambridge: Harvard University Press, 1966), p. 137.

3. Edmund Burke, *First Letter on a Regicide Peace,* cited in ibid., p. 97.

4. Edward V. Gulick, *Europe's Classical Balance of Power* (New York: Norton, 1967 ed.), p. 61.

5. Stanley Hoffman, *The State of War* (New York: Praeger, 1965), pp. 79–80, 86.

6. Leopold von Ranke, *The Great Powers* (1833), in G. G. Iggers and Konrad von Moltke (eds.), *The Theory and Practice of History* (Indianapolis: Bobbs-Merrill, 1973), p. 101.

7. James Bryce, *International Relations* (Port Washington, N.Y.: Kennikat Press, 1966 ed.), pp. 235–238.

8. Thucydides, *The Peloponnesian War,* trans. by Rex Warner (Baltimore: Penguin Books, 1972), especially pp. 54–67, 198–199.

9. Felix Gilbert, *To the Farewell Address* (Princeton: Princeton University Press, 1961), pp. 45–48.

10. Patrick J. McGowan and Robert M. Rood, "Alliance Behavior in Balance of Power Systems: Applying a Poisson Model to Nineteenth Century Europe," *American Political Science Review* 69 (September 1975): 859–860; Edwin H. Fedder,

"The Concept of Alliance," *International Studies Quarterly* 12 (March 1968): 80; Julian Friedman et al., *Alliance in International Relations* (Boston: Allyn and Bacon, 1970), pp. 4–5.

11. Ole R. Holsti, P. Terrence Hopmann, and John D. Sullivan, *Unity and Disintegration in International Alliances: Comparative Studies* (New York: Wiley, 1973).

12. Fedder, "The Concept of Alliances," p. 68.

13. Bruce Russett, *Community and Contention: Britain and America in the Twentieth Century* (Cambridge: MIT Press, 1963).

14. See, for example, McGowan and Rood, "Alliance Behavior"; Charles Ostrom, Jr., and Francis W. Hoole, "Alliances and Wars Revisited," *International Studies Quarterly* 22 (June 1978): 215–236; Frederick H. Lawson, "Alliance Behavior in Nineteenth Century Europe," *American Political Science Review* 70 (September 1976): 932–934; and Bruce Bueno de Mesquita, "Systemic Polarization and the Occurrence and Duration of War," *Journal of Conflict Resolution* 22 (June 1978): 241–267; among others. Many of these studies have utilized the useful compendia of statistical data provided in the studies by J. David Singer and Melvin Small. These include J. David Singer and Melvin Small, *The Wages of War, 1816–1945: A Statistical Handbook* (New York: Wiley, 1972); and "Formal Alliances, Extension of the Basic Data," *Journal of Peace Research* 3 (1969): 257–282; "Formal Alliances," *Journal of Peace Research* 1 (1966): 1–32; and "Alliance Aggregation and the Onset of War, 1815–1945," reprinted in Francis A. Beer (ed.), *Alliances* (New York: Holt, Rinehart and Winston, 1970), pp. 13–67. For a larger discussion of the quantitative approach, see Melvin Small's chapter elsewhere in this volume.

15. Holsti et al., *Unity and Disintegration*, pp. 61–65, 74, 143, 223.

16. Robert A. Kann, "Alliances versus Ententes," *World Politics* 14 (July 1976): 611–621.

17. Ian H. Nish, *Alliance in Decline* (London: Athlone Press, 1972), p. 74.

18. William L. Langer, *European Alliances and Alignments, 1871–1890* (New York: Vintage Books, 1964 ed.), pp. 503–504; Joachim Remak, *The Origins of World War I 1871–1914* (Hinsdale, Ill.: Dryden Press, 1967), p. 20.

19. Among the many evaluations of Dulles' impact on Anglo–American relations, perhaps Churchill's was the most piquant. The Prime Minister said that the American Secretary of State was "the only case of a bull I know who carries his own china closet with him." Cited by Townsend Hoopes, *The Devil and John Foster Dulles* (Boston: Little, Brown, 1973), p. 221.

20. Hosoya Chihiro, "The Tripartite Pact," in James W. Morley (ed.), *Deterrent Diplomacy* (New York: Columbia University Press, 1976), pp. 201, 210, 220–221, 239–240. All Japanese names in this essay are given in the normal Japanese order, surname preceding given name.

21. Holsti et al., *Unity and Disintegration*, p. 6.

22. Russell H. Fifield, *Americans in Southeast Asia* (New York: Crowell, 1973), p. 237.

23. Roger Dingman, *Power in the Pacific* (Chicago: University of Chicago Press, 1976), pp. 164–169.

24. Samuel R. Williamson, Jr., *The Politics of Grand Strategy* (Cambridge: Harvard University Press, 1969), Chapter 7ff.

25. My thoughts on this phase of alliance decision making were stimulated by Gordon Craig, "The Military Alliance against Napoleon," in his *War, Politics, and Diplomacy: Selected Essays* (New York: Praeger, 1966), pp. 22–45.

26. Joseph P. Lash, *Roosevelt and Churchill, 1939–1941* (New York: Norton, 1976), offers an insightful treatment of this process.

27. Dingman, *Power in the Pacific,* pp. 67–75.

28. George C. Herring, Jr., *Aid to Russia, 1941–1946* (New York: Columbia University Press, 1973), pp. 204–211.

29. The term is Johanna Meskill's. Cf. her *Hitler and Japan: The Hollow Alliance* (New York: Atherton Press, 1966).

30. Security treaty between the United States and Japan, September 8, 1951, in Martin Weinstein, *Japan's Postwar Defense Policy, 1947–1968* (New York: Columbia University Press, 1971), pp. 187–188.

31. George Packard, III, *Protest in Tokyo* (Princeton: Princeton University Press, 1966), offers the most detailed account of the security treaty revision crisis.

32. Historical Office, Department of State, *Foreign Relations of the United States, 1950,* vol. 6, *East Asia and The Pacific* (Washington, D.C.: Government Printing Office, 1976), pp. 1243, 1289, 1299, 1340, 1369, 1951, vol. 6, pt. 1, pp. 706, 834, 851, 856–857, 860, 875. [This documentary series will hereinafter be cited simply as *FRUS,* with appropriate date, volume, and page references.]

33. Graham Allison, *Essence of Decision* (Boston: Little, Brown, 1971), pp. 13, 29–35.

34. Nishimura Kumao, *San Furanshisuko heiwa jōyaku,* vol. 27, Nihon gaikō shi (Tokyo: Kajima heiwa kenkyū jo shuppan kai, 1971), pp. 88–90; *FRUS,* 1951, VI: 829.

35. John Foster Dulles, *War or Peace?* (New York: Macmillan, 1950), pp. 5–16, 168–170. Michael A. Guhin, *John Foster Dulles* (New York; Columbia University Press, 1972), pp. 129ff., analyzes Dulles' writings at midcentury. See also *FRUS,* 1950, VI: 1335; *FRUS,* 1950, VII: 620; *FRUS,* 1951, VI: 780–783, 858–859.

36. John Steinbruner, *The Cybernetic Theory of Decision* (Princeton: Princeton University Press, 1974), pp. 93, 103, 112, 115–121. Alexander George has propounded similar ideas, focusing on the origins and nature of the values which decision makers seek to protect in his "The 'Operational Code': A Neglected Approach to the Study of Political Leaders and Decision-Making," *International Studies Quarterly* 13 (June 1969), especially pp. 191, 220. Ernest R. May, *"Lessons" of the Past* (New York: Oxford University Press, 1973), and Robert Jervis, *Perception and Misperception in International Politics* (Princeton: Princeton University Press, 1976), Chapter 6, demonstrate and discuss this mode of analysis.

37. *FRUS,* 1951, VI: 820, 830–832.

38. Curriculum vitae, 1946, Yoshida Shigeru file, Book I, item 104, Biographies Files, Central Files of Government Section, Supreme Commander Allied Powers papers, Record Group 331, National Archives.

39. Ben Ami Shillonoy, *Revolt in Japan* (Princeton: Princeton University Press, 1973), pp. 135, 139.

40. Allison, *Essence of Decision,* pp. 5–6, 78–86. Morton Halperin has outlined and categorized standard operating procedures within the American governmental bureaucracy. He concludes that governmental subunits do structure choices in

terms of their mission or "vital essence," acting so as to minimize threats to their ability to carry out such a mission independently. Cf. his *Bureaucratic Politics and Foreign Policy* (Washington, D.C.: Brookings Institution, 1974), especially pp. 39–40.

41. Nishimura, *San Furanshisuko heiwa jōyaku,* pp. 21–53.

42. Michael K. Blaker, *Japanese International Negotiating Style* (New York: Columbia University Press, 1977), analyzes and categorizes Tokyo's diplomatic procedural norms.

43. *FRUS,* 1950, VI: 1279–1282, 1289; *FRUS,* 1951, VI: 782; JCS 1380/97, January 30, 1951; JCS 1380/103, March 22, 1951, CCS 383.21 Japan (3-13-45), section 24, Joint Chiefs of Staff papers, Record Group 218, National Archives; Joseph L. Collins, *War in Peacetime* (Boston: Houghton Mufflin, 1969), pp. 252–255.

44. *FRUS,* 1951, VI: 781–783, 787–788.

45. Army Chief of Staff to Joint Chiefs of Staff, July 5, 1951, included in JCS 2180/21, July 9, 1951, CCS-092 Japan (12-12-50), section 4, Joint Chiefs of Staff papers, Record Group 218, National Archives.

46. Richard Neustadt, *Alliance Politics* (New York: Columbia University Press, 1970), p. 143. See also Allison, *Essence of Decision,* pp. 162–181.

47. Notes on meeting with Under-Secretary of State James Webb, March 25, 1950, President's Secretary's File, Harry S. Truman papers, Truman Library; memorandum of Acheson–Truman telephone conversation, April 4, 1950; memorandum of Acheson–Dulles telephone conversation, Box 65, Dean Acheson papers, Truman Library.

48. Dulles to Acheson, March 29, 1950, J. S. Cooper file, 1971 addendum; and Dulles memorandum of conversation with President Truman, April 28, 1950, Japanese peace treaty file, John Foster Dulles papers, Princeton University Library, provide insights into the special ambassador's domestic political concerns.

49. *FRUS,* 1951, VI: 839.

50. Frederick S. Dunn, *Peacemaking and the Settlement with Japan* (Princeton: Princeton University Press, 1963), p. 92.

51. The expression came to me by way of Professor Clarence Ferguson of the Harvard University Law School.

52. Thucydides, *The Peloponnesian War,* p. 48.

PART III

11
History and Policy

❦   ❦

Samuel F. Wells, Jr.

THE FOREGOING CHAPTERS have examined diverse ways to enhance the cooperation and mutual support between historians and political scientists working in international affairs. The authors have also either explicitly or implicitly explored how studies in diplomatic history and international relations can become more useful to policy makers. Before discussing in greater detail the question of how scholarship can be more relevant to the policy process, let me advance a tentative statement about the prospects for collaboration between scholars in the two disciplines.

The Bases of Interdisciplinary Cooperation

We should recall that history and political science were a single field of study not much more than a generation ago. The schism occurred largely because those scholars interested in refining political analysis came to believe that history as a discipline was too broad in focus, too descriptive, and too concerned with events from remote eras to allow a new subfield to prosper. Most historians, then and now, believed it was a good thing to cleanse their discipline of people who wanted to develop the scientific study of politics.

The principal obstacle to increased cooperation between the fields today remains the historians' mindset. As every student has observed, historians are a perverse and fiercely independent breed. They insist that every conceivable side and source of an issue should be investigated, that facts and interpretations are inextricably bound together, that no model can possibly do justice to more than a single case, and that correct or definitive history cannot exist. It is well known that historians seldom work in teams voluntarily. If forced to do so, they invariably divide the project into segments which can be done independently, and which ultimately bear little relation to what goes before and

269

after. All these elements combine to make any properly trained historian a poor collaborator.

But some of the constraints of mental orientation and training appear to be eroding. A recognition of problems in past scholarship, as well as difficulties in the marketplace (in the competition for both student registrations and jobs for graduates), are forcing historians to make their lectures and writing of greater interest to the general citizen and ultimately more relevant to his concerns. Increasingly, diplomatic historians are studying events within the last twenty years and experimenting with new modes of analysis which include psychology, quantification, and decision theory. They are striving to relate their subjects from the past to contemporary issues and attempting to develop generalizations which will explain more than an isolated episode. There are growing numbers of international historians who prefer to work within highly analytical frames of reference so long as their methodology allows them to do full justice to the diversity of their data. Thus, recent developments indicate that the possibilities for historians to collaborate with political scientists on international affairs research have improved considerably.

The difficulties in increasing interdisciplinary cooperation from the political scientists' point of view are decreasing. The intense love affair and infatuation with behavioral methods has waned, especially among international relations specialists. Many scholars are searching for new research approaches, and there is ample evidence in the published literature and at professional meetings that political scientists are interested in incorporating into their work the data and methods used in cognitive psychology and the empirical evidence in archival history.

The bases for fruitful collaboration between the disciplines of history and political science are now available for the first time. The most promising avenue of research is that of structured, focused comparison developed and explicated so well in this volume by Alexander L. George. The best applications of this method are in George and Smoke, *Deterrence in American Foreign Policy* (1974) and in Richard Smoke's recent *War: Controlling Escalation* (1977).[1] Now we need a series of new studies in which international relations scholars refine models and common questions which allow the evaluation of the differences as well as the similarities in a diverse set of cases. At the same time diplomatic historians can select the appropriate episodes from the past and provide the evidence and analysis necessary to test the models and theories. Upon completion of a group of such studies, we should then return to a more comprehensive mode of quantified analysis of large numbers of cases to see how our understanding of international processes has improved and what predictive value we can expect from our work. Historians can play a crucial role in this stage as well by providing the case studies and assuring the historical validity of the analysis.

While collaboration can be very beneficial in advancing the quality of research in both the history and the theory of international affairs, additional requirements must be met in order to make the results useful to policy makers. The first step in this process is to develop a clear understanding of what historical evidence and analysis can offer to the policy process.

The Uses of History in Policy Formulation

History can serve policy makers by improving their understanding of contemporary issues through studies of prior cases of comparable nature. In making decisions about the strategic arms competition with the Soviet Union, officials in Washington today have to act in a highly complex technical area with only the crudest estimates of their potential opponents' goals and motives. Their basis for choosing one set of assumptions over another could be strengthened if there were available a concise study which examined prior arms races such as the Anglo–German naval competition before 1914 and the Japanese–American rivalry before 1941 in terms of precise questions addressed to archival materials. A study of this type could investigate the options considered, the motives behind decisions, and the accuracy with which intentions were communicated from one side to the other much more fully than we can ever know these matters in a current situation. And if properly focused toward today's Soviet–American arms decisions, it would identify the similarities as well as the differences between cases from the past and present circumstances.

Historical studies shaped to current requirements can provide a type of vicarious experience which tempers decision makers against the belief that each aspect of today's international environment is unique. While prior episodes will hardly prove identical to the present or provide specific courses of action which can be repeated, elements of past situations and patterns of events do recur. Sound studies will help officials avoid the all-too-common problem of basing assumptions on poor analogies from the past. They will serve as a sensitizing device by providing a checklist of potential actors, collateral issues, and unanticipated consequences which can be consulted while formulating important decisions. In the broadly synthetic works of which Gordon A. Craig has given us a superb recent example, historians can pull together the details and the trends from past eras which have gone to make up national diplomatic style and operating behavior.[2]

A specific study on whether the atomic age is without parallel in previous history would be valuable in clarifying much of our analysis about the military and political value of nuclear weapons. Most social scientists and many policy analysts who do not work directly with nuclear weapons accept the view that 1945 marks a fundamental turning point in international affairs. They contend that such destructive power in the hands of so few states has meant that no episode before 1945 can provide relevant insight into any apparently equivalent event since this time. They argue that the advent of nuclear weapons marked such a great quantitative change in firepower that it actually represented a qualitative increase. Along this same line, it is clear that most American policy makers from 1945 until about 1965 acted as if the nuclear age were totally without precedent. Yet there is good reason to believe that this very assumption, which remains untested, was part of the complex of attitudes that fueled the Cold War.

Substantial evidence suggests that in several important aspects of international behavior the nuclear age is not different from previous eras. Our principal nuclear rival has never acted as if atomic weapons were qualitatively different from conventional arms. Even in the extreme case of the Cuban missile crisis, Soviet withdrawal can be explained in terms of overwhelming United States non-nuclear naval and air power in the Caribbean and political pledges to withdraw the American missiles in Turkey. As the two superpowers approached nuclear parity, leaders in Washington came to accept the fact that atomic weapons were usable only at the margin of diplomacy as instruments of bargaining. They might well have reexamined the preceding twenty years to realize that this had been essentially the case during the period of American nuclear superiority, all the talk about massive retaliation notwithstanding. Today our strategic systems are designed not to be used, and the chance of their use is extremely remote. Current officials would find comparisons of international power politics in the 1870s and today not strikingly dissimilar. But few scholars have adopted this changed viewpoint, and leaders of the administration and Congress occasionally revert to the old rhetoric about a nuclear holocaust.[3]

There is a pressing need for studies which examine what changed with the advent of nuclear weapons and what did not. This, of course, involves the historians' classic concern with change and continuity. With massive quantities of records for the 1950s now being declassified and opened for research, scholars should investigate the validity of the assumptions which lay behind American diplomatic and defense policy. To explore these issues properly, historians should compare how nations acted in times of crisis and calm when they confronted opponents of greater and lesser strength. A comparison, for example, of the Soviet Union's policy during the 1930s toward Germany and Finland with its policy in the 1960s toward the United States and Poland would be very informative. Carefully executed focused comparisons of a set of cases from Soviet and American policy basically could establish what can be fruitfully compared before and after 1945 and what cannot.

The use of history in comparative terms can also warn against reliance on excessively rational or culture-bound analysis. Detailed archival research frequently shows the disorder and unpredictability of human affairs, and as Samuel R. Williamson skillfully has demonstrated in a preceding chapter, such research can identify the unusual effects which the Austro–Hungarian policy of annual crop leave for the army had on mobilization decisions in the crisis of July 1914. By pointing out the irrationality, misperception, poor communication, and lapses of control over government units in crisis situations by people, history can provide a cautionary brake against too ready acceptance of coldly rational models or the implications of bargaining and systems theories. It can also, through an examination of how other societies respond to specific situations, demonstrate the pitfalls of attributing our national values and interests to other nations. A valuable study could be done about how American leaders developed a plan to overthrow Fidel Castro on the assumption that a small landing force was all that was needed to generate a rebellion against his regime. It would be instructive to examine how the planners of the Bay of Pigs invasion reasoned away or ignored such widely available evidence as Lloyd Free's published study of Cuban opinion, which showed that 86 percent of the people viewed the Castro government favorably in the spring of 1960.[4] Numerous other cases could be investigated to show the problems created by basing foreign decisions on ethnocentric assumptions.

Evidence from the past can help to develop and refine techniques such as integrative bargaining. This application of mathematical decision theory, used for some years in complicated labor disputes, was recently applied in the Panama Canal treaty negotiations to rate the value to each side of the various points at issue and arrive at a solution better for both than what would have resulted from single-issue bargains and tradeoffs. Studies applying integrative bargaining analysis to complex international settlements such as the Congress of Vienna in 1815 and the Paris Peace Conference of 1919 could shed additional light on the techniques used by skilled negotiators in the past and on how their performance might have been improved. It could also provide insight into future approaches to the Strategic Arms Limitation Talks (SALT) and the Mutual and Balanced Force Reduction (MBFR) negotiations.

Historians can make a significant contribution to the policy process in identifying large questions of importance in future decades and in forecasting the limits and lines of development for these issues. Trained especially to analyze the process of change and continuity over time, historians should reject the old canard that they are better at facts than lessons or futures. Students of the past have as much (or more) reason to engage in forecasting future issues and trends as do lawyers, journalists, and systems analysts. They possess a perspective of proportion and the principal experience within society in analyzing such likely problems of the 1980s and 1990s as ethnic separatist movements, nationalism within alliances, and competition for vital resources. They sould seize the opportunity provided and demonstrate their abilities to assist government officials in developing better public policy.

273

The Problems of Access to the Policy Process

This step will not be easy, however, because gaining the attention of decision makers is fraught with obstacles. Exercising influence on policy formulation is, in fact, difficult for people in official positions. The whole school of bureaucratic politics developed from a perception that personal and organizational interests shape and misshape policy outcomes. The opportunities for scholars outside the government to influence decisions are necessarily more restricted than for those inside the system, and these chances are further reduced through the operation of "Halperin's Law," which declares that "bureaucrats are too busy to change their minds."[5] Government officials, especially political appointees who come into top-level policy organizations such as the National Security Council, work with the assumptions and information they bring to the office. Despite being in those positions which place a premium on fresh ideas, these busy decision makers seldom have time to replenish their intellectual capital. In Washington one hears frequent lamentations that senior officials devote all their time to efforts at coordination, communication, and control, leaving no opportunity for reflection or acquiring new information.

Further complications for scholarly access stem from the divergent assumptions of bureaucrats and academicians about the policy process and the nature of the international environment. Most of the theories discussed in this volume rest on the basic premise that, if sufficient knowledge is made available, it will produce better policy and ultimately a state of international harmony. In contrast, the belief systems of most officials place a high value on conflict within and between governments, on utility rather than validity, and on the uniqueness of the current situation. Since they are also convinced that most scholars do not understand how the system really functions, bureaucrats seldom feel they can profit from social science research. With regard to the goals of international policy, historians and political scientists studying crisis management and escalation generally assume that government officials seek to enhance peace and stability while advancing national interests. Yet, for most policy makers having to sort through complex options in chaotic situations in which they are personally involved with various individuals and events, it is extremely difficult to be analytical and objective. In current bureaucratese, their goal is often "to optimize their personal stakes," or to win!

Still, these obstacles are not insurmountable, and a clear appreciation of their characteristics and magnitude is the first step toward conquering them. The greatest advantages social scientists have in their effort to influence policy are the bureaucrats' desire to develop policy that succeeds and their realization that their track record is not very good. With this understanding, a reasonable strategy for increasing the use of historical evidence and analysis in the policy process can be developed.

The Increased Use of the Past to Shape the Future

The basic objective of such a strategy is to demonstrate the value of history to policy formulation. The current state of the disciplines of diplomatic history and international relations persuades us that they can provide significant benefits to decision makers and that the recognition of these gains will lead to an increased reliance on historical methods and materials. The problem of how to achieve this recognition becomes essentially an issue of research design and transmission. In this regard, the value of history for policy decisions can increase if scholars are prepared to produce studies designed and packaged to the consumers' specifications.

In order to serve the needs of policy makers, social science studies must be brief, related to issues presently under consideration, and linked to more detailed backup materials for subsequent reference. They must also make clear exactly how their findings relate to whatever limited set of practical options the policy makers are considering. The first and most basic task is to improve the general quality and policy relevance of the literature on international affairs. This may not be as large a job as it appears. A recent study demonstrates that a substantial amount of the external research sponsored by government agencies in fiscal year 1975 was global in scope and not designed for use in immediate future circumstances.[6] Thus, an incremental improvement in the quality and relevance of this body of work would be easily attainable.

Scholars wanting to shape the future should conduct studies of present policies analyzed against a broad historical background. For example, given the Carter administration's stated belief that arms sales aggravate international tensions and increase the chances of war, a valuable study could be made of arms competitions since the eighteenth century to see whether increased levels of armament have aggravated conflicts or perhaps have had the reverse effect. We should also develop forecasts of future issues based on shifts over past decades. And to highlight the differences with other nations, we should conduct studies of comparative episodes which isolate such issues as national values and style, means of protecting interests, and ways of resolving problems.

A final element of design is to accommodate the senior bureaucrat's dependence on executive summaries, imposed in part by the press of time and demand for immediate decisions. For each comprehensive study, a brief overview not over two pages in length should present in concise, intelligible prose free of jargon and equations the main points of the argument, their relevance to immediate issues, and recommendations for action. Such summaries will be the main instrument for achieving recognition. Only if they prove stimulating and useful will the full studies be read.

The remaining task is transmitting the carefully focused insights from the past to policy makers. The most direct way to accomplish this is through sponsored external research or projects done as consultants and contractors. Scholars whose services are not sought by the government can send summaries of their work to the offices which coordinate external research or academic liaison. The same technique can be used for members of Congress known to be interested in specific subjects and for staff members of the appropriate committees. In order to get their views before the policy community, social scientists can write for the daily press and contribute to journals such as *Foreign Policy, International Security, Orbis,* and the *Washington Review of Strategic and International Studies.* It is useful to recall the experience of former Senate majority leader Mike Mansfield, who frequently found that the only way he could get his views before President Lyndon B. Johnson was to travel at least a hundred miles from the Capitol to make a speech which would get reported in the *New York Times* and the *Washington Post.*[7]

A longer range approach to the transmission problem is to encourage recent graduate students to take jobs in the bureaucracy. They could introduce historical perspective into their own work and into their evaluations of the work of others. We must recognize that, in light of the longevity of officials such as Clark Clifford and W. Averell Harriman and given natural human sensitivity to the revival of past episodes that were less than successful, there are potential costs to introducing historical lessons into some debates. In such cases, the junior bureaucrat may wish to adopt the technique of intelligence operatives and function as "a mole historian," putting anonymous historically based policy papers on the desk of his superior in the dark of night. Alternatively, he could follow the time-tested practice of leaking the same information to the press.

The ultimate long shot is to rely on principal decision makers of future decades absorbing the lessons of applied historical research as students in the classroom. The nation has not had a President who was a serious student of history since John F. Kennedy, and the prospects among likely contenders are not strong. The Special Advisers to the President for National Security Affairs have since 1961 all been highly trained in historical analysis, but one must note that large numbers of social scientists were not pleased with the policies that flowed from the service of their high-powered academic colleagues.

While we would not expect the combined elements of this strategy to succeed in transforming the nature of policy in the foreseeable future, it has a good chance of making marginal improvements in the short run. And as the people of the United States and their leaders come to accept the implications of the end of the era of American omnipotence, the potential for using the experience of other ages and other peoples should increase sharply.

Notes

1. Alexander L. George and Richard Smoke, *Deterrence in American Foreign Policy: Theory and Practice* (New York: Columbia University Press, 1974); and Richard Smoke, *War: Controlling Escalation* (Cambridge: Harvard University Press, 1977).

2. See Gordon A. Craig, "The Democratic Roots of American Diplomatic Style," in Helmut Berding et al., *Vom Staat des Ancien Regime zum Modernen Parteienstaat: Festschrift für Theodor Schieder* (Munich: R. Oldenbourg Verlag, 1978), pp. 117–131.

3. For more discussion on this point, see Paul Gordon Lauren's chapter on bargaining in this book.

4. Lloyd A. Free, *Attitudes of the Cuban People Toward the Castro Regime: In the Late Spring of 1960* (Princeton: Institute for International Social Research, 1960), p. 1–9.

5. Enunciated by Morton H. Halperin of the Center for National Security Studies on September 12, 1978, at a conference entitled "History as an Instrument of Policy Analysis," held at the Woodrow Wilson International Center for Scholars in Washington, D.C.

6. See J. Martin Rochester and Michael Segalla, "What Foreign Policy Makers Want From Foreign Policy Researchers: A Data-Based Assessment of FAR Research," *International Studies Quarterly* 22 (September 1978): 435–461. Unfortunately, the authors did not have access to an index of the research sponsored by the National Security Council or the Central Intelligence Agency, and their data shows only what research the funding offices ordered, not what policy makers used.

7. Author's interview with former Senator (now Ambassador) Mike Mansfield, May 5, 1968, Chapel Hill, N.C.

277

Index

An interdisciplinary book of this nature bridges several different areas and academic specialities in diplomacy. Its contents range in time from Thucydides to SALT II, in geographical scope from the United States to China, in approach from stylized literature to computerized tables and charts, and in subject matter from Clausewitz to cognitive mapping. In an effort to assist those readers searching for individual cases, people, theories, methodologies, or issues, each entry is listed with terminology most familiar to particular disciplines. Then, to facilitate the process of relating specific historical items to larger theoretical concepts or methodological approaches, many entries are either simultaneously listed or cross-referenced under several topics.

Index